FLORIDA STATE
UNIVERSITY LIBRARIES

MAY 7 1996

TALLAHASSEE, FLORIDA

The crisis of the Spanish old regime traditionally has been interpreted as a result of a bourgeois revolution. Historians have argued that the ascendant class was formed by a group of new landowners, merchants, and bureaucrats who dismantled the old feudal state and began to transform Spain into a capitalist society. In this book, Professor Cruz challenges this viewpoint by arguing that in Spain, as in the rest of continental Europe, a national bourgeoisie did not exist before the second half of the nineteenth century. He proves the model of bourgeois revolution inadequate to explain any movement toward mobilization before 1850.

Historiography based on the bourgeois revolution theory portrays Spain as an exceptional model whose main feature is the "failure" resulting from the immobility of its ruling class. Basing his conclusions in part on an impressive study of over five hundred merchants, bankers, bureaucrats, and politicians who lived in Madrid, Cruz argues that the nature of the crisis of the old regime in Spain was mainly political and in part economic, but never the consequence of a social revolution. This work revises the standard interpretive model of the crisis and relocates Spain in the mainstream for industrialization, urbanization, and democratization that characterizes the history of modern Europe.

Gentlemen, bourgeois, and revolutionaries

Gentlemen, bourgeois, and revolutionaries

Political change and cultural persistence among the Spanish dominant groups 1750–1850

JESUS CRUZ

University of Delaware

Published by the Press Syndicate of the University of Cambridge
The Pitt Building, Trumpington Street, Cambridge CB2 1RP
40 West 20th Street, New York, NY 10011-4211, USA
10 Stamford Road, Oakleigh, Melbourne 3166, Australia

© Cambridge University Press 1996

First published 1996

Printed in the United States of America

Library of Congress Cataloging-in-Publication Data
Cruz, Jesus.
Gentlemen, bourgeois, and revolutionaries : political change and cultural persistence among the Spanish dominant groups, 1750–1850 / Jesus Cruz.
p.   cm.
Includes bibliographical references and index.
ISBN 0-521-48198-8 (hc)
1. Middle class – Spain – Madris – Economic conditions.   2. Middle class – Spain – Madris – Social conditions.   3. Spain – Politics and government – 18th century.   4. Spain – Politics and government – 19th century.   I. Title.
HT690.S7C78   1996
305.5'094641 – dc20
                                                                95-14694
                                                                    CIP

A catalog record for this book is available from the British Library.

ISBN 0-521-48198-8 Hardback

To my parents:
José Cruz and
Ana Valenciano

Contents

Acknowledgments *page* ix

Part I: Careers, business, and fortunes

1. Introduction — 3
2. Merchants — 16
3. Bankers — 58
4. Bureaucrats and professionals — 87
5. Politicians — 128

Part II: The museum of families

6. Habitus, solidarity, and authority — 169
7. Kinship, friendship, and patronage — 208
8. Conclusion: Rethinking the Spanish revolution — 259

Appendix A: The sample — 277

Appendix B: Analysis of assets — 293

Appendix C: Archival sources — 317

References — 321

Index — 343

Acknowledgments

This book has grown out of a doctoral dissertation project that started ten years ago in Madrid. Its initial idea was inspired by the teaching of María Victoria López-Cordón, who awakened my interest in the social history of eighteenth-century Spanish elites. Then, David Ringrose encouraged me to go ahead with a project that seemed too ambitious in the beginning. Without his wise mentorship, criticism, and personal support during the years of doctoral work at the University of California, San Diego, this book would never have been written.

The original manuscript was dramatically improved thanks to the critical comments of my fellow graduate students Doug Cremer, Ed Beaseley, Stefan Fodor, Connie Meale, and David Ortiz, active participants in the UCSD's Department of History thesis seminar. I always enjoyed our dissertation gatherings and appreciated their critical commentaries. The book has also benefited from John Marino's insightful suggestions regarding its original version. My doctoral coursework with Eric Van Young, Russel Jacoby, and Anthony Sutcliffe has been especially important in generating the kind of intellectual commitment needed in the historical profession. Carlos Blanco-Aguinaga and Susan Kirkpatrick helped me approach the history of Spain through its literature. Javier Morillo did a superb job translating chapters I originally wrote in Spanish and editing the whole manuscript. Pamela Racliff, Josep María Delgado, Mauro Hernández, Pompeu Casanovas, and Pedro Pérez Herrero also read parts of my work; I owe all of them my thanks for their advice. My colleagues at the University of Delaware – especially George Basalla – have contributed to the completion of this work in creating the favorable atmosphere needed for intellectual accomplishment. Valuable suggestions have also been made by a number of anonymous readers.

Acknowledgments

I have a special debt to the staff of the Archivo Histórico de Protocolos de Madrid, where I spent most of my time during 1989. The Spanish Ministries of Education and Culture, the University of California, San Diego, the Center for Iberian and Latin American Studies, and the University of Delaware deserve special mention for their economic and institutional support.

My last thanks go to my wife Cynthia Schmidt-Cruz, who read patiently and critically all versions of my manuscript, making a number of perceptive suggestions. Thanks, Cindy, for your patience, understanding, and intellectual support. Thanks Cristina por ser una niña adorable. . . .

Part I

Careers, business, and fortunes

1

Introduction

This book has as its protagonists a group of families who belonged to what Spanish writers of the first half of the nineteenth century called the "middle classes" and contemporary scholars call the "bourgeoisie." Its object is the study of social and economic practices of this group in the transition from the eighteenth to the nineteenth centuries. Its main argument is based on the conviction that the historical changes which characterized the crisis of the old regime in Spain were mainly of a political nature. While they also in part reflected economic necessities, only to a very small degree were they the result of alterations in the traditional social structure of Spain between 1750 and 1850.

Madrid is the setting for most of this story. Because Madrid was the political capital of the Spanish state, in addition to being an important business center, most of the historical transformations related to the crisis of the Spanish old regime took place in this city. However, although my analysis focuses on Madrid, my intention is to go beyond the limits of the old wall that surrounded the town until the first third of the nineteenth century. First of all, this study aims to offer the reader a comparative perspective of the formative process of Madrid's dominant groups. This process will be analyzed in comparison to similar occurrences in other Spanish regions and in other European countries during the same period. The ultimate goal of the project, however, is to study the formation of the group which has been called the "Spanish bourgeoisie": that ascendant social class which, according to some historians, transformed the course of Spanish history in a revolutionary manner.

Historians have analyzed Spanish history using two basic models of interpretation that were formulated in response to the need for an explanation of modern Spain's economic backwardness and political instability.

Careers, business, and fortunes

The first model offers a sociopolitical explanation based on the so-called process of the bourgeois revolution between 1812 and 1843. It has been elaborated primarily by Marxist historians, although important representatives of non-Marxist historiography have accepted this approach.[1] According to the defenders of this model, a new social class, the bourgeoisie, seized power and then reformed law and society to serve its own interests, that is, to promote capitalist development. With the passage of time this bourgeoisie, consisting of a group of new landowners, merchants, and bureaucrats, who had maintained a revolutionary position between 1812 and 1843, became increasingly more conservative until they merged with the landed aristocracy. The threat of a popular revolution inspired by the rural and urban proletariat led to this confluence of interests between the new bourgeoisie and the old aristocracy. Thus, a sociopolitical block was formed which, according to these historians, impeded industrialization and democratization. Nevertheless, there exists only limited agreement among historians regarding the historical content of this "process of bourgeois revolution." They only coincide in the use of the term; the interpretation of facts differs so greatly from one scholar to the next that at times it seems as if they are describing different Spanish bourgeois revolutions.

The second model, which complements the first, offers an economic explanation based on the failure of agrarian and industrial revolutions in Spain. According to this theory, agrarian revolution failed because the processes of disentailment did not change traditional property structures. The old landed aristocracy was merely augmented by a new class of landowners. Spanish agriculture continued to be immobilized by a social minority with minimal interest in raising their yields and productivity.[2] This lack of an agrarian revolution stifled the demand for and accumulation of capital necessary for a large-scale industrial revolution. Consequently, industrialization occurred only on a regional scale in Catalonia and the Basque country.

---

[1] Pérez Garzón (1980) summarizes the origin and development of the paradigm in Spanish historiography. About the conflicting application of the general model of bourgeois revolution to the Spanish case, see Clavero and Ruiz Torres (1979); Alvarez Junco (1985 and 1986); Gil Novales (1985); Ringrose (1986); Pérez Ledesma (1991). For general works in which the paradigm has been defined see Fontana (1979 and 1987); Tuñón de Lara (1983); Sebastià and Piqueras (1987: 13–19). The works of Artola (1983) and Marichal (1977) offer an interpretive variable emphasizing the political nature of the revolution, though never questioning the role of the bourgeoisie. Jover (1992) and Bahamonde and Martínez (1994) offer new revisionist approaches to the nature of the nineteenth-century revolutions and the role of the bourgeoisie.

[2] See the already classic works of Tomás y Valiente (1971: 87–96); Simón Segura (1973: 278–279). See also Fontana (1977: 162).

Introduction

In addition, the occasional spurts of industrial modernization in the rest of Spain were sponsored by foreign investors whose economic behavior was colonial. For these reasons, according to this view, the Spanish economy maintained a level of backwardness which made social and political stability impossible.[3]

In the past few years, an important revision of the second model – the well-known thesis of "failures" – has been made. By means of a minutely detailed reconstruction of series of production, prices, exports, and so forth, historians have arrived at the conclusion that Spanish agriculture maintained a slow but sustained growth (per capita as well as overall) from the decade of the 1830s until 1931.[4] Among other factors this growth reflected changes introduced in property structure by disentailment. The revisionists have also concluded that foreign investments, far from hurting the Spanish economy, were a dynamic factor. The failure to obtain access to foreign markets, rather than the narrow scope of the interior market or the colonization of domestic productive sectors, lies behind the mediocre performance of Spanish manufacturing. Thus relative delay, rather than failure or stagnation, is a more appropriate term to describe the performance of the Spanish economy up to 1931. From the perspective of the new economic history, Spain is not seen as an economically stagnant or failed country, but rather as a country whose economy remained submerged in a slow, although constant, process of modernization.[5]

Although historians have revised the economic paradigm, the old sociopolitical paradigm of the bourgeois revolution remains[6] in spite of the fact that the two concepts no longer complement each other. Indeed, if the failure of the Spanish economy has been explained by virtue of an agreement between an appeased bourgeoisie and a recovered aristocracy, how can the same argument be maintained after changing the terms of the paradigm? If we accept the existence of steady economic modernization, there is no reason to explain any economic "failure" by hypothesizing the existence of a

---

[3] Nadal (1981 and 1987).
[4] For an update on the progress of Spanish economic history, see Harrison (1990) and Martín Aceña and Prados (1985). Concerning agrarian history, see García Sanz and Garrabou (1985), whose works continue a research line initiated earlier by Artola (1978), Anes (1970), and Tortella (1973).
[5] Part of the debate on the adequacy of the term "failure" to characterize the performance of nineteenth-century Spanish economy can be found in Sánchez Albornoz (1985); Prados de la Escosura (1988) finds it more appropriate to speak of "delay with slow modernization" instead of "failure" to define the achievements of the Spanish economy during the nineteenth century.
[6] That is the case of the collective work of García Sanz and Garrabou (1985: 43, v. I), otherwise very innovative.

bourgeoisie which abandoned its historical function. The revised economic paradigm leaves us with a piece that does not fit into this puzzle of contemporary Spanish history. I believe that this ill-fitting piece is the theory of bourgeois revolution and the concept of bourgeoisie as an emerging new and revolutionary social class.

Thus, the central objective of this study is the revision of the existing paradigm of the bourgeois revolution. In my analysis, I use tools similar to those utilized by economic historians in their revision of the growth rhythms of modern Spanish economy. In other words, I study the details of the formative process of the social class known as the "bourgeoisie." Curiously, historians have formulated a theoretical model – the bourgeois revolution – without a concrete empirical foundation. Because of this, the model is no more than a cliché, and its use limits the understanding of specific aspects of contemporary Spanish history.[7]

The revision proposed by this book requires an approach to the problem based on new methodological frameworks. The first framework deals with the characteristics and the treatment of the historical sample to be studied. This sample must be situated in a broad chronological context in order to perceive rhythms of change or continuity in the evolution of the social group under study. The model of bourgeois revolution articulates a fundamental premise: the existence of an emergent and revolutionary social class. The spark of this revolution is placed at 1812; thus, the formative process of the revolutionary social group presumably occurred in the second half of the eighteenth century. My work is based upon a statistical sample of 549 cases of families who lived in Madrid between 1750 and 1850. Most of the data of this sample comes from notarial sources, although these have been supplemented by sources from familial archives and from literary and periodical texts. My intention is to study changes and continuities in the history of these families taking two basic analytical variables: economic strategies and patterns of social behavior.

This study begins with the variations and continuities detected in economic activities. I analyze the manner in which individuals or groups of

---

[7] As Cobban (1964: 22) mentioned some years ago regarding the French example, "an empirical examination of social facts is needed, such as a contemporary sociologist would make of his own society. An estimate of social position must not be based on a single criterion, legal, political or economic, as it often has been in the past, but on a plurality of tests – actual wealth and its nature, sources of income, social status and prestige, origin and direction of social movement of the individual and his family, legal order, political orientation, contemporary esteem, economic function, personal aspirations and grievances, and so on."

Introduction

individuals established their fortunes, focusing on the most frequent forms of capital accumulation and investment. The purpose is to discover the way these families contributed to the development of the capitalist system in Spain between 1750 and 1850. The next topic of study is the patterns of social reproduction within this sample to determine when its members truly began to constitute a new social class. I examine issues regarding their demographic behavior and biological reproduction, to verify the articulation (or the lack thereof) of a culture that could define their identification as a social group. I also attend, when such information exists, to the cultural preferences and political positions adopted by our protagonists throughout their lives. Once we obtain a profile of the families that make up the sample, I place the results in comparative perspective. As I have already indicated, the ultimate goal of this study is to analyze the problem of integration of an ascendant social class on a national scale. I believe that with the currently existing regional studies it is possible to establish some preliminary features to characterize the so-called Spanish bourgeoisie.[8]

The second methodological assumption refers to the analytical framework that couches the argument of this work. One global observation is that its focus is decidedly interdisciplinary; therefore, its analytical frameworks have to be understood in a complementary manner. Throughout these pages, the reader will notice the interaction of concepts such as region, class, group, culture, and hegemony. From the beginning it is essential to reflect upon their significance and their theoretical content.

Although this study does not deal exclusively with one region, and it is not a work of economic history, nevertheless its first analytical frame of reference is the theory of regional systems analysis. I would like to take as my point of departure William Skinner's assertion that

> human activity or social action is in the last analysis systemic, and . . . systems of human interaction are at once, spatial, temporal, and hierarchical. Methodologies that ignore even one of these dimensions necessarily yield inadequate explanations. Social-science history needs models that bring space, time, hierarchy, and scale into a single analytical paradigm.[9]

---

[8] The following list of works published in recent years illustrates this progress: Bahamonde Magro (1981 and 1986); Caro Baroja (1985); Cruz (1986 and 1990); Fernández (1982); Franch (1986); Eiras (1981); García Baquero (1966); Guimera (1985); Maruri (1990); Molas (1985); Otazu (1987); Pérez Garzón (1978); Ramos Santana (1987); Tedde (1983); Villar (1982); Zylberberg (1979 and 1983).
[9] Skinner (1977:37).

The basic unit of spatial analysis is the nodal region, understood as a socioeconomic space of interaction which is differentiated and organized hierarchically. Every nodal region has a temporal structure; that is, all of its systems of interaction are reproduced with the passage of time. Based on this combination of temporal and spatial variables, models of interpretation applicable to distinct fields of the social sciences have been constructed. The application of this methodology has obtained best results in the study of economic spaces through the analysis of the formation and evolution of markets. Starting with the basic model of the nodal region, that is, a geographical space with a sole center of articulation, models of greater complexity have been constructed.[10] In these models, cities are crucial insofar as they almost always are the centers of regional spaces and, therefore, form the networks of hierarchy. But the cities are more than nodes of economic activity. As places of residence of the elite, cities are centers of political and cultural decision. Therefore, the significance of the analysis is not limited to the field of economics but is also very useful for understanding a wide variety of political, social, and cultural phenomena.[11] As a consequence, any approach to articulation of a social formation which ignores its regional dimension runs the danger of offering an inadequate explanation.

Following these theoretical assumptions, it seems logical that any analysis of the peculiarities of Madrid society should take into account the role of the city as the center of a regional space. The same can be said of the rest of Spanish cities. Finally, the problem of articulation of regional markets, and later of the national market, along with their respective social formations, will have to be understood within an analytical paradigm that considers the three dimensions defined by Skinner: space (region), time (history), and hierarchy (power).

Despite the abundance of regional studies of eighteenth-century Spain, there still does not exist a model of regionalization that offers an integrated vision. In the light of recent research, the classic paradigm of a dynamic periphery and a stagnant center seems only partially valid. Nevertheless, some studies undertaken in recent years in this field have produced noteworthy results.[12] Prime examples are Pierre Vilar's already classic study of Catalonia, and the more recent study of Madrid by David Ringrose. Both

---

[10] See Smith (1976); Christaller (1966); and Rozman (1973).
[11] About the role played by the city in history, see Bairoch (1989) and Reher (1990: chap. I); see also Madrazo (1986) and Ringrose (1988).
[12] Fernández (1985).

Introduction

works offer an alternative model in which the region is understood as an interactive space between the urban centers and their respective hinterlands. Vilar demonstrates how Barcelona, during the eighteenth century, was transformed into a center of production which connected a regional market with an international one. Unlike Barcelona, Madrid maintained its character as political center of the old Spanish empire and, according to Ringrose, was only a place for the redistribution of goods and services. The capital acted as a drain that absorbed the income generated in much of Spain. While at the end of the eighteenth century Catalonia began to integrate an urban network with its center in Barcelona, Madrid failed in this role as an integrating center. This had immediate consequences on the formation of the middle classes and the elites. While in Barcelona, as Jordi Maluquer has pointed out, the bourgeois elite was renewed by access to new social groups from the artisan and rural world, the elite of Madrid remained static. In other words, what differentiated Madrid from Barcelona was the reproduction there of an elite from within the same social realm as compared with the renewal of Barcelona's elite via the opening of access to new social groups.[13] This example serves to demonstrate the importance of the regional systems analysis theory for any study of social history.

The second analytical framework on which this study is based comes from cultural anthropology and refers to the interaction between the concepts of culture, class or group, and hegemony. I work with the assumption that any social relation is fundamentally cultural, and that in every social formation there always exists a hegemonic culture.[14] In a traditional sense, to be a cultured person means to master certain areas of academic knowledge, which also implies a different type of social behavior. A person is considered a cultured man or woman because he or she behaves in a distinctive manner, knows conventions, and is an educated person. This concept of culture is the result of the transfer of certain patterns of behavior of the elite to the rest of society. It reflects, therefore, a partial view regarding education in particular. On account of this, some social scientists prefer to speak of "cultural capital" rather than simply culture, when it is understood in this sense of exclusivity.[15]

---

[13] Vilar (1987: vol. III); Ringrose (1987: 125–137); Maluquer (1989: 188–89).
[14] The original definition of the concept of hegemony appears in Gramsci (1971: 57) and (1979: 17 and 110). See also Mouffe (1979).
[15] For a definition of cultural capital, see Bourdieu (1977: 191; 1988: 78–83). Its application for a study of the formation of a Spanish social group can be found in McDonogh (1986: 166–201).

Careers, business, and fortunes

In this book I will use the concept of culture as it is defined by anthropologists and ethnologists: the life style of a people. This life style consists of conventional models of thought and behavior, which include value systems, beliefs, norms of conduct, and even forms of political organization and economic activity. These models of thought and behavior are transmitted from one generation to the next by means of a learning process, never by means of genetic inheritance. Individuals or groups learn modes of behavior; therefore, culture is something malleable, and should not be considered outside of its economic and social context.[16] Finally, cultural models influence the structuring of thought and perception; this is what anthropologists call cultural conventions or cultural prejudices. The importance of conventions is decisive in understanding the articulation of value systems in diverse societies. The application of this principle helps historians to understand the variety of responses in different spaces with similar levels of historical development.

In every social space, one can locate several cultures which, in turn, are the product of the action of different social groups. To the extent that every social relationship is also a relationship of domination, we find that there are always one or several social groups which end up imposing their culture. This is what Gramsci called "cultural hegemony," and he particularly defined it as the usurpation of language by the dominant classes. Following this line of analysis, the bourgeois revolution should be understood fundamentally as the attempt of the bourgeoisie to hegemonize their culture, in the same way that feudal society was characterized by the hegemony of the values of aristocratic culture. The central question that I will pose in this book concerns the existence of a bourgeois culture in Spain before 1850, a culture which should have been the expression of a new class consciousness acquired by the protagonists of the Spanish revolution between 1812 and 1843.

This leads us to a new problem of particular importance for historians: how to explain alterations in different hegemonic cultures. Durkheim only partially resolved the problem by introducing the notion of "collective conscience" to explain the basis of certain manifestations of collective action. His great contribution consisted of combining two analytical categories that in the Cartesian and Kantian traditions fit together rather poorly: knowledge and action. For Durkheim, social life should be explained not

---

[16] For a definition of culture see Williams (1981:10–13); Hatch (1973); Kroeber and Kluckhohn (1963).

Introduction

only according to the conception of those who participate in it, but also by profound unconscious causes. However, in spite of the value which knowledge and logical structures have in his theory, Durkheim, like Marx, located definitive reason on the level of objective structures to explain social change.[17]

The Marxist tradition solved the problem by subordinating ideological changes – the superstructure – to the equilibrium between productive forces and the means of production. In the end, the superstructure is always determined by the infrastructure. History is thus explained by a succession of modes of production which are basically defined by the dominant means of production in their interior. The well-known debate about the transition from feudalism to capitalism is in part inherited from this conception, which concentrates on the development of the productive forces in order to explain historical change.[18] Beginning in the 1960s, the influence of Gramsci, structuralism, and modernization theory opened the way for a revision of this model of interpretation. This helped to form a more pragmatic attitude leading to a new definition of the concept of social class which was less dependent on economics, and more concerned with ideology. In *The Making of the English Working Class*, E.P. Thompson showed how a class is not only defined by objective categories, but also by its own self-conception. For this reason, a class is not defined as an aggregate of agents that share the same position in the productive process, but rather as a cluster of norms, habits, meanings, customs, and symbols with which groups of individuals identify.[19] Using a cultural approach, I will attempt to determine how the individuals or groups under study represent themselves – to see to what degree these dominant families were capable of creating a new symbolic space or a new culture. But above all, I wish to determine whether this culture arose as an alternative to another which was displaced, and if that process was the result of the consciousness, raising of new social agents.

The model of bourgeois revolution focuses its attention on the fact that during the first half of the nineteenth century radical changes occurred in the political systems of Western European countries. These changes profoundly affected economies and, in large part, favored more dynamic social spaces. However, this interpretative model is based on the acceptance of the existence of a social class which promoted revolutionary changes. At the

---

[17] Thompson (1985: 14–20).
[18] See Mooers (1991: 17–26); Aston and Philpin (eds.) (1987); Barceló (1987).
[19] Thompson (1966: 9–12).

foundation of this model is the classic Marxist premise of class struggle as the driving force of history, and the definition of social class based on its place in the process of production. Certainly, the new role of the bourgeoisie in the capitalist mode of production would explain this class necessity to carry out its revolution.[20] Nevertheless, in the two last decades, social scientists have been revising this interpretive model, questioning not only its validity but even the premises on which it is based: (a) the existence of a new social class with the ability to incite a revolution; (b) the relationship between economic, political, and social change in the historical process; and (c) the very concept of social class and of class struggle as the sole explanatory element of social change.[21]

To the extent that the French Revolution has been presented as the most developed example of bourgeois revolution, it seems logical that the revision of the paradigm began by using the historical process initiated in 1789 as a point of reference. Once the institutional developments were studied, historians began to research which groups moved the revolution forward. Their conclusion is that in those years a real bourgeoisie did not exist in France, and that a large part of the nobility was never opposed to revolutionary liberalism.[22] Similar studies in Germany and England arrived at similar conclusions regarding the existence of a revolutionary bourgeoisie.[23]

With regard to the relationship between economic changes and politicocultural changes, or in other words the relationship between infrastructure and superstructure, current historiography has rejected all forms of economic determinism. The studies of Abner Cohen and, especially, Pierre Bourdieu, demonstrate how the structures of domination are more than the product of control of the means of production by a social class. The forms of domination depend, in great part, on the capacity of a specific social group

---

[20] Marx and Engels (1934: 11–12); Marx (1920: 455); Ossowsky (1956); Dahrendorf (1959: 34).
[21] Reddy (1987: 1–23).
[22] Cobban (1964) opened the debate criticizing the thesis of Lefebvre (1963) and Soboul (1981) which emphasized the bourgeois character of the revolution. Regarding the social nature of the groups that protagonized the revolutionary process, see Furet (1971: 255–289). A general vision of the debate can be found in Doyle (1980). Chaussinand-Nogaret (1976: 39–64) revised the political role played by the nobility during the revolution.
[23] The revision in Germany was initiated when historians debated the causes of the failure of the 1848 revolutions – Krieger (1957). On the lack of a bourgeoisie or a bourgeois culture in nineteenth-century Germany, see Bleiber (1977: 193–95). Also see Mayer (1981: 79–127); Diefendorf (1984); Harris and Thane (1984: 215–234). On the nature of the English revolution, see Russel (1979); Stone (1972). One of the central themes in the debate about the lack of a revolution in England refers to the standards of living of the English working class during the nineteenth century – Taylor (1975); Deane (1986: 255–271).

to impose their culture upon others. However, this culture is not the product of the exclusive action of objective structures, as is the case with means of production. For Bourdieu, a fundamental element in the shaping of a class culture is what he calls "habitus." According to this author every social process is dynamic, and its dynamism is made possible by what he calls "fields" or "groups" – in other words, social classes. Habitus is understood as a series of internal structures of perception, of thought and action, which have a relative autonomy and which change more slowly than economic structures. These internal structures of perception, thought, and action are deeply rooted in the human conscience through custom and norm. Even where historians have perceived revolutionary changes, habitus is barely altered. It is as if we constructed a functional skyscraper with materials from a medieval castle. We could, perhaps, succeed in creating an innovative building in its exterior appearance, but its structure would remain old. Thus, where we actually should look for revolutionary social change is in those behaviors that signal a different habitus. Obviously, those changes operate in less conventional historical cycles than those which historians are accustomed to using.[24] In this book, I will try to define the most characteristic habitus of Madrid's dominant groups. Their comparison with that of other groups outside Madrid helps us to know more about the reality of social change in Spain beginning in the first half of the nineteenth century.

A more complicated issue is the concept of social class, its theoretical content, and its use as a category of historical analysis. It is clear that the term "social class," as it is used in this book, does not refer exclusively to a group of people who share a common position in the productive system. This does not mean that I completely reject the economic content of the concept. Wealth – defined as control over means of production – is always a clear element of social distinction. But it is not the sole determinant. Social rank depends not only on money but on many other factors that fall into the category which Bourdieu called cultural capital.[25] Prestige, influence, and power are categories which are not necessarily associated with wealth, although those who possess money have greater possibilities of acquiring these social goods. Most of the time, cultural capital is not the patrimony of a single class, but of several. Whether we call them class factions, social layers, or social blocs, the idea of group always prevails. Thus when I use the

---

[24] For a definition of habitus, see Bourdieu (1988: 127 and 128).
[25] Status according to Weber (1978).

Careers, business, and fortunes

concept "social group," I take into account that this category implies multiplicity and, therefore, does not contradict the concept of social class.

As stated earlier, this study deals with the group that the Spaniards of the first half of the nineteenth century called the *clases medias*. Although the word "bourgeoisie" appeared as early as the eighteenth century, it did not then have the connotations it has acquired since around 1870. It seems that the term was initially used with more of a political meaning than a social one. It began to be used systematically in the political vocabulary of the first workers' unions.[26] Returning to the period we are studying, what did the historians, journalists, and writers who discuss social themes in the first half of the 1800s understand by middle class? We can consider the example of Marquis de Miraflores in his *Apuntes histórico-críticos para escribir la historia de la revolución de España*, one of the most important works of the period. According to this author, Spain's great problem resided in the isolation which the Spanish monarchy imposed upon its elites, especially the aristocracy. Since the end of the sixteenth century, a tacit alliance was established between the monarchs, the people, and the clergy, in order to weaken the aristocracy. The people benefited from this alliance by obtaining advantages "that made their civil existence superior to any other in Europe before the eighteenth and nineteenth century revolutions." The crown, in its way, was able to exercise absolute power with scarcely any opposition. "But," writes Miraflores, "the ruin of the aristocracy also involved the ruin of prosperity and of enlightenment, and the lower class, although a blind instrument of its own ruin, retained better conditions than did the aristocracy, the middle class, and the industrial classes." This explanation has doubtful historical validity because Miraflores was only interested in legitimizing his opposition to absolute monarchy from an aristocratic perspective. But it is interesting to note two points from this reasoning: first, that the political projected presented by the enlightened aristocracy was compatible with that of the middle class, and second, that the author makes a distinction between middle class and industrial groups. From 1830 on, according to Miraflores, a cycle of history closed, thanks to the reconciliation between the crown and the aristocracy, with the consent of the middle class and industrial classes.[27]

There is no consensus with regard to the real influence of this middle class in Spanish society of those years. Concerning the social definition of

---

[26] See Botrel and Le Bouil (1973: 137–160).
[27] Marqués de Miraflores (1834: 4–10). Saint Simon made the same distinction concerning the groups who made the French Revolution possible. Quoted by Cobban (1964: 58).

Introduction

this group, however, there seems to be general agreement about two distinctive features: their exclusivity – which distinguished them from the old aristocracy as much as from the industrial classes – and their leadership role. Perhaps Miraflores had a very Castilian way of understanding the middle class, but the immense majority of his contemporaries concurred with his view of this social group. Obviously, the vantage point from which they viewed Madrid society determined their definitions of social groups. They saw it as a society whose intermediate layer consisted of bureaucrats, businessmen, professionals, and property owners, and as a society that tended to exclude all those who depended, directly or indirectly, on manual labor.

Contemporary characterization of the middle class contradicts the use of the term "bourgeoisie" in the sense employed by the Marxist tradition. Thus, the Spanish middle class, like its European counterparts in the same period, did not necessarily have to be a new social class which defined itself in opposition to the aristocracy. To the contrary, a substantial portion of these middle classes consisted of families of unequivocally noble origins.

To summarize, this work attempts to fill a vacuum in Spanish historiography of the last decade as it treats the social history of the first half of the nineteenth century. For diverse reasons the attention of historians has been displaced from this topic. On the one hand, there exist a greater number of works about the eighteenth century, especially its second half. Social history has benefited from this first displacement. In recent years, there have appeared several high-quality monographs dealing precisely with the problem of the formation of the bourgeoisie.[28] However, they all end in 1800, thus limiting themselves to the frame of the old regime. Furthermore, they are mostly regional studies which, on occasion, do not concern themselves with general historical processes.

On the other hand, interest has focused on twentieth-century studies, with some interest in the second half of the nineteenth century. Thus, research on the crisis of the old regime, fashionable during the 1970s, has suffered from a certain lethargy which only began to dissipate in the late 1980s.[29] Meanwhile, the tendency in other European countries has been just the opposite. I hope that my study works toward restoring the continuity of process between eighteenth and nineteenth centuries that has been overlooked by Spanish historiography.

---

[28] See fn. 10.
[29] Alvarez Junco and Santos Juliá (1989: 53–63).

2

Merchants

It is not surprising that a society such as Madrid's, dominated by noble families, ecclesiastical dignitaries, and prestigious bureaucrats, would pay little attention to its merchants,[1] even as commerce constituted the raison d'être of other European cities. The character of Venetian society, for example, had long been determined by its wealthy business classes.[2] The life style of the merchant elites of several Dutch cities played a fundamental role in defining a national culture.[3] Even Paris and London, cities with prominent political-administrative establishments, had prestigious merchant communities. However, Spain – like Italy and to a certain degree Russia also – created a dual image for its principal urban centers. Madrid, like Rome and St. Petersburg, has served as an archetype for the powerful and parasitic city, while Barcelona, Milan, and Moscow stood out for their industriousness and commercial activity.[4] Before exploring this urban image further, we should first ask whether this dichotomy in fact existed. To what extent was it true that merchants were a subordinate group in Madrid society at the end of the eighteenth century? How important was Madrid's commercial community relative to its counterparts in other regions of Spain?

---

[1] "Those who set the pace of the capital were not the few hundred merchants settled in the city, but rather the great mass of clerics, rentiers, officeholders, and professionals." See Domínguez Ortiz (1976: 398).
[2] Burke (1974); Lane (1973).
[3] The "bourgeois" nature of Dutch nationalism in its formation period has been a matter of historiographical debate. See Schama (1988: 6); Huizinga (1968: 112); Wallerstein (1980: 65).
[4] That was the perception of some English travelers in Spain between 1750 and 1850. See Robertson (1988: 138); On the parasitism of Madrid see Juliá (1989: 140 and 1994: 255–258).

16

Merchants

Madrid as a commercial town

It is true that Madrid was not primarily a trade city as were Cadiz, Bilbao, and Marseille.[5] Madrid and Vienna were the only imperial capitals in Europe that lacked direct access to the ocean. Vienna's isolation was ameliorated by the Danube, but Madrid had no similar means of water-based communication. Transportation to the interior of Spain was slow and difficult; travel to the capital was possible only by foot or on horseback.[6] There are few similar examples of an urban center whose geographic and environmental adversity is matched only by its importance as a center of political power. Aside from cities in central Asia that appear to fit this type,[7] Mexico City and Tehran seem to be the only cities outside Europe comparable to Madrid in this respect. Tehran had always been a prominent trading center on the legendary Silk Route.[8] Mexico City, the center of an ancient civilization, was converted into a political-administrative center by the Spanish, while at the same time it established itself as the nucleus of an important regional market. The tone of its society was set by the creole aristocracy, the colonial bureaucracy, and the Church, but was also affected by a sizable community of merchants who were an important part of the power elite in the city.[9] A similar influence was felt in Madrid, although this is a part of the city's history that has gone somewhat unnoticed.

In the following pages I reevaluate Madrid's role as a commercial center, focusing on the groups that made up the business community in the city. In general, contemporary historians of Spanish society have identified merchants as an essential part of the bourgeoisie.[10] In studies of the social and economic history of Madrid this characterization is unmistakable, to such an extent that when the rise of the bourgeois class and the bourgeois revolution are discussed, most of the individuals referred to are merchants.[11] It is assumed that in the first half of the nineteenth century a new kind of business developed – some of the strongest examples of which could be

---

[5] García Baquero (1976: 104); Basurto (1983: 19); Carriere (1973: 27).
[6] Ringrose (1970: xxi–xiii).
[7] Skinner (1977b).
[8] Curzon (1966: 330).
[9] Brading (1971: 97); Kicza (1983: 173).
[10] In an interpretive model which started with the works of Vicens Vives and Nadal (1971: 128 and 1985: 130).
[11] Pérez Garzón (1978), for instance, emphasizes the role played by Madrid merchants in the formation of the *milicia nacional* – a civic army made up of the middle classes. This *milicia* was, according to Pérez Garzón, the instrument of the bourgeoisie to implement the revolution.

found among merchants – and that this new method was the deus ex machina of a new capitalism that blossomed at the dawn of the Alfonsian restoration.[12] This chapter tests such assumptions by analyzing businesses and family fortunes. The questions is whether the business elite present in Madrid in the second quarter of the nineteenth century was in fact the bearer of a new capitalism that differed from that of the second half of the eighteenth century.

A world of diversity dominated by the Cinco Gremios Mayores

At least two features demonstrate the importance of the Spanish capital as a commercial center. The first is the existence in the city of the most influential merchant corporation of the old regime Spain.[13] The second concerns the wealth and level of sophistication of some of the trading firms, which on occasion were much greater than those of similar firms in other Spanish provinces.

Indeed, in the Cinco Gremios Mayores Madrid had a merchants' guild similar in its structure and function to those in other European capitals.[14] Apart from its function as a guild, this institution contributed to the development of a number of capitalist practices in the interior. Capella and Matilla emphasized the absence of a tradition of guilds in Madrid until it became a capital.[15] But once that happened, as Molas has written, the growth of the guild conglomerate was extraordinary.[16] Whereas toward the end of the seventeenth century the activity of the Cinco Gremios was limited exclusively to the purchase and sale of merchandise, by the last decade of the following century it was the only Spanish enterprise with a presence in principal economic centers both within and outside of Spain. The Cinco Gremios had a branch in Cadiz out of which it conducted its commercial and financial operations with America and northern Europe. It had offices and representatives in Valencia, Barcelona, Paris, and London, among other cities. It managed some of the most important industries of the period, such as the textile mills of Guadalajara and Ezcaray, the linen mills

---

[12] Bahamonde and Toro (1978: 8–11); Bahamonde (1986: 365 and 366).
[13] According to Ruiz Martín (1970: 158) it was "the most powerful capitalist institution in Castile."
[14] Like the Six Corps in Paris and the Twelve Great Livery Companies in London. See Molas (1985: 17 and 28); Bergeron (1978: 19). The Madrid corporation was formed by the guilds for silk, linen, jewelry, clothes, and drugs.
[15] Capella and Matilla (1957: 7).
[16] Molas (1985: 82).

of Madrid, and the silk-working shops of Valencia. Just a few steps from the Santa Cruz church, in one of the prime sections of Madrid's Atocha street, the Cinco Gremios erected a building that bore testimony to the corporation's importance at the time.[17] When in 1808 the French government conducted a financial survey in an effort to raise funds through compulsory loans, the Cinco Gremios was considered the strongest financial institution in Spain. While the lending capacity of the Banco Nacional de San Carlos was of some 3 million reales, for example, the Cinco Gremios was able to lend 50 million reales to the state. The importance of this Madrid-based trading group did not go unnoticed by contemporary observers.[18]

Nor did Bonaparte's officials ignore the importance of some of Madrid's individual trading firms. Their survey included a report on the banking firms operating in Madrid, whose combined capital totaled 147 million reales; I discuss this group in the next chapter. At this point I focus on the principal commercial establishments that remained open in Madrid during those years, when the operations of a number of other firms were interrupted by the French occupation. Among the entries in the survey appear the firms of Francisco Antonio Bringas, with estimated assets of 36 million reales, the firms of the Caballero brothers with combined assets of 30 million reales, and the firm of García de la Prada, whose assets were valued at 20 million reales. Of a total of 11 establishments cited in the survey, 8 had assets worth more than 14 million reales and all of them had more than 5 million reales in assets.[19] Some of the most important businesses of the time do not appear in the survey, such as those of Iruegas-Sobrevilla, Angulo, Pérez Roldán, and Trasviña. In addition, the survey noted the existence of some 70 clothing stores, 43 firms specializing in the sale of silk goods, 78 haberdasheries, and 120 dry goods shops. Although the document does not provide precise figures for the value of their assets, in all cases they were worth at least 1 million reales. These data reflect the importance, at least qualitatively, of Madrid's traders. It may seem exaggerated to say that Bringas was the wealthiest merchant in Spain at the dawn of the nineteenth century, but with the information currently available such a statement is perfectly valid.

Madrid's business community in the mid-1700s, according to estimates

---

[17] See Marín Perellón (1988).
[18] ANF, leg. afIV 1608b, p. 8. See Tedde (1983: 309).
[19] ANF, leg. afIV 1608b, p. 11. The estimates of the fortunes agrees with the my own information obtained from different sources in the Madrid notarial archives. See the samples of the García de la Prada and Caballero families in AHPM, P. 21098 and 21782.

calculated by the property tax authorities of Ensenada, consisted of roughly 1,900 individuals.[20] This figure included a number of occupations not directly related to the purchase and sale of merchandise. For example, neither business agents, who offered a service similar to that performed by today's administrative managers, nor the money brokers who specialized in handling bills of exchange and other financial services, were included. The censuses of the late eighteenth and early nineteenth centuries offer a figure of nearly 1,400 people involved in commerce,[21] of which one-fourth were classified as large-scale merchants; the rest were simply shopkeepers. What was the significance of this division? Molas has observed that a hierarchy of merchant groups existed based primarily on economic differences but also according to increased status with greater distance from manual labor.[22] Throughout the eighteenth century in Madrid this hierarchy was based on whether or not one belonged to the Cinco Gremios Mayores, and it had strong social implications. But the distinction was maintained in the nineteenth century, as evidenced by the occupational categories given by the population censuses. Why was this hierarchy maintained when it was so clearly contrary to the spirit of the liberal revolution?

Two features characterized the economy of the capital: the importance of its consumer market and the nearly complete lack of involvement by the merchant sector in the manufacture of consumer goods. The consumer market was broadly divided between two types of products: basic and luxury goods. Among the former, wheat, beef, fuel, and wine accounted for the majority of demand.[23] But the distinctive feature of this market compared to others in Spain was the importance of the demand for luxury goods in the capital.[24] Only Madrid was home to royalty, and for this reason home also to families with the greatest purchasing power of the time. The Cinco Gremios Mayores controlled that portion of the market until its disintegration in the 1830s. Nevertheless, the disappearance of the institution did not mean the disappearance of the social sector that had sustained it. Its absence merely

---

[20] Ringrose (1985: 89 and 416–418).
[21] Merchant occupational categories are very confused in the *Censo de Floridablanca* (1787). According to the *Censo de Godoy* (1797) data, there were in Madrid 1,442 merchants divided in two categories: 351 *comerciantes* (merchants) and 1,091 *mercaderes* (retailers). A very similar figure appears in the *demostración general de la población de Madrid* (1804): of 1,364 individuals dedicated to commercial activities, 365 were merchants and 999 retailers. See Pérez Moreda (1983) and AVM 4-4-37.
[22] Molas (1985: 47).
[23] More details about the supply market of Madrid can be found in Ringrose (1985: chap. VII), Castro (1987), and Fernández García (1971).
[24] Ringrose (1985: 105–108).

meant that the latter had adapted to a changing institutional environment. The 1830 registry of merchants recorded the names of 878 individuals, many of whom managed businesses already in existence in the eighteenth century.[25] In reality the new registry was made up of the same sectors that formed the Cinco Gremios, with the addition of the financial sector and new specializations. But in Madrid, unlike other cities such as Barcelona and Paris, the world of production remained separate from that of distribution. The bulk of the luxury products that were sold in Madrid originated in distant export markets. This dissociation of production and distribution explains the chronic separation between commerce and industry that characterized Madrid society until well into the nineteenth century.

The Cinco Gremios was not made up exclusively of wholesale merchants. They, in fact, were a minority of the guild's members. Of the more than 300 trading firms belong to the Cinco Gremios operating in Madrid at the end of the eighteenth century, only 30 percent could be considered large-scale merchandisers.[26] The remainder were closer to retailers, although they were distinguished from the *mercaderes* by the kind and quality of their products as well as by their membership in the prestigious corporation. Later I will analyze the significance of this exclusivity; for the moment it suffices to note that membership provided an excellent base from which to establish business relationships and, on occasion, for access to credit. Although the Cinco Gremios developed in the seventeenth century as a group of retailers, as time passed it came to include a complete network of merchant companies.

Outside of the Gremios Mayores there were two quite different groups of merchants: the specialized merchants and the small retailers. Specialized merchants rivaled the members of the Cinco Gremios in influence and wealth. Some of these merchants had strong mutual economic and family ties, creating groups dedicated to importing products that were either targeted for specific regional markets or found only in certain international markets. Such was the case with the Basque iron merchants, the Catalonian textile dealers, and some foreign merchants who imported goods from their native countries.[27] The list of close-knit merchant groups would also have

---

[25] AVM, Secretaría, 2-428-1.

[26] According to their volume of business, their clients, and their activity in the markets. The sample is based in the study of the family fortunes of 99 members of the CGM. According to different editions of the *Almanak Mercantil* (between 1797 and 1808) the number of commercial firms affiliated to the CGM is as follows: 374 in 1797; 340 in 1800; 303 in 1807.

[27] The survey made by the Bonapartist government in 1808 mentioned the Catalonian firm of Jaime Mas as one of the most important in Madrid, with a capital of 18 million reales. ANF, leg. afIV 1608b,

to include families such as the Gardoquis, the Pandos and the Quintanas, whose principal offices were located in Cádiz and Bilbao but who ran wholesale distributorships of overseas products in Madrid. Booksellers, although they were a separate group, given the characteristics of their trade and their proximity to the world of culture, could also be counted as specialized merchants, considering the structure of their businesses and the extent of their fortunes.

Small retailers accounted for the bulk – approximately 80 percent – of trade in Madrid. It is impossible to establish a classification of the distinct sectors that made up this category, given the diversity of occupations involved. As a whole they were defined by their smaller individual sales volume, their greater proximity to the crafts sector, and their absolute exclusion from the power centers of the time. A few of these retailers ran profitable businesses, judging by their wealth and their sales income, but they were virtually irrelevant within the merchant community.[28] One distinction to be made within this group was between shopkeepers, who operated out of fixed storefront space, and traveling vendors. Both kinds could be found in all corners of the capital; their stores, stands, and carts were a part of daily life on Madrid's crowded streets. The sale of specialized products, on the other hand – whether by a member of a guild or an independent – was confined to the best areas of the city, near the Plaza Mayor and the Puerta del Sol.

In this chapter I analyze the characteristics of the conglomerate of family enterprises that constituted the most noteworthy part of Madrid's merchant community. Table 2.1 shows the composition of the sample for analysis by type of specialization. The sample used throughout this research consists of 202 merchants who lived and died in Madrid between 1750 and 1850, although the majority of the cases are from between 1783 and 1816. Ninety-two percent of the cases are merchants who either belonged to the Cinco Gremios Mayores or were specialized traders. This means that my analysis focuses on the groups that controlled the majority of the market for luxury consumer goods, that is, the economically better-off sector of Madrid's merchant community. This does not mean that it was an elite in the sense of

---

f. 11. Other important firms registered were the Wercruyse Brothers, specialized in trade of Flemish commodities, Galarza y Goycoechea, specialized in iron products, and Casariego, specialized in clothes from Segovia.

[28] Data from the *Catastro de Ensenada* show that some Madrid merchants not members of the CGM had similar or even superior levels of income. See Ringrose (1985: 418 and 421).

Merchants

Table 2.1. *Occupational distribution. 202 Madrid-based merchants, 1750-1850*

Occupation	No. of cases	%
Cinco Gremios Mayores	164	81.2
Booksellers	6	3.0
Specialized traders	22	10.9
Clothiers	3	1.4
Shopkeepers	7	3.5
Total sample	202	

constituting a powerful minority; their economic power, although considerable in some cases, was not extraordinary overall. Their potential for penetrating the circles of power in the city or the state apparatus, though extant, was limited.

More than an elite, the merchants who are the subjects of this study should be considered a significant part of Madrid's upper middle class toward the end of the eighteenth and the beginning of the nineteenth centuries. Perhaps neither the most important nor the most representative part, but certainly, as noted, the group most viewed by historians as the sector that played the largest role in the downfall of the old regime. In the literature of Spanish history – and the history of Madrid in particular – there is a nearly universal tendency to identify commerce with the bourgeoisie and to accord to merchants the role of protagonists in the bourgeois revolution. This line of argument is based on two commonly accepted assumptions about the role of merchants in Western societies during the early modern period. The first of these generally considers the merchant classes as having constituted a group foreign to the aristocratic society that in the end subverted the traditional order. The second is based on the fact that all trading activity is fundamentally capitalist, and therefore merchants have been the best guardians of capitalism since early history.[29]

---

[29] This assumption is based on Adam Smith's definition of *Homo economicus*, which identifies human nature with commercial activity (Smith 1937: 13). The German school, the Marxist historiography, as much as the modernization theorists had traditionally emphasized the connections between commercial activities, bourgeoisie, and capitalism. See Theda Skocpol (1979: 3f.). A good example for the case of England can be found in Brewer (1982: 201). Most studies of the Spanish bourgeoisie during the eighteenth and nineteenth centuries focus mainly on commercial groups. See fn. 10 in the Introduction.

By analyzing the economic activity of the 202 merchants in the sample I attempt to verify both assumptions for the case of Madrid. In the following pages I discuss the nature of their businesses, their behavior in the markets, and how they used money. In brief, this study is an attempt to define the contribution, or lack thereof, of Madrid's merchants to the consolidation of the capitalist system in Spain.

Business strategies

Family groups were at the core of the vast majority of merchant enterprises operating in Madrid between 1750 and 1850. These businesses not only depended on families for their survival and propagation, but their organization was also patterned after hierarchical family structures.[30] This form of family-centered business was relatively constant throughout the period in question.

At the more general level of market control, family groups made use of diverse associational forms. While these associations were driven by shared economic interests and by a common understanding about proper market behavior, they were equally propelled by feelings of solidarity. The first of these was family solidarity; all forms of association were strengthened if the parties were united by blood ties. The second was geographic solidarity, based on regional or hometown bonds. Such bonds were especially important in a society such as Madrid's, composed largely of immigrants from almost all regions of the country. People from the same region, county, or town identified with each other out of love of the *patria chica* (little fatherland) and in order to maintain their local culture in the big city.[31] Regional compatriots established networks of tacit brotherhood and mutual protection, used in many cases to control specific sources of power in the city.[32]

---

[30] This, however, was not a peculiarity of the Madrid case but rather a common practice among most European merchant communities of the period. See Bergeron (1978: 34); Davidoff and Hall (1987: 200).

[31] "Upon arrival in town, and probably for several years, the migrants carried with them their 'rural' attitudes toward marriage, fertility, family, social relations and just about every other aspect of urban life," according to Reher (1990: 300).

[32] Jaume Torras, in an interesting article that questioned the traditional assumption of the nonexistence of an integrated market in eighteenth-century Spain, illustrates the case of the Catalonian merchant community in Madrid. This community, according to Torras, constituted an example of what Curtin called "commercial diasporas" (mercantile groups linked by kin and geographical ties that controlled certain channels of international trade). See Torras (1989); Curtin (1984). A brief introduction of the Catalonian merchant community in Madrid during the eighteenth century can be found in Zylberberg (1983: 283 and 284).

Table 2.2. *Regional origin of the merchants of Madrid, 1750-1850*

Region	No.	%
Northwest (Galicia, Asturias)	7	3.8
North (Basque Country, Navarre, Rioja)	146	78.9
Old Castile	8	4.3
New Castile	2	1.1
Catalonia, Aragón	3	1.6
Madrid	14	7.6
Andalusia	1	0.5
Foreigners	4	2.2
Subtotal	185	
Unknown	17	
Total sample	202	

Source: Author's compilation from AHPM data; Merchants.dat

Table 2.2 shows the regional origins of 187 merchants who conducted business in Madrid between 1750 and 1850. The predominance of the North as the place of origin of 79% of the cases gives us a picture of a homogeneous community as far as regionally based culture is concerned. Refining the data somewhat further, we observe that of the 146 cases of northern merchants, 85.2% came from two regions with similar environment and cultural characteristics: the valleys of Cantabrian Mountains and of the Basque country.[33] The northern predominance was nearly total – 90% – among those merchants belonging to the Cinco Gremios, so that it was common to find groups within the membership from the same town. All told, this data is fairly indicative of the closed nature of this community and the important role that regional connections must have played in its social reproduction. I will return to the nature of such connections and their historical implications at a later point in this study.

From familial and regional ties arose a third kind of solidarity, one that stemmed from friendship. When friendship was shared by persons from the same social stratum, it produced a relationship based on trust. Individuals, for example, placed the destiny of their families in each other's hands in the

---

[33] An area in the Spanish Atlantic fringe which, according to Arensberg's categorization, constituted a cultural and ecological space with similar forms of communal organization. See Arensberg (1963: 77); Moore (1984: 37).

Careers, business, and fortunes

event of a sudden death. But when friendships were formed between persons of different social standing, as was fairly frequent, the relationship became one of loyalty, something that anthropologists have termed patronage.[34]

Economic relations valued personal prestige, generally associated with a name or location, over any sort of evaluation based on personal merit. This can be seen clearly in the array of corporate forms that existed in Madrid during the period of this study. Approximately 60% of the 202 merchants making up the sample belonged to some sort of collective or general association. An even greater percentage – 82.7% – shared in the ownership of a publicly held corporation, and just 2.7% were silent partnerships. Sole proprietorships constituted 8.3% of the cases.[35] The data demonstrate a high degree of acceptance by Madrid's merchants of various forms of ownership, which could be interpreted as a sign of capitalist vitality in the city. One should not be overly optimistic, however. Out of a total of 82 companies (both publicly held and silent partnerships) studied between 1750 and 1850, 53.3% involved people with direct family ties. Employer–employee relations characterized 32.3% of these; among this group family and regional origins frequently played a role. In only 14.4% of the cases was no apparent linkage found among managers and/or employees of the firms. A similar phenomenon occurred in the publicly held companies, although here there was more of a mixture of both traditional and modern elements. The larger companies, whether government protected or independent, were dominated by specific groups that were part of the client economy. These companies nevertheless attracted investments, as what would now be considered demand deposits, from a varied spectrum of independent sources (see Appendix B).[36]

Between 1750 and 1850, the forms of merchant associations grew in complexity and, probably, effectiveness. On occasion they changed their legal basis, and as a result new forms of association appeared. But the legal

---

[34] "'Vertical friendship', a durable two-way relationship between patrons and clients permeating the whole of society, was a social nexus peculiar to the old society, less formal and inescapable than feudal homage, more personal and comprehensive than the contractual, employment relationships of capitalist 'Cash Payment'," according to Perkin (1969: 49).

[35] An evaluation of the systems of commercial association in Spain during the eighteenth and nineteenth centuries can be found in Franch (1986: chap. V); Petit (1979); Matilla Quizá (1982).

[36] A good example was the stock companies network established around the Cinco Gremios Mayores (Compañía de Lienzos de La Salceda, Compañía de Paños, Compañía de Lienzos de la Soledad, etc.). The Compañía de Lonjistas, for instance, generated a mean of 3 million reales a year in stocks. Buyers were mainly (70% of cases) individuals related to the state bureaucracy. AHPM, P. 19969–77.

Merchants

system as well as the associative practices remained backward compared to the advances taking place in other European countries. The Commercial Code of 1829, for example, did not resolve the problem of limited liability, nor was there a property register until 1886.[37] Furthermore, the classic systems of promotion based on family, regional, and friendship ties remained embedded in these innovative legal measures.[38]

Businesses increased in complexity as they grew in size, so that little by little their original specializations faded. For this reason the notion of a specialized trading system must be qualified, since such specialization took place in the context of great diversity. Only retail vendors specialized in the sale of a few products; larger-scale merchants diversified their lines to include a wide range of merchandise and, on occasion, financial services. The largest of Madrid's merchants, both members of the Cinco Gremios and the specialized traders outside of that guild, functioned also as lenders and foreign exchange bankers, at times even participating in other sectors of the city's economy such as the government provisioning and tax collection.

The best stores, generally affiliated with the Cinco Gremios, were located in the city center. According to some contemporary observers, Madrid's stores underwent a significant transformation in the period covered by this study. Nevertheless, the majority of the businesses in eighteenth-century Madrid still lacked the luxury and comfort of their contemporaries in the great European capitals.[39] Only a few modernized their exteriors, adding display windows and improving their interiors to match the style of Parisian stores. Most stores had no exterior signs or any other public advertising, a custom that would continue well into the nineteenth century. From without, the only sign indicating the existence of a store was a sliding door that in the summer allowed the shop to expand its display space. A few stands, a display case, and the shelving filled up the interior space, which was generally poorly illuminated and austerely decorated. A religious image invariably decorated the interior, most commonly the Virgin Mary, if not the patron saint of the merchant guild to which the proprietor belonged. The lack of light at times made an adequate examination of the quality of the merchandise very difficult, so that complaints and accusations of fraud were part of everyday life for the vendor. The poor ventilation produced a heavy atmosphere in which the smells that vied for dominance were as diverse as the goods for sale.

---

[37] Toro (1986: 528); to establish a comparison with other European countries, see Pollard (1965).
[38] As one can conclude from the studies of Otazu (1987: 312 ff.) and Bahamonde (1989: 541).
[39] Aulnoy (1691; 330–338).

Careers, business, and fortunes

Nevertheless, all this began to change fairly rapidly in the first half of the nineteenth century. By 1850 Madrid already boasted a number of businesses that had nothing to envy of their counterparts in other European capitals. Customers could sit comfortably in front of a mirror in some of the elegant department stores along Mayor street, peruse the *Journal des modes* or *Le Petit courrier* to catch up with the latest Parisian styles, and make their selections. They would almost always find what they sought, especially if it was a French product (even if, in fact, it had been manufactured in Barcelona). By those years some stores already had been transformed into places where the city's well-to-do socialized. These spots offered entertainment for the idle, prestige for the established aristocracy, an opportunity for the nouveau riche to strut, and, not infrequently, an occasion for the start of a romance.[40]

Despite this activity, the renovation was rather superficial. Much about the nitty-gritty of commercial life remained as it had been one hundred years before: the social origin of the merchants, how businesses were established, how they were managed, their role in the marketplace, the very nature of trade, and even the geographic heritage of those the merchant community comprised.

Mancebos, *masters, and inheritors: Sources of capital*

Breaking into the business world was not an easy task and demanded a number of conditions that very few people could meet. Those with access to capital found it much easier, but it was also necessary to have adequate connections. As long as the Cinco Gremios kept a grip on the market for luxury products, access to the merchant community was even more complicated. The criteria for admission to each of the guilds were established in the successive ordinances of 1731, 1741, and 1783. The tenth ordinance, for example, excluded those with Muslim or Jewish blood, those who had been persecuted by the Inquisition or by any other tribunal for any notorious transgressions, and those who had been manual laborers.[41] Many guild members came from farmer families (*labradores*) of the Cantabrian and Basque valleys.[42] They were generally midlevel landowners who in most

---

[40] Mesonero (1851: 38).   [41] Molas (1985: 82).
[42] In the genealogical guide of Maza Solano (1953–57) one can find scattered information about some of these families.

cases depended on their own manual labor to such an extent that the term "manual labor" as a status maker was used exclusively as a description of the work of craftsmen. Of course, the *hidalgo* lineages of these northern families were well recognized, and the purity of their bloodlines was therefore above question. While, with the disintegration of the Cinco Gremios discriminatory legal hurdles also disappeared, day-to-day practice changed very little. We know that wealth in the second half of the nineteenth century remained in the hands of a small group whose social and regional origins were very similar to those of the members of the Cinco Gremios.[43] Access to the world of business, as with access to the worlds of bureaucracy and politics, did not really open to society as a whole until the first third of the twentieth century.

The most common means of becoming part of the merchant community was by serving an apprenticeship. The *mancebos*, as apprentices were called, were a very characteristic feature of Madrid society. The trading firm was organized, as mentioned previously, along hierarchical lines that mimicked those of the patriarchal extended family. The owner of the business was at the same time the head of the family and exercised his authority over employees and servants. The relationship between masters and *mancebos* was neither contractual in nature nor based solely on the payment of a salary. The master took in the apprentice as one more member of his family, so that the mutual commitment they established was essentially personal. During the first years of the apprenticeship a *mancebo* received nothing more than room and board in exchange for work. As time passed, if his apprenticeship was productive and his behavior proper, the *mancebo* began to collect a salary that increased every four or five years. A good career as an apprentice ended with his participation as a full partner in the company. This was the step that led to emancipation, every apprentice's dream.

Apprentices left their home towns when they were still children. Manuel Caballero, for example, relates that he left his parents in his most "tender years" to seek his fortune in Madrid. In the capital he was taken in by his cousin, who offered him employment in his business, one of the richest and most luxurious of the time. Manuel's attitude toward his employers was always one of sincere gratitude and deep respect, "like that of a child for his

---

[43] The most significant cases were those of the Marquis of Salamanca and Fernández Casariego, both with familial backgrounds in the lower levels of the provincial *hidalguía*, who succeeded in Madrid thanks to their integration in the economic and political client networks which controlled the capital power structures. See Bahamonde (1981: 387, 429 and 1989: 526). Otazu (1987: 300) has noticed the regional connections of those who formed the Madrid bourgeois elite toward 1850.

father." They were, he stated, his best counselors. He owed his education to them, and thanks to them he had learned a profession that accorded him social status. In addition to his instruction Manuel indicated that he had accumulated considerable savings in the years that he worked as head apprentice in his cousin's silk trade.[44]

Some of the prospective *mancebos* arrived in the city with a small sum given them by their parents to assist them in their initial assimilation.[45] The apprentices were almost always relatives of their employers, or came from the same home town or region, so that business groups were created and sustained based on family ties and regional solidarity. This group system facilitated upward mobility, but since it was constrained to the limits of a very well-defined group it was an imperfect mobility. Thus it was that Madrid's merchant class, unlike those of other Spanish cities, constituted a closed circle with relatively homogeneous social behavior. Yet as late as 1930, Manuel Azaña identified the image of Madrid with that of an idle aristocrat who, among other things, lives off the profits from a small business managed by one of his poor relatives brought in from the provinces.[46] At times those poor relatives ended up surpassing their mentors in skills or status, but even in these cases they depended on them. On not a few occasions the *mancebo mayor* – that is, the most important employee after the owner – assumed the role of the patriarch when the latter was away. A prolonged illness, absence from the business due to a long trip, and death would likely produce this transfer of responsibilities.

Only very rarely would a widow take over a firm's reins, and in those few cases it was only a temporary measure until she found a new partner. Sometimes the situation would be resolved by the marriage of the widow to the head apprentice, an occurrence that was considered respectable since it involved people from the same social circle. The marriage also served in many cases as a vehicle for social climbing. Juan Sixto García de la Prada, one of the wealthiest merchants in late-eighteenth-century Madrid, was able to emancipate himself economically thanks to a good marriage and his wife's dowry.[47] Marrying one's daughter to a head apprentice was an act of gratitude by the patriarch toward his underling. This type of marriage not

---

[44] AHPM, P. 22975 (wp).
[45] Nevertheless, the already installed Madrid merchants did not formally require any amount of money to admit apprentices in their business, as was the case in London. In Madrid masters never signed legal apprenticeship contracts. Most *mancebos* were members of the family, or their ties with their masters were strong enough to bypass any contractual formality. See Earle (1989: 94).
[46] Quoted by Juliá (1989: 140). [47] AHPM, P. 21047, p. 58.

Merchants

only gave continuity to the business and, for that matter, to the family, but it also served as an incentive for young men just starting on a business career.

Life as an apprentice did not always mean a career leading to higher social stature, however, not all stories had a happy ending; more often than not the trainee ended his days as they had begun: at the orders of his master. Bartolomé de los Heros is one apprentice plagued by misfortune. A native of Valmaseda, a district in Vizcaya, de los Heros belonged to a noble family with good connections in the capital and in the colonies. His first steps led him to America, assisted by a good sum of money from his father. There he found the protection of his relatives and fellow Vizcayans, but for unknown reasons his experience in America produced only expenses and disasters. So badly did it go that he decided to try his luck in Madrid. Once there he set to work in a business owned by his uncle, Juan Antonio de los Heros, but a few months later an illness he had contracted in the West Indies took his life. This misfortune occurred in September 1782 when Bartolomé was still a minor.[48]

It was easier to start a business as a retail vendor, since this sector was not controlled by any specific group. Starting up a luxury merchandising or wholesale business was another matter; considerable capital was required, in addition to the social requirements and the contacts mentioned in previous paragraphs. Capital for such ventures was almost always derived from two sources: family and personal work. Table 2.3 gives the start-up capital for 55 merchants who lived in Madrid between 1750 and 1850, although more than 90% of the cases fall within the period between 1750 and 1816. Forty-six of the 55 cases, or 84%, belonged to the category of luxury good merchants, and a majority of these belonged also to the Cinco Gremios. Precise information is not available for the quantity of money necessary to open a business in Madrid; we can nevertheless make some observations from the analysis of the asset levels in the sample. Almost 22% were below 100,000 reales, indicating that one in four merchants started business with some 50,000 reales – and some with even less. The median initial capital was approximately 200,000 reales, distributed so that 40% – a little more than one-third – of the merchants had between 100,000 and 300,000 reales. Within this group could be found the majority of the upwardly mobile businessmen, that is, the fortunate *mancebos*. Last, the initial net assets of a significant proportion – 32.7% – surpassed 500,000 reales, and the majority

---

[48] AHPM, P. 21721, p. 84.

Table 2.3. *Initial capital of Madrid merchants, 1750-1850*
(reales de vellón)

Capital	1750-83	1783-1816	1816-50	Total	%
1-100,000	7	5	0	12	21.8
100,000-200,000	9	4	1	14	25.5
200,000-300,000	2	5	1	8	14.5
300,000-500,000	0	3	0	3	5.5
500,000-1,000,000	2	5	0	7	12.7
1,000,000+	2	6	3	11	20.0
Total cases	22	28	5	55	
% in periods	40.0	50.9	9.1		
Median of capitals	207,902				

Source: See Appendix B.

of these in fact exceeded 1 million reales. Rather than accumulated capital, these amounts represented inherited wealth.

Most of the small-scale investments were made out of personal savings earned from working in a store. Juan Posadillo, for example, earned 1,500 reales per year for his employment as an apprentice in his brother's store. This salary did not include the costs of room and board, which were paid by the patron as head of the family. After nine years of apprenticeship, Juan became a partner in the firm; this radically changed his situation. For seven years he received one-tenth of the total profits, which meant an increase of more than 3,000 reales in his annual income. In 1771 he was finally promoted to *mancebo mayor* and increased his percentage of the profits to one-third. By 1777, Juan had accumulated 150,000 reales and opened his own business.[49] Occasionally salaries were paid in kind, merchandise was given to the trainee, or he was given a share of the high-quality debt instruments acquired by his employers, but this was a relatively infrequent practice used only in times of economic difficulty.

The portion of assets obtained via inheritances was also very important. One fairly common type of inheritance was that received by nephews from an uncle. Among all relatives, merchants preferred nephews for those posi-

[49] AHPM, P. 19967, p. 29.

tions that demanded most responsibility within the business. When there were no direct heirs, these nephews became the guardians of the family business for future generations. Most common, however, were those merchants who, like Santiago Sancho, inherited their businesses from their parents.[50] Inheritance was the principal vehicle for the continued presence of the most important family names in the merchant community of Madrid, names like Posadillo Caballero, Iruegas, Sáinz de Baranda, Sáaenz de Tejada, etc. Of course, if the son's behavior was dubious his parents could also opt to disinherit him, as did Manuel de los Heros, who refused to give one single coin of his fortune to his son due to the latter's "tendency to squander and frivolously waste his money."[51]

Approximately 30% of the initial assets of the 55 cases studied had been accumulated through commerce and implied the continuation of family fortunes through the generations. But there were also significant assets – around 10% of the total – that came from family fortunes not reaped through business activity. A significant portion of Madrid's merchant elite came from well-off families of provincial nobility, and thus had sufficient capital to launch their business careers. That was the case of the Iruegas family, present in Madrid since the mid-1700s, and proprietors of one of the most elegant shops in the city during the first half of the nineteenth century.[52]

Last, it is necessary to point out the occasions on which the novice merchant obtained economic assistance from a family member or a friend. Ramón de Angulo, for example, received 50,000 reales on loan from his father as a start-up fund for his store. Ramón's father lived in Ranero, a small village in the valley of Carranza in the Basque country.[53] Ignacio Sáenz de Prado received 70,000 reales in 1791 from a relative of his living in Torrecilla de Cameros to make improvements to his business.[54] Such loans were not made altruistically, however; either interest was collected on them or the money was entrusted to the businessman for investment purposes. This sort of transaction, as with the inherited assets that originated in the hometowns of merchants operating in Madrid, demonstrates the existence of an economic interaction between the capital and other peripheral regions

---

[50] He inherited his father's shop located in Atocha Street near the CGM building. AHPM, P. 19988 (wp).
[51] AHPM, P. 18823, p. 432.   [52] AHPM, P. 21409, p. 243.
[53] AHPM, P. 19969, p. 819.   [54] AHPM, P. 20070 (wp).

of Spain. In this sense, Madrid was not only an agent for the absorption of assets, but also served to redistribute the surpluses generated in some of the more dynamic regions of Spain at the time, as in the case of the Cantabrian border. Only through an analysis of the nature of the business conducted by these merchant firms in Madrid can we come to understand the characteristics of that interaction between the capital and the regional markets.

Markets and business

The size of a business determined its character and the extent of its specialization. In general, businesses tended to be diversified in nature, corresponding to the backwardness of Madrid's economic development during that period. Indeed, what is termed here "specialized trade" often included activities as diverse as the sale of woolens and military supply contracting. Only small merchants specialized somewhat narrowly; the majority of the traveling vendors, small shopkeepers, and retailers in general carried a modest range of merchandise. Their economic function was to meet the household demand of the popular classes, whose purchasing power was very slight. There was also a segment of the firms belonging to the Cinco Gremios that specialized in some way, but even these showed a clear trend toward business diversification. It was very rare, for example, to find a member of the Gremios who did not function at one time or another as a moneylender,[55] or who had not offered some financial service at a local scale such as guaranteeing a bill of exchange or accepting private money as a checking account. Finally, those businesses with sales volumes surpassing 1 million reales yearly income – 56.6% of the sample used here – tended to participate in multiple markets.

In this section I use a number of specific examples to analyze the nature of those operations that were sufficiently large to allow their proprietors to diversify their lines of business. This means that retailers and those small merchants not belonging to the Cinco Gremios Mayores will be left out of the analysis. Between 1750 and 1850 historical changes significantly transformed the Spanish economy. To illuminate the extent to which these changes affected Madrid's economy I next examine the role played by Madrid's merchant capital in regional and national markets.

Generally speaking the nature of the merchandising business remained

[55] Zilberberg (1983: 288).

unchanged over the hundred-year period of this study, and businesses usually fitted a common model. The basis of this model was diversification, as has been noted, and it was characterized by participation in three sectors of Madrid's economy: the provision of basic goods for the city, the sale of luxury goods, and filling contracts for the state. The first of these sectors linked the capital with a wide hinterland that included various regions of the interior of Spain. The luxury goods trade, by contrast, was based on the exchange of products with markets in other regions and countries. During the period of this study important transformations occurred in the last of these sectors: that portion of the market driven by governmental services. The basic good market was also liberalized, and the volume of luxury trade increased, although fairly modestly. These changes did not, however, affect the structure of Madrid's market, which remained basically unaltered.

The Posadillo family business during the second half of the eighteenth century offers a clear example of the model generally adopted by merchants. Originally from Zérdigo, a village in the Castrourdiales jurisdiction, the Posadillo Llaguno clan appears to have arrived in Madrid close to the year 1740. Domingo was the eldest of the three sons who eventually established businesses in Madrid, and therefore the trail blazer. His first steps were thoroughly standard: he began as a *mancebo* in the store operated by his cousin Gregorio Llaguno and, by 1765 or so had saved enough capital to launch his own business, replete with his own assistants.[56] In a few years Domingo owned two stores located near Madrid's Plaza Mayor. His family and other from the village of Zérdigo had helped him get started in the city, and in this first step into the luxury goods market Posadillo again made use of his family to consolidate his business. In 1769 he rented a store from Joaquina de Sobrado, a widow, and installed his brother Juan Santos there.[57] Years later his brother Francisco received ownership of another store as a present for his marriage to a first cousin.

In the 1770s Posadillo expanded his business into regional markets. The pharmaceutical market was not limited to the capital, but in fact extended into nearby areas. Every year Posadillo rented a store in Almagro during its annual town fair. His apprentices and salesmen sold products there that could otherwise only be found in Madrid's specialty stores. This link to regional markets was quite significant and reached considerable distances, including the country of la Vera and the Campo de Calatrava. In this

[56] AHPM, P. 19963, p. 291. [57] AHPM, P. 19962, p. 513.

manner Madrid's merchants forged connections among a number of regions in the interior of the peninsula, regional markets elsewhere, and the international market. Normally, druggists in Madrid had as clients their colleagues in those regions that enjoyed easier access to the capital than to the coast. But among the Posadillo family's clients were also found a number of families of the local elite and a good number of rural churches.[58]

In 1776 Domingo Posadillo signed a partnership contract with a brandy manufacturer in the town of Miguelturra in La Mancha. Posadillo invested part of his capital in a liquor distillery owned by Manuel López, who in turn agreed to furnish liquor to his new partner's business in Madrid. Posadillo would collect two reales for each *arroba* of brandy marketed, in addition to the interest on his investment.[59] The next year, Posadillo purchased from the Marquis of Ensenada, in the town of Valdepeñas, "a wine cellar with equipment for bottling wine."[60] Four years later Posadillo was already producing wine which he sold to the municipal authorities of Madrid.[61]

In 1782 the Posadillo family business offered a clear example of diversification. Thanks to the close relationships he shared with family and regional comrades, Domingo Posadillo controlled several stores in Madrid – at least three of which he owned – that belonged to the Cinco Gremios, one wine cellar in Valdepeñas and another in Manzanares complete with its own vineyard, a store in Aranjuez, and stores leased out for the annual fairs of various towns in la Mancha. In 1783 his brother Francisco obtained a position as treasurer of the branch office that the Cinco Gremios operated in Cádiz. From this post the family obtained a greatly expanded credit line to finance its businesses and a much more reliable supplier for their varied product lines. In addition, Posadillo began to invest part of his profits in leasing the *tercias* and tithes of the grape taxes of the townships of Manzanares and Miguelturra.[62] In 1787 Posadillo leased the liquor distributorship for Madrid for five years. During those same years the House of Domingo Posadillo was also accepting money from individuals as, in effect, demand deposits.[63]

Domingo Posadillo had five sons and many nephews, of whom only two followed him into the business world. Carlos, his second, became a Francis-

---

[58] AHPM, P. 19971, p. 244 and 245; 19972, p. 88 and 19975, p. 209.
[59] AHPM, P. 19966, p. 33.   [60] Ibid, p. 527.
[61] AHPM, P. 19968, p. 321.   [62] AHPM, P. 19969, p. 93.
[63] AHPM, P. 19973, p. 442.

can friar. Antonio undertook legal studies, his career culminating as a lawyer of the Royal Council. Josée, with his father's help, became manager of the *encomineda* of Manzanares in 1793. Manuel and Juan Antonio remained with the family businesses. Manuel, however, died young and Juan Antonio eventually dedicated himself exclusively to wine production, becoming in effect an agribusinessman. In this way the family left the world of business for those of civil service and real property ownership, a path followed by many of Madrid's merchant families.

Illustrating more effectively the model of business diversification is the small group of families that made up the elite of Madrid's merchant community: that is, the directors of the Cinco Gremios and their descendants. This group was distinguished by its influence over the economic and political life of Madrid. An analysis of their businesses shows that they remained essentially unchanged with the turn of the century, and that the new generation continued to operate within the same economic framework. The economic history of the García de la Prada family, for example, extends throughout the time period covered by this study. Juan Sixto arrived in Madrid in the mid-1700s to be initiated into the business of selling linens with his uncle Juan Bautista Ruiz de la Prada. The Prada family was of the nobility of the mountains of Santander whose members settled in Madrid and the American colonies. Fernando, brother of Juan Sixto, followed an ecclesiastical career and eventually rose to a high position in the tribunal of the Inquisition.[64] Juan Sixto's linen shop was one of the most exclusive of the early nineteenth century. García de la Prada supplied the major firms of the capital and served as a wholesaler for countless small and midsized businesses. For a number of years Juan Sixto was the chief director of the Cinco Gremios Mayores, with an additional salary of 50,000 reales per year, not including the indirect benefits that such a position afforded.

Without a doubt the greatest of these benefits, as far as his business was concerned, was the various contracts signed by the Cinco Gremios and the Public Treasury for the procurement of army uniforms. Juan Sixto invested a good portion of the income from such contracts in city taxes; with the remainder he began to make mortgage loans to noblemen with problems of liquidity. Both activities produced for García de la Prada one of the most impressive fortunes of those years and one that was, needless to say, consid-

---

[64] AHN, Estado, Pruebas de Carlos III, exp. 767.

Table 2.4. *Garcia de la Prada's loans to the Marquis of Cogolludo, 1778-88*
(reales de vellón)

Statement: March, 1778 September, 1784	3,238,528
Statement, March 1784 September, 1785	18,468
Statement, February 1787 August, 1788	153,789
Loan at 2.5 percent	862,845
Total debts	4,274,630

Source: AHPM, P. 21,080 (wp)

erably larger than those of many members of the old aristocracy.[65] How the mortgage business worked is demonstrated by the business García de la Prada conducted with the House of Medinaceli. Table 2.4 gives the amount of the first debt contracted by the Marquis of Cogolludo in the form of merchandise and loans between 1778 and 1788. The debt was guaranteed with the rents earned from the estate of Castellar and the *novenos* and *tercias* of Ecija. Three years later a *censo* was reached between the duke of Medinaceli and García de la Prada with a value of 8 million reales and an interest rate of 3%, guaranteed by the duke's estate. In effect it was a short-term mortgage, since the agreement called for the 8 million reales to be repaid in only eight years.[66]

This entire fortune was passed on to Juan Sixto's sole heir, his son Manuel, who continued to run the family businesses. The second generation Prada did not have to pass through the purgatory of apprenticeship as a *mancebo* to gain high social standing. Manuel came into his father's business at an early age and, more important, was the scion of an estate that generated a sufficiently abundant income to assure a very comfortable and early retirement. Thus Manuel was nominated member of the Orden of Carlos III when he was only 30 years of age, whereas his father received this distinction only in his later years. By 1800, when he was only thirty-three years old, Manuel was Comisario Ordenador of the Royal Armies and director general of the Royal Provisions of the State, as well as being a director on the

---

[65] Recent works demonstrate the economic troubles of many aristocratic families between 1750 and 1850. Whether the aristocrats lost social leadership as a consequence of their indebtedness is a matter of debate. See Atienza (1987: 327 and ss.) and Bahamonde (1986).
[66] AHPM, P. 21080 (wp).

governing council of the Bank of San Carlos.[67] During the war years Manuel's profits from procurement contracts increased as he took advantage of his position as magistrate of Madrid. The third generation of Pradas – now well into the nineteenth century – continued to hold very high posts in the financial world and Madrid politics and, of course, continued making good use of their family influence and their connections with the state to do business.[68]

Government supply contracts and the sale of luxury goods also produced fortunes for the Iruegas and Bringas families, two of the most important among Madrid's business elite from the end of the eighteenth century to the middle of the next. Their histories were parallel to some extent, in that they were from the same regions, were in fact relatives, and owned similar businesses. The Iruegas formed one of the wealthiest merchant families in Madrid around the 1780s. Baltasar de Iruegas, the sire of the family, was director of the Cinco Gremios, a position he used as an entry into the government procurement business.[69] On August 16, 1790, Iruegas, along with other Madrid merchants, lost a portion of his store in a fire that destroyed part of the Plaza Mayor. This mishap led him to begin a partnership with his in-laws nephew and fellow countryman Francisco Antonio Bringas to rebuild his business and also to speculate on the vacant lots left by the fire.[70] Baltasar did not have a direct descendant, so his fortune passed on to his nephews, some of whom continued in the business world at a much lower level. The man who really gained from the wealth that Iruegas had amassed was his relative, compatriot, and partner Francisco Antonio Bringas y Presilla, himself the founder of another well-known dynasty of businessmen.[71]

The first Bringas about whom anything is known, Francisco de Bringas López, probably arrived in Madrid in the first half of the eighteenth century with little more than a small sum of money in his pocket and the document that established his noble lineage. I do not know how Francisco began his business career, but he clearly chose a fortuitous path; by 1780 he enjoyed the title of "supplier of the Court and Royal Residences," which gave him

---

[67] AHPM, P. 21094, p. 427.
[68] On the Manuel García de la Prada offspring see AHPM, P. 22274, f. 363; 23028, f. 81 and 25778, f. 1.
[69] There existed a provisioning company founded by Manuel de Iruegas in which the most powerful members of the CGM and the Compañía de Lonjistas participated. AHPM, P. 21102 (wp). AHN, Estado, Pruebas de Carlos III, exp. 1055.
[70] AHPM, P. 23093, p. 738.   [71] Pérez Galdós (1951: vol. VI, 1750).

control of a significant part of the fuel market in Madrid.[72] We also know that he was a member of the Cinco Gremios and that he entailed real estate properties – worth 6.5 million reales – that his nephew Francisco Antonio would inherit along with his businesses and positions. The enrichment of Francisco Antonio, the true author of the saga, actually started long before he came into his uncle's substantial inheritance. Francisco Antonio de Bringas y Presilla had been born in the valley of Mena and he had heard many stories of fellow townspeople and relatives who had made their fortune in the capital. With the help of his uncle he soon became involved in the world of commerce, and especially in the government supply business. In 1797 he founded the Bringas company with 2 million reales in assets derived from the stores he had inherited from Francisco Bringas López.[73]

His business activities were quite diverse in those years; in addition to his stores, Francisco Antonio was one of the largest lenders in the capital.[74] During those early years of the new century Bringas was "quartermaster of the royal armies" and also kept up his uncle's sales operation in the city. But the heart of his economic activity was real estate speculation. Bringas knew how to take advantage of the fallen values of the lots around the Plaza Mayor after the fire, investing a considerable portion of his assets. He surely never regretted the investment, since it produced the economic security necessary for his family to survive the many crises of the nineteenth century. The war was, in fact, something of a blow to his businesses, forcing some of them to close, but Bringas maintained his military supply business and his real estate properties in Madrid.[75] Francisco Antonio died in 1822. A few years before, his son of the same name had enlisted in the *guardia de Corps*, but around 1827 he left the army to take over his father's businesses and to marry the daughter of a very important Madrid banker. Upon his untimely death in 1834, his entire fortune was passed on to his daughter and only heir, María Pilar Bringas, who later married an ambitious provincial lawyer. From that time on the descendants of those eighteenth-century merchants lived off their inherited estates and their positions in the state bureaucracy. Thus did their forebears' struggle to accumulate capital evolve into a struggle for a different kind of capital whose currency was political power and titles of nobility.

[72] AHN, Diversos, Títulos y Familias, legs. 2227 and 2246.
[73] AHPM, P. 21393, p. 52.   [74] Ibid. p. 838.
[75] AHN, Diversos, Títulos y Familias, leg. 2225.

Merchants

The last example that I will examine in this section is that of the Caballero family, whose history truly belongs to the nineteenth century. Andrés and José Caballero del Moral were brothers from the Valle de Guriezo in the Santander mountains who arrived in Madrid toward the end of the 1780s to live with relatives. Part of the Caballeros' success was due to their knack for strategic marriages. Solidarity among regional compatriots helped Andrés win the hand of Francisca del Mazo, niece of Juan Sixto García del la Prada, while José made good use of his good connections in Madrid's business community to exchange matrimonial vows with the widow of Diego Pérez Donis, once a director of the Cinco Gremios Mayores.[76] Between 1790 and 1810 the Caballeros built their own financial empire, which combined their showroom business with a wholesaling enterprise for the capital and mortgage lending to the aristocracy.[77]

The children of Andrés became the second generation of the House of Caballero, since José had left no direct heirs. Andrés and José Caballero y Mazo continued to control the Caballero firm and at the same time participated actively in Madrid's public life during the mid-1800s. The second generation of brothers – the Caballero y Mazo – were fully a part of Madrid's power elite in the first half of the century. By 1835 Andrés was director of the Bank of San Fernando, councilman in Madrid's municipality representing the *cuerpo colegiado de la nobleza* (noble estate), his brother José was a knight of Santiago and married a daughter of the wealthy merchant José Collado, with whom he culminated his career in business. Successive generations of Caballeros never left the business world, even though their social status by 1865 was quite different from that enjoyed by their forebears when they had arrived in Madrid some eighty-five years earlier.

This review of the business characteristics of Madrid's commercial community demonstrates the limited extent of the structural transformation of markets in the Spanish interior between 1750 and 1850. Of course, the economic reform measures adopted between 1798 and 1855 prompted renewed activity in a number of markets that had shown clear signs of saturation, as was the case with the real estate market. It is also true that over the course of this period there was a rejuvenation of the society comprising the world of business in Madrid. New families appeared, the means for ac-

---

[76] AHPM, P. 23079, p. 245; 21404, p. 72. AHN, Estado, Pruebas de Carlos III, exp. 1826.
[77] AHPM, P. 21782., p. 529.

cumulating capital multiplied, and there were more opportunities to make money and to make it fast. But all this took place within a framework that continued to be dominated by a system of patronage and clientage that reflected the persistence of a traditional economy.

Family fortunes and investment practices

The study of accumulated personal fortunes sheds light on the investment practices of each of the groups represented in this study, as well as on the structural changes that were observed in Madrid's economy over the long term. Understanding both phenomena is essential to evaluating the changes in and the continuities of the economy of the Spanish interior in an age of supposed transformation.

Information is available about the estates of 99 merchants who lived in Madrid between 1750 and 1850. The data come for the most part from posthumous inventories carried out on occasion for the purpose of dividing up inheritances. These inventories provide information about the values and compositions of the varied assets of each estate. In only nine cases is such information lacking, because the data have been derived from sources other than inventories, usually from declarations annexed to wills or other official documents. Although some of these cases are quite significant, like that of García de la Prada, I do not believe that they would alter the overall results. Unfortunately, between 1740 and 1791 families almost never tool inventories of their assets, or if they did, they did not do it in a legally documented manner.[78] This is the reason that the majority of the cases included here – 56% of them – are taken from the period between 1783 and 1816.

There was no generally accepted norm for partitioning estates. Most of the time this was accomplished by compiling an inventory of the deceased's assets that began by valuing household items and ended with an appraisal of any income-generating assets, but this order was not followed on many occasions. In one way or another, however, all agreements for dividing estates concluded with an estimate of total value, termed the "body of the assets" or "body of the estate," from which were subtracted the usual deductions to calculate the net assets to be shared. There were two kinds of

---

[78] Through a Royal Order enacted in November 4, 1791, probate inventories could be completed by family and friends of the testator without intervention of the Royal Justice, as was required by the previous law. AHPM, P. 21885, p. 113.

Table 2.5. *Net assets of merchants in Madrid, 1750-1850*
(*reales de vellón*)

Net Assets	1	2	3	4	Total%
1-500,000	17	1	5	1	24.2
500,000-1,000,000	13	1	2	3	19.2
1,000,000-1,500,000	16	1		5	22.2
1,500,000-2,000,000	10	1			11.1
2,000,000-5,000,000	5			4	9.1
5,000,000-10,000,000	6			3	9.1
10,000,000+	5				5.1
Total cases	72	4	7	16	99
Net Assets Median	1,149,683				

Key: 1. Cinco Gremios Mayores; 2. Booksellers; 3. Shopkeepers; 4. Special Commerce.
Source: Probate Inventories, AHPM. See Appendix B.

deductions: those that were required by the law, as was the case with dowries and the *lecho cotidiano;* and any outstanding debts contracted by the deceased. The data examined in this work refers to the net assets.[79]

Table 2.5 shows the distribution of the size of estates according to the occupation of each of the persons in the sample. As can be seen, the bulk of the data – 72% – refers to merchants affiliated with the Cinco Gremios, who constituted the authentic "merchant bourgeoisie" of Madrid. The category of shopkeepers includes clothes dealers whose business consisted of buying and selling used apparel, and who constituted a very distinct group within Madrid's merchant community. The estates of the seven shopkeepers in the sample were valued below 1 million reales, indicating that the social category of the occupation was correlated with its economic importance. However, the subsample included in this work is too small to be significant; a thorough examination of this category of merchants would benefit from monographic study and is beyond the scope of this work. A similar effect can be seen within the booksellers, a profession located between the commercial, cultural, and artisan spheres. The four cases that appear in our

[79] Detailed information on the nature and value of this kind of source can be found in García Baquero (1976: 503); Castañeda (1984: 757–760); Bennassar (1984).

analysis demonstrate their dispersion along the social spectrum. Toward the end of the eighteenth century, bookselling was a profession bestowing more social prestige than income, although for the most part booksellers were an honorable and relatively influential middle class, a group that in itself deserves further study.[80]

The sixteen cases categorized as specialized traders offer a profile closer to that of the members of the Cinco Gremios. Their median wealth was some 1,481,146 reales, compared to 1,165,776 for the merchants in the Cinco Gremios. However, 43.7% of the specialized traders in the sample had assets greater than 2 million reales, as opposed to 19.4% of the merchant guild members. This should not come as a surprise, since specialized merchants unaffiliated with the Cinco Gremios represented the most dynamic sector of the merchant class in Madrid, and indeed of the merchant class in the country during the period. This sector's function was to link the market in the capital with those regions showing the greatest level of economic activity – such as the textile traders of Catalonia and the Basque ironworkers. Their "specialization" – keeping in mind the imprecision of the term – placed them in a propitious position for enrichment, since they often controlled very well-differentiated market segments of the demand generated in the capital.

One-fourth of the estates were valued below 500,000 reales. This group includes shopkeepers and the less-diversified merchant guild members. Nevertheless, more than half of the merchants in the sample held assets that ranged from 500,000 to 2 million reales, a range that brackets the median estate value of 1,149,683 reales. The upper one-fourth of the sample exceeded 2 million reales in value, but only a fraction possessed a fortune surpassing 10 million reales. But what is the significance of these figures? What information do they reveal? In the first place, they can give a good idea of the importance of Madrid's merchant community relative to others in the period of the study. Second, they indicate how these groups invested their surplus capital. And last, comparison of data for the groups that made up the middle class of Madrid can help shape an understanding of merchants' contribution to the financing of a developing capitalist economy.

The levels of wealth accumulated by the merchants of Madrid make clear that this group was well established in Spanish society toward the end of the

---

[80] Thomas (1983) studied the institutional developments of the Real Compañía de Impresores y Libreros de Madrid. Still we do not know anything about the sociology of its members.

Merchants

eighteenth century. According to available data, the wealth of Madrid's merchants was surpassed only by that of merchants based in Cádiz, and was well above that found in other provincial communities. The estates of 21 merchants operating in Cádiz and García Baquero studied had a median net worth over 3 million reales, and one-third of these were valued at more than 7 million reales, significantly higher than those of their Madrid counterparts.[81] There is no doubt that the great trading companies of the era were centered in Cádiz, and it is very possible that the greatest merchant fortunes were made there also. Nevertheless, the sample analyzed by García Baquero is sparse. The correlation of 22 cases with a surrounding community of 600 individuals is insufficient by an measure. In addition, the sample covers only registered merchants, that is, the sector that enjoyed the largest profit margins; its social equivalent in Madrid would be the elite of the Cinco Gremios and, as will be seen later, the financial community. A more complete study is required before we can make this comparison with greater confidence.

The panorama changes substantially when we turn to compare data for the merchants of Valencia, Málaga, and Seville. Nearly 38% of the 52 Valencia merchants studied by Franch possessed estates smaller than 300,000 reales, and none of them reached 5 million reales. Their median wealth was around 750,000 reales, considerably below that of their counterparts in Madrid, which is all the more significant given that Franch's sample includes only the most successful merchants in the city.[82] Madrid's merchant community was also wealthier than that of Málaga, which consisted largely of foreigners who specialized in agricultural exports. Fifty-eight percent of the 36 cases studied by Villar had estates worth less than 500,000, compared to only 24% in Madrid. A similar result is obtained by comparing the greatest fortunes of the two communities: only 27% of Málaga's merchants controlled more than 1 million reales in assets, while 56% of those in Madrid did. The median values of the two communities' estates also differed significantly, being 270,984 reales in the case of Málaga versus 1,149,683 in Madrid. Despite these statistics, a few isolated cases, such as that of the Irishman Galwey and the Frenchman Laclau, involved estates that surpassed those of the merchants of Valencia and were comparable to those of the wealthy merchants of Cádiz and Madrid.[83] Alvarez Santalo and García Baquero's study of Seville shows that 77% of the merchant wealth of that community was below 1 million reales, while only 22% fell between 1

[81] García Baquero (1976: 510). [82] Franch (1986: 293).
[83] Villar (1982: 135–138).

and 5 million, and the median wealth was even less than that calculated for Málaga.[84]

The last case to consider is that of the exporters of the port city of Bilbao, some of whom maintained close contacts with Madrid.[85] Of the more than 20 cases studied by Basurto, none involved an estate worth more than 2.5 million reales, and one gets the impression that the median wealth was below those in the other communities discussed here.[86] Thus, judging by these comparisons, it seems clear that the route to enrichment as a merchant was easier in Madrid than in other regions of the country. In addition, the merchants of Madrid, who in a city of aristocrats, ecclesiastical dignitaries, and high government functionaries, appeared to pass somewhat unnoticed, regain their importance as a group when viewed as an integral part of the whole of Spanish society. This explains in part why Madrid's market attracted immigrants from certain provincial middle classes, and why a very narrow group of these immigrants would go to great lengths to keep it under their control.

Figure 2.1 and Table 2.6 show the structure of wealth and its evolution from 1750 to 1850. That period has been divided into three time segments chosen to illustrate the changes that occurred in this structure over the long term. The historical literature on Spain commonly places the birth of modern capitalism in the first half of the nineteenth century, in conjunction with the disentailment processes.[87] In the case of Madrid, various authors have frequently postulated a profound transformation of the economic structure and the corresponding enrichment of a new social class.[88] The evidence offered by the data analyzed here contradicts that interpretation. The inventories of assets tend to establish a simplified division of the inheritances between household goods and real estate. Such a division is insufficient for the sort of analysis I am attempting, given that under the rubric of household goods can be found anything that was not urban or rural real estate property. Therefore I have divided this heading into four separate categories. In the first are included what we could call "true household goods" – that is, items of general domestic use, including luxury goods and

---

[84] Alvarez Santalo and García Baquero (1980: 129).
[85] Especially those in the business of international wool trade who frequently were agents of export firms established in Madrid (see Chapter 3). Also the owners of prestigious export firms in the main Spanish ports (Bilbao and Cádiz) ended up establishing businesses in the capital. See AHPM, P. 20073 and 20075 (wp).
[86] Basurto (1983: chap. V).
[87] Herr (1989: 720–725) offers a revision for this model of interpretation.
[88] The book written by Bahamonde and Toro (1974) represents a good example of this interpretive model that these same authors have revised in subsequent publications.

Merchants

Table 2.6. *Composition of the fortunes. Merchants of Madrid, 1750-1850*

Total sample: 99 cases			1	2	3	4
1750-1783	Total cases: 23	23.2%	73.9%	8.7%	4.3%	13.1%
1783-1816	Total cases: 56	56.6%	75.9%	3.6%	4.4%	16.1%
1815-1850	Total cases: 20	20.2%	65%	0	15%	20%

	1750-1783	1783-1816	1816-1850
Personal Estate			
Domestic	2.88	3.63	3.30
Cash/silver	7.40	8.08	5.47
Real Estate			
Rural	4.39	2.55	5.32
Urban	6.56	11.22	21.63
Revenues			
Government debt	9.77	10.98	14.43
Company stocks	13.24	10.78	3.80
Loans/censos	5.17	3.28	5.74
Business			
Trade credit	26.56	27.35	17.39
Commodities	23.80	22.14	22.90
Industry	0.23		0.02

1. Cinco Gremios; 2. Booksellers; 3. Shopkeepers; 4. Specialized Commerce.
Source: See appendix B.

money, be it in the form of currency or precious metals.[89] The second category includes real estate. I have included those assets related to the business in the third category: in the case of merchant, commodities and trade credits. The only type of business in which we can find equipment is among the booksellers, whose goods have been included in the category of commodities, since the number of cases and amount of capital involved are too small to alter the conclusions from the sample.

More complicated, however, is the fourth category, titled "other investments," which contains all investments other than real estate. That portion termed "Debt" is perhaps the most subject to question, since within it have been included holdings in part of the various government debt instruments floated by the state in the one hundred years encompassed by this study.

---

[89] The storage of silver and gold was not the result of a desire for ostentation, rather a necessity imposed by the deficiencies of the monetary system prior to the first third of the nineteenth century. See Pérez Herrero (1988: chap. 8). On the lack of currency in Spain at the end of the eighteenth century see Artola (1982: 389 and 398).

Careers, business, and fortunes

1750-1783

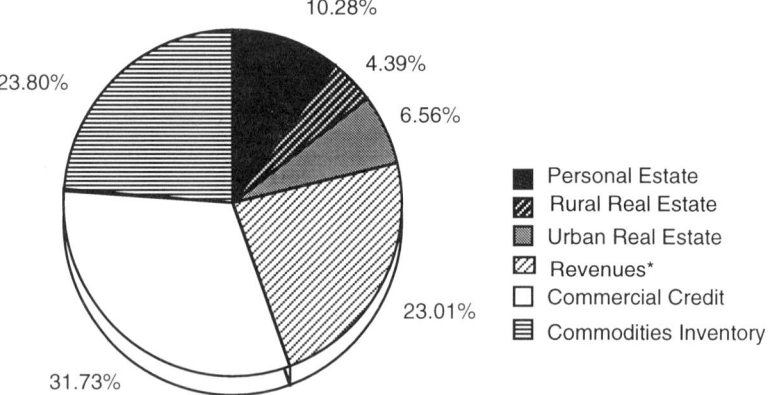

* Government Bonds and Public Companies Stocks

1783-1816

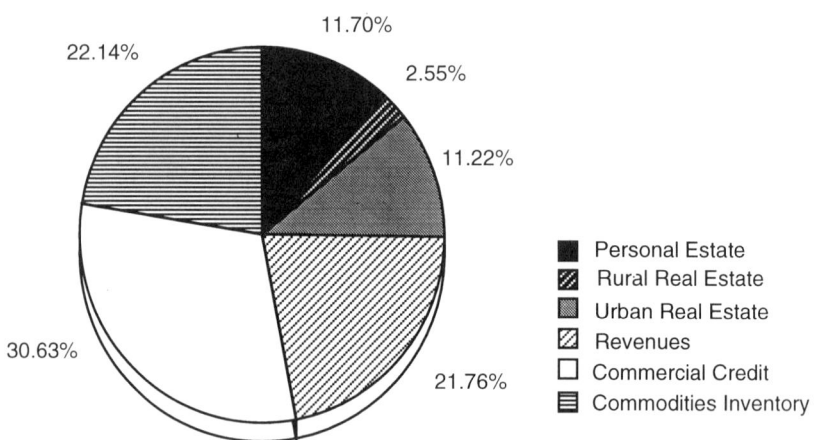

Merchants

1816-1850

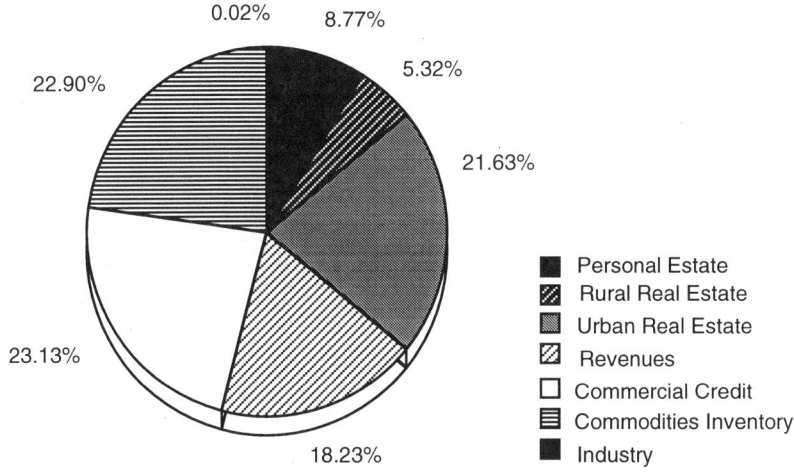

Figure 2.1. Percentage distribution of gross assets: Merchants, 1750–1783

Placing the *vales reales* – which were very abundant in the inheritances that were passed on in the last years of the eighteenth century – together with the leasing of municipal taxes and the purchase of stocks could be questioned, but these investments share an essential character as government-generated. This, along with the small but secure return they provided, leads me to believe that grouping them together offers a more precise historical understanding. Last, under the heading of loans are interest-bearing lending activities and *censos* – a sort of finance instrument similar to today's mortgages.

The picture painted by the charts in Figure 2.1 is one of a steady trend with neither radical changes nor stagnation. The charts illustrate the trajectories of change followed by some kinds of assets and the more stable proportions represented by others; nevertheless, with one exception, each of the trajectories was the product of a gradual transition rather than a sudden change. I begin my analysis with the continuities that distinguish the overall picture generated by the charts.

Domestic goods maintained a stability matched only by that portion of the estates invested in industrial activities. The fact that domestic consumer goods did not vary in their proportion of assets does not mean that merchant households failed to grow more comfortable over time, but does indicate a certain shrinkage of the consumer market. Explaining the stability of industrial investment is a much more complicated matter and carries great historical implications. García Sanz correctly observes that one of the greatest downfalls of the economy of Madrid – and consequently of the economy of the Spanish interior – was due to the very slight investment of merchant capital in the sphere of production. This separation, he concludes, was the result of a long-term process that had more to do with the attitude of a portion of the urban classes than with the context within which the Spanish market had been developing since the end of the sixteenth century. García Sanz views the problem through the lens of Braudel's classic thesis of the "treason of the bourgeoisie," which explains the apathy of this social class toward production as a cultural problem stemming from certain social prejudices.[90] Thus Madrid's merchants preferred to employ their money where the cultural returns were higher – that is, in those sectors that brought social prestige – instead of in productive activities. To what degree should we accept this interpretation? In my opinion Garcí Sanz is on target in his identification of the symptoms, but his diagnosis is somewhat less certain.

There is one feature that differentiates the merchant community in Madrid from those in other Spanish regions in which the production–distribution dichotomy was not as sharp. This is the fact that the majority of Madrid's merchants immigrated to the city from distant regions, and their social composition was primarily of regional low and medium levels of *hidalguía*. Of course the migration of this class of people from the provinces to large cities was not a phenomenon exclusive to Madrid. During the modern age the growth of the urban middle classes of all European capitals was fed by an influx of provincial job-seekers who generally settled into the various economic niches found in these cities. At first these groups were fairly homogeneous in their social and regional origins,[91] but with the passage of time and in step with economic specialization, the patterns of immigration became more complex. The bulk of the merchant and financial class of Paris at the start of the nineteenth century came from the provinces,

---

[90] García Sanz (1985a: 673), (1985b: 24).
[91] A large percentage of the London merchants and craftsmen in the beginning of the nineteenth century came from the southeast of England. See Earle (1989: 86); Wareign (1980).

but their origins were as varied as their own market.[92] Nevertheless, in Madrid – with greater intensity than even in Cádiz, Málaga, or Mexico City – a pattern of long-distance immigration persisted that maintained a certain integration with social and geographic origins. These immigrants were from a middle-lower, or in some cases even humble, social bracket, but they always proceeded from a social sphere that did not include artisans, who were the ones who participated in the productive sector of the city. Of course their aristocratic heritage, laden with prejudices, contributed very little to the integration of the two worlds. Up to this point García Sanz's argument could prove valid. But the evidence shows that some of the provincial noblemen – very few, to be sure – sporadically risked a portion of their capital in some productive investment without concern for social prejudice.

To understand the divide between production and commerce one would have to take into account at least two more factors. In the first place, it would be necessary to examine the evolution of Madrid's market and its failure to integrate with nearby markets to form a regional economy. The demand generated by Madrid society was not conducive to the development of a regional market. A significant proportion of the products that flowed into Madrid's market were shipped in from distant economies. Contacts between these remote economies and the capital were established and maintained entirely by a specialized group. These specialized traders were native to the regions or neighboring regions of the products sources. Thus the merchant communities of Madrid maintained their previously mentioned integration of geographic origins and their marked dependence on family ties. Insofar as this state of affairs remained constant, it was these small groups of provincial noblemen who maintained control over a considerable portion of Madrid's market without breaking historical continuity. The absence of an integrated regional economy undoubtedly favored a social model that, among other things, made possible the separation between production and merchant capital.

Second, we must keep in mind the fact that all investors seek maximum returns on their capital, within the limits of what is socially acceptable. Industrial investment in Madrid was not among the most profitable options until well into the nineteenth century, due to the lucrative state-related businesses and the profitability of the real estate market and the narrowness

---

[92] See Bergeron (1978: chap. II).

of the consumption market in Madrid and the interior.[93] Therefore a significant portion of surplus capital, as will be seen below, was invested in the real estate market and in the various forms of public debt, instead of flowing into the productive sector.

Commodities, with commercial credit, constituted the largest portion of the estates of merchants, and their proportion thereof varied very little in the hundred years covered here. This indicates that an essential part of merchants' assets were dedicated to what we could call "active investment," that is, investments allocated to maintaining and improving the business. Nonetheless, around the turn of the century this form of active investment lost ground to "passive investment" – that undertaken in sectors outside of the merchandising business. Undoubtedly this presupposed a certain degree of economic transformation, as evidenced by the increasing liquidity of investors' assets. That transformation, positive from any perspective, was manifested in two very specific, and probably complementary, aspects that were reflected in merchants' estates. On the one hand, the liberation of property allowed for greater activity to develop in the assets market, one which more than any other in the capital had shown clear signs of saturation around the last three decades of the eighteenth century. On the other hand, available data indicate that something similar to a process of rationalization of the individual economies occurred, probably as a reaction to the new investment possibilities opened up in the market. The result of this was an increase in passive investments so that in the period from 1816 to 1850 they represented over 50% of estate assets, as opposed to approximately 38% in the prior period (see Table 2.7).

These trends showed up in two clear ways: first in the growth of investment in urban property and, to a lesser degree, the growth of public debt and rural property; and second in the reduction in the volume of trade credits in relation to total net assets. Nevertheless, as Table 2.6 demonstrates, the growth in investments varied significantly with the size of the patrimonies. The increased investment in urban property implies neither a new trend nor even one peculiar to Madrid. Merchants, whether in Cádiz, Málaga, or Paris, found rental property ownership to be a sufficiently profitable and low-risk sector to merit the investment of their surpluses.[94] The rental property market in Madrid was consistently very active and mer-

---

[93] The problem of the surplus is analyzed in Appendix B.
[94] García Baquero (1976: 517); Villar (1982: 142); Bergeron (1978: 26); Mas (1986: 48).

Merchants

Table 2.7. *Net assets and investment of merchants in Madrid, 1750-1850*
(reales de vellón)

	Personal Estate		Investment			Real Estate	
	1	2	3	4	5	6	7
1750-1816							
Total	3.42	7.89	10.63	11.48	3.62	3.07	9.89
Net Asset							
1-1,000,000	4.84	9.24	7.93	14.04	2.03	5.34	5.34
100,000-2,000,000	2.47	6.20	10.3	11.16	5.45	2.05	6.61
2,000,000+	1.76	8.43	14.84	2.71	12.23	3.45	19.20
1816-1850							
Total	3.30	5.47	14.43	3.80	5.74	17.39	14.43
Net Asset							
1-1,000,000	5.36	5.60	8.93	2.78	6.17	2.13	17.10
1,000,000-2,000,000	2.28	5.31	17.52	4.45	1.41	8.85	29.32
2,000,000+	0.40	5.56	21.06	4.80	16.48	4.36	13.20

1. Domestic; 2. Silver/cash; 3. Government debt; 4. Company stocks; 5. Loans; 6. Rural; 7. Urban.
Source: Probate Inventories. See Appendix B.

chants contributed to this activity.[95] Nevertheless, in the last years of the eighteenth century signs of market saturation began to appear caused by the existence of a considerable number of entailed properties. A good example of this problem was the large number of applications submitted in those years for royal licenses to release these entailed properties. The repeated liberalizations of entailed property eventually remedied this state of affairs so that the entrance of urban property into the free market served to straighten out the tangled inheritances of many aristocratic families of the period. But as indicated by the trend evident in Figure 2.1, the expansion of the rental property market was not the result of a sudden change but rather of a long-term trend. The same conclusion holds for public debt, whose market underwent notable growth beginning with the issuance of the first royal bonds and the establishment of pensions, and lasting until the speculative fever of the 1830s and '40s. In any case, there were other groups that benefited more from this market than the merchants; Table 2.6 shows only

[95] Cruz (1990: 255).

Careers, business, and fortunes

how this form of investment attracted one sector of the merchant classes: that with the greatest investment capacity.

Between 1750 and 1850 there was without question a clear improvement of the merchant patrimonies, clearing the way for an increase in liquid assets for investment. This improvement was seen in the reduction in the amount of assets held in precious metals and cash, which fell by two percentage points,[96] and most of all in the decrease in the proportion of assets tied up in trade credit – some 9% over the time period. The merchant estates of the first half of the nineteenth century had gained liquidity and bore the signs of a more active market. However, this change did not reflect a change in the economic structure of the Iberian interior. To the contrary, it reinforced several traditional features of that economy, such as the significance of the rental property market and its dependence on business with the state. This analysis of merchant estates demonstrates that there were no radical changes in the nature of sales and distribution activities, despite the modernization of certain markets prompted by a new juridical framework.

By way of conclusion: The intermission of an economy

As in a dramatic work, the climax and denouement of Spanish capitalism was preceded by an intermission that lasted longer than that envisioned by its author. To be sure, the political class of the last third of the eighteenth century began to grow aware that the era of plans was coming to an end and that it was necessary to inaugurate the era of reforms. Between 1798 and 1855 the eventually prevalent reformist spirit was transformed into a determined drive for change that became radical on not a few occasions. During those years the legal apparatus of the Spanish monarchy began a transition toward the consolidation of a system of free competition, both in the area of individual legal rights and, most of all, in the area of economic relations. Historians have tended to attribute these changes to the revolutionary impulses of a new social class. But what we must question is whether these changes really were caused by a new class and if those changes produced a new economy. In other words, to what degree was there in the 1850s in Spain a free market economy and a society based on the unquestionable principle of legal equality for all individuals?

[96] The ratio between precious metal in storage and cash in the fortunes after 1816 was 0.70 in favor of cash.

Merchants

The evidence derived from our analysis is that, at least in Madrid and in the Castilian interior, there was no freely competitive market in 1850. As a consequence, the predominant socioeconomic structure was closer to that of a premodern society than the ideal pursued by the vanguard of the liberal society.[97] This is not to say that certain economic practices did not have an unmistakable capitalist character, or that the "revolutionary" force of early liberalism didn't have its modernizing effects. But the fact is that the economy of Madrid offered a complex contrast of light and shade indicative more of a system that was in the process of transformation but that had not yet undergone any revolutionary change. In 1850, for example, light shone on the markets for capital and for real estate – urban as well as rural – both of which were clearly in a period of expansion, while the shadows were cast along the chronic restriction of the consumer goods market. This consumer goods market was confined by the ramparts of a very limited demand and the absence of a regional market, resulting in the redirection of the majority of the factors of production toward state-dependent businesses. In the end these latter traits were those that defined the character of Madrid's economy, which continued functioning on a foundation of a clientele system that was as ancient as the capital itself. In sum, the political forces, first reformist and later revolutionary, produced only partial results insofar as they did not alter Madrid's market structure. In Madrid, in contrast to Barcelona, Paris, and London, the profits of traders and merchants did not find their way into the productive sector of the economy.[98] The capital market continued to depend heavily on goods manufactured outside its region; its industry would remain essentially artisan-based until after 1900.

From the analysis of the economic behavior of the merchant community of Madrid between 1750 and 1850, as of its process of social reproduction, emerges an image of historical continuity. Historians of the bourgeois revolution or liberal bourgeoisie have tended to focus more on the trees of political change than the forest of the society that lies behind such change, perhaps because it has been assumed, as a result of a reductionist perspec-

---

[97] Liberal politicians, either *moderados* or *progresistas*, introduced in Spain the practices of English political economy and the laissez-faire principles of the French revolutionaries. See Artola (1978: 295–305).

[98] Differences between the economies of Madrid and Barcelona in the old regime have been summarized on several occasions. See Vicens (1968: 28–30); Ringrose (1987: 128). The case of the Overkampf manufactures in Paris illustrates the use of commercial capital for productive purposes. See Bergeron (1978: 223–265); Pinkney (1950: 55–60); Gille (1963: 27 ff). About London, see Wrigley (1975).

tive, that all political change implies prior socioeconomic change. The fact is that Madrid's market in the first half of the nineteenth century had basically the same structure as that of the end of the seventeenth, and the groups that controlled it reflected the same pattern of socioeconomic behavior.

Of course we know little about the origins of the merchant community of Madrid and its growth after the city became the capital of the Spanish empire, but available information, though sparse, supports my argument. Comparing the economic biography of the Horcasitas family, which accumulated its fortune throughout the seventeenth century, with other families from the eighteenth and nineteenth centuries, it is difficult to maintain the idea that the merchant dynasties operating in Madrid – which were, for the most part, protagonists of the bourgeois revolution – qualified them to be considered a new social class. Francisco de Horcasitas was born around 1624 in the valley of Arcentales, in the area surrounding the province of Viscaya. Being a second son, he had to emigrate to Madrid: "El Dorado for the youth of the entire kingdom," as Jesús Bravo has written. Thanks to the help of his relatives and Viscayan compatriots, he was able to make his fortune in Madrid, so that toward the end of the seventeenth century he was actively participating in the luxury goods market, in the sale of metal goods, and in the market for woolens. Although specific data are not available, it is certain that the state would have been among his most prominent clients. In fact, he invested a very substantial part of his wealth in the purchase of different types of public debt, while he used the rest to purchase houses and to assure the perpetuation of the family line through the establishment of a trust. Indeed, Francisco's successors enjoyed such a favorable social position that throughout the eighteenth century they were counted among the economic and political elite of Madrid.[99]

Two centuries later, in 1882 to be precise, Francisco de las Rivas y Ubieta, the first marquis of Mudela and one of the wealthiest men in nineteenth-century Madrid, died in that city. To his biographers, Rivas was the model of "a self-made bourgeois man."[100] To his contemporaries he represented the paradigm of that new middle class that was driving Spanish society along the path of liberalism. Nevertheless, his biography contained nothing new; it mirrored a pattern as ancient as the history of Madrid since its establishment as a capital. His origin was that of a provincial nobleman from the Basque country who tried his luck first in America and later in Madrid.

---

[99] See Bravo Lozano (1986: 497–521).   [100] See Bahamonde and Otero (1989: 525).

He used relationships based on family, regional, and friendship ties to enter the business world. And, last, his dizzying enrichment was due to the diversification of his business activities into the classic markets of luxury goods, state contracts, and wholesale supplies for the capital. Would Rivas have been a model of a self-made businessman if instead of coming from the noble Valle de Gordejuela he had been an Asturian coal supplier or a Galician water vendor? Would he even have had an opportunity to improve his social position? Of course we know of no case of bourgeois enrichment in nineteenth-century Madrid that was not launched with the assistance of parents, regional compatriots, or, at the very least, political friends. Madrid's market was controlled by a series of exclusive circles that dominated the economy of the capital until well into the twentieth century, a model that is quite distant from the idea of a market economy based on the principle of laissez faire.

Between the Horcasitas and the Marquis of Mudela came many families, some of which have served to illustrate our analysis. Their economic biographies demonstrate that the social history of the Spanish interior needs to be reshaped to fit a paradigm of transformation over the long term, rather than a revolutionary rupture. As in the theater, the stage crew took advantage of the intermission to prepare the new sets, and the actors to change their costumes. However, the climax represented by the unequivocal modernization of Spanish took somewhat longer to occur than its authors had desired. Meanwhile, a portion of the public seemed to allow itself to be seduced by the new sets and costumes, without noticing that the plot was unfolding on the same stage and without substantial variation in the cast of characters.

3

Bankers

Between the Fuggers and Ruizes in the sixteenth century and the formation of the first Spanish national bank under the direction of Cabarrú, there is a long history of banking that has scarcely begun to be written. The events in this history center around Madrid, beginning in the days when it became the capital of the Spanish empire. Until very recently, Madrid had an almost complete monopoly of the banking scene, comparable only to its near-monopoly of Spanish politics. A discerning historian has defined Madrid as "the capital of Spanish capital." Although that assertion was intended to refer only to the nineteenth century, Madrid's financial dominance began much earlier.[1] The city has always fit that definition because of a natural tendency in the history of European finances, according to which the bankers have had to settle in next to the administration of the state.[2] The reason is simple enough, then as now: the state is the major client of the banks.

In this chapter I study the economic behavior of Madrid's financial community, which parallels the activities of the merchants described in the previous chapter. I am interested in understanding the nature and evolution of their businesses in order to determine the degree of transformation toward a modern system based on economic freedom. Furthermore, I would like to analyze the social origins of the individuals of this group, how they created their fortunes, and how they invested their surpluses. In the process, I intend to determine whether the financial elite of mid-nineteenth century Madrid were qualitatively distinct from their counterparts in 1750. As pointed out in the previous chapter, scholars traditionally identify Madrid as the place where radical changes occurred both in the way business was

---

[1] Sanz Ayán (1988); Domínguez Ortiz (1978); and Caro Baroja (1985).
[2] "En Espagne *sólo Madrid es Banca*" asserted Zylberberg (1983: 266); see also Tortella (1989: 338).

carried out as well as in the social composition of the business groups during the first half of the nineteenth century. Although economic change took place, I shall argue that it was not extensive enough to alter the traditional structure of Madrid's economy; it revolved around the business of the state machinery and was controlled by a patron–client system that neutralized mechanisms of free competition and regulated access to new social groups.

Madrid and Spanish finances

It seems that until 1640, Seville and Barcelona shared with Madrid the presence of important groups of *hombres de negocios*, the term used to describe the bankers of the era. Italians in their majority, specifically Genoese, were responsible for the "burials" of precious metals to which Quevedo referred in one of his best-known verses. Indeed, the Genoese took the lion's share of the financial trades of the Spanish crown until the middle of the seventeenth century.[3] Nevertheless, Italian financial capitalism did not survive the different bankruptcies of the Spanish monarchy and the monetary problems derived from the introduction of copper as a substitute for silver in the Castilian monetary system.[4] Little by little, in the seventeenth century the Italians were replaced by *asentistas* of Portuguese origin, who earned success in the financial market during the reign of Charles II. The Portuguese, most of them *conversos*, had to install their firms in Madrid, thus guaranteeing the role of the capital as a financial center.[5] Many of those families ended up holding government posts and even, in spite of their unequivocal Jewish origins, were named knights of some of the *ordenes militares* and given aristocratic titles. Others were less lucky, suffering financial difficulties in addition to being persecuted by the Inquisition.[6] As Spain was losing leadership on the international scene, however, its financial needs became less dramatic. It was only then that the country began to feel the greater presence of Spanish bankers competing for control of the finances of the state.[7]

The first half of the eighteenth century was tortuous for the new Bour-

---

[3] "Nace en la Indias honrrado/Donde el mundo le acompaña/Viene a morir en España/Y es en Génova enterrado." On the role of the *asentistas* of Genoese origin during the seventeenth century, see Sanz Ayán (1988: 316f.).
[4] Ruiz Martín (1970: 113–117).
[5] That was the case of Montesinos, Fonseca Piña, Baez Eminente, etc. See Sanz Ayán (1988: 336f.).
[6] That was the case of the Montesinos family. Sanz Ayán (1988: 336ff.).
[7] Zylberberg (1983: 268).

bon monarchy as it attempted to gain financial stability. However, monetary stability, combined with decreasing public spending due to the absence of warfare, allowed for a reduction of public debt. Spanish administrators began to feel more relieved from about 1750 onward. Their worries were no longer limited to seeking ways out of financial difficulties, and included finding a way of rationalizing the fiscal system so that its yields might improve. Most of the reforms after 1750 were aimed at both halting the growth of the deficit and at creating conditions favorable to the long-term development of the Spanish economy. The beginning of hostilities with England in 1770, however, renewed the threat of bankruptcy.[8] By then Madrid was the virtually undisputed capital of Spanish capital, and this financial terrain was dominated almost completely by groups of Spanish origin. From then on, it was in Madrid that all plans for the financial system of the country were orchestrated and it was in this city that those plans found success or failure. Bankers also preferred to house their headquarters in the capital city, although practically none of these *hombres de negocio* were of *madrileño* origin. Thus the country saw the consolidation of a tendency which, as we have seen, began in the mid-seventeenth century.

But let us return our narrative thread to the second half of the eighteenth century. What was the situation of Spanish financial capital at this time? There is no doubt that from 1780 onward the history of Spanish finances saw significant changes in direction. Belatedly as compared to some European countries, while outpacing others, Spain organized its first national bank. Pedro Tedde aptly described the atmosphere that surrounded the formation of the Bank of San Carlos, as well as its tortuous history and eventual closure.[9] His book shows how the formation of a national bank, the culmination of a series of organizational attempts, was the project of a group of government officials and *hombres de negocios* who were established in Madrid or who at least had strong ties to its economy. The fact that the initiative came from the capital should not go unnoticed. Like other national banks of the era, the Bank of San Carlos had as its primary mission the handling of the finances of the state. But at the same time many of those who moved the project forward were trustees of important interests in agriculture, commerce, and state finances – that is to say, in the three basic sectors of the Spanish economy at the end of the eighteenth century. As a result, the innovation implied by the creation of a modern institution of credit was

---

[8] Artola (1982: 321f.). [9] Tedde Lorca (1988).

undermined by the objectives of those who created it and by its particular urban context. On the one hand, the bank was originally created in order to prop up the battered public treasury of the absolute monarchy suffering a cash flow crisis precipitated by Spanish involvement in the American wars of independence. At the same time, however, many of its founders also envisioned an endless number of projects directed at favoring the development of capitalism. On the other hand, these same founders belonged to a social world that was embedded in the old regime. The social dynamic of the old regime depended on Madrid's role as political capital. That is to say, it belonged to a traditional society that was characterized more by its ability for self-reproduction than by its flexibility in integrating new social groups.

Banks provided three fundamental types of financial services in the second half of the eighteenth century. First were services related to foreign exchange and money orders – in other words, services related to the contact between a given city and the international market. Second were all services for credit, both short-term loans with low interest and long-term loans with higher interest. Finally, there existed a variety of services related to the creation and management of private capital, mainly through accounts that had many of the characteristics of modern checking accounts. The banker became trustee of the money that his clients handed over and made it profitable through his investments in government debt, in the leasing of state or municipal taxes, or simply in commercial operations. These could be considered, above all, commercial credit banks. Agrarian credit remained under the control of a vast group of local moneylenders who, in general, practiced usury as a complementary activity.[10]

The bankers of Madrid controlled almost all of the services mentioned. They were involved, of course, in most operations of money order and foreign exchange, since only certain well-established firms of the capital had the adequate infrastructure necessary to put the provincial Spanish markets in contact with the international market.[11] I shall study this aspect further on; for the moment, let it suffice to say that this specialization was the result of long experience in the domestic and international markets. In the long term bankers built networks of contacts which involved family and friends, and, in many cases, their *paisanos* (fellow countrymen). Many of the banking

---

[10] About money-lending activities during the nineteenth century, see Martínez Andaluz (1986: 492–504).

[11] "Madrid was the place where most bills of exchange were negotiated, since the appropriate kind of merchant-banker specialists were established there." Fernández (1982: 39–40).

establishments studied here were the result of the persistent work of successive generations of the same family group.[12] Cádiz was Madrid's only competition in money order operations, but many of the firms of Cádiz maintained close contact with the capital, if they were not themselves simply branches of Madrid banks.[13]

Large private credit operations also operated in the capital, because it was there that firms with sufficient borrowing power were established. These were generally limited to commercial activities related to the export of wool or the importation of colonial products. We will see further on how the bankers of Madrid provided the credit needed to charter shipments of wool that left from the port of Bilbao, or for shipments of cocoa and sugar that arrived in Cádiz. Of course, in these operations they often competed with local merchants with sufficient means to risk part of their capital on commercial credit operations.

The dominant role of Madrid's *hombres de negocios* was clearly evident in all of the activities related to the finances of the state and to the administration of private capital. The importance of the capital city is logical, given the slow pace of internal communication in this era. In order to accomplish business transactions, a banker had to be at the right place at the right time or risk losing the initiative. This was also true of other European capitals like London, Paris, or Vienna – where the cities symbolized political power.[14] What was unique to Madrid was the fact that although the Spanish capital was poorly communicated with the most dynamic regions of the Spanish economy of that era, it held a complete monopoly over the world of peninsular finances.[15] In England, for example, London established itself as the principal financial center of the nation and, subsequently, of the Empire. Nonetheless, since the last years of the seventeenth century and, especially, during the eighteenth century, there existed an important money market outside the capital. This market was in the hands of private groups that had arisen in the provinces. They specialized in long-term mortgage loans, and their support was fundamental to the industrialization process.[16] The regions of Essex and Suffolk, situated between London and Birmingham, had

---

[12] That was particularly the case of some foreign firms installed in Spain at the beginning of the eighteenth century such as Gnecco & Cia, Rossi and Joyes. Zylberberg (1983: 275–279).
[13] That was the case of the Cinco Gremios Mayores, whose importance as a financial entity has been noted in the previous chapter.
[14] E. A. Wrigley (1987).
[15] Ringrose (1985); de Vries (1984: 318f.).
[16] Anderson and Cotrell (1974: 150–158); Anderson (1970: 85–101).

only five banks until 1780. By the first decades of the nineteenth century, however, they could already count on a network of banking firms with branches open even in small localities.[17] In 1790, James Oakes decided to abandon his wool fabric firm in order to become a banker. For this purpose he remodeled his home, situated in the center of the locality of Bury St. Edmunds, with the help of a London architect. At the time, Bury had fewer than 7,000 inhabitants and already had a fully operational bank.[18] England, of course, was in the vanguard of the process of economic modernization which began in Europe during the second half of the eighteenth century. Other European countries took several decades longer to establish a solid financial market comparable to the English one. France's growth potential, for example, was delayed by, among other reasons, the inadequate banking system monopolized by the Bank of France, which was excessively centralized and dominated by the inflexible attitudes of the men who controlled it.[19] Something similar occurred contemporaneously in Spain, where Madrid's dominance defined the context of Spanish finances. Although it lost its role as center of an empire and did not become an industrial center until very recent times, Madrid never stopped being Spain's financial capital.

As of 1797, Madrid had a total of 30 banking establishments according to the *Almanak Mercantil*. This number remained more or less constant until 1808, although the tendency was toward growth. In 1800 there were 34 registered banks, while in 1807 the number rose to 37.[20] A list compiled by the Bonaparte administration in 1808 noted the existence of 38 firms, while the aforementioned *Almanak* indicated only 35. These lists refer only to the *cambistas* – the firms that specialized in bills of exchange, thus excluding some of the *hombres de negocios* whose specialty was credit to the state. I do not know of a source similar to the *Almanak* for the first half of the nineteenth century, but taking the works of Angel Bahamonde and Jesús Martinez as points of reference, I have studied a total of 30 cases up to 1868.[21] In Table 3.1, I have noted those firms which appeared in at least three of the aforementioned lists between 1797 and 1808. Table 3.2 records the names of

---

[17] Davidoff and Hall (1987: 245).
[18] Ibid. p. 246.
[19] Cameron (1967: 127); Asselain (1984).
[20] According to Zylberberg (1983: 275) toward 1750 there existed in Madrid twenty-five bank firms.
[21] For data between 1797 and 1808 see Tedde (1983: 301–331). See also Gallard (1797–1808). For information on the period between 1808 and 1868 see Bahamonde (1981 and 1986); Martínez Martín (1986: 80–125).

Careers, business, and fortunes

Table 3.1. *Cambistas of Madrid, 1797-1808*

Abad de Aparicio	Gorbea
*Aguirre e Hijos	*Gonzalo del Río
*Alvaro Benito	*González de Lobera
Amandi	*Iranda, Marqués (de)
*Avancino	*Joyes
Barrueta	Nadal
*Bartelemi Hermanos	Nafarrondo
*Colonilla, Marqués (de la)	*Ravara e Hijo
*Daudinot Bouhebent	Rigal
*Drouillet	Romero
*Dutari Hermanos	Urquijo
	Zapater

* Cases studied in this sample

Table 3.2. *Bankers of Madrid, 1808-1868*

•Aguirre Solarte, José Ventura	*Muguiro Iriarte, Rafael
Anduaga Mejia, Manuel	Muñoz Sánchez, José (M. de Remisa)
*Balmaseda, Juan Domingo	*Murga Michelena, Bartolomé
Barbería, Pedro	•Norzagaray, Mateo
*Barcenas, Francisco (de las)	•Pérez Seoane, Manuel
Beronda y de Espina, Juan	Riansares, Duque (de)
*•Caballero y Mazo, Andrés	Rivas, Francisco (de las) (M. Mudela)
Casa Gaviria, Marqués (de)	*•Ruiz de la Prada, Manuel
Ceriola Flaquer, José (de)	*Ruiz Garcia de la Prada, Manuel
Ceriola, Jaime (de)	Ruiz, José Segundo
*•Chavarri, Basilio	Sevillano, Duque (de)
*•Chavarri, Francisco Antonio	•Soriano Moreta, Ricardo
•Collado, José (M. de Laguna)	•Soriano Sánchez, Antonio
Finat, Andrés	Soriano y Pelayo, Ramón
Gaviria, Antonio	Vegamar, Conde (de)
*•Gil de Santibañez, Manuel	Velle, Conde (de)
•Maltrana Monasterio, Antonio	Vicente, Juan José (de)

Source: see footnote 21
* Continuity of business already established during the eighteenth century
• Cases studied in this sample

Bankers

bankers from the first half of the nineteenth century, some of whom were running establishments that were begun in the eighteenth century.

My analysis is based on the study of 27 bankers whose businesses were operating for at least part of the period 1750 and 1850. Of these, at least 13 were themselves *cambistas* who appeared on the lists to which I have referred. In all societies, bankers tend to constitute a distinctive group. Their life style was comparable to that of the aristocracy of the old regime. Because of the way in which many of them ascended on the social scale, they have been considered the paradigmatic upper bourgeoisie of a liberal society. The truth is that as a social group they never clearly belonged to the aristocratic stratum, but neither do I believe that they could be considered a prototypical bourgeois group. In Madrid, as in other urban societies of Europe in the transition from the eighteenth to the nineteenth centuries, the bankers were an elite with clearly defined traits. Let us see what these traits were.

Commerce and finances as complementary activities

In general, historical literature has tended to associate the banker's life with luxury and opulence, but seldom has that literature focused on the precariousness of their life. The *hombres de negocios* had to act in an economy which still lacked integration, where slow communications and poor legal resources created permanent insecurity. Even the most conservative businessman lived with the constant threat of suspension of payments looming over his head. In general, the stability of the banking business depended upon two factors: its diversification, and the control of information about the markets. Regarding the first factor, we can safely say that the bankers of the era were a combination of merchants and financiers, with the former occupation almost always being the more important. The pure financier – one who owned a firm which specialized exclusively in the administration of capital – did not yet exist. The lack of pure financiers was true for all European societies of the period, even the most advanced.[22] In Madrid, for example, it was extremely difficult to distinguish a banker from a merchant. As we have seen, the former were called *cambistas* because their business was mostly oriented toward the negotiation of bills of exchange. During all of the eighteenth century and the beginning of the nineteenth, however, the

---

[22] Lisle-Williams (1984: 352f.); Wilson (1988: 14f.).

Cinco Gremios were the most substantial institution of credit. There were also some important businessmen within the structure of the Gremios Mayores who accepted bills of exchange and offered credits with interest, even though they were not considered *cambistas*.

The main business of most of Madrid's houses of exchange was the wool trade, but this was never their only activity. Many bankers owned commercial enterprises that were administered either by a reliable manager or by a family member. The firm of Manuel Francisco de Aguirre, one of the most important of the period, maintained a haberdashery warehouse in the *Puerta de Guadalajara*, managed by one of Don Manuel's sons-in-law. The same occurred with the firm of Dutari Hermanos. Juan Bautista Dutari, the founder, had entered business life as a druggist in Postas street, and kept it open throughout his life.[23] This participation in commerce holds true for the more prominent bankers of the first half of the nineteenth century. By then the wool market had already declined, but many had already entered other spheres, either in retail or wholesale commerce in Madrid.

The eighteenth century seems to have been a second golden age for the wool trade. Between 1700 and 1780, the nomadic herds of Castilian livestock grew from two to five million heads, as foreign demand for quality wool enhanced the profitability of the export business.[24] Madrid's bankers benefited especially from this situation because they served as intermediary agents for the marketing of the product. Many even ended up being distinguished members of the Honrado Concejo de la Mesta, making them a part of a very select minority.[25] But why did a city relatively far from the centers of production, and definitely distant from points of exportation, control this market? First of all, most of the great livestock owners resided in Madrid, many of them old aristocrats with some position in the Court. Second, the very nature of the sales contracts for wool, which always involved an important credit operation, drew the trade to the peninsular banking center. The banker would contract with an owner to purchase the *cortes* ("cuts") of wool for one or several reasons. Simultaneously, he would agree to extend to the sheep owner credit equal to the estimated amount of production at the contracted price. It was subsequently the banker himself who got in touch with his correspondents, who were established in places between the centers of production and those of exportation. Finally, while

---

[23] AHPM, P. 19972, p. 224 and AHBE, Secretaría, book 18570.
[24] García Sanz (1985a: 655–656).
[25] That was the case of Manuel Francisco de Aguirre; AHPM, P. 19114.

Bankers

Table 3.3. *Bankers and public activity*

	No. cases	%
City Hall	3	20.0
National Treasury	11	73.3
Other	1	6.7
Total known	15	100.0
Unknown	12	
Total sample	27	

Source: Author's compilation from AHPM; Bankers.dat

the shippers of the ports transported the product to the purchasing firms, the bankers of Madrid retained control of foreign exchange and money order operations.[26]

The second element that has been seen as a factor of stability in the banking business regards the control of information about the markets. Securing this control was not an easy task. It was necessary to compete with a state accustomed to intervening in the commercial networks.[27] Competition revolved around having contacts inside the spheres of power. Businessmen established these contacts by making use of their influence in order to obtain public positions. Table 3.3 shows that in 73 percent of the cases where bankers were involved in the public sphere, they worked for the Public Treasury. Bankers, like the commercial elite, obtained appointments as advisers on the Junta de Comercio or in other institutions dependent upon the Public Treasury. Holding a public position generally ensured the necessary contacts in order to obtain a supplying contract, or to negotiate a government loan. Thus, public positions were pursued not only for social prestige, but also as a business imperative.[28]

Besides tending to business with the state, bankers had to have control over regional and international markets. Networks of family and friends were an indispensable tool in achieving this goal. The family served to

---

[26] Some examples of wool trade contracts can be found in AHPM, PP. 21092, p. 743 and 21094 p. 237 and 300. On the role of the shippers in the port of Bilbao, see Basurto (1983: chap. III).

[27] This public control over the markets was particularly evident in regard to city provisioning. Ringrose (1985); Castro (1987); Fernández García (Madrid: 1971).

[28] The government of the National Bank of San Carlos was one of the bankers' favorite public positions. See Tedde (1988: 290 and 335).

guarantee the continuity of the business through strategically arranged marriages. These family networks, moreover, extended into secondary lateral kinship. The Dutaris, for example, relied on family members involved in business in cities as distant as Zaragoza, Ecija, and Pamplona.[29] These kinship networks were reinforced by the existence of strong bonds of regional solidarity. We will see this more clearly in the next section when we analyze the clienteles of the banking houses; let it suffice to point out that an analysis of commercial correspondence shows solid mutual confidence between kinship groups from the same region.[30]

Consequently, the diversification of businesses and the utilization of personal influence constituted the pillars that guaranteed security. These factors were not always sufficient, and instability inevitably accompanied the lives of bankers. The larger the volume of business, the greater the risk, so that almost all of the banking establishments used in this sample went through difficult periods at some moment in their history. Some of them survived several suspensions of payments while others lost their businesses in the process. What were the causes of this insecurity? To what degree did this insecurity accentuate the conservatism of these businessmen?

The insecurity was to a great degree the result of factors external to the administration of the businesses. Information lag caused by the difficulty of communication was a significant risk factor, especially for a group as dependent upon long-distance commerce as were the bankers of Madrid.[31] The banker Agustín de Queneau committed the Bank of San Carlos to the purchase of French government debt a few months before the revolution broke out. Queneau served as the agent of several French firms in different areas of Spain. The operation surpassed 29.5 million reales and was realized with the guarantee of the Lecoteulx firm of Paris, which Queneau represented in Spain. Neither the knowledge that Queneau and Cabarrús undoubtedly had about France, nor even the solvency of a bank as solid as that of the Lecoteulx family turned out to be enough. The fact is that poor information cost Queneau his business and began a legal battle with the Bank of San Carlos that lasted several years.[32]

---

[29] The information about Dutari comes from AHPM, PP. 19627 and 19628; AHBE, Secretaría, book 18648. Information about Aguirre: AHBE, Secretaría, leg. 725. Regarding Fernández Gonzalo del Río, see Basurto (1983: 132).

[30] See business correspondence of the Dutari firm. AHBE, Secretaría, leg. 725.

[31] Ringrose (1970); Madrazo (1984).

[32] AHBE, Secretaría, leg. 782. International crises were another factor of instability just as or more important than internal conflicts. Between 1793 and 1794, as a consequence of the war with France,

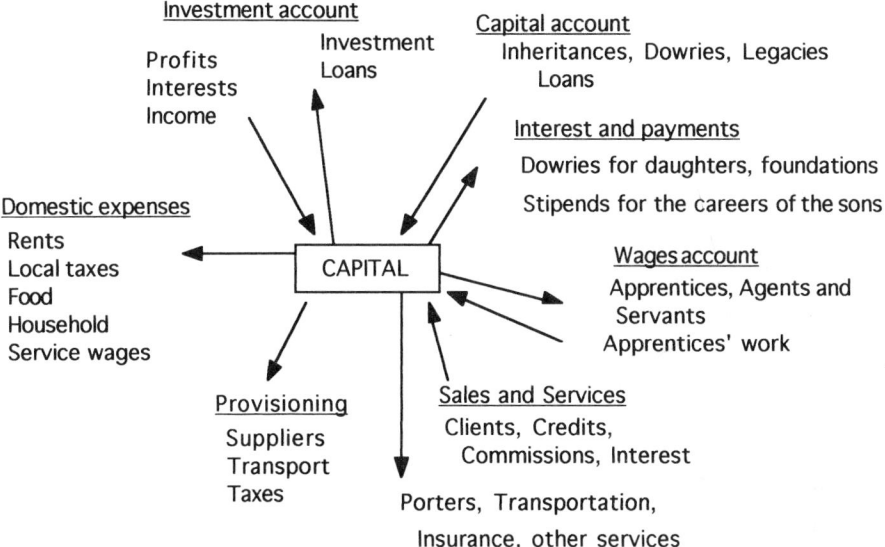

Figure 3.1. Circulation of bankers' trade capital

The main problem of both bankers and merchants, however, was the persistent scarcity of circulating capital that characterized the economy of those years. Most commercial transactions were based on credit, but there were never any clear guarantees for collection. Many times debt redemption spanned several generations, so that many of their commercial loans came to be regarded as uncollectible. Besides having to deal with war, primitive communications, and lack of legal protection, the banker and the merchant had to maintain a large enough flow of incoming capital so as to service his large operating debts. In Figure 3.1, I have tried to represent graphically the flow of operating capital within what could be a model for a family business of the era. The success of a firm depended to a great degree on the good reputation of its owners and on their careful selection of debtors. This is why the commercial and financial economy of the era was based on a complex system of mutual trust. A banker's family and its social standing was his most important capital, as it established his ability to generate

the firms of Dutari, Aguirre, and Rosi Gosse all underwent suspensions of payment. Other firms, like Barthelemi, Drouillet, and Daudinot also went through difficult periods. Nevertheless, they all managed to survive. See AHBE, Secretaría, leg. 725; books 18648 and 480.

Table 3.4. *Credit in proportion to total capital, 1750-1860*

% regarding total capital	No. of cases	%
0-10	4	26.6
10-24	3	20.0
25-49	3	20.0
50-74	4	26.6
75-100	1	6.6
Total known	15	
Total sample	27	

Source: Author's compilation with data from AHPM, AHBE; Bankers.dat

guarantees. The firms of Dutari and Aguirre overcame the crisis of 1794 thanks to their good name.[33] A malicious rumor or a family scandal, by the same token, could hinder the progress of a family's businesses. Commercial credit accounted for a very significant portion of banking fortunes (Table 3.4), and always entailed a constant factor of instability. This was because both wholesale operations – requiring a large amount of capital – and the retail purchase of products for immediate consumption were done on credit. The problem for the *hombres de negocios* was to make sure that collections were sufficiently timely so that they could sustain their expenses. People were frequently late in their payments, however, if they paid at all. Of course, there were operations that offered a high level of security. Bills of exchange were always negotiated at a fixed term, which guaranteed collection, but high rates were resisted, causing delays in payments.[34] The state tended to delay payments of debts, although it always did pay in the end. Aside from this, doing business with the state always offered the advantage of a possible mortgage of royal or local taxes. Offering credit to individuals was a bit more risky.[35] If it was a government official or someone dependent upon the administration, the creditor knew that collection was going to be intermittent. Some noble houses that went through difficult times at the

---

[33] AHBE, Secretaría, leg. 725.
[34] Roover (1957); Pérez Herrero (1988: 45–78).
[35] The bank of Carranza, for instance, lost more than 5 million reales between 1740 and 1840 in credits that were never collected. Around 1850 the firm was still trying to collect debts that were established more than a hundred years before. AHN, Diversos, Títulos y Familias, leg. 2246.

Bankers

beginning of the crisis of the old regime were a greater credit risk.[36] The account books of Madrid's bankers are replete with operations of credit to the old Spanish aristocracy that, on many occasions, ended in foreclosure.[37]

Obviously, each banker made his own estimates about acceptable levels of risk for his business. Regarding management Madrid bankers adopted a combination of risk and caution. On the one hand, doing business on commission, the negotiation of bills of exchange or short-term loans at a moderate premium were all investments that entailed little risk. Long-distance commerce and wholesale marketing, high-interest credit operations, and speculation in public debt, on the other hand, all bore a major risk. Our bankers combined both types of business with a major inclination toward the more risky operations. How are we to understand this logic? We can only find the answer by looking at the levels of profitability of each one of these businesses.

Casas de Negocios

Before becoming bankers, the Gibson family, from the tiny English locality of Saffron Waldon in Essex, owned a brewery. The Twinings of Colchester had been in the business of tea manufacturing. In Birmingham, the Lloyds, before becoming bankers, manufactured iron; the Galtons, weapons; and the Gibbons were dedicated to the trade of metals.[38] All of them were of heterogenous social origin, and their activities responded to the necessities of a regional market that by the end of the eighteenth century already encompassed an extended urban network between the political financial-commercial center of London and the industrial city of Birmingham.[39] Most of these families were originally from the same region where they had made their fortunes, a reality quite different from that offered by Madrid in the same era.

None of the bankers from our Spanish sample were originally from the capital or from its adjacent regions. Only Frutos Alvaro Benito, who achieved notable success during the French invasion, was from the neighboring province of Segovia. Like the merchants, more than half of the

---

[36] Atienza (1987); Bahamonde (1986: 369); Carmona (1986: 505–514).
[37] According to some scholars it seems the aristocracy lived in a kind of permanent status of economic agony since the end of the sixteenth century. Nevertheless, they found ways to maintain their hegemonic position in all levels of life. See Fayard (1982: 366–367); Hernández Benítez (1991: 229f.).
[38] Davidoff and Hall (1987: 245).
[39] Wrigley (1975); Saville (1969: 32); Booker (1974).

Table 3.5. *Regional origins of the bankers of Madrid, 1750-1850*

	No.	%
North (Basque Country, Navarre, Rioja)	13	56.5
Old Castile	1	4.3
Madrid	1	4.3
Andalusia	1	4.3
Foreigners	7	30.4
Total known	23	
Unknown	4	
Total sample	27	

Source: Bankers.dat

bankers were from the northern Spanish provinces, almost one-third of them were foreigners; the rest, as can be seen in Table 3.5, were fairly well distributed.

The Dutaris, for example, were originally from Zugarramurdi, a small village next to the French border, in a place of difficult access from the Navarrese valley of Baztán.[40] The Carranzas were from Castrourdiales, on the coast of Cantabría, while the Chávarris, Abrisquetas, Aragorris, Murgas, and Aguirres were of Basque origin, the first two from the noble countryside of Ayala, the rest from Vizcaya. The foreigners were all of French or Italian origin. Many of the French, like the Marquis de la Colonilla or Drouillet, were from the French Basque country. The Italians were all of Genoese origin. All of the bankers' places of origin were several days' travel from the capital. However, what was especially curious about this pattern of regional origins is that, once again, it was part of a long-term tendency that began in the seventeenth century and persisted until the end of the nineteenth.[41]

A similar pattern occurred with regard to the social origins and the professional careers characteristic of the financial elite of Madrid. We have seen how English bankers had accumulated their capital in activities as diverse as the manufacture of swords or tea. It was a long time before Madrid's financial elite began to receive capital from industrial sectors. The

---
[40] On Zugarramurdi see Caro Baroja (1968: 12f.)
[41] Otazu (1987: 300); Ringrose (1986: 302–323); Bahamonde and Otero (1989: 524–594).

prototype of the Madrid banker accumulated his capital in trade, foreign exchange, and money orders, or in speculation with the finances of the state, a model closer to the old regime than to a laissez-faire society.[42] In this respect Spain seemed less like England and more like the French model or that of other Southern European countries.[43]

Two functionally distinct groups stand out in this pattern of business continuity, although there were no differences in the social origins of the people who formed these two groups. The distinction appears between those firms that did business with the state, excluding trade and money orders, and those concentrated on the latter activities with modest amounts of speculation in the finances of the state. Both groups represent social models well known to the urban societies of early modern Europe: the royal financiers, known as *asentistas* in Spain, and the merchant-bankers or *cambistas*.[44] All were members of the provincial *hidalguía* and constituted a fairly select group that in Madrid was unequivocally noble.

The Carranza family provides us with a good example of pure *asentistas* in the second half of the eighteenth century, as do the Aguerris in the era of Philip IV, and, in a certain sense, the Gavirias in the time of Isabel II. The Carranza firm was opened under the direction of Don Domingo Carranza around 1730. The family belonged to a lineage of Santander nobility, one of whose branches was from Castrourdiales.[45] During the reign of Carlos III, the Carranza firm was one of the most stable in the kingdom. At that time, they held substantial contracts for provisioning the navy and administered a sizable loan for the construction of the palace of Aranjuez.[46] After government loans and the administration of taxes, the Carranzas' main business was in the wool trade and in supplying interest-earning loans to the great noble houses.[47] The firm as such disappeared at the beginning of the nineteenth century, but the Carranzas' ties to the highest levels of the administration of the state remained strong for several generations.

The model provided by the examples of the Carranzas can be extended to other families of national and foreign origins like the Patricio Joyes, Avan-

---

[42] Molas (1985: 26–27).
[43] See Chaussinand-Nogaret (1970). A noteworthy difference is that at the end of the eighteenth century in Paris there already existed connections between financial and industrial capital. See Bergeron (1978: 318).
[44] Roover (1963 and 1974).
[45] AHN, Estado, Caballeros de Carlos III, exp. 715.
[46] AHPM, P. 21669, p. 642f.
[47] AHPM, P. 21670, p. 82.

cinos, the Marquis of Iranda, Juan Bautista Rossi, etc.[48] All of their businesses prospered in the framework of the "old corruption," the term used by W. Rubenstein to categorize certain practices common in the administration of the English monarchy at the end of the eighteenth century. According to Rubinstein, the administration of the state was at the mercy of a network of internal solidarities in which influence, privilege, venality, and bribery were more important than personal merit when it came to advancement.[49] The old corruption began to disappear in England after 1810 when the expansion of electoral suffrage introduced political competition. Since this kind of electoral competition was not really evident in Spain until the first third of the twentieth century, we can say with some assurrance that the old corruption took quite some time to disappear from the country's political administration.[50]

But the most prevalent prototype in Madrilinean business society was that of the banker-merchants. Mesonero referred to them in his memoirs as the children and grandchildren of the "wealthy druggist in the Postas street or of the merchants at Santa Cruz square and Puerta de Guadalajara who actually were bankers, reside in grand palaces, ride in golden calashes, and stamp their letters with heraldic coats of arms embossed with the crown of Count or Marquis."[51] Mesonero may have been thinking of the Aguirre-Murga family when he wrote these lines, or perhaps the Dutari-Fagoagas, the Chávarris, the Muguiros, the Caballeros or any one of a large group of families that fit the paradigm. Many men began their careers as mere clerks in the establishments that their families or *paisanos* had opened in Madrid. Good behavior and demonstrated business ability facilitated their rise in the company's ranks to the status of partner.

Most of the banker-merchants began their careers as members of Madrid's Cinco Gremios Mayores, and many ended up in the Honrado Concejo de la Mesta, in the administration of the monarchy, or with a noble title. This career path was always accompanied by a process of capital accumulation derived from a diversified business portfolio, as we saw in the preceding section. Table 3.6 summarizes the profits of the Dutari Hermanos firm during the height of its business, providing an example of such

---

[48] AHPM, P. 21002, p. 281; AHPM, PP. 21044, p. 267; 21002, p. 281; 22867, p. 235 and 21693, p. 510. See also Zylberberg (1983: 279).
[49] Rubinstein (1987: 265f.).
[50] Artola (1974: 128, v. I).
[51] Mesonero (Madrid: 1975: 27).

Table 3.6. *Profits of Dutari Brothers, 1785-1825*
(reales de vellón)

1785		1787	
Total assets	13,671,374	Credit	14,522,106
Debts	3,777,605	Debit	3,714,162
Capital	9,893,768	Capital	10,807,944
		Profits	914,175
		Relative increase	9.23%
1794		1798	
Credit	11,863,291	Credit	13,414,522
Debit	8,210,924	Debit	9,762,097
Capital	3,652,367	Capital	3,652,425
Negative balance	7,155,557	Profits	58
Relative increase	-66.10%	Relative increase	0.0015%
1803		1804	
Credit	15,576,721	Credit	19,617,413
Debit	10,975,369	Debit	14,225,881
Capital	4,619,352	Capital	5,391,532
Profits	966,927	Profits	772,180
Relative increase	26.47%	Relative increase	16.71%
1810		1814	
Credit	14,612,697	Credit	19,237,964
Debit	12,877,205	Debit	15,221,963
Capital	1,735,429	Capital	4,016,001
Negative balance	3,584,040	Profits	2,280,572
Relative increase	-66.24%	Relative increase	131.41%
1823		1825	
Credit	13,340,749	Credit	10,629,939
Debit	11,763,185	Debit	4,769,029
Capital	1,577,564	Capital	5,923,910
Negative balance	2,438,437	Uncollectible	5,915,229
Relative increase	-60.71%	Total capital	8,869
		Negative balance	1,568,883

Source: Author's compilation departing from data in: ABE, Secretaría, Libro 18.648

an enterprise in action. The information is from the "inventory book" of the firm, where all profits were recorded. Because these are general accounting amounts and not a summary of each partner's profits, the numbers reflect net profits. Given the family structure of the society, there were a variety of expenses such as domestic maintenance, costs of representation, payment of salaries, sumptuary expenses, etc., which were included in the debit section. In a later chapter I will focus on these particular expenses which are extremely important in understanding the details of the bankers' everyday life. For the moment I am only interested in the general accounting of profits. Two things can be concluded from an analysis of these profits: first, that capital surpluses occurred irregularly, and second, that the business was extremely volatile, something which has been stressed previously. It seems that the fluctuations depended upon very specific situations. For example, the 1812–14 war affected profits positively, while crises in 1793–94 and 1808–10 hurt income. These crises, however, never definitively affected the stability of the firms, except in very specific cases.[52] Moreover, some bankers, like Frutos Alvaro Benito, Colonilla, or the same Dutaris, made quite a profit from speculation during times of war. The accounting sheets of the Dutari firm show that the period from 1812–14 was one of its most lucrative.

Table 3.7 shows the profits of the firm Aguirre and Sons once it overcame the suspension of payment sof 1794. The advantage of this source is that it reflects the gross income before deductions for expenses. In this accounting, better than in that of Dutari, we can appreciate the profit-making possibilities offered by the trade in wool over other operations, despite its risks. While the interest rate of a loan fluctuated between 3% and 5%, and the brokerage fee for the discount of a bill of exchange was somewhere between 0.5% and 2% over its value, the percentage of profits earned from the sale and resale of a product like cocoa or sugar was about 17%. Trading in the wool market was much much more profitable, almost always providing profit margins of over 40%. Of course, these profit margins entailed a high-risk factor and required a sizable capital investment.[53] Consequently, given the nature of the wool business and the considerable

---

[52] Those who particularly suffered the hostilities with France between 1793 and 1814 were the bankers of French origin. Agustín de Queneau, for instance, had to leave Spain in 1794 as a consequence of the legal restrictions imposed by the government over French citizens who were residents in Spanish territory. AHBE, Secretaría, leg. 782.

[53] These data have been collected from the records of the Dutari and Sons firm: AHBE, Secretaría, book 18570, pp. 1–53 and 298–255; AHBE, Secretaría, book 18564 (years 1771–78).

Table 3.7. *Profits of Aguirre and Sons firm, 1787-1801*
(reales de vellon)

Company formed in 1787	
Credit	10,742,556
Debit	7,207,078
Capital	3,535,478
Balance made in 1801	
Net capital (debts subtracted)	16,497,436
Capital retained in France	10,000,000
Subtotal	6,497,436
Profits 1789-1800	6,000,000
Capital	12,497,436
Net Profits	8,961,958
Relative increase	253.49%

Source: AHPM, P. 21095, p. 213

risks that it entailed, we cannot accurately depict the *cambistas* as a business elite that played it safe by embarking only on speculation ventures. This role was played by the *asentistas*, whose better connections enabled them to speculate on the state's money. Nevertheless, some *asentista* families like the Carranzas also risked their capital on long-distance trade.[54] In reality, all of these *hombres de negocios* adjusted themselves to the possibilities that Madrid's market offered, a market whose main reason for being was derived from the city's role as political capital.

Family fortunes and investment habits

Through the analysis of family fortunes we learn about investment habits and, in turn, about the long-term changes in the market of capital. We have available to us information about the fortunes of 24 bankers who lived between 1750 and 1867. Data are also provided by the inventories of properties for inheritance purposes, and by declarations of capital. As is the case of businessmen between 1740 and 1791, the families of bankers rarely inventoried their assets, and when they did, it was not through legal channels (due

---

[54] For more details of the businesses of the Carranza family, see AHPM, P. 21670, p. 82.

Careers, business, and fortunes

1750-1816

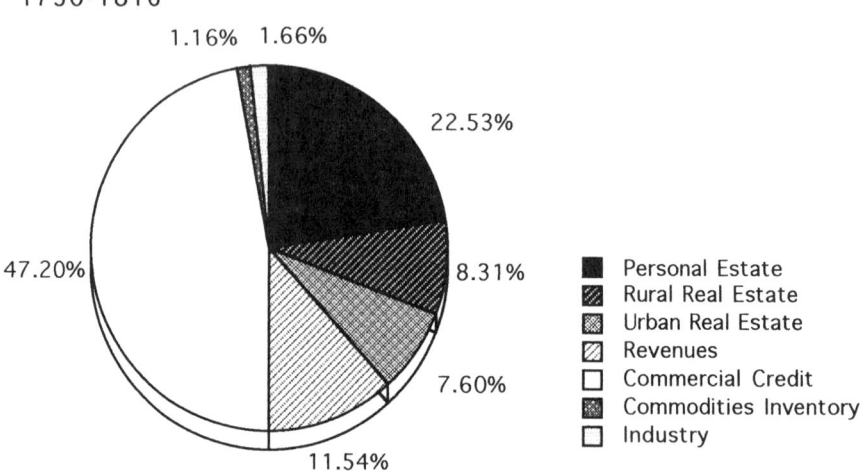

1816-1867

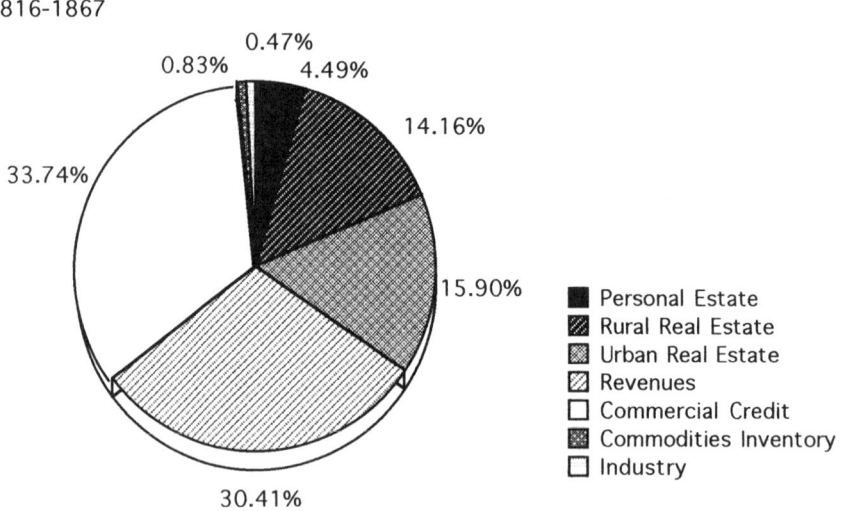

Figure 3.2. Percentage distribution of gross assets: Bankers, 1750–1867

Table 3.8. *Composition of the fortunes. Bankers of Madrid, 1750-1867*

	1750-1816 Total cases: 11	1816-1867 Total cases: 13
Personal Estate		
Domestic	4.01%	1.38%
Cash/silver	18.52%	3.11%
Real Estate		
Rural	8.31%	14.16%
Urban	7.60%	15.90%
Revenues		
Government debt	9.45%	28.34%
Company Stocks	2.09%	2.07%
Loans/censos	11.02%	7.79%
Business		
Commodities	1.16%	0.83%
Commercial credit	36.18%	25.95%
Industry	1.66%	0.47%

Source: See Appendix B

to the law of 1791). In this case, the scarcity of sources is more apparent because the group is so small.

Figure 3.2 and Table 3.8 show the composition of the fortunes of 24 bankers who consolidated their holdings between 1750 and 1867. "Final capital" refers to net assets divided between the heirs. As with the merchants, the analysis of bankers' family fortunes helps gauge their contribution to the consolidation of modern capitalsim in Spain up to the middle of the nineteenth century.[55] The median value of the total capital in the first period (1750–1816) is 4,758,272 reales; in the second period (1816–67) is 156,391,348 reales. Much of the difference between the two figures is explained by inflation between the final years of the eighteenth century and the later years of the French invasion.[56] On the other hand, some of the families used in the 1816–17 sample were continuing businesses begun in the second half of the eighteenth century, and thus their patrimonies were more solid.[57] These figures also show that the bankers of Madrid con-

---

[55] Tortella (1973: 112) has historically placed the first phase of modern Spanish capitalism between the end of the French invasion and the decade beginning 1860.
[56] See C. Barciella (1989: 501 and 518); Hamilton (1969).
[57] To compare the levels of continuity of some financial firms see Table 2.2 in this same chapter.

stituted a true moneyed elite that was in a privileged position over the rest of the business elite, not only of Madrid, but also of other Spanish provinces. In the second half of the eighteenth century, we have seen that the median net asset capital of the rich businessmen of Cadiz was 3,626,165 reales, while the median in Málaga's trading community was 270,984 reales.[58] Only the wealthiest businessmen of the Cinco Gremios Mayores attained fortunes comparable to those of the bankers, which were surpassed only by the patrimonies of some aristocratic families.

The global structure of the fortunes in the two periods reflects substantial changes that point to the existence of new conditions in the markets. We cannot detect, however, a transformation that radically altered the means of production of the economic system. I will first note the continuities. Although the patrimonies after 1816 had reduced by 10% their dependency on trade and financial credits, these were still a very important part of their fortunes. In both the first and second periods, credit accounted for a third of the inventoried goods. Approximately 10% of these were considered uncollectible, in some cases up to 30%. The specter of insecurity did not entirely disappear from the world of finances in the nineteenth century.

Where we do see changes that reflect new conditions in the market of capital is in investments. Between 1750 and 1816, capital owned in the form of silver, money, and gems made up 18.5% of the patrimonies. This tendency reversed itself radically in the first half of the nineteenth century, when government debentures and real estate began to displace this hoarded capital. Government paper went on to constitute 28% of family fortunes, increasing 19% from the first period. As Angel Bahamonde has pointed out, the decades of 1830 and 1840 were the "Golden Age" for speculation in public debt.[59] The Royal Treasury provided a continuing and varied emission of public debt: *vales reales*, leasing of taxes, stocks, etc. All of these served to activate the market of capital. This change, however, was a response to the financial needs of the state and not to a profound alteration of the conditions of the market. The problems of state finances were not new to Spain but the solutions that were attempted were innovative and expanded investment possibilities.

Something similar occurred with the process of disentailment which undoubtedly breathed new life into a real estate market that was showing

---

[58] García-Baquero (1966: chap. XI); Villar (1982: 135).
[59] Bahamonde (1981: 9f.).

signs of a shortage of supply. Hence, real estate, which accounted for 16% of the patrimonies of the first period, reached 30% in the second. This change was not as spectacular as the increase in investments in government debt, but it was nonetheless significant. The trend varied, though only moderately, in terms of geographic preference of real estate investments. In the first period ownership of rural versus urban properties was fairly balanced, while starting in 1816 the preference shifted more heavily toward urban property. These investments became more attractive as the cities grew, increasing the value of urban land and of rents. The profits coming from the leasing of urban properties stayed at about 6%, although sometimes it reached 10%. Besides being secure and profitable, investment in urban property was a mark of social prestige.[60] The elites' investments in urban and rural property was not, however, a novelty. To the contrary, it was part of a general historical tendency of urban elites of Western Europe.[61]

Other investments played a secondary role in the composition of fortunes. Loans, considered a low-risk investment, went from being 11% of family fortunes to being just 7.7% in the second period. Despite their security, loans were the least profitable investment, which explains why the Madrid bankers had only a moderate interest in usury. As time passed, loan services became a more specialized activity, considered of secondary importance in the financial world. Usurious loans were generally only offered by individual small lenders or as a complementary activity of larger companies, although some moneylenders came to amass considerable fortunes.[62] Stocks in state-protected companies or in the Bank of San Carlos (later called Bank of Isabel II and of Spain) constituted 2.9% of the patrimonies of the first period. Practically all of the bankers set aside a small portion of their money to buy stocks in the Cinco Gremios Mayores. The securities market saw a revitalization that began in the 1830s. State-protected companies had disappeared, but they were replaced by a larger number of private and public companies. The market's momentum was supplied by the construction of the railway. Notwithstanding, the amount of money invested in stocks remained proportionately small.

Industrial investment, which had only accounted for 1.65% of the fortunes of the first period, practically disappeared in the second. Why did the

---

[60] Mas Hernández (1986: 24–87); Bahamonde (1986: 369).
[61] See de Vries (1976: 219); Allen (1988); Clay (1974); for the case of Madrid see Cruz (1990).
[62] The novelist Pérez Galdós reflected this social archetype in his fictitious character Torquemada. On the social meaning of moneylending in Madrid, see Martínez Andaluz (1986: 492–504).

Careers, business, and fortunes

Table 3.9. *Structure of the investments of the firm of Aguirre and Sons, 1780-1804 (reales de vellón)*

Type of investment	Capital invested	%
Purchase of land	2,134,940	35.0
Leasing of land for herding and livestock	1,229,007	20.2
Purchase of livestock	1,720,050	28.2
Soap factory	250,439	4.1
Company stocks	320,000	5.2
Houses in Madrid and Aranjuez	342,000	5.6
Carts and oxes	90,000	1.5
Total	6,086,436	99.8

Source: See Appendix B.

bankers not invest in activities that favored industrial development? Could one characterize the investment behavior of this group as unproductive? When explanations for the lack of productive investments in internal Castile are attempted, three types of reasons are invoked. First, cultural norms are said to have stood in the way. Those who support this explanation characterize the bankers and the entire economic elite as being excessively aristocratic.[63] Second, the state is blamed for not providing favorable commercial and fiscal policies. Finally, the lack of industrial investment is seen as the result of the peculiarities of Madrid's market and the lack of regional integration.[64]

Looking at the example provided by the investments of the firm of Aguirre and Sons between 1780 and 1803 (Table 3.9), we can see how a substantial portion of these investments were aimed at improving the business. These could not be considered unproductive investments. Another matter to consider is that the nature of the wool export business favored an exclusively export-oriented economy and not the consolidation of an internal market. We should also understand the investment habits of any social

---

[63] Regarding the problem of the compatibility between nobility and manual labor see Morales Moya, (1987: 959–976). According to this scholar such incompatibility was more a legal issue than a real practice. García Sanz (1983: 11–27), however, emphasizes the negative influence of prejudice toward manual labor in the development of the Spanish economy.
[64] That would be the explanation of David Ringrose (1985).

Bankers

group as a function of the possible profitability of the investments. Except in extraordinary cases, it makes no sense to think that an *hombre de negocios* might risk his money for any reason other than achieving the largest profit possible. Investment in the wool market is understandable given that, as we have seen, profits were very high, sometimes 40% over the amount of invested capital. In the first half of the nineteenth century, after the collapse of the wool market, businessmen had to look for other venues for investment. The restrengthening of the role of the state coincided with an era of growth in public expenditures and with the desperate need to find new ways to finance the deficit.[65] Investors found greater profitability for their capital in new issues of government debt or in the purchase of disentailed properties. By using their money in this manner, instead of building factories or improving the country's infrastructure, the bankers were acting rationally in a market that did not offer other options.[66] This state of things reinforced the mechanisms of the "old corruption," whether by old groups or new ones.

In order to understand the investment habits of Madrid's bankers we need to take into account their social origins and relationship to the provincial nobility. Only one of the bankers from the sample was born in Madrid; the rest were descended from small rural nobility from the north of Spain. The business elite of Madrid accumulated most of its capital in markets that had nothing to do with the agrarian development of their region. The opposite was true in Catalonia where, as Pierre Vilar has described, capital accumulation had its origin in a process of transformation of the regional agrarian world.[67] The case of the Gloria family, studied by Roberto Fernández, offers a good example for comparison.[68] The Glorias were from a middle class of craftsmen and laborers who prospered in the environment of Barcelona's regional market. Because of their involvement in craftsmanship, it is reasonable to think that the Glorias' industrial initiatives came rather naturally. The Madrid *cambista*, belonging to a family of rural nobility who had left for Madrid in search of fortune, knew little or nothing of the world of craftsmanship and had no interest in learning about it. Trade and finances were more lucrative and, consequently, offered a better social position. The form of investments opted by the elite financiers of Madrid responded, above all, to the conditions of the market. The proof of this is in the fact that some of them did not hesitate to invest in industries if these were considered

[65] Fontana (1971: 13). [66] Cerutti (1989: 11–21).
[67] Vilar (1987: 452, vol. 3). [68] Fernández (1982: 1–151).

profitable. Nicolás de Aragorri, Marquis of Iranda, owned an iron foundry in Vizcaya and several sugar mills in Santo Domingo.[69] The Dutaris and the Aguirres invested some capital in the establishment of soap factories near Madrid. Frutos Alvaro Benito manufactured *marraga* (cloth made from goat fur) in Sepulveda.[70] All of these examples demonstrate that the bankers of Madrid, despite their ties to the provincial nobility, did not share a prejudice against investing part of their surplus capital in industrial ventures. If the Castilian bourgeoisie was less productive than the Catalonian, the English, or the French of the same era, it was fundamentally due to structural reasons, and not the result of whimsical personal decisions.

Conclusion: Parallel lives

Around the middle of the nineteenth century the bankers left their offices in the old Aduana for the comfortable salons of the newly created Madrid Stock Exchange. Since Britain's textile industry no longer demanded Spanish wool, this industry ceased to be profitable. The money which was formerly invested in the wool trade was displaced to other sectors of the economy. All attention turned to speculation in the new stock market. Everywhere Madrid saw anonymous societies spring up and disappear just as quickly after stock transactions were completed. There were days, as a contemporary observed, that transactions exceeding 200 million reales were completed with barely a change in the rate of exchange being felt.[71] Banks facilitated loans with only the guarantee of paper assets, whether this was in the form of bank bills or drafts on a current account that were passed on from one person to the next. The rapidity of growth of some fortunes was matched only by their rate of extinction. This speculation fever, as it has been called by some historians, was undoubtedly a response to a new set of economic relations. But to what degree can we say that the basis of this economy was the result of profound structural changes?

The evidence provided by this chapter points to a market in Madrid that remained fundamentally dependent upon the strong presence of the state in the city. The city continued to be an administrative financial center, very distant from the most important centers of production of the country. Although the trade and financial sectors saw a dynamic upsurge, the productive sector stayed at the level of craftsmanship. The city remained de-

---

[69] AHPM, P. 21764, p. 645.   [70] AHPM, P. 21092, p. 103.
[71] Torrente Fortuño (1969: 158, vol. II).

pendent on a long-distance market of consumer goods and proved incapable of stimulating a regional market. The new framework of economic relations to which I refer was not the result of a profound structural change in the economy of the city and its regional space, but rather the consequence of a process of adjustment to which the state was forced to submit during the first half of the nineteenth century. The loss of the colonies and the consequent loss of revenues caused the state's role in Madrid's economy to expand. Now more than ever the administration needed financial credit, making this period one of the most outstanding in the history of the banking sector of the economy. Institutions like the stock market testify to the existence of a more specialized capitalism, but its structural bases did not vary substantially from those of the middle of the eighteenth century. In a certain sense we can see parallels in the problems of the monarchy's treasury in both periods.

The economic elites of both periods also have their parallels. Of course, the nature and ways of doing business had evolved during such an extended period of time. The banking community in the time of Charles II, for example, consisted of families of foreign origins, while in 1850 the overwhelming majority of Madrid's established financiers were nationals.[72] This notwithstanding, their biographies seem replete with parallel experiences. The clue to these commonalities has to be found in the persistence of a clientelistic economy fueled by the different economic roles of the state: taking out loans, issuing public debt, and offering contracts for provisioning. In this economic framework, the mechanisms and social configuration of the financial elite conformed to a model that was stable in the long term. This model was characterized by relations between immigrants and patrons, not class conflict.

From the beginnings of Madrid's consolidation as an economic center, immigrants made up its merchant community. This immigration was a result of the existence of economic links between the city, the country, and the rest of the empire. At first it was foreign families (Italians, Portuguese, French, and Irish) who controlled the Spanish world of finance. By the beginning of the seventeenth century northerners began to appear on the financial scene, and by the middle of the nineteenth century they became the nucleus. However, this immigration was not the result of a spontaneous process incited by self-made men, or adventurers inspired by enthusiasm and

---

[72] See Ayán (1988: 334f.); Zylberberg (1983).

ambition. The elite had very measured mechanisms of social reproduction that were not altered even during the liberal period. The immigrants arrived in Madrid under the protection of a patron. They always either belonged to a family with connections or had at their disposal a group of friends and *paisanos* who could provide the necessary network. This explains how some families, like the Dutari, continued to be a forceful presence in the circles of economic power for more than three generations.

4

Bureaucrats and professionals

If there is one thing that historians agree upon it is that both the ideas and attitudes that provided the momentum for the fall of the old regime in Spain came mostly from the social groups with ties to the administration of the state and the professional world. Although the Spanish Enlightenment evolved most visibly in gatherings held in fashionable salons and in meetings of the *sociedades de amigos del país*, some of its staunchest supporters could be found in the offices of the royal palace and the government councils.[1] By the same token, liberalism found some of its strongest adherents among the ranks of government officials, professionals, and landowners – groups that were by no means mutually exclusive.[2] Only a few financiers or merchants were among the prominent liberal politicians of the first half of the nineteenth century, while the industrial bourgeoisie did not yet even exist as a definable social group.[3] The introduction of electoral systems after 1812 did not change this pattern even though part of the political class now had to be elected.[4] Although restricted suffrage permitted a limited opening of the system to new social categories, the political class through 1850 mostly consisted of administrative officials and professionals.

---

[1] It was, according to Sarrailh a "select minority" of politicians, writers, and economists connected to the administrative life and not from the university world. See Sarrailh (1957: chaps. VI–VII); Herr (1975: 136).

[2] In this respect, Comellas wrote, referring to the years after 1840, that "approximately half of the court deputies of the distinguished legislations are well-known lawyers, and it would not be improbable, rather much to the contrary, that a considerable portion of the rest studied law as well." See Comellas (1970: 76–77); Suárez (1982: 46–47); Chávarri (1988); Burdiel (1987: 127–66).

[3] 3 Vicens Vives (1971: 128); Marichal (1977: 23); Marti (1981: 189).

[4] In reality, during the nineteenth century the developed elites serving in Europe showed a strong tendency to link their interests with the minority groups, instead of with the "average citizens" or with the egalitarian conceptions of civil rights and political liberty. This in fact demonstrates the vitality of the old aristocratic society. Rosenberg (1966: 14); Mayer (1981: 128f.).

Careers, business, and fortunes

Most historians also agree that the changes that led to the fall of the old regime in Spain were the result of a social revolution ignited by a new bourgeoisie.[5] But here we run into an interesting interpretive paradox. Historians of the eighteenth century, as we saw earlier, tend to define this bourgeoisie as consisting of merchants and financiers. Those who write about the first half of the nineteenth century, however, portray this new class as made up mostly of agrarian property owners,[6] administrative officials, professionals, and to a lesser degree including merchants, industrialists, and bankers. The explanation for this inconsistency is simple. The more we know about the individuals and groups prominent in the revolution, the more difficult it becomes to classify them as bourgeois, in the sense that this concept has acquired in both the Marxist and liberal traditions.[7] This is why the consensus over the social definition of the founders of the liberal state becomes more and more controversial. Some see the bourgeoisie as revolutionary, and although they might define the group as stemming from an agrarian base and quite separate from the productive sector, they are nonetheless seen as a bourgeoisie with sufficient ability to lead the revolution. Others interpret this bourgeoisie as always having been very weak and ultimately dependent upon the old aristocracy.[8]

In this chapter I am going to study the familial economies of a group of people who held position in the administration of the state and in Madrid's professional world between 1750 and 1850. Many of them, because of their administrative functions, were part of the political class.[9] A select group of them could be considered members of the administrative elite, but along with them in the sample are persons from what could be described as the middle to high levels of the state administration. In the second half of this study I define more specifically the social classification of these men, using a

---

[5] Be it because of the existence of disagreement among the elites, as Morales Moya (1987: 66) has suggested, or simply as a consequence of a social revolution, according to Pérez Garzón (1980: 123).

[6] Artola (1978: chap. III).

[7] Be it the result of a change in the relations of production that prevailed in the feudal mode of production, or the rise of a new urban class linked to the development of mercantile circuits. See Skocpol (1979: 3–43).

[8] Fontana (1975: 162–165).

[9] By political class I understand that fraction of the ruling class which, in the political domain, exerts an influence on the government of its society. I would include, first of all, those who compose the executive and legislative power. In second place are the specialized functionaries (state technocrats). In last place are all those individuals or groups who intervene directly in the political process through clientele, parties, or other pressure groups. Of course, between 1750 and 1850, this was an extremely limited group if we compare it with contemporary societies. See Weber (1978: 54–56); Pérez Díaz (1987: 48).

Table 4.1. *Occupational distribution: Bureaucrats and professionals in Madrid, 1750-1865*

Occupation	No. of cases	%
1. *Bureaucracy*		
Councilors	107	56.1
Other	28	14.7
Middle ranks administration	20	10.4
Total	155	
2. *Professionals*		
Lawyers	7	3.6
Physicians/Apothecaries	20	10.4
Procuradores/Agentes	9	4.7
Total	36	
Total bureaucrats and professionals	191	

series of variables that takes into account their culture, and not just their political positionings, as historians have tended to do. The ultimate objective of this analysis is to either verify or revise the thesis that there was a rise to power of an entirely new social class and to suggest that we might have been asking the wrong question. The best way to test the thesis would be to come to a closer understanding of the groups that were central to the revolutionary process, whether they encouraged it or opposed it, as many bureaucrats did.

It is not my intention to offer a study of the entire Spanish political class during the crisis of the old regime. The very important sectors of the military and the regional administrations are just two of the groups left out of my analysis.[10] I can obviously not presume to capture in one chapter the whole of a social history as complex as that of the decay of the old regime, a time when so much was changing and so much was staying the same. Nor will this be a study of the core group of the political class that traces their careers, salaries, and social standing. My aim is less ambitious: The analysis of a series of personal biographies, with the goal of obtaining a collective portrait of the social group that was most visible in the political debate that led to the liberal state. The sample is based on 191 cases of families that were

---

[10] Following Pérez Díaz (1987: 49) I refer only to the analysis of the civilian political class in the central government.

involved in either the government administration, the political life, or the professional world of Madrid between 1750 and 186.[11] Table 4.1 details their distribution according to occupational category. The diversity of the group calls for separate treatment for each category, and even the creation of subcategories. These subdivisions notwithstanding, the sample presumes an internal coherence that will become evident both in the analysis of family wealth and in observations about social behavior.

This is not statistically a random sample but rather a selection imposed upon us by the availability of sources. Although it may seem surprising, the history of the sociology of power for an era as important as the period of the "bourgeois revolution" has many gaps. This analysis should serve to fill some of those gaps, albeit only partially.

Officeholders and politics: Familial economies

Under the absolute monarchy service to the state and political practice were generally complementary activities. For this reason, until 1808 the Spanish political class was made up mostly of government officeholders, as it was in other European countries. This hegemony of administrative officials became more apparent, of course, in the second half of the eighteenth century, when the Spanish monarchy, like most other in Europe, began delegating more and more authority to a very select group of specialists. In time dynastic absolutism began to give way to a kind of bureaucratic absolutism founded on the existence of a specialized elite.[12] This elite gained enough power to eventually achieve some autonomy, the product of the monarch's confidence in leaving his administrative and judicial duties to them. From this select minority of royal employees also evolved a spirit of change that could be perceived, in the times of both Charles III and his successor, in the political and intellectual atmospheres of the era.

The liberal state began to undermine the identification of political practice with service to the crown when it introduced the division of powers and the principle of national sovereignty.[13] Little by little the pledge of service to the dynasty was replaced by the notion of civil service, although this was an extremely slow transformation that lasted through the nineteenth cen-

---

[11] See Appendix A. [12] Rosenberg (1966: 18–19).
[13] Marichal (1977: chap. V).

tury. These changes, along with the introduction of restricted suffrage, energized Spanish political life in an unprecedented manner. Officially, all citizens were equal in the eyes of the law, free to express their ideas, and had greater access to the centers of power. Did, however, the sociopolitical transformation implied by these institutional changes really take place? Did the Spanish political class of the first half of the nineteenth century consist of persons from a new social class?

To answer these questions we will look at the economic behavior and the origins of wealth of the 155 persons who make up the sample of administrative officials (see Table 4.1). The data are derived from an analysis of 76 family inventories written up as patrimonies were being divided among surviving heirs. The composition of this group was much more complex than the bankers and, to a lesser degree, the merchants previously discussed. For this reason the analysis will start off with the establishment of a series of subcategories of occupations that correspond to the organizing scheme of the era. This criterion for classification may seem a bit conventional, as it does not always come from exclusively sociological criteria, but I think it will offer a clearer historical understanding. I start with the assumption that being a member of the Council of Castile was much more socially prestigious than being a councilor in Hacienda (Public Treasury), despite the fact that the difference in salaries earned by each would have been insignificant. The same was true of the middle and high positions in these institutions; salary level was not necessarily indicative of social status. After 1812 and, especially, after 1834 liberal reforms curbed these differences somewhat, although a few areas of government administration like justice or diplomacy maintained a certain air of exclusivity that made them more prestigious.

Table 4.2 shows the composition of the subcategories of specialization for the officials in the sample. Well over three-fourths of the sample – 87.1% – are men who worked in what could be called the high administrative and political levels. Of these, 68.3% served as members – either as councilors or ministers *(secretarios del despacho)* – of one or other of the councils that were the traditional power centers of the absolute monarchy. Many were active participants in the creation of the liberal state, while others remained loyal to absolutism or enlightened despotism. Some 18.8% of the men were officials in the administration of the councils, later called ministries, and although they never actually became councilors or ministers their social

Table 4.2. *Occupational distribution: Royal bureaucrats in Madrid, 1750-1865*

Occupation	Councilors*	%	Other	%	Total
Justice	29*	18.8	11	7.1	40
Public Treasury	33	21.3	28	18.1	61
State	21	13.6	2	1.2	23
Other	24	15.1	7	4.5	30
Total	107		49		155

* Most of them belonged to the Council and Camera of Castile abolished by liberal politics in the nineteenth century.
Source: Func.dat.

status and salaries were comparable. Most of the men in this category worked in Hacienda, an institution whose complexity required this horizontal diversity (accountants, intendants, managers, etc.). Public servants in the administration of justice make 6.1% of the sample. They served as judges in the *Audiencias* and chanceries, as *Alcaldes de Casa y Corte* and as members of the reformed nineteenth-century magistracy. The remaining 12.9% were midlevel employees of the various institutions (secondary officials, accountants, and the like). The reader will understand that my interest in those groups that were influential in the historic changes of the beginning of the nineteenth century justifies the exclusion of the employees and subordinates who were the vast majority of the state bureaucracy.

It is somewhat difficult to determine exactly what portion of Madrid's active population between 1750 and 1850 participated in the government bureaucracy or the political class. Contemporary censuses used categories that do not translate easily to the terms used by modern social sciences. Table 4.3 shows the evolution of the portion of Madrid's active population between 1757 and 1857 that made up the administration and professional groups. Two things can be inferred from the table: first, that the group grew at a steady rate the entire period, and second, that it was an extremely important nucleus relative to the rest of the population if compared to the situation in other Spanish cities. Their expansion was the logical consequence of an increasingly complex state. In effect, the bureaucratic machinery of the liberal state was a good deal more complex than it was under

Table 4.3. *Administrative officials, professionals, and active population in Madrid, 1757-1857*

		% total
1757		
Population		
Royal and municipal governments	3,000	2.3
Professionals*	556	
1787		
Crown, Military	5,407	3.7
Professionals	799	
1799		
Officeholders	6,482	4.0
Professionals	1,082	
1856-1857		
Government employees	7,332	3.9
Cesantes	3,091	
Professionals	737	

* I have included in this category only lawyers, physicians, and *escribanos*, because those are the best quantified professions in all population censuses.
Sources:
1757: Extrapolation from "Catastro de Ensenada," see Ringrose (1985: 416)
1786: "Censo de Floridablanca," Jiménez de Gregorio (1980: 221)
1799: "Diccionario de Hacienda" Canga Argüelles. Quoted by Ringrose (1985: 127-128)
1857: "Censo general de población." AVM, Secretaría, legs. 6-63-29 y 6-41-69
Data of total population from Carbajo Isla (1987: 225).

absolutism as a result of the introduction of the division of powers.[14] The portions of the populations of France and England employed by the state in the first years of the nineteenth century were both proportionately larger than Spain's. Likewise, the proportions of the active populations of Paris and London working for the state were also larger than Madrid's. The Spanish capital, however, always gave the impression of a city weighed down by its bureaucracy, due to the chronic weakness of its industrial sector. The impression was nonetheless rooted in the reality of a society divided between those who sought jobs *(pretendientes)* and those already employed.

[14] Mesonero coined the term *empleomanía* (hiring mania) to signify the desire of most members of the elite to obtain jobs in the state administration. See Mesonero Romanos: 63.

Careers, business, and fortunes

Select officeholders: The consejeros

Until 1834 the most specialized members of the public administration were the members of the *consejos*, the government councils. The councilors, officials appointed by the king, played a double role in the absolutist state. On the one hand they were members of what we know today as the state technocracy, while on the other they served as the legislative power of government. Practically all of the *secretarios de estado y despacho*, who together were a kind of executive branch before 1812, had previously been councilors.[15] The councils, in the meantime, controlled some of the executive power, especially in Castile, and all of the legislative and judicial powers. This was true despite the decline into which some of them had fallen by the end of the eighteenth century.[16] Between February and March of 1834 the liberal government definitively suspended all activities of the councils of Castile, Hacienda, War, and the Indies, all of which still had significant power.[17] The Council of State was the only agency to survive until the end of the nineteenth century.[18] By the end of the eighteenth century some of the councils served only as consulting bodies. Some, like the Council of Orders, were residual organisms whose membership was merely honorary. After 1834 the councils of the past were replaced by the ministries. Their legislative functions were passed on to the parliament and senate, while their executive powers were taken by the council of ministers.

A significant number of ministers and parliamentarians between 1820 and 1840 had previously been councilors. The last names of some of the most notable liberals like Argüelles, Gareli, Queipo de Llano, Pérez de Castro, Alcalá Galiano, Bardají y Azara, and Riva Herrera are also found in the history of the old regime bureaucracy.[19] Until the reforms of López

---

[15] And I say a type because the executive power wasn't held exclusively by the king. Nevertheless, "Unlike other Secretaries and even Council presidents, the Secretario de Estado y del Despacho did not need a royal decree for his dictates to have executive power; it sufficed with a notice containing the phrase 'the King orders me to say' or 'upon order of the King' or something like that to be immediately carried out" Bermejo (1982: 38).

[16] The Council of Castile was the maximum legislative institution by means of a consulting process which always had the king as its point of reference. The reinforcement of the role of the Secretarios de Estado y del despacho, first in the Junta Suprema de Estado, next in the State Council and finally in the Council of Ministers exemplify the loss of power of that rancid institution. The participation of other councilors in the legislative process was very secondary and was limited to consulting. Cabrera (1982: 264).

[17] Sánchez Bella (1974: 655–57).

[18] Carrasco (1975: 426).

[19] Paredes (1991: 23); Fayard (1982a: 534, 547, and 557); Chávarri (1988: 191).

Bureaucrats and professionals

Ballesteros in 1827, Spain cannot really be said to have had any norms to regulate the staffs, systems of access, and salaries of administrative officeholders. There was no set criteria for entrance into an administrative career, and this remained true until the end of the nineteenth century.[20] When someone was considered for a position a variety of factors came into play, among which the candidate's preparedness was not always primary. Of course, both entering into the bureaucracy and securing a political future required a certain level of specialization not available to just anybody. But what one most needed, above all else, were good contacts. Adequate influential connections had to be cultivated. The selection of officeholders and politicians was based exclusively on clientelistic principles. In Spain, as in the rest of continental Europe in the nineteenth century, power and dominance was achieved through a system of patrons and clients. This system was much more important as a factor of social interaction than was the confrontation of opposing classes. The liberal system even reinforced clientelism as it demanded more forcefully than ever that those granted administrative positions remain politically loyal. The state consequently remained under the control of a small minority of men who came almost exclusively from the same social groups that held power under the absolutist state.

Through an analysis of family fortunes we can detect this social continuity. In the great majority of the cases studied patrimonies kept a certain structural similarity to each other, despite chronological distance between them. Personal biographies can shed light on the lack of objective criteria for entering and rising in the administration. The biographies will show the diversity of experience among the professionals and, on occasion, point to the inequalities of wealth between individuals from similar administrative or political categories. The fortune of the prominent *hacendista* Joaquín Iturbide, for example, was worth only 2 percent of that of his colleague Ambrosio Garro Micheloterena, when both estates were inventoried at the end of the eighteenth century.[21] The fortune of Julián Aquilino Pérez, inventoried in 1857, was exactly 170 times larger than Antonio Espinosa Brun's, inventoried in 1837.[22] These inequalities show that social status and ability were not necessarily complementary elements among those in positions of

---

[20] It was Bravo Murillo, beginning in 1852, who established the basis for an overall reform of the Spanish administration. See Carrasco (1975: 230f.).
[21] AHPM, P. 21741, p. 579 and 20067.
[22] AHPM, P. 24619, p. 132 and 25942, p. 830.

Careers, business, and fortunes

Table 4.4. *Councilors' fortunes, 1750-1850*
(reales de vellón)

Council of	Castile	Public Treasury	State	Other	Total	%
Net value of fortune						
1-500,000	7	6	2	3	18	38.3
500,000-1,000,000	2	3	0	0	5	10.7
1,000,000-1,500,000	2	1	2	0	5	10.7
1,500,000-2,000,000	1	2	2	2	7	14.9
2,000,000-5,000,000	0	6	2	1	9	19.1
5,000,000-10,000,000	0	0	0	1	1	2.1
10,000,000+	0	2	0	0	2	4.2
Total cases	12	20	8	7	47	100.0

Source: Probate inventories, AHPM. See Appendix B.

power in the era in question.[23] Although in all of the cases studied there existed a reasonable level of wealth, the presence of moderately sized fortunes shows that the ability to rise among the ranks of the bureaucracy did not depend exclusively on financial advantages; social status also proved to be extremely important.[24]

The forty-seven patrimonies of individuals who were or had been councilors illustrate the difference between social position (status, in the Weberian tradition) and wealth (Table 4.4). The members of the Council of Castile, whose nobility was practically a requirement of office and whose social status was highly valued, were among the "less fortunate" of the sample. The mean for their fortunes in the eighteenth century was at 385,335 reales, while the median was at 467,411. Adding the four cases of former members of the council registered between 1839 and 1860 raises both figures, placing the mean at 927,284 reales and the median at 1,016,399. In any case, after adjusting their fortunes for inflation they still

---

[23] This is a proven tendency in some power elites since the seventeenth century. The data offered by Hernández Benítez (1991: 220) in his study of the councilmen of Madrid prove patrimonial differences, which in some cases are surprising. Likewise, Fayard (1982a: 354) detected important differences between the diverse "cuerpos de hacienda" of the Councilors of Castile between 1621 and 1743.

[24] Regarding the difference between social position (status) and economic position, see Weber (1978: 302–7).

remain below those of their colleagues sitting on other councils.²⁵ Of course, these figures do not include the value of entailed properties *(mayorazgos)* which were never inventoried and which were more common among the members of the Council of Castile. Even so the relative levels of wealth is remain, since in only 59 percent of the cases is there evidence of the existence of a *mayorazgo*. The modest size of these fortunes has to be understood within the context of a process begun in the time of Philip V and which Fayard has described somewhat exaggeratedly as the "impoverishment of the high magistrates."²⁶ This process was probably the result of a greater specialization of the functions of the institution, which demanded greater selectivity in order to obtain better service.²⁷

The greatest level of wealth was found among the members of the Consejo de Hacienda (Public Treasury). The mean of the twelve fortunes in the sample from the eighteenth century is of 2,794,623 reales, while the median is at 1,574,359. Considerable wealth seemed to be common among the *hacendistas*. The mean of the eight cases listed for the period after 1816 is of 3,961,699 reales. This difference is explained by the greater inequality found among the patrimonies analyzed for the second period. The councilors' wealth was often the result of their careers as *hombres de negocios*. Hacienda was always in need of specialists in accounting and finances, and so it was the logical choice for businessmen who wanted to enter the government administration. The liberal state had this in common with the absolutist state. The distance between the councilors under Philip IV and Charles II and Cabarrús in the eighteenth century, and the liberals Mendizábal, Madóz, or Salamanca was more chronological than social or political. The state's occasional dependency on private capital was the result of a secular tendency of the Spanish economy.²⁸

The sixteen remaining cases, nine members of the Council of State and seven from various other councils, show intermediate levels of wealth, falling between the members of the councils of Castile and Hacienda. The mean and the median of the first nine cases is at 1,400,000 reales. The seven

---

[25] For the deflation of these values I have used the price series from Barciella (1989: 501 and 518) and Cuenca-Esteban (1990: 373–99).
[26] Fayard (1982a: 355).
[27] The ascents of personalities like Floridablanca or Campomanes or lesser known councilors like Bernardo Cantero de la Cueva, José García Herreros, or Andrés Simón Pontero are a good example of this tendency. Fayard (1982b: 122–23); Hernández Franco (1986).
[28] In this, the Spanish model resembles more the other countries of continental Europe than the English model. See Wrigley (1987: 190–91).

remaining show a mean of 2,008,579 reales and a median of 1,534,494. A little over 81 percent of the fortunes were inventoried between 1788 and 1816, meaning they obviously belonged to the world of the second half of the eighteenth century.

As a whole the councilors were a social strata characterized more by their social position than by their wealth. Figure 4.1 offers a comparison between the mean values of the fortunes relative to merchants and bankers. Their level of wealth gave bankers a position of privilege that was comparable only to that of the old aristocracy. Merchants also had superior levels of wealth, especially in the nineteenth century. Of course, the patrimonies of the government officials do not take into account what could have been the most valuable assets of this group: their education and social prestige. Together these resources guaranteed social success, which translated into a well-paying administrative position. The fortunes of the councilors were also much more solid in their structure than those of merchants and bankers. Let us now turn to the nature of this stability.

The importance of property is a major factor in the solidity of the councilors' wealth. First we have the *mayorazgos*, the entailed properties which represented the steadiest way of passing on wealth. As stated earlier, these properties were never mentioned in the documents written up for the division of goods among heirs. This concealment is a result of the very nature of these writings, which were needed when parts of the inheritance were contested.[29] There was rarely any doubt as to who was to inherit the *mayorazgo*: the law of primogeniture demanded that the eldest son, or the closest descendant if there were no sons, inherited the property. A sizable number of the councilors' patrimonies – 59 percent of them – included a *mayorazgo*, although there were far fewer cases of councilors who petitioned the state to create new entailments. In her study of the councilors of Castile, Janine Fayard gives the *mayorazgo* central importance in the evolution of family wealth. How significant was the *mayorazgo* to the subjects of our study, these families who lived through the agony of the old regime? To what degree were our councilors affected by the liberal laws after 1836 which sought to suppress property entailments? Why were they so inactive in petitioning for the foundation of new *mayorazgos*, especially after 1814?

The relevance of this institution to the social and economic history of modern Spain has been the subject of very different interpretations. The

---

[29] Fayard (1982a: 321).

Bureaucrats and professionals

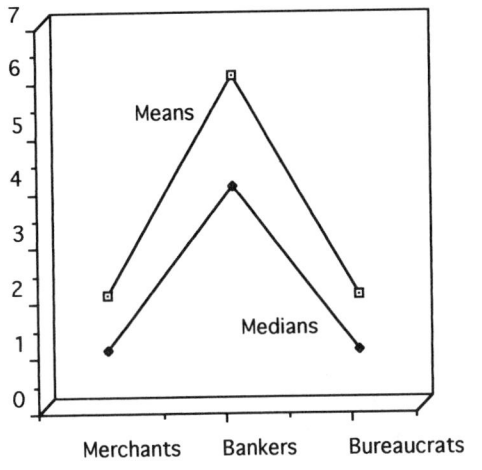

1750-1816

Means	
Merc	2,258,128
Bank	6,943,612
Bureaucrats	2,289,002

Medians	
Merchants	1,104,714
Banke	4,856,565
Bureaucrats	1,327,226

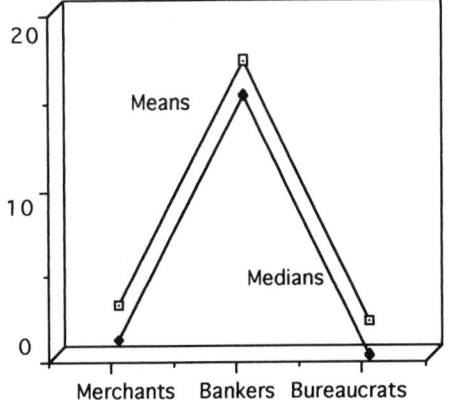

1816-1866

Means	
Merchants	3,637,992
Bankers	17,362,380
Bureaucrats	2,256,629

Medians	
Merchants	1,373,485
Bankers	15,400,000
Bureaucrats	557,363

Figure 4.1. Compared fortunes: Means and medians, 1750–1866 (reales de vellón)

debate over its nature, socioeconomic function, and disappearance is at the center of a by now old debate among historians: that of the factors and processes that led to the abandonment of feudalism and which made possible the development of capitalism. Clavero and his followers consider mostly the *mayorazgo's* juridical aspect when they define it as a form of feudal territorial property ruled predominantly by extraeconomic coercion. These coercive relations are a result of the property owner's eminent domain over the property, a condition which gives him powers above and beyond those of a mere contractual relation. The *mayorazgo* is then the most obvious expression of a socioeconomic formation dominated by feudal methods of production. This, the explanation goes, is why the *mayorazgo* was the nobility's (the feudal class's) instrument of control over the means of production. Thus is explained the fact that they were "radically opposed to the new framework of economic relations which the revolutionary bourgeoisie was trying to impose."[30]

In a different interpretation, Domínguez Ortiz has defined the *mayorazgo* as the instrument to which the nobility resorted in order to guarantee their historical continuity. According to the author the *mayorazgo* was much more than a mechanism for the control of the relations of production; it was, above all, a way to assure the continuity of a lineage. Thus, the entailed property's importance was not exclusively economic: it was replete with social implications.[31] As an instrument of social domination the *mayorazgo* was extremely successful. Cabarrús, one of its most persistent detractors at the end of the eighteenth century, did not think twice about resorting to the foundation of his own *mayorazgo* in order to perpetuate his family line.[32] This being said, as an economic tool its success was much more limited because in practice it was forced to adapt to the rhythm imposed by the development of the market.

Some years ago Artola first pointed this out. For him the nature of the land leases often set up between the *mayorazgo* landowners and local peasants was solely contractual. That is to say, they did not exemplify the practice of eminent domain but rather of mere capitalist relations. This would mean that the validity of the entailment of the property was fairly relative and, on many occasions, more symbolic than effective. Entailment

---

[30] See Clavero (1989: 107 and 408–14); Ruiz Torres (1981: 31–42).
[31] Domínguez Ortiz (1976: 329).
[32] A detail ignored by all the historians who have studied this illustrious precursor of the nineteenth-century liberalism. See AHPM, P. 20733, p. 653.

Bureaucrats and professionals

did not mean that the affected lands were outside of the market.[33] This is confirmed by the more recent studies of Mauro Hernández and Bartolomé Yun in which we see, especially in the latter's work, countless examples of voluntary disentailments brought about by the desire to bring the property into the market. When entailed property became less profitable, or if the proprietor simply needed money, he could resort to petitioning for a royal license. "From what I have seen," Hernández points out, referring mostly to the second half of the seventeenth century, "the *solicitudes de facultades* (petitions for licenses) for this era are very common in the *Cámara de Castilla* section of the Simancas Archives."[34] The eighteenth century increased this practice to the degree that entailed properties, among which the *mayorazgo* was the most important, often became more of an obstacle than a benefit to landowners. This was the logical consequence for a sector of the economy that was undergoing a steady transformation. As Richard Herr has shown, during the second half of the eighteenth century the agrarian property market had experienced unprecedented expansion.[35] When population growth sparked a general rise in the demand for agrarian products, the immediate consequence was the development of commercial agriculture. My own impression, based on the still fragmentary available evidence, is that at the end of the eighteenth century the *mayorazgo* was losing its economic value, although its symbolic value was less affected.

Of the 107 councilors in the sample, I have been able to document the existence of *mayorazgos* in 64 instances, 59.8% of the total. Only nine of those had been founded in the latter years of the eighteenth century, while the rest stemmed from earlier family inheritances. Looking at the whole of the sample – the full 155 cases – we can see how the councilors, who make up 68.3% of the total, held 80% of the registered *mayorazgos*, while all other groups – the remaining 31.6% – held only 20% of the entailed properties. The councilors also held proportionately more *mayorazgos* than merchants and bankers. As we saw earlier, these latter two groups were on the whole wealthier than the councilors.

The councilors of state held the greatest proportion of entailed property was 16 of 21 cases, or 76.1%. They were followed by members of the Council of Castile: 18 (62%) of 29 cases. By contrast, of the 33 members of the Consejo de Hacienda only 15 (45% of them) owned one or more

[33] Artola (1978: 100–2).
[34] Hernández Benítez (1991: 208, 22) Yun Casalilla (1987: 236).
[35] Herr (1989: 733–43).

mayorazgos. This once again points to the more socially open atmosphere of this council in the context of a system that offered few social fissures.[36]

At the end of the seventeenth century 90% of the members of the Council of Castile had either inherited or founded their own *mayorazgos*.[37] One hundred years later we see quite a different picture, with about half of the councilors neither inheriting nor founding entailed properties. Does this reflect, as some historians have claimed, a tendency of the Spanish administration to become increasingly bourgeois?[38] There is no reason to think that this is the case. As we shall see later on, the ranks of the political class, even in the nineteenth century, consisted of the different groups that made up the provincial elites. These elite groups consisted mostly of nobles of varying degrees of wealth who nonetheless enjoyed similar social status. The fact that by the end of the eighteenth century fewer of the less wealthy noblemen were resorting to the foundation of *mayorazgos*, relative to their predecessors in the seventeenth century, points to the decline of the social and, above all, economic function of this institution not to a decline of the families involved. The fact that these were noblemen excludes the possibility that this was the result of a lack of legal resources to entail properties. In fact, some of the families considered paradigmatic examples of the new, bourgeois political class are ones identified in my sample as having founded *mayorazgos* before 1816. This is the case of José Moñino, Count of Floridablanca, who entailed his properties in Zarza de los Vaqueros in the province of Murica with an annual rent of some 120,000 reales.[39] Miguel de Múzqiz, Secretario del Despacho Universal de Hacienda, also founded a *mayorazgo* over his holdings in Naples and Navarre which provided him with 95,000 reales of profit a year.[40]

The examples of Moñino and Múzquiz illustrate the value of the institution as a symbol of social success and, to a great degree, the guarantee of economic continuity. It was often the case, however, that profits generated by *mayorazgos* were modest, which explains why many of their holders opted to enter administrative careers. The country manor of Golpelleira,

---

[36] The Council of the Public Treasury lacks studies similar to those carried out for the councils of Castile and the Indies, even though that institution had the greatest number of employees of the Spanish administration. Regarding the history of the institution see García-Cuenca (1982); Alvarez Morales (1982).
[37] Fayard (1982a: 322).
[38] Rodriguez Casado (1953: 372).
[39] AHPM, P. 21104, p. 389.
[40] AHPM, P. 21265, p. 723.

the *mayorazgo* estate inherited by Luis López Ballesteros, in 1843 turned a meager profit of 12,000 reales. An exemplary father, if the exminister of Hacienda divided such paltry benefits among the most needy of his twelve children, he would have had a difficult time surviving had it not been for the pension he received as a former government official.

As mentioned earlier, many petitions for royal licenses to disentail properties were filed. We know that beginning in the seventeenth century it was a common practice of the Spanish nobility. The lack of research on the subject keeps us from knowing if petitions were made continuously or if they came in cycles, and if the latter is true if these cycles corresponded with economic turns. In the sample at hand most of the examples stem from the last decade of the eighteenth century. Among them is the case of Antonio González Yebra, who sat on the Council of Castile. He was granted a license to sell his home on Turco street, one of his *mayorazgos*, at 165,000 reales. Fernando de Nestarés, also a councilor of Castile, was forced to transfer some of his properties in order to pay his daughter's dowry and finance her wedding.[41]

The composition of entailed properties did not differ much from previous periods. In the few cases where we are supplied with specific information, the *mayorazgo* was made up of more real estate than domestic property, and more rural land than urban property. In most cases the lands were held in the area from where the lineage originated. A person's accumulation of several entailments was the best way of guaranteeing greater stability of the properties' yield. The Marquis de Caballero, councilor of state and minister under Joseph Bonaparte, had inherited four entailments over lands and homes in the province of Salamanca, which together rendered him over 100,000 reales in profit a year.[42] The heir of the Villavicencio house enjoyed over 200,000 reales in rents from his no less than fifty *mayorazgos*.[43] Approximately 21 percent of the cases registered in this sample held more than one mayorazgo. All of these families came from old lineages that were well established in their home region; the accumulation of entailments was the product of a long family history.[44] There were very few cases, besides those

---

[41] AHPM, P. 21115, p. 985. [42] AHN, Diversos, Títulos y Familias, Leg. 14.
[43] Lasso de la Vega (1951: 145).
[44] It was the case of the families Colón Larreátegui, Escobedo de Aragón, González Yebra, Nestarés y Grijalba, Ortíz de Guinea, Caballero, Riega, and Villanueva y Pacheco-Alvarado. This accumulation of connections (ties) of a single person was a source of constant worry for the crown, which in 1789 dictated a new regulation for *mayorazgos* which proved to be ineffective. See Clavero (1989: 295 and 300).

of families who founded new entailments, of a person taking initiative to revitalize and old *mayorazgo*.[45] The fact that the nobility often chose to disentail properties rather than to try to make concrete improvements on them shows how this group preferred to follow the logic of the laws of the market, rather than the principles established by the old society. That is why in 1836 nobody rose against laws that suppressed *mayorazgos*, even though some of the ministers and not a few deputies who put them into effect themselves came from families who held entailed properties.

Liberated property was just as or even more important than entailed property in councilors' patrimonies. The councilors of state held the largest proportion of entailed estates relative to free ones: of eight cases five – or 62 percent – consisted of a combination of both categories. The smallest proportion is found among the councilors of Hacienda: in only 30 percent of the cases was there a combination of free and entailed properties.

Not all of the inventories showed positive gains in terms of common property, something which was not frequent among merchants and bankers.[46] The councilors' fortunes were often the result of inheritances, as they tended to be from important families with long histories. It was not rare for the poor administration of an inheritance to cause balances of common property. We should also keep in mind, though, that these patrimonial imbalances were affected by the political instability of the period, especially after 1808. María Antonia Sáenz de Tejada, for example, had brought into her marriage to the councilor of State Bernardo de Iriarte about 869,000 reales, while his own capital exceeded 1 million reales. In his

---

[45] This was the case of the Councilor of Castile, Fernando Nestarés y Grijalba, who joined the *mayorazgo* of his wife and title of Marqués de la Hinojosa, which included the jurisdiction of the *dehesa* of la Hinojosa, the *dehesa* of la Serena, a position of councilman for life, and a flock of 8,333 sheep. AHPM, P. 22989, p. 418.

[46] *Bienes gananciales* (common property) was the term given to the earnings of any of the spouses after the marriage, regardless of the origin of the properties generating those earnings. Generally, they reflected the difference between the possessions brought by the spouses to the marriage (the capital and the dowry) and the final fortune. Nevertheless, its estimation incurs many errors, for which reason one must be very cautious in weighing the importance of this information. My guess is that in less than 30 percent among the cases used in this book were the possessions brought by the spouses to the marriage officially estimated (in the presence of a public notary). Whether because the operation was so costly, or because of the difficulty in estimating the value of future inheritances, the fact is that in most occasions the inheritors carried out privately the estimation of their capital in order to be able to proceed with the inventory of their possessions. There is no need to insist about the relative value which such estimations deserve. Besides, the division of the final goods often included goods which should have formed part of the family fortune, such as the education expenses of one of the inheritors or the dowries of the daughters. All these observations lead one to utilize the variable earnings with much caution and not a little skepticism.

Bureaucrats and professionals

last will and testament, dictated shortly before his death, Iriarte lamented how "diminished his fortune had become due to the costly travels and moves which war and service to the fatherland had required him to take." In effect, the Iriarte family's fortune in the end did not even match the value of the marriage dowry.[47] The Iriarte case is representative of the general instability that characterized the political class in the midst of the liberal revolution and which was accentuated by the definitive practice of the system of *cesantias* (political layoffs).[48] Exactly 12 percent of the forty-seven cases studied lacked any increase in common property. However, in no cases was the final balance of goods negative, meaning debts (debit) were larger than capital (assets). The lack of gains in terms of common property did not mean the financial ruin of a family; it simply meant an inappropriate development of the patrimony. The councilors actually had in their salaries a guarantee of their well-being.[49]

Figure 4.2 shows the composition of forty-seven fortunes during the period they were inventoried.[50] Once again I insist that what I am trying to compare is the structure of the patrimonies, that is to say, their relative rather than absolute value. To do this we must keep in mind the change in the value of money throughout the period studied. Seen as a whole the fortunes of the councilors offer two distinctive characteristics relative to the groups discussed previously. The first is the relative homogeneity of their composition despite the diversity in the sample in terms of professions represented and level of wealth. This structural homogeneity in the pa-

---

[47] AHPM, P. 21693, p. 90 and 478. Something similar happened to Juan José Alesón y Bueno, of the Consejo de Indias, for whom leaving Madrid in 1808 meant financial ruin: "in order to survive, my wife had to sell many of our treasured possessions" AHPM, P. 22279, p. 888.

[48] The cases of Cabarrús, Floridablanca, or Godoy show that political fortune in the times of Despotismo Ilustrado was also a variable value, but not compared with what happened after 1814. The *cesantes* (workers who were temporarily laid off) formed a social type characteristic of Spanish society of the nineteenth century. See Mesonero (1851: 116).

[49] I have no concrete information about the salary of a councilor between 1750 and 1834. One can make an estimation using the data revealed by Bernard (1976: 157–246) and Gómez-Rivero (1988: 48–54 and 153) for the personnel of the secretary of justice. The regular salary in the epoch of Charles III was 120,000 reales per year, to which one would have to add grants which ranged from 30,000 to 90,000 reales. There was a spectacular rise in the salary of the ministers of the epoch of Porlier Sopranis, but afterward they returned to levels of the period of Charles III or even lower. The salary of an official mayor oscillated between 40,000 reales (1714) and 42,000 (1807).

[50] See Appendix B. In order to compare these patrimonies with those studied by Fayard (1982a: 350–87), I have decided to follow her classification criteria to define the different components which form a personal fortune. The difference with the classification used in the two preceding chapters refers to the sections labeled revenues and credits. The first includes all the capital revenues (public debt, stock, etc.) and the profits from the rent of lands and houses. The section of credit includes basically the credits and loans.

Councilors of Castile
1790-1809

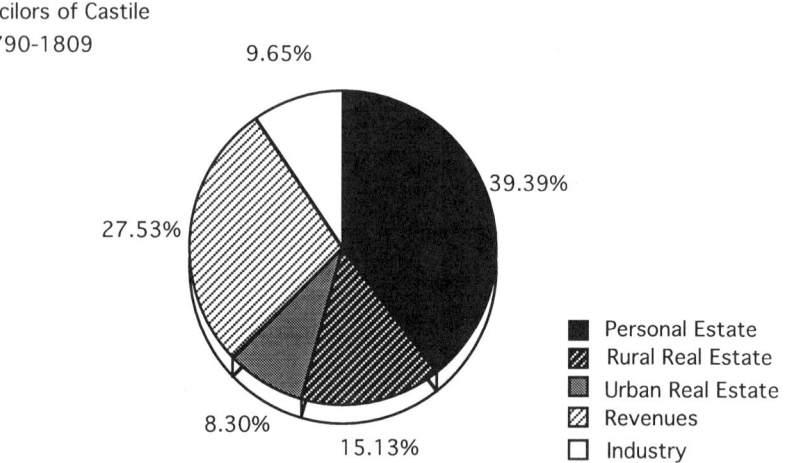

Councilors of Castile
1839-1860

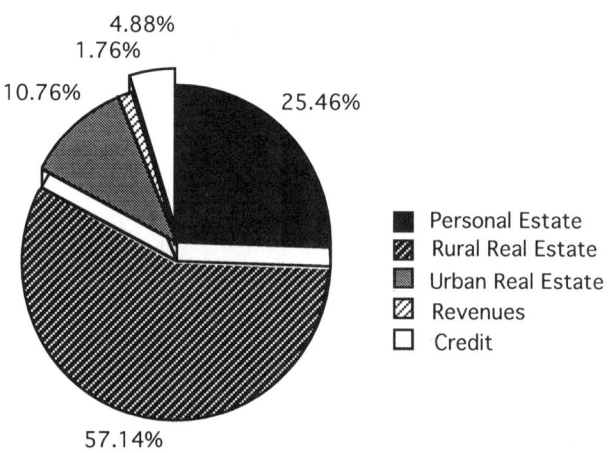

Figure 4.2

Bureaucrats and professionals

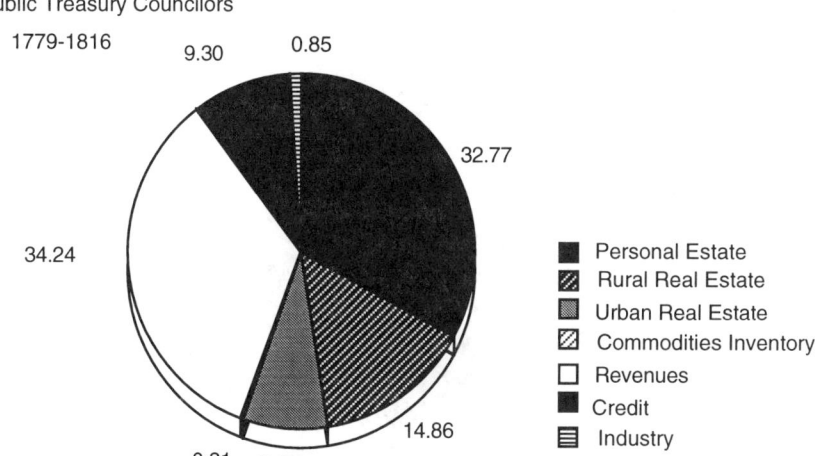

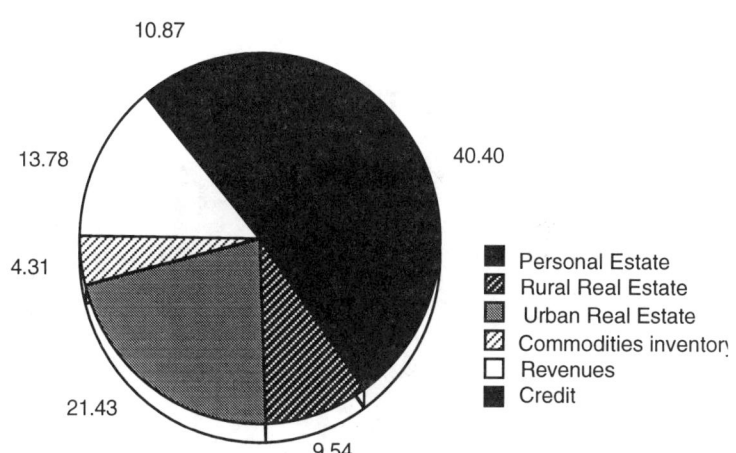

Figure 4.2 (cont.)

Careers, business, and fortunes

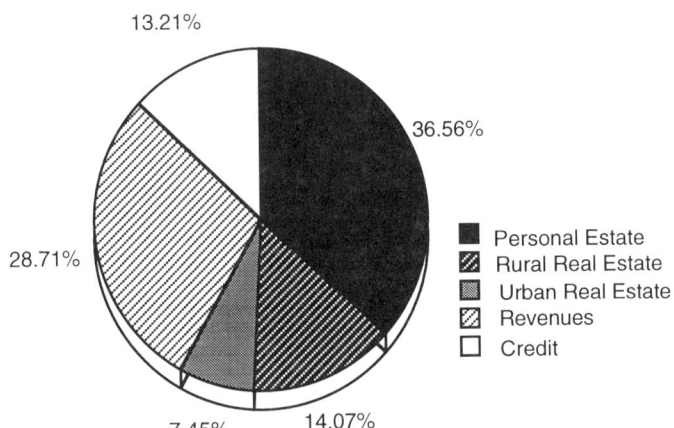

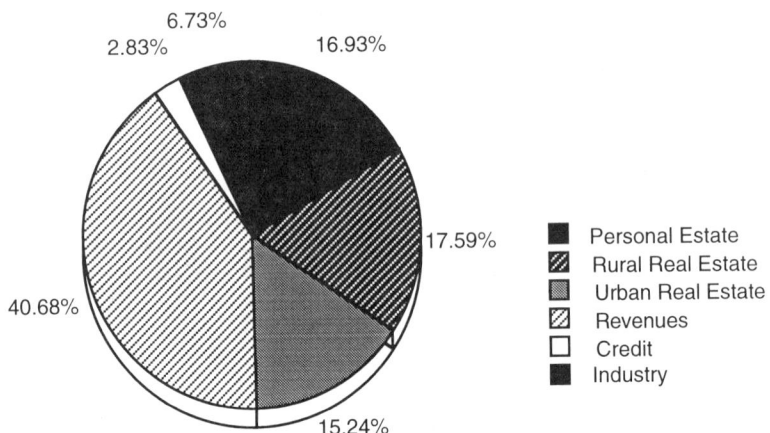

Figure 4.2 (cont.)

Bureaucrats and professionals

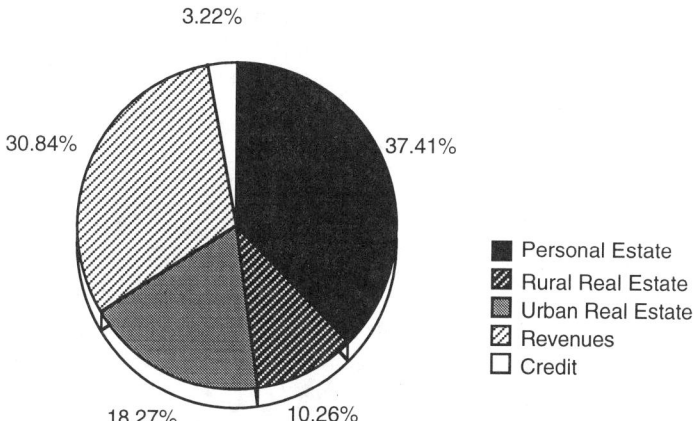

Figure 4.2. Composition of fortunes: Councilors

trimonies of the group is not causal, and it confirms their coherence as a collective social group. The second characteristic that stands out in the continuity of its composition, that is to say, in the elements – land, money, personal objects, etc. – that made up an individual's wealth. As a whole, personal property accounted for approximately one-third of the patrimonies, a figure much higher than the proportion found among merchants and bankers. Money and amassed capital (silver and gems) surpassed holdings in domestic property (furniture, clothing, etc.) at a ratio of two to one. In the meantime, capital assets were three times greater than holdings in money between 1750 and 1816, while between 1816 and 1864 the two items were at almost equal levels, with case being slightly favored. In the nineteenth century cash began to substitute amassed capital. Salaries and rents – though irregular, more or less guaranteed – favored a greater influx of money into the homes of government officials, a tendency also evidenced among merchants and bankers.

The importance of personal property in the whole of the councilors' patrimonies is explained by two complementary reasons. First is the very nature of the fortunes, whose level of working capital was very small. In contrast to the merchants and bankers, the wealth of the councilors stemmed fundamentally from their salaries and the profits from their fixed capital. The second reason is the social function of the group, which had a variety of symbolic repercussions. Expenditures on clothing, furniture, carriages, etc. were necessary investments of a people that had to watch very carefully the maintenance of their social status. Care of the wardrobe and the use of carriages were two fundamental elements of symbolic capital, and so a health portion of the family's budget was spent on them. Francisco Moñino, the count of Floridablanca's brother and the future governor of the Council of Indies, owned a wardrobe valued at more than 120,000 reales in the declaration he made at the time of his wedding.[51] Some of his garments were valued at 9,000 reales – twice the amount of money estimated that a middle-class family of four needs to live one year.[52] For Moñino and his colleagues on the Council of the Indies, clothing was a symbol of authority, as well as something that distinguished them from subordinate social groups.

The decor of homes also followed this symbolic language of domination. Comfort seems to have been a secondary consideration when purchasing furniture and household equipment. Heating for protection against sometimes harsh Madrid winters was limited to a couple of braziers in the main rooms. Bedrooms often lacked ventilation and, except for the master bedroom, were furnished sparsely. They sometimes contained only a couple of chairs and one or more cots instead of beds. In the main rooms of the house, however, careful attention was paid to curtains, furniture, painting, and decor. The Council of Castile's Juan Antonio Paz y Merino lived in a home on Carrera de San Jerónimo that had a living room in which he could entertain about forty guests. A crystal chandelier hung from the ceiling, the windows and door frames were decorated with crimson curtains, and the walls were covered with religious paintings. Against the walls sat thirty-four plush chairs and a walnut sofa that seated three people. In the center of the hall was a walnut table, while several other pine tables in the room completed the furnishings.[53] Living room furnishings are a part of all of the

---

[51] In 1787, Francisco Moñino, the brother of Floridablanca, married María Pontejos y Sandoval, the daughter of the Marqueses de Pontejos, one of the most prestigious families in Madrid at that time. On several occasions the adversaries of Floridablanca criticized his favoritism toward his brother Paco, as he was familiarly known, who besides his administrative position and his good marriage accumulated more honors than he probably deserved. See Hernández Franco (1984: 29 and 30). AHPM, P. 21104, p. 389.
[52] Ringrose (1985: 102).
[53] AHPM, P. 20087, wp.

Bureaucrats and professionals

inventories of holdings of the middle and high classes of the era. That room was the central area of the house and was used by the owners to socialize with their family, friends, *paisanos,* and protégés. A large number of chairs was always a feature of the decor, illustrating the importance of sociability as an element of social distinction.

Another third of the councilors' patrimonies consisted of real estate (land and homes). Among the councilors of Castile rural properties surpassed urban holdings in much greater proportion than they did among other councilors. Thirty-six inventories – 76.5% of the sample – include real estate; in twenty-seven of the cases, 57.4% of the total, the estate held rural properties while in twenty-two of the inventories, or 47% of the total, showed urban property holdings. Only eleven inventories – 23.4% – had no real estate whatsoever. Just one of those eleven cases was of a family that owned entailed properties, which were not normally inventoried. So it is certain that ten families in the sample lacked entirely any kind of real estate. This was the case of Antonio Espinosa Brun, whose patrimony was limited to his domestic property, some money, and a few titles of consolidated debt.[54] In some cases, the unimpressive size of the fortune was due to the instability of the historical moment or as a result of having been disgraced politically. Francisco de Cabarrús asserted that his capital exceeded 12 million reales, "purely and legitimately acquired," before his incarceration.[55] But in a good number of the cases the absence of real estate was the result of personal decisions about how to invest surpluses and not of patrimonial limitations. Half of Councilor of the State Francisco de la Vega's wealth, for example, was invested in public debt and in stocks in the *Cinco Gremios*.[56]

A significant portion of the rural property that appears in the inventories came from family inheritances.[57] Because of this they tended to be far from Madrid, in the regions of origin of the families. Most of the farms that José Cabanilles owned, for example, were in Valencia, his father's home town. His mother left him lands in Asturias valued at 50,000 reales, but he centered his activities as agrarian property owner in Valencia. The lands were put to various uses, from the cultivation of olives and cereals to rice. With

---

[54] AHPM, P. 24619, p. 132.
[55] AHN, Diversos, Serie General, leg. 7.
[56] AHPM, P. 21679, wp.
[57] It is nearly impossible to establish an exact measure since the fortunes do not always offer this type of information. In only four cases of the twenty-six in which rural estates appear, do these not proceed mainly from inheritance. AHPM, P. 23003; 22279; 18193. AHN, Diversos, Serie General, leg. 35.

Careers, business, and fortunes

the exception of a recreation garden near the ocean, in which the Cabanilles had built a farmstead, the properties were all leased. When the inventory of goods was taken, it was calculated that 20,000 reales in rent, dating from July of 1844, had been collected. By far most of these rents were half-year debits that expired the holiday of San Juan. Although I do not have exact figures, I estimate that the family received over 40,000 reales in rent from the indirect exploitation of their agrarian lands.[58] Very few councilors started an agrarian patrimony from scratch. It was more common for someone to make improvements on inherited properties. Among the men who did this was Pedro Martínez de la Mata, from Hacienda, who invested 740,000 reales in the purchase of the Soterraña meadow in Extremadura, a property recently disentailed. He also bought lands and a farmhouse in Colmenar de Oreja valued at nearly 200,000 reales. These investments significantly improved his original, inherited patrimony, which consisted of houses, lands, and wine cellars in Rioja – valued together at 300,000 reales.[59] Half of Juan Alesón y Bueno's properties were left him by his father and were located in Navarre, the latter's birthplace. The other half had been acquired in state auctions and were located in Orihuela.[60] Finally, we have the example of the Council of Castile's Joseé Pérez de Hita, who added to his patrimony the hacienda San Estanislao, located near Granada. Pérez de Hita had inherited a *mayorazgo* in Atarfe that included lands that produced cereals, wine, oil, flax, and wool.[61]

In only nine cases were real estate holdings entirely urban. The small percentage is not surprising, given that this type of property tended to play a complementary role in the patrimonies studied. Many times a councilor never owned the home he lived in while in Madrid. Those fortunes in which urban properties figure more prominently deserve different treatment. They were generally families with distinguished ties to the urban oligarchy, which was the case of the Salazar or Santa Clara families in Madrid, or others from provinces.[62] Francisco Salazar y Agüero, from the Council of Castile, had inherited from his father several houses in various parts of the capital. According to the *planimetría de Madrid*, recorded in 1749, the six properties owned by Francisco Salazar Rogibal, father of Francisco, brought

---

[58] AHPM, P. 25219, p. 2057.
[59] AHPM, P. 23003, p. 2.
[60] AHPM, P. 22279, p. 888.
[61] AHPM, P. 182005, p. 25 and 18193, p. 176.
[62] Ignacio Santa Clara Villota, of the Consejo de Castilla, bought the title of Councilman of Madrid which his son Manuel inherited. AHPM, P. 21659, p. 717. See Hernández Benítez (1986: 658).

Bureaucrats and professionals

in rents of over 30,000 reales.[63] The Salazars' ties to Madrid can be seen in the nature of their patrimony, two-thirds of which was made up of money from rents and *efectos de Villa* (municipal bonds).[64] Sometimes councilors owned urban properties because they participated in the active urban market of the first half of the nineteenth century. Among these were the Canga Argüelles family, which invested more than 1 million reales in urban lands, and Julián Aquilino Pérez and his brothers, who were among the biggest buyers of disentailed properties in Madrid.[65]

Most of the councilors' urban property, however, stemmed from family inheritances or purchases made in a family's home town. Houses, warehouses, and lots were all of secondary importance in these patrimonies. Often these holdings consisted of a home the family once lived in. A family's property just served to show the provincial roots of the clan. To invest in the purchase of a house in the place of origin was a very frequent practice among merchants and bankers, but some bureaucrats also did the same.[66]

One-fourth of the typical patrimony consisted of rents of very diverse natures. A very small number of cases, a total of four, included provincial land rents. Of course, the information the inventories provide us with is insufficient. They usually were adequate amounts for the owners when it came time to divide up the inheritance. An administrator was always appointed to account for the *mayorazgos* or nonentailed properties. Sometimes this person was a family member, normally a member of the rural community who had enough education to be able to handle basic accounting.[67] However, very few accounting books survive from the time, and so even though we know that between 1750 and 1850 agrarian rents saw a sustained increase with momentary interruptions, we cannot determine to what degree this occurred in the cases studied here.[68]

---

[63] Cruz (1990: 264).
[64] AHPM, P. 22520, wp.
[65] AHPM, P. 21000, p. 431; 25132, p. 201; 24994, p. 684; 25942, p. 901. See Mas Hernández (1986: 54).
[66] José López Juana, senator and former Councilor of the Indies, bought several houses near the cathedral in his native Sigüenza. AHPM, P. 25371, p. 499. Pedro Domínguez Lorente, member of the council of the Public Treasury, owned a house in Ceuta valued at 75,000 reales AHPM, P. 23090, p. 1208. Francisco de Campo y Haza inherited from his wife houses in Cádiz valued at more than 250,000 reales. AHPM, P. 21774, p. 667 and 21775, p. 9.
[67] A son of the minister López Ballesteros combined his chaplaincy with the administration of the *mayorazgo* of his family. See González López (1987: 186).
[68] With a depressive phase between 1820 and 1840. See Robledo Hernández (1984: 211); Fernández de Pinedo (1980: 66).

Careers, business, and fortunes

The inventories show that investments in public debt accounted for a significant portion of the income revenued by the councilors. Twenty-nine of the forty-seven inventories studied, 61.7%, include some form of state bonds. Several reasons explain the tendency toward this kind of investment. First is that for many of those who served in the administration these investments were not voluntary. Because of the persistent state deficit, intensified after 1779, government officials' salaries were often delayed for long periods of time. The state offered the alternative of receiving these payments in the form of government debentures.[69] Second, we can assume that high administrative officials trusted these kind of investments. They were the promoters of this type of debt and were often privy to privilege information. Francisco de Cabarrús, for example, was the largest individual stockholder of the Bank of San Carlos. He paid out of his own pocket for 1,750 shares of stock, while he purchased another 1,630 through his trading company. It is also significant that the rest of the bank's largest stockholders, whether they were individuals or companies, were in his circle of influence.[70] Finally we should mention that the state guaranteed, at least partially, the security of the investment. Despite the problems of the government's treasury, practically all of the wealthy class of Madrid between 1750 and 1850 dabbled in some sort of business with the state.

The other significant portion of income from rents came from investments in commercial and financial stock. These types of holdings are found in twenty-eight inventories, 59.6% of the forty-seven in the sample. The patrimonies of the second half of the eighteenth century generally tended more toward this kind of investment. The fact that the early nineteenth century saw the collapse of many of these companies explains this tendency. A similar situation is found in the commercial and financial patrimonies of the period; it seems that between 1814 and 1840 the portfolios of Madrid investors were significantly reorganized. The limits of the period are probably marked by the disappearance of the Cinco Gremios and the arrival of the railroad and the proliferation of insurance companies.[71] In 57.6% of the cases, in fact, councilors chose to invest in stock in the Cinco Gremios and

---

[69] In 1789 a commission was created to review the state of the current credits against the Public Treasury. The result was that 80% of the titles given out and 65% of the value came from unpaid salaries and pensions and unpaid loans. See Artola (1982: 389).

[70] For the main part it was a matter of French businessmen such as Lecouteulx, Lenormand, Hoüet, Beaumont, Queneau, et al. – Tortella (1986: 389f.).

[71] Bahamonde (1981: 138f.).

Bureaucrats and professionals

their complex financial and commercial working;[72] investments in the Bank of San Carlos followed close behind in number.[73] Only in a couple of instances is there any diversity in the kind of stock held. For example, the portfolio of the councilor of Hacienda Francisco de Campo y Haza looked something like this: 87.7% in stock in the Companñía de la Vega de Ribadeo, the rest divided proportionally among the Compañía de Filipinas and the Cádiz consulate.[74] Buying stocks in the state-protected companies (most of them were) was generally a sound investment. They were less profitable than agrarian and urban investments, but their security made them more attractive. The political class's participation in institutions that channeled commercial and financial capitalism in the period is a positive trait, although their actions took place under the patronage the state exercised over these institutions.

Where we do see a generalized coincidence is in the scant relevance of industrial investments for our select bureaucrats. None of the councilors directly put money into industrial ventures the way they did in the commercial sector (investments in the trading houses, the Cinco Gremios, or the state-protected companies). Industrial wealth, seen in only two cases, consisted of one factory and several smithies owned directly by the individuals being inventoried. The smithies belonged to the members of the Isla Fernández family, several of whom served on the Council of Castile, while the factory was owned by Antonio de Ibarrola Llaguno, member of the council of Hacienda.[75] Like other northern noble families, the Islas leased several smithies and mills on the Isla de Siete Villas, where their lineage began. Ibarrola, who owned the royal leather tanning factory established in Aravaca, offers us a more interesting example of northern noblemen who combined service to the state with business practices in Madrid. Being a coun-

---

[72] Through the purchase of stock or impositions of the Cinco Gremios and their satellite commercial institutions. The amount of some investments reveals its importance. José Antonio de Santa María, for example, has taxes of more than 1.6 million reales. Pedro Martínez de la Mata bought stocks valued at 273,742 reales; Francisco Javier de la Vega invested 46,240 reales; Melchor Jacot 300,000; Vicente Rodríguez Rivas had investments of 162,500; Ignacio Santa Clara Villota 110,000; Francisco de la Dehesa had 180,000 in the CGM and 38,056 in bonds of the Diputación de Comercio. AHPM, P. 21692, p. 512; 23003, p. 2; 21697 wp; 21670, p. 44; 21855, p. 173; 21659, p. 717; 22873, p. 14.

[73] It was the case of the Councilor of State José de Anduaga, who possessed stock in the Bank of San Carlos with a value of 240,000 reales. The stock of Francisco de la Herrán was more than 126,000 reales, the total of his investments. Sixty-five percent of the stocks of Luis Losada, of the Council of Ordenes, were from the Bank of San Carlos, the remaining 35% were from the dry goods company. Those of Francisco Martínez de Sobral exceeded 52,000 reales. AHPM, P. 22277, p. 717; 23388, p. 1027; 21042, p. 147; 21418, p. 196.

[74] The total investment exceeded 170,736 reales. AHPM, P. 21774, p. 667 and 21775, p. 9.

[75] Fayard (1982a: 512–14); AHPM, P. 22424; 21103, p. 305.

cilor in Hacienda, in 1800 Ibarrola held a position on the Junta de Comercio, another on the board of directors of the Bank of San Carlos, managed his factor's silk warehouse in Madrid, and occupied his traditional role as director of the royal factory in Aravaca. He applied his business aptitude to his service to the crown. He was not exactly an independent industrial entrepreneur but rather, above all, a public servant who knew how to exploit the means the state put at his disposal.[76] Ibarrola did not represent the modern, self-made capitalist entrepreneur, but he can be considered the historical antecedent of the modern technocrat in service to the state.

What conclusions can we draw from the analysis of the nature and origins of the councilors' wealth? What historical implications can be found in the way that the councilors acquired their wealth? The composition of their fortunes – or, stated differently, – their position in the productive process, shows that councilors constituted a sort of rentier group. The fact that 76.6% of the patrimonies studied included some form of real property, and that 74.5% some form of rent, supports this conclusion.[77] The manner in which the councilors chose to acquire their wealth shows a certain historical continuity with small, though important, variations. Figure 4.3 shows graphically the structure of the fortunes of the councilors in Fayard's study of the period of 1621 to 1746, along with structure of the patrimonies looked at here. The similarities are obvious. Some of the elements varied substantially between periods, but their similarities are nonetheless striking. *Censos* and *juros* were replaced by *vales reales, renta del tabaco,* or the most modern *imposiciones al 3%*. The substitution of investment in companies for stocks was also an important novelty. The amount of working capital was smaller than one hundred years earlier, due mostly to credits and loans. Some of these changes were the result of a more complex economy, an unequivocal sign of a transition to capitalism. In essence, however, the fortunes in both cases follow a similar patrimonial model based on salaries received from the state, rents coming in from the exploitation of rural and urban lands, and the value of their personal belongings. The occasional exuberance of the latter is a reflection of the councilors' privileged social status. Given these

[76] Ibarrola was not an industrialist like his contemporaries Fernando Rodríguez, the owner of a company that made carriages, or Juan Kastler, who owned a brewery, or Gerónimo Daguerre, who like Ibarrola, owned tanneries in Madrid. AHPM, P. 23084, p. 136; 23830, p. 13; 23090, p. 1646 and 21081, p. 543f.

[77] Almost two-thirds of the patrimonial wealth of the councilors was composed of real estate and rents. In the case of the bankers, both elements constituted 43.9 percent, while for the businessmen they formed slightly more than one-third.

Bureaucrats and professionals

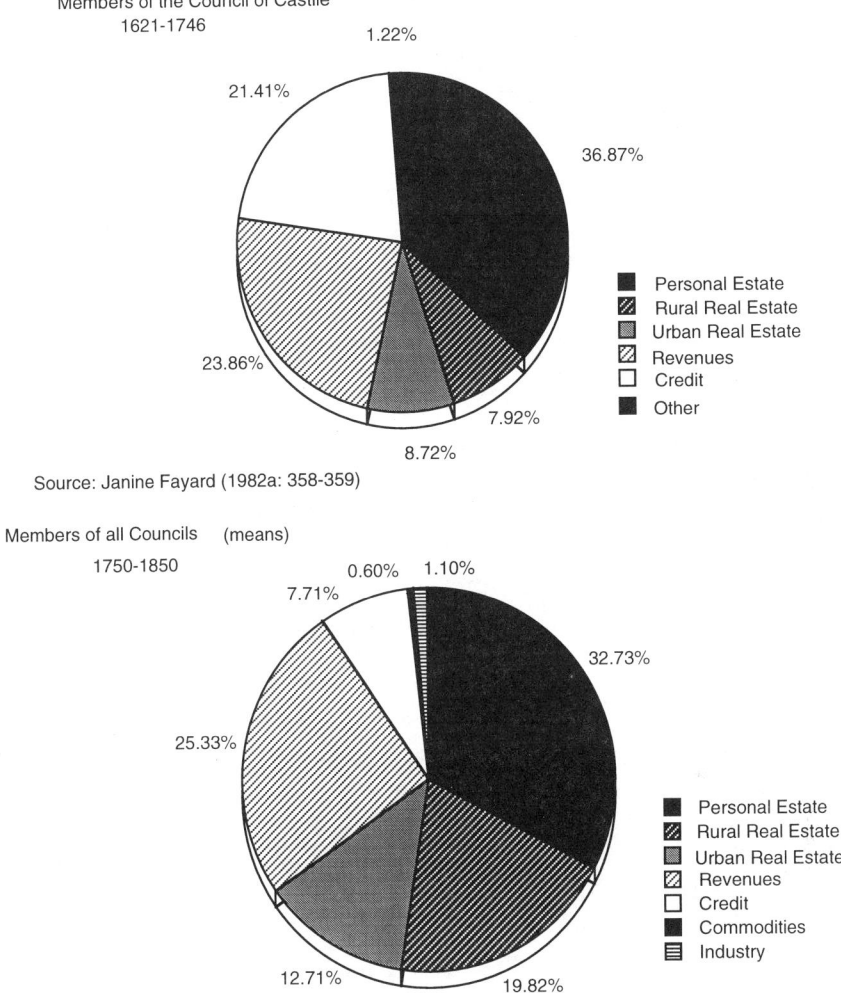

Figure 4.3. Comparative distribution of gross assets: Councilors, 17th–19th centuries

Careers, business, and fortunes

characteristics, it seems to me the social position of the objects of this study can only be defined as being a model of continuity.

High and middle ranks of the administration

The high levels of administration did not consist entirely of those who sat on one or another council. There were also a series of analogous categories and also positions directly under the councilors in the administrative echelons, which had similar social prestige (*Oidores, Alcaldes de Casa y Corte, ministros contadores, intendentes, secretarios, etc*). In this section I will look at a small number of these cases. I have only selected officials who, going by the date of their inventories, served in the administration while the system of councils was still in place. This notwithstanding, some of them lived through or were even played prominent roles in the institutional changes that liberalism introduced. Most of the men in the sample served in Hacienda, because this council employed more of this kind of specialized high official. There tended to be virtually no social distance between the officials studied here and the ones in the previous sample. There are, however, some cases with nuances that point to differences in social origin.

I have also included in my sample fourteen cases of men from what could be called the middle ranks of the administration, a series of very diverse administrative categories. Despite this diversity, if we look at the nature and origins of the wealth of the men in these ranks, they do seem to make up a coherent social group (Appendix B).

The members of the first group of high officials were not generally as wealthy as the councilors. The median of the four cases from the administration of justice was at 169,546 reales, while those from Hacienda had a median of 777,602 reales. The latter group included at least three patrimonies that surpassed 1 million reales, but on the whole the accumulation of wealth was inferior to that found for councilors. One of the millionaire fortunes belonged to Juan Ignacio Güell, minister in the Tribunal de la Contaduría Mayor de Cuentas. Juan Ignacio was the son of a councilor of Hacienda and the grandson of a councilor of Castile – this family was not new to the world of government service.[78] His holdings included several *mayorazgos*, including a position as *regidor* in Barcelona, but the bulk of his wealth came from the many houses in Madrid that his family had owned

---

[78] Fayard (1982a: 304); AHPM, P. 23400, p. 304.

Bureaucrats and professionals

since the first half of the eighteenth century.[79] Unlike the Güels, the Azofras present a good example of an ascendant family. José Azofra Delgado, the head of the family, was born in the valley of Vizcaya, also in the northern side of the peninsula. The son of a provincial *notario*, Azofra amassed his fortune while working in the Contaduría del Real Tribunal de Cuentas of Lima, where he served as general accountant for several years. Like many of his friends, neighbors, and kin, Don José had a successful career in the colonial administration. He founded a *mayorazgo*, inherited by his son Domingo, in order to assure the continuity of his lineage.[80] Family members continued working in the high administration of Hacienda for at least another generation, but we have no information about them for the second half of the nineteenth century. The Azofras are, of course, an obvious example of an ascendant family, but their social ascent does not seem to be the work of "self-made men." They owed their social rise to multiple networks of kin, *paisanos*, and friends that controlled access to positions in the government administration. This social ascent does point to the fact that Madrid's dominant groups allowed a certain amount of flexibility for upward mobility in order to guarantee renewal. Later we will see in greater detail the nature of this mobility, but for the moment suffice it to say that its existence can be perceived by looking at the origin and consolidation of the family fortunes.

Indeed, the amount of property changing generational hands in the twenty-nine inventories of high and midlevel administration officials that form this sample is inferior to what we saw for the councilors. Inheritances were most frequent among the members of the high administration and fairly rare among those in the middle ranks. Of the fifteen fortunes of high officials in the sample, we have found inherited goods in at least eight – 53.3 percent. For example, Manuel Carrancio, judge of the Chancery of Valladolid, inherited a farm and home in a town in the province of Palencia, where his family originated. Although his father was only a provincial lawyer, the Carrancios were a well-to-do family in the region.[81] Their status was similar to that of José Agustín de Ussoz y Mozi, who inherited several farms around Madrid, and Fernando Ibarrola Layseca, who served in the Secretaria de Gracia y Justicia and who inherited the bulk of his fortune

---

[79] Cruz (1990a: 257).
[80] AHPM, P. 20927, p. 295.
[81] AHPM, P. 22869, p. 1065.

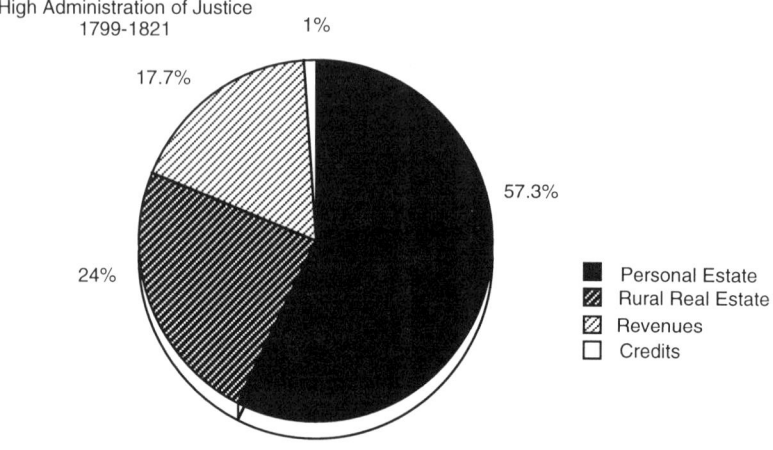

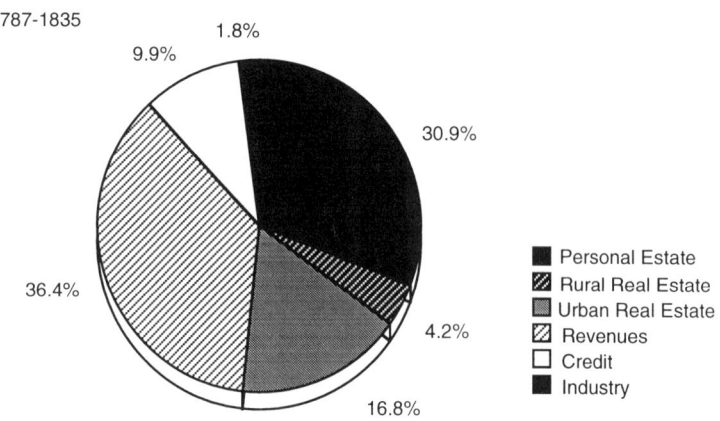

Figure 4.4. Composition of fortunes: High administration, 18th–19th centuries

from his uncle.[82] In many cases, however, the officials began their careers with no fortune at all, as was the case of the aforementioned treasurer of army, Domingo de Marcoleta.[83]

[82] AHPM, P. 21750, p. 476. [83] AHPM, P. 21658, p. 866.

Bureaucrats and professionals

Among middle-level officeholders inheritances were more rare. The overall level of wealth of this group – the median of their patrimonies was at 214,000 reales – and the composition of the fortunes indicates that this group consisted of men of inferior social rank. Possibilities of inheritance, of course, were lower the smaller the amount of accumulated wealth. Personal property accounted for the most important portion of the patrimonies of the high officials, followed by revenues and real estate. The structure of the fortunes does not differ significantly from the councilors; variations are found mostly in their content (Figure 4.4). The greatest difference is the importance of urban properties in the patrimonies, especially among those in the administration of Hacienda. In this they are closer to the fortunes of the merchants studied in previous chapters than the councilors'. A sizable portion of these properties came as a result of the group's participation in Madrid's real estate market, which was especially active after the disentailments of 1798. Francisco Gorbea, who belonged to a merchant family established in Madrid since the beginning of the eighteenth century, was one of those active in the market.[84] A clear example of an ascendant family, the Gorbeas were originally from the valley of Gordejuela in the Basque country and upon arriving in Madrid began trading in hardware. Francisco Gorbea, a member of the family's second generation, cemented his privileged social status by reaching the position of *oficial mayor en la Contaduría Mayor de Hacienda*. The family's third generation continued in the high administration of the state and became tied through marriage to the Santa Clara family, members of the oligarchy that controlled municipal power in Madrid.[85]

Investment in urban real estate marked the difference between the old bureaucratic dynasties and families in the process of social ascent. Buying houses made more sense to those families who consolidated their fortunes in Madrid's clientelistic economy. The presence of this type of ascendant family was felt the most in the administration of Hacienda. They are especially visible in this sector's high and middle ranks, although many of them ended up being incorporated into the administrative elite. After all, in order to enter the administration of justice, the army, or diplomacy one needed a degree of specialization that usually required a university degree, making these institutions more socially selective. But for those who did not have the means or influence to obtain a university degree, there did exist other

[84] Capella and Matilla (1957).
[85] Hernández Benítez (1990); AHPM, P. 21656, p. 854.

Careers, business, and fortunes

venues through which they could enter the state bureaucracy, reach a respectable social status, and create a network for themselves through which they could help their friends and family.

Does this mean that any person, regardless of their social origins, could use the administration of Hacienda as a way of climbing the social ladder? Should we be looking among these subordinate sectors of the administration and the economy, which did often provide the opportunity for upward mobility, to find our revolutionary bourgeoisie? Absolutely not. As I have pointed out from the beginning, social forces were such that, even in Hacienda, very few people had the opportunity to follow the path to social ascent. The chosen few were always those who had at their disposal direct or indirect clientelistic networks that were moved by the forces of solidarity between family, friends, or persons from the same geographic region. Social ascent was impossible for those who had no access to these networks, who lacked the necessary contacts, and who were not protected by a powerful patron. Besides, participation in public life and the achievement of political or economic relevance was dependent upon the absorption of ascendant groups by the traditionally dominant class and not upon the formation of a new social elite that was in opposition to the preexisting one. Greater detail about this process will be provided in the following chapter, when we look at the liberal political class.

Furthermore, while examples of social ascent certainly did exist, they were not the norm. After all, the dominant model in both the middle and high sectors of the administration was one of social reproduction. Most of the sample – 62.1 percent of the forty-nine cases – fits this profile. The norm consisted of men like Juan José de Ugalde, *oficial mayor en la secretaría de Gracia y Justicia*, who belonged to a family that for several generations had been serving in this sector. In his will Don Juan José took care to stress the fact that he belonged to an old lineage of Castilian nobility. His father served the king in the colonial administration, where he rose to the position of permanent royal judge of Guatemala. Don Juan José was not rich – his fortune in 1805 was of less than 100,000 reales. This would have been a decent level of wealth for one with no descendants, but it was by no means excessive. This notwithstanding, his luxurious belongings included a Spanish coach with a white cloth interior and glass windows, as well as a white berlin that he used to get around Madrid.[86] The Ugaldes, like most of the

---

[86] AHPM, P. 22975, p. 855.

families in this sample, started off at a socially favorable rank and tried throughout their lives to maintain it. This social position was often based more on the maintenance of status – belonging to a family group, etc. – than on the accumulation of wealth. The Ugaldes shared a social space with other ascendant families and sometimes, as we shall see later, created marriage ties to them. By so doing they guaranteed the continuity of their social collective without losing their hegemonic position. In my opinion they are, once again, representative of a society that favored continuity over change, though always within the context of dynamic social activity.

Professionals

The same combination of established families and newly rising families was apparent among the ranks of professionals. Sociologists and historians have traditionally considered this group to be the bourgeoisie that moved the revolutions of the nineteenth century. This is partially because many of the ideologues and politicians of the revolutions that took place between 1789 and 1848 were lawyers, journalists, ecclesiastics, and professors. This interpretation is also, however, the result of the fact that professionals fit the traditional conception of what is considered "bourgeois": they were educated, technologically competent, secure and independent. It seems, though, that the group's identification with the bourgeoisie, as well as the development of an independent specialized professionalism, were consequences of the liberal revolution and not its causes.[87] And so the automatic connections drawn between professionals and bourgeoisie do not seem to be entirely adequate for the period being studied. The professional world was for many a route to social advancement in the same way that the merchant and administrative spheres were for others. In this section we will look at a small number of family histories that illustrate incidents of social ascent. In most of the cases, however, the families were from the middle and high levels of the social spectrum, which meant that they were fairly well established socially. This makes me doubt that the professional class in Spain, as well as in the rest of Europe, was the prototype of a new, ascendant bourgeoisie.

Like all groups in this study, the professionals also experienced important changes brought about by liberal legislative action after 1823.[88] The new

[87] Millerson (1964: 3).
[88] Villacorta Baños (1989: 2).

Table 4.5. *Occupational distribution: Madrid professionals, 1750-1865*

	No. of cases	%
Lawyers	7	19.4
Physicians/Apothecaries	20	55.5
Procuradores/Agentes	9	25.0
Total	36	

laws did away with certain professional categories, recognized others for the first time, and favored the development of new careers. I will not delve into this complex area here, nor will I provide a detailed classification of professions existing before the period in question. This could be the subject of extensive research which I hope someday might be undertaken. I would like to simply analyze the origins and compositions of the fortunes of thirty-six cases taken from five different professional categories (Table 4.5). The size of the sample does not allow for definitive conclusions to be drawn – my intention is to offer a series of hypotheses that might be analyzed more fully in the future. The cases were happened upon by chance, as often happens in historical research, and are not the result of a selection based on pre-established criteria.

Their level of wealth and the composition of their fortunes (Appendix B) point to differences between the various categories of professions. Millionaire fortunes were most common among *agentes* and *procuradores*. However, imbalances in the amount of accumulated wealth within these two groups are also relatively larger. The fortune of Santiago Sáenz de Azofra, *agente de Indias*, was thirty times larger than those of two other *agentes* in the sample. Procurador Manuel Esteban de San Vicente's fortune was fourteen times larger than Pedro Manuel Rueda's, who was a *procurador*. Similar imbalances are found only among doctors, while apothecaries and lawyers were generally more homogeneous with regard to level of wealth.

As for the composition of their wealth, there is a clear difference between, on the one hand, *agentes*, *procuradores*, and apothecaries, and on the other hand lawyers and doctors. The former two were characterized by ample amounts of working capital (generally in the form of credits) and by the absence of rural real estate. *Agentes* and *procuradores* also tended to invest in public debt and urban real estate. The fortunes of the apothecaries show a similar structure as far as investments in urban real estate and public debt, but they differ in that all included valuable pharmaceutical merchandise as part of their wealth. Unlike these first three groups, working capital was scarcely found among the fortunes of lawyers and doctors. Rural real estate investments were more prevalent than urban ones, although types did exist. Public debt, however, was just as attractive to this group as it was to the others.

Do these structural differences have social implications? Of course, they do. The forms of wealth accumulation, investments preferences, and the diversity of the origins of fortunes are all marks of the social position of the men in the sample. The structure of patrimonies of the *agentes*, *procuradores*, and, to a certain degree, the apothecaries is fairly similar to that of merchants and bankers as seen in previous chapters. The patrimonies of lawyers and doctors, in the meantime, were closer in structure to those of councilors and high administrative officials. The differences and similarities are clear indicators of the social provenance of those in the various groups.

The positions of *procurador* and *agente* were bought and did not require university degrees. Very little is known about these professions, except that they provided substantial benefits for those in them. Both shared a similar function of mediating between civil society and the administration of justice. *Procuradores* and *agentes* oriented and usually represented those who had legal disputes with the crown. The activity of the *procuradores* was not completely independent, since they were few in umber and were paid salaries as administrative officials. But they cannot entirely be considered government employees, since most of their income came from the commissions they charged their clients for representation. Positions of *agentes* were also purchasable, but their numbers were restricted by the crown. They offered their services to the best-paying clients, and their activity was not restricted just to the administration of justice.[89] Both groups, especially the *agentes*, were infamously corrupt. They were undoubtedly the most visible elements of the clientelistic system that dominated all walks of Spanish life. The liberal revolution abolished the position of *agentes* and attempted to reform the *procuradores*, but their functions were merely subsumed by those in similar professional categories (*gestores administrativos*, for example).

The fact that these positions could be bought meant that attaining them was sometimes the result of social ascent. The 80,000 reales that Juan de

---

[89] Fayard (1982a: 29).

Aramayona paid for a position as *procurador* came from his businesses with the trading firm of Francisco Antonio Bringas. The fact that he was originally from the valley of Carranza, along with his ties to the Bringas firm, probably helped him in getting started a business in Madrid.[90] Other cases, like those of Manuel Esteban de San Vicente or Juan Herrezuela, seem to indicate that *procuradurías* were also sought by members of families of already elevated social status.[91]

The career path of the *agentes* was more likely to be used as a way of climbing the social ladder. Santiago Sáenz de Azofra, for example, started his career with no money and died having amassed a fortune of over 6 million reales. He was the son of a small property owner in the region of Rioja. The bulk of his fortune was in money and public debt. His patrimony shows no sign of having been increased by inheritances – it was all community property. Although we do not know the details of his career, it is obvious that Sáenz de Azofra made the best of the commissions and bribes that so often came into the hands of *agentes*.

Social promotion among doctors and lawyers was far less frequent. We have seen how the composition of their fortunes was very similar to the model provided by members of the political and administrative elite. Inheritances were very common among lawyers – most of the six cases studied included some kind of inherited wealth. Domingo Rico Villademores, lawyer of the Reales Consejos, inherited lands in Valencia and Madrid valued at over 300,000 reales. Rico belonged to one of those families of provincial nobility that are so common in our story. What was not at all common about his life was the way it ended: he was executed for having served Joseph Bonaparte while an *Alcalde de Corte*.[92] Vicente González Arnao also belonged to a well-known family of professionals and bureaucrats – his father had served on the Council of the Indies. His marriage to Rosa Ruiz de la Prada, daughter of the successful banker Manuel García de la Prada, shows that he belonged to the upper crust of society.[93]

Continuity among the ranks of the doctors is evidenced by their inherited wealth and by a tendency toward professional endogamy. Juan Gámez, the king's personal physician, was the son of a doctor who practiced in Ubeda. Juan José García Sevillano, who also treated the king, was the son of a doctor, and he married Magdalena Casal, the daughter of another palace

---

[90] AHPM, P. 21704, p. 387.   [91] AHPM, P. 23570, p. 1342 and 21782, p. 35.
[92] AHPM, P. 21430, 21769 and 21786 wp.   [93] AHPM, P. 23072, p. 1094.

physician.[94] Two of Iñigo Lorente's sons followed in their father's footsteps, becoming lecturers in medicine. A third son went into the military and the last became an ecclesiastic.[95]

As a whole the doctors in the sample were an economically well-off group, though their wealth was not extraordinary. Some of them were able to amass millionaire fortunes, but most of them just lived comfortably off their wealth. The group's first priority seems to have been to guarantee university educations for their sons. Bartolomé Piñeira, a member of the governing board of medicine, spent most of the capital brought in during his first marriage to pay for his sons-in-law's university training. Piñeira's social status was representative of the group as a whole. The son of a lawyer who practiced in the province of Jaén, he inherited some real estate from his father. His second marriage was to Nicasia Soldevilla, the daughter of the royal doctor Juan Bautista Soldevilla.[96]

The tendency among lawyers and doctors, unlike the *procuradores* and *agentes*, was toward social reproduction and not social ascent. The model of reproduction was most evident among the lawyers, who were also the most influential professionals. This point is important. In the end the *procuradores* and *agentes* represented professions with ties to the old regime that fell prey to the liberal whirlwind, while lawyers played a central role in the political process of Spanish liberalism. We will see this in greater detail in the following chapter. For now let it suffice to say that lawyers were at the center of the political class that first articulated and established the liberal state. This was a political class that, if it follows the model presented here, came together not through a process of social ascent but rather through social reproduction and the cooptation of an old, dominant elite. The diversity in the nature, origins, and methods of accumulation of wealth in this small sample once again confirms the assertion.

[94] AHPM, P. 18819, p. 1.   [95] AHPM, P. 21403, p. 768.
[96] AHPM, P. 21789, p. 116 and 21783, p. 140.

5

Politicians

Mesonero Romanos argued that by 1845 the councilor was a relic of forgotten times.[1] In the new century of haste and horse races, as Antonio Flores called it, the councilor was replaced by the professional politician.[2] While the former represented perseverance in attaining a position of power, the politician embodied spontaneity and immediate success, values more in tune with new times.[3]

Without a doubt, the speed with which one could rise in a political career was one of the things that most impressed those who witnessed the fall of the old regime. The men of 1808 still remembered how slowly political careers advanced under the absolute monarchy, and so to many it seemed unfathomable that the most distinguished men of 1812 were only thirty years old. In the times of Charles III nobody would have become a minister at the mere age of twenty-eight as did Castro y Orozco in 1837. This speed, together with the reception of liberal ideas, were the factors that led contemporaries to declare that Spain had undergone a middle-class revolution between 1812 and 1837.[4]

---

[1] Mesonero (1964: 1340–55).   [2] Flores (1969: 18).   [3] Mesonero (1964: 1342).
[4] For the writers of the era this revolution was a triumph of the middle classes [see Botrel and LeBouil (1973: 138–39)], an argument that has been rescued by contemporary Marxist historians to construct the paradigm of the bourgeois revolution. The problem is still the lack of systemic studies to define what "middle classes" meant for the contemporaries of the revolution and what the term "bourgeoisie" means for the Marxist school. *The History of Spain* recently published by Planeta Editorial is a good example of this reality. In Chapter 7 Marc Baldó Lacomba (1988: 214f.) describes what he calls the "ascendant bourgeoisie." According to this scholar, this was a class formed by a conglomerate of landowners – many of them with noble backgrounds – farmers, professionals, bureaucrats, artisans, merchants, financiers, and industrialists. However, his classification is merely descriptive and places a provincial noblemen, a high bureaucrat, an urban craftsman, and a local farmer all in the same social class. In the same book, the chapter by Sisinio Pérez Garzón (1988: 307f.) focuses on the period of Isabel II in the hegemony of the bourgeoisie and the bourgeois revolution, but his analysis refers to the political occurrence, ignoring the problem of the historical formation of this social class.

Politicians

In the previous chapter I considered the councilors to be one of the groups that smoothed the way for liberal change. In this sense they were a part of the middle classes, or at least they represented, to some extent, the interests of these groups. But if we are to believe Mesonero, after 1834 they were no longer the archetype of the Spanish political class. The institutional changes set in motion by liberalism brought to the scene new archetypes. In the new liberal state the councilors left a vacuum that was quickly filled by the deputies and ministers of the new era. Both groups were an essential part of the Spanish political class. In an era of change, as was the time between 1812 and 1837, many institutions were transitory. Only the cabinet and the parliament maintained continuous control of executive and legislative power, respectively. Did these institutional changes respond to a process of social revolution? To what degree did the ministers and parliamentarians proceed from different social strata than those of the former councilors? Can we speak of the existence of a new political class in 1850?

This chapter will attempt to answer these three questions. My intention is to provide new evidence for the historiographic revision of the model of the Spanish bourgeois revolution. I will show that the political class which was the moving force behind the liberal revolution – independent of political allegiances within liberalism – came, for the most part, from the same social ranks as the politicians of the old regime. In my opinion what we know as the Spanish revolution was a process of political change but not the consequence of a social revolution. In order to show this I will analyze sociological variables that characterized the members of the cabinet and the parliament. The first of these is wealth, or their status with respect to the means of production. Second, I will look at occupational structure, taking into consideration that access to professional specialization was a privilege restricted to certain social strata. The third variable is their geographic location, looking at the degree to which the Spanish political class conformed to a certain model of regional integration, and the fourth is the family origins of the class as measures of their position in society. I will finally analyze the cultural identity of this political class, meaning its affinity for a determined system of values, norms, meanings, and symbols. The first four variables have an independent character, while the last can only be defined as a function of a series of other variables that complement it (family, religiosity, attitudes, etc.). For this reason this section will only address the first four, saving the analysis of cultural identification for the next chapter.

Careers, business, and fortunes

The sample is based on 129 individuals who occupied political posts between 1800 and 1850. Of these, 119 were ministers one or more times, while the remaining 10 were deputies, senators, or simply people with influence in the court. As a result, the sample is based fundamentally on a group of persons who reached the highest levels of politics in those years.[5] With some exceptions, the majority of individuals who were prominent politically between 1812 and 1853 were cabinet members at some time or another. Additionally, the majority – 71.2 percent – of the ministers had been deputies before occupying cabinet seats. They all, as a result, reached the cabinet with some political experience, although, as we have seen, this experience was less extensive than in previous eras. The ministers on the cabinet, therefore, constituted the most important element of the political class of the liberal state.

Family fortunes

The nature and origin of personal wealth are decisive indicators for social classification. An analysis of their personal fortunes may reveal the political elites' level of integration in the new capitalist economy. As Janine Fayard has pointed out, rent from land, income from government debt, private loans, and salaries constituted the bulk of personal holdings of the political class between 1621 and 1746. Only in a few instances did Fayard detect the existence of productive investment in industries and commercial activities.[6] Taking these old regime fortunes as a point of reference, I will analyze the extent to which the personal holdings of the ministers differed from those of the political classes of the previous era.

Table 5.1 shows the value of the fortunes of twenty-two ministers and ten politicians of the first half of the nineteenth century.[7] The first observation that can be made is the considerable level of wealth of the group. The median of the fortunes of the ministers is at 1,755,235 reales, while the mean exceeds 16.6 million reales, figures somewhat above what has been

---

[5] I have selected 119 ministers who mainly held positions in reformist and liberal governments, or in other words, those who endorsed *Ilustrado* and liberal politics in Spain. I have excluded cabinets between 1814–20 and 1823–34. Angel Bahamone (1981: 36) estimated a total of 202 ministers for the period 1834–54.

[6] Fayard (1982a: 322–387).

[7] Information on the fortunes of Garro and Caballero has been extracted from documents other than their probate inventories. I have rebuilt the first from the inventory made after Garro's wife deceased: AHPM, P. 20092 (complete). In the case of Caballero, the information was compiled from his 1810 will: AHPM, P. 22980, p. 648.

Politicians

Table 5.1. *Fortunes of politicians, 1800-1866*
(reales de vellón)

Net Assets	Ministers	%	Other	%
1-500,000	4	18.2	0	0
500,000-1,000,000	2	9.1	2	20
1,000,000-1,500,000	4	18.2	0	0
1,500,000-2,000,000	2	9.1	2	20
2,000,000-5,000,000	3	13.7	5	50
5,000,000-10,000,000	4	18.2	0	0
10,000,000+	3	13.5	1	10
Total Cases	22		10	
Median	1,755,235		2,700,000	
Mean	15,913,448		6,596,214	

Source: Probate Inventories, AHPM. See Appendix B.

calculated for councilors and entrepreneurs in the same period.[8] This increase in wealth was no doubt due to the thaw introduced by constitutionalism into political life. The electoral system made of politics a more competitive activity and, consequently, a more professionalized one. For this reason, certain sectors of the traditional elites abandoned the comfortable lethargy to which patriarchal absolutism had accustomed them. It is symptomatic that, for the first time in three hundred years, the old Spanish aristocracy returned to the political scene.[9]

The inequities among fortunes also reflect a certain diversity in the occupational structure of the ministers. The great fortunes belonged to the bankers Collado, Aguirre Solarte, and Salamanca, while the more modest fortunes belonged to Cortázar, García de la Torre, and Riva Herrera, all of these administration officials.[10] To be sure, as a whole the different pa-

---

[8] For the deflation of these values I have used the price series from Barciella (1989: 501 and 518) and Cuenca-Esteban (1990: 373–399).

[9] According to Comellas (1970: 66), what characterized this era was, above all, the creation of a new nobility. However, this was not a new practice in the Spanish monarchy; since the Middle Ages, kings and queens granted noble titles in return for personal services. What we need to know better is whether the nature of those services changed under the constitutional monarchy. Regarding the activity of some old aristocratic families during the liberal period, see Marichal (1977: 131f.) and Janke (1974: chap. XVI).

[10] The two first were Councilors of State while Riva Herrera was a high bureaucrat in the Council of the Public Treasury. Riva Herrera's fortune was greater than his inventory indicates; he held several *mayorazgos*, the value of which is impossible to estimate. AHPM, P. 25219, p. 1496.

trimonies do not present considerable inequities and indicate fairly well-off economic positions. Besides, we have not found one case of a loss in terms of common property and, with the exception of the fortunes of the Marquis of Salamanca, the rest ended with a positive balance when liabilities were evaluated.[11]

Personal property constituted less than a fourth of the patrimonies of the ministers (Figure 5.1). Domestic property roughly equaled the amount of wealth in money and silver. The proportion of domestic goods in important fortunes, such as the ones of Salamanca or Collado,[12] do not reflect their real value. Salamanca, for example, had a painting collection valued at more than 7 million reales and his palace was replete with valuable artifacts. Other fortunes, like those of Ramón Gil de la Cuadra and Modesto Cortázar were made up mostly of this kind of property. Both owned important collections of paintings leading one to look at the value of these as investments. Cortázar's collection was valued at 84,000 reales, but unfortunately, it was never inventoried. The value of Gil de la Cuadra's collection surpassed 900,000 reales and included paintings by Velázquez, Titian, Murillo, and Zurbarán, among others. It was made up mostly of classical paintings in which the works of the Spanish school were well represented, but the collection also contained more recent works, such as a portrait of the Duchess of Alba painted by Goya.[13]

In nineteen inventories – 86.3 percent – one can find some real estate property, while in eleven cases it formed the major part of the holdings. Interestingly, a considerable part of this real estate was composed of inherited property; most politicians belonged to wealthy, established families. In six inventories urban real estate was more important than rural holdings. The patrimonies with the greatest proportion of urban property were the ones of Canga Argüelles, Aguirre Solarte, Cortázar, Ferrer y Cafranga y Salamanca. Canga Argüelles, a member of a prominent family of Asturian nobility, owned properties in Madrid valued at close to 900,000 reales. Only a third of those properties had been acquired by Canga himself, the rest proceeded from his marriage to Eulalia de Ventadés, daughter of a high-ranking official of the public treasury.[14] The other three cases consisted of

---

[11] Information on Salamanca comes from the work of Angel Bahamonde (1981: 403). It refers to the years after 1860 and before his bankruptcy. When he died in 1883, his personal patrimony had a deficit of 6 million reales.
[12] Both ministers of the Public Treasury in 1874 and 1854, respectively.
[13] AHPM, P. 27101, p. 1896.
[14] AHPM, PP. 21000, p. 431, 24994, p. 696 and 25132, p. 201.

Politicians

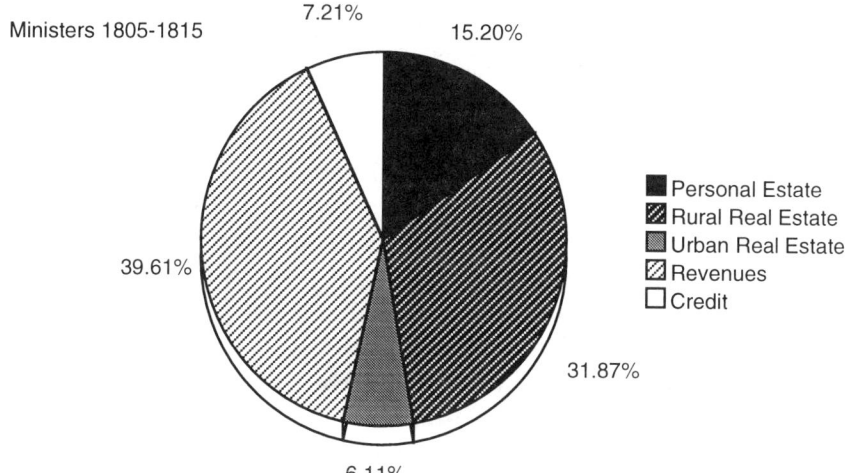

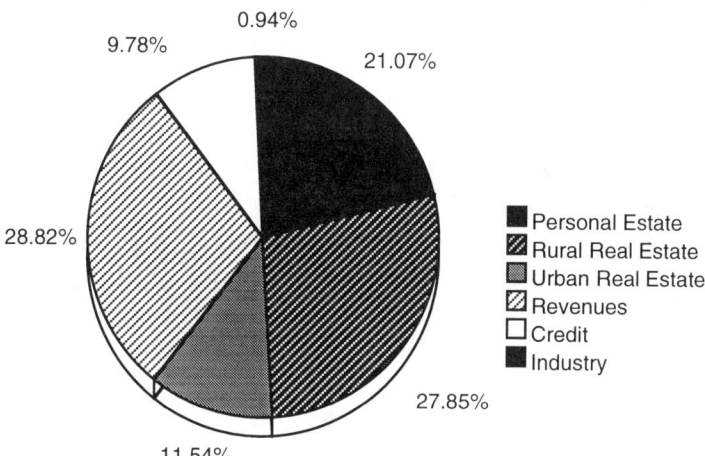

Figure 5.1. Composition of fortunes, 1805–1864

recent acquisitions resulting from participation in Madrid's real estate market.

Family residences of the ministers tended to occupy an entire building in one of Madrid's central streets. The Ferrer family, for example, inhabited the principal floor of a building situated at number 13 of Desengaño Street. Don Joaquín María Ferrer y Cafranga had invested more than a million reales in a purchase made profitable with the rental of several rooms in the building.[15] Like the Bueno de Guzmán family, the fictional characters of Galdós's *Lo Prohibido,* the second generation of the Ferrer family began to install itself in each of the floors of the building.[16] The descendants of Ferrer, the man who would be mayor of Madrid and minister with General Espartero, would be for many years the inhabitants of Desengaño 13, sharing the building with their tenants. For others, such as the bankers Aguirre Solarte and Salamanca, the purchase of urban property constituted a primary part of their investment strategies.

In the thirteen remaining inventories rural properties exceeded urban holdings and, in at least five cases, constituted the most important share of the patrimonies. This was the case of José Antonio Caballero, Councilor and Minister of Gracia y Justicia in 1800, whose real estate was valued at 4.5 million reales. One-fourth of this he inherited from his uncle in the province of Salamanca, while the rest stemmed from his own investments in lands and certain grants of Charles IV.[17] Lands made up the greatest part of the patrimony of Francisco Agustín Silvela, a member of a family prominent in Spanish politics since the second half of the eighteenth century. Approximately half of his properties, valued at more than 1 million reales, were inherited from his father. These were lands in the province of Valladolid, where the Silvela family had a family seat. Notwithstanding, Don Francisco invested more than 500,000 reales in the purchase of disentailed properties in various areas in Old Castile.[18]

---

[15] AHPM, P. 28758, p. 1016.   [16] Pérez Galdós (1951, IV: 1661).
[17] Jerónimo Caballero, General of the Royal Army, was granted the title of Marquis of Caballero by Charles IV in 1794. He belonged to a well-established noble family from Salamanca. His nephew, José Antonio Caballero y Pozo, inherited the title and the *mayorazgo.* José Antonio, second Marquis of Caballero, started his career as *Alcalde de Corte* in Seville, and was later promoted to a chair in the Council of State. In 1808 he sided with Napoleon. When the French were defeated, Caballero was prosecuted and accused of collaboration with the enemy. That was the end of his career. See AHN, Diversos, Títulos y Familias, leg. 14.; AHPM, P. 22980, p. 648; Gómez-Rivero (1988: 95).
[18] AHPM, P. 26376, p. 3394.

Politicians

Inherited property was a part of 85 percent of the fortunes that included real estate. A large share of these were or had been at one time entailed family properties. Manuel de la Riva Herrera, for example, inherited the whole of his lands in several *mayorazgos*. This was also the case with José García de la Torre, Councilor of State, who inherited the lands that his ancestors owned in a place called Torre de Esteban Amban.[19] A portion of Ferrer y Cafranga's real estate around Pasajes proceeded from his *mayorazgo* of Echéverri, which had belonged to his family since 1762.[20] Modesto Cortázar's parents had bequeathed him a small property in Vizcaya valued at only 13,000 reales.[21]

In most cases, however, patrimonies were improved with new investments, in many instances tending toward the purchase of disentailed properties. In this aspect there is very little difference between the ministers of the final years of the absolute monarchy and the ministers under constitutionalism. Among the former are the cases of Pedro Cevallos and Ambrosio de Garro. Pedro Cevallos, Minister of State between 1808 and 1809, inherited properties valued at 1.9 million reales, not counting several of his and his wife's *mayorazgos*. They consisted mostly of lands in the province of Santander, where his family originated. Cevallos improved his properties with the purchases of ecclesiastical properties after 1798. His investments exceeded 400,000 reales.[22] Ambrosio de Garro y Arizcun, Marqués de las Hormazas, was one of several bankers of Navarrese origin who influenced the political life of the eighteenth century. He held the positions in Ministry of the Treasury and later the Ministry of the State between 1809 and 1810. His properties included land in Orihuela inherited by his wife and his own paternal inheritance of land in the valley of Baztán. However, the greatest part of the patrimonial base of Hormazas was acquired in purchases made between 1793 and 1808. The investments were in excess of 1 million reales and the purchases were located in the areas of Rojales, Guardamar, and Getafe. Hormazas's buying euphoria was directed at the market of private property and not at disentailed properties. His example typifies once again the existence of an active free market of property preceding that of disentailments.[23]

---

[19] He was minister of Gracia y Justicia in 1820 and 1823. AHPM, P. 25446, wp.
[20] AHPM, P. 26813, p. 529.   [21] AHPM, P. 27380, wp.
[22] Escudero (1975: 13f.); AHPM, P. 25030, p. 142.
[23] Caro (1985: 384f.); AHPM, P. 20092 (complete protocolo).

Careers, business, and fortunes

The case of Javier de Burgos brings us right into the liberal era. Known for his contributions to the field of administrative law, he was nominated minister of Fomento in 1833 and *gobernación* in 1846 under the *moderados*. The Burgoses were a well-known family of Motril at the end of the seventeenth century. Javier's father, Diego Antonio de Burgos, managed several family estates and a sugar mill. The lands were from the family inheritance and their exploitation allowed the Burgoses to live a rather comfortable life. Javier's inventory, undertaken in 1854, shows improvements made to the family patrimony. To the lands and factories of Motril, Burgos added an estate of 320 hectares in the province of Toledo, with the investment costing more than 600,000 reales. At the time of his death Javier de Burgos lived practically off of his leased properties alone.[24]

Only in two cases were rural properties purely the result of purchases and not inheritances. One of those was Canga Argüelles and the other was the Marquis of Salamanca. The former case consisted of investments of over 400,000 reales. Most of the estates were located in Asturias and some of them in León. The Marquis of Salamanca shows us the greatest investment effort of the cases studied here, with estates valued at 25.4 million reales. The possessions of the flamboyant Marquis extended through several Spanish provinces and even included properties in France and Portugal. Nonetheless, his patrimony ended up completely decimated by successive bankruptcies.

Revenues constituted one-third of the patrimonies and after real estate they were the most important group of assets. These consisted primarily of investments in public debt. Sixteen of the twenty-two inventories of ministers – 72.7 percent – included some kind of government debt. In at least five cases this portion was the most important part of the patrimony. This was the case with Antonio Porlier Sopranis, Minister of Gracia y Justicia under Charles IV, who had two-thirds of his patrimony invested in *vales reales* and Treasury bonds. Like most ministers before 1834, a portion of these investments was forced, since it was the result of withheld salaries.[25] This notwithstanding, Porlier had invested more than 500,000 reales in the purchase of *vales* in different editions.[26] It was the first half of the

---

[24] AHPM, P. 26804, p. 1367.
[25] In 1810, for instance, the administration owed almost 750,000 reales in salaries to the Marquis of Caballero. Most of this money was paid in public debt bonds. See AHPM, P. 22980, p. 650.
[26] AHPM, P. 21410, p. 478.

nineteenth century, however, which was the true golden age for speculation in government debt.[27] The patrimonies of these ministers also reflect the ability to take advantage of profitable business opportunities, as occurred with investment in disentailed properties. In addition, for the first time a portion of these investments went to other European countries in a systematic manner. This process was the result of the existence of a more specialized network of information services and commercialization. Practically all of the greatest investors in government debt in this sample also held titles to foreign debt.[28]

Company stocks were far less important elements of the ministers' fortunes than they were to the fortunes of the councilors of the eighteenth century. As noted previously, the disappearance of privileged companies would explain this tendency. The money that the political class had previously invested in this area was apparently rerouted in the nineteenth century toward the purchase of public debt, while the financing of societies through company stocks involved mainly the commercial and financier groups.[29] This tendency was corrected, however, by the 1840s as a result of the railway and the subsequent greater accessibility to exterior markets. The company stocks that made up the patrimony of Angel Calderón de la Barca, for example, were worth approximately 1 million reales. They consisted entirely of holdings in foreign companies, mostly in the United States.[30]

Industrial investment is once again almost entirely absent from the fortunes of the political class. The only case where we see this kind of investment is that of Javier de Burgos. The most important part of his industrial capital stemmed from the leasing of his sugar mills. These, however, were inherited from his ancestors and not something that he exploited directly.[31] Burgos had, however, invested almost 300,000 reales in the lead mines of the mountains of Almagrera, which provided him with some benefits stemming from the smelting of the mineral.[32] Burgos is an example of the frustrated premature industrialization of Andalucía reported by some economic histo-

---

[27] Financiers, politicians, and courtiers controlled basic channels of information in the recently created Madrid stock market. This control allowed incredible occurrences of speculation. Perhaps one of the most spectacular stories of rapid enrichment was that of the Marquis of Salamanca. See Torrente (1969: 62f.).
[28] Canga Arguelles is the only exception. His stocks concentrated in *deuda corriente sin consolidar al 5%*. AHPM, P. 25132, p. 210.
[29] Otazu (1987: 312f.) [30] AHPM, P. 25248, p. 433.
[31] He sold most of his sugar mills a few years before his death. AHPM, P. 26792, p. 125.
[32] AHPM, P. 26804, p. 1375.

rians.³³ The fact that the Burgos case is so isolated illustrates the practical absence of an industrial bourgeoisie in the so-called Spanish revolution. This social group was without a doubt extremely weak in 1840. There did, however, exist nuclei – especially in Catalonia – that showed great social and, more importantly, economic dynamism.³⁴ National politics remained under the control of a society that had secularly excluded the purely industrial world, at least until the latter half of the nineteenth century.

The profile of the fortunes of the ten politicians who were not cabinet members does not offer great variation (see Appendix B). Together they also show considerable wealth, with a median at 3.2 million reales and a mean at 6.6 million. Seven of these fortunes have their origins in the second half of the eighteenth century and even earlier. At least six of them came from families that had combined business with the state with positions in the Public Treasury Administration. In two cases, Ignacio Goyeneche and Domingo Cabarrú, the families had obtained noble titles as rewards for their services. Of the four remaining fortunes two belonged to high officials of the Treasury, one to a professional, and the last to an important family of businessmen of the nineteenth century. In these we see an even greater importance placed on real estate, which in this last case constituted almost two-thirds of the value of the patrimonies. All of the inventories contain some kind of rural or urban property, which in 80 percent of the cases was the most important portion of the family patrimony. The distribution of rural and urban properties is fairly proportional, with urban properties having a slight advantage.

All of the patrimonies included rural estates whose origins were also fairly diverse. In at least four cases the lands were mostly the product of inheritances or marriages. Among the inheritors Ignacio de Goyeneche, Count of Saceda, stands out. He owned extensive properties in several areas of Castilla and Navarra.³⁵ Domingo de Cabarrús, the second Count of Cabarrús, gives the example of the well-married. Domingo had inherited from his father, besides the title, the lands that the latter had acquired in the *términos* (counties) of Torrelaguna and Uceda in the last years of his life.³⁶ But the most substantial portion of his patrimony proceeded from his

---

³³ Nadal (1987: 106 and 1981).   ³⁴ Solá (1986: 157f.).
³⁵ AHPM, P. 25424, p. 4005.
³⁶ His father planned the construction of an irrigation canal in these lands. See Zylbelberg (1979: 423 and 424).

Politicians

marriage to Rosa Quilty, the only daughter of a very wealthy landowner family of Irish origins installed in the province of Málaga.[37]

In five of the remaining patrimonies we see a combination of inheritances with purchases, with only one of the fortunes consisting entirely of properties from recent acquisitions. Among the former Carlos Calderón Molina stands out. His lands, two-thirds of which were inherited, were valued at 13.6 million reales. Manuel Calderón, Carlos's father, was an important businessman who was part of the circle of the intendant Gaviria. An important part of his capital, stemming from his deals of loans and military supplies, was invested in disentailed properties in Andalucía. Carlos's life seemed more like that of a wealthy bondholding property-owner than that of a businessman, although he did invest more than 2 million reales in stocks in railroads and mining enterprises.[38] Only Manuel Ortiz de Taranco, an official of the treasury and senator, had acquired the entirety of the base of his patrimony in disentailed estates, valued at 1.5 million reales.[39]

Real estate was followed in importance by personal property and commercial credits, although the proportions of each were very different. It was the fortunes of commercial or financial origins, like those of Francisco del Mazo and Carlos Calderón, that held the greatest amount of working capital. Collectively, politicians outside of the cabinet showed less interest in investment in public debt. The reason for this disinterest might have been that they were farther away from information circles than the ministers, but the fact that many of them had no salaries from the administration must have also been a factor.

These fortunes are somewhat more active in the realm of industrial investments. If we compare them with the other groups studied in this work, the ten patrimonies represent the highest rate of these types of investments. They were mostly investments in agrarian industries, in many cases leased to third parties or managed from a distance. This was the case of Pérez Moltó, the owner of a flour mill in La Roda, as it was also with the aforementioned sugar mills of the Count of Cabarrús. These men were not, then, industrial entrepreneurs in the sense that the Bonaplatas or the Peels or Oberkampfs were, that is to say, people who directly administered their

---

[37] Villar (1982: 131 and 135).
[38] Carlos Calderón Molina was nominated to the Senate in 1845. On the Calderón family see Otazu (1987: 314). AHPM, P. 28431, p. 652.
[39] AHPM, P. 26369, p. 1555.

production.⁴⁰ They did represent, however, the advance of a certain kind of agrarian capitalism that benefited from the process of disentailment and that dynamized a sector of the Spanish economy.⁴¹

Looking at these patrimonies, what preliminary conclusions can we come to regarding the social position of their holders? First, they were a wealthy group whose sources of revenue had a tripartite origin: property rents, income from professional activities, and capital profit. This was a socioeconomic position typical of a rentier class. Besides, their wealth was not acquired in a recent process of usurpation of the means of production, as some historians of the bourgeois revolution have claimed. To the contrary, most of the cases analyzed are of families whose patrimonies were built, in part, through the means provided by a precapitalist economy. The political elite of the liberal state, as far as their economic position is concerned, seems to be more the result of a process of social reproduction than of the emergence of a new social class. So far, the piece defined as social revolution does not fit well into the puzzle of nineteenth-century Spanish history.

Occupational structure and political affiliation

Something similar occurs if we look at the occupations of men installed in the parliament and the cabinet, the most important centers of political decision making in the first half of the nineteenth century. Although occupational status, especially in the case of professionals, is a category of relative sociological validity, it can nonetheless aid us in uncovering certain social tendencies. This notwithstanding, any use of this type of variable should not step out of its historical context, nor can it be looked at independently. We have to keep in mind that a lawyer or an officer in the military could also be an owner of property, while those who registered solely as property owners could also hold a university title.⁴² While the category of property holder may be useful as a tool to identify a social group, it is doubtful that the categories of doctor of laws, lecturer, or lawyer held the same social implications. The relativeness of their sociological validity would be a function of the major or minor existence of mechanisms that favor social mobility. This

---

⁴⁰ Nadal (1985: 22–23); Bergeron (1978: 251f.); Chapman and Chassagne (1981: 12–17).
⁴¹ Herr (1989) Héran (1990: 160–170).
⁴² For instance, among the six parliamentarians elected in Valencia in 1834 only one defined himself as a landowner. They registered first as military (3), lawyer (1), and engineer (1). Despite this classification, all of them were owners of large lots of land in Valencia's suburbs and the province. Burdiel (1987: 66–69).

mobility would be defined not solely at a juridical level, in terms of equality of rights, access to education, free market and so on, but also at a cultural level, in terms of a person's ability to overcome social prejudices, the value of personal merit over loyalty, the disappearance of clientelist mechanisms and of patronage, and so on.

Changes in the occupational structure of the organs of power within a given spacial and temporal context can, nonetheless, point to the existence of a general social change. The discovery of a greater number of merchants and artisans in the municipal life of revolutionary France has helped Lynn Hunt reinforce her argument that this country saw the rise of a new political class.[43] Did something similar occur in Spain? If we are to accept the existence of a social revolution, then at least one of the following circumstances must have occurred: a change in the occupational structure in the centers of power or, as a counterpart, a profound democratization of the mechanisms of access to the occupational world established in these centers. Let us see if this was the case. We should first look at the occupational structure of some of the legislative assemblies that met between 1812 and 1836. We know with fair certainty the composition of the assemblies of 1812, 1822, 1834, and 1836, and with less certainty that of 1820.[44] Both from the political perspective and in terms of the continuity of its components there is a greater similarity between the assemblies of 1812 and 1820–23 compared with those of 1834 and later. There existed a very select group of liberal politicians who were able to hold power from 1812 onward. They were, according to the description of *El filósofo rancio*, very young people, between the ages of fifteen and thirty, who as early as 1820 had become heroes of Spanish liberalism.[45] Because of the absence of concrete data, we have to accept the impression given by Gil Novales of the presence of the most important men of Cádiz in the Cortes of the *Trienio*.[46] The distance in time separates the men of 1812 from the legislature of 1834. However, it is

---

[43] Hunt (1984: 149–178), criticizes Cobban's thesis although she considers the French Revolution was essentially political in nature.

[44] Data offered by Marichal (1977: 31), compiled from Fermin Caballero's works, are incomplete and difficult to compare with the data extant for other legislatures:
Landowners, merchants, and economically independent: 45   30.2%
Officeholders and military   69   46.3%
Ecclesiastics   35   23.5

[45] I am referring to people like Argüelles, Alcalá Galiano, Florez Estrada, Istúriz, Martinez de la Rosa, Toreno, and others. The quotation comes from Pérez Ledesma (1991: 172–173); see also Girón (1979: 91, vol. 2).

[46] Gil Novales (1980: 15).

more difficult to explain the fact that only 27 of the deputies of 1822 – a minuscule 14.3% – were to return to their seats in 1834.[47]

The experience of 1812 became somewhat isolated, and its influence dissipated as liberalism began solidifying its ideas and perfecting its institutions. Alcalá Galiano realized that the Cortes of 1812 came about in very special circumstances. The French occupation and the system of indirect voting favored the influence of a few notable writers and educated men who had taken refuge in the very small nation created in the area between the bridge of Zuazo and the ocean that beat against the walls of Cádiz.[48] The work of the deputies of Cádiz, as Pérez Ledesma has shown, was fundamentally to find a way to dismantle the existing highly stratified society. The main part of the discussion centered around how to create a society based on the principle of equality, understood to be juridical equality, and a society run above all by the principle of merit and the ability of the individual. This debate was more ideological than pragmatic and was the result, according to Pérez Ledesma, of the sociological composition of the assembly. They were mostly jurist and ecclesiastical professionals and nobles, people that can hardly be identified with a bourgeois class. This author adds that this general purpose of the 1812 Cortes was opposed to what occurred in later legislatures, that were more oriented toward the defense of property than to the promotion of "merits and abilities."[49] I agree with Pérez Ledesma with regard to the characterization of the political debate and his understanding of it as a product of the sociological roots of the deputies of 1812. However, I doubt that the changes in the political debate which occurred after 1834, were the result of the incorporation of different social groups into the parliament.

Table 5.2 shows the occupations of the deputies and members of parliament of the aforementioned legislatures.[50] The legislative term of 1812 had the highest number of deputies, and the 1834 term was the smallest. The mean amount of deputies present at the rest of the Cortes was 240. Collectively, only two occupations, *hacendado* and ecclesiastical official, appear

---

[47] Nevertheless they formed a very select group of politicians who played a leading role in the history of the first Spanish liberalism. Burdiel (1987: 95).
[48] Alcalá Galiano (1955: 357, vol. II). [49] Pérez Ledesma (1991: 169).
[50] All authors point out the difficulty in calculating the exact number of representatives in the 1812 Cortes de Cádiz. Elections took place in a country divided by war. The figures in Table 4.2 have been elaborated taking into account the contrast between the various sources I have mentioned. In particular, I have utilized the works of Chávarri and Suárez because I consider them to be the most complete. See also Morodo and Díaz (1966); Busquets (1972: 213).

Table 5.2. Deputies, 1820-1836. Occupational structure

Occupation	1812	%	1822	%	1834	%	1836*	%	1836**	%
Ecclesiastics	87	28.9	27	11.1	4	2.1	4	2.7	14	9.3
Lawyers	44	14.7	30	12.4	45	24.0	40	27.1	27	18
Officeholders	58	19.3	60	24.8	20	10.6	30	20.2	26	17.3
Military	43	14.3	28	11.7	49	26.1	17	11.5	22	14.7
Professionals	9	2.9	17	7.0					10	6.7
Comm./Indust.	6	2.0	17	7.0	17	9.0	12	8.1	16	10.7
Landowners	3	1.0	60	24.8	53	28.2	39	26.3	35	23.3
Municipal Govern.	14	4.6								
Unknown	37	12.3	3	1.2			6	4.1		
Total	301		242		188		148		150	

*February parliament.
**October parliament.
Sources: For 1812, see Suárez (1982: 28-46); Chávarri (1988: 31-77); Solis (1987: 189-190). For 1822-1836, see Marichal (1977: 31 and 95); Burdiel (1987: 92 and 311)[50].

unevenly represented throughout the period. The term *hacendado* generally refers to those deputies who identified themselves as such because they were property holders, whether the properties were urban or rural. The virtual absence of this category in 1812 can only be explained, once again, by the special circumstances surrounding that calling of the Cortes. What it does not mean is that those social groups that were defined by their dependence on the production of their properties were excluded from the legislative body. I am certain that a study of the nature of the fortunes of the deputies of Cádiz, as well as a look at their social origins, would show them to be not too different from this social group. The table demonstrates the importance of the *hacendados* in all of the legislative terms beginning with the *Trienio*, and eventually become the best represented interest in the legislature.

I do not think it necessary to detail here the importance of this elite of landowners that Artola defined as an "agrarian bourgeoisie" to the process of consolidation of the liberal system.[51] The problem continues to be the scarcity of historical knowledge about this group, making its social definition a difficult task. It has been generally accepted that this "agrarian

[51] Artola (1978: 97, 157, and 175).

bourgeoisie" was the result of a melding of two social strata. The first would be made up of a group of farmers who were able to benefit from the various systems of free leasing of land which were fairly common in some regions of Spain throughout the eighteenth century. Although this group's character would be eminently rural, the nature of their economic practice was essentially capitalist. The other stratum would have a mixed character as it evolved, with on the one hand a series of capitalists of urban origins that decided to place part of their surpluses in land, and on the other hand a group of agrarian property owners whose investments were aimed at simply bettering their patrimonies. This stratum of property holders was the principal beneficiary of the disentailments and the most important component of that "rural bourgeoisie."[52] However, we are just beginning to see historical studies that systematize the sociology of these social strata. The work of Francois Heran about the Vázquez family, for instance, points to the path future investigations of this sort should follow. Heran, using the example of a powerful property-owning family of Andalusia, shows how the so-called agrarian bourgeoisie was the result of a consolidation of a system of family networks extending back to the old regime. These kinship networks did not consolidate their dominance in a process of replacement of one class with another, nor was it the result of a pact drawn up between adversaries that were forced to come to terms with each other. It was the result of an adaptation of a preexisting social dynamic to the demands of a new framework for economic and political relations. In the second half of the nineteenth century those family networks made up a system of lineages whose culture was similar to that of the old regime, despite the fact that its economic practices responded perfectly to the demands of modern capitalism.[53] The work of Heran on the Sevillian agrarian bourgeoisie, as well as the works of Rueda and Herr concerning groups that benefited from disentailments, show the weaknesses of the concept of an agrarian bourgeoisie as a way of socially defining the rural elites of the first half of the nineteenth century.[54]

---

[52] In a recent article Mariano Peset (1990: 166) vindicates the importance of the urban sectors in the process of the formation of this new class of owners. It is Peset's opinion that this class existed before the disentailments occurred, although they consolidated their hegemony through their control of land purchases in the new disentailed market.

[53] Heran (1990: 15).

[54] Rueda (1986: 154–178) defines the purchasers of land in the Mendizábal and Espartero disentailments as people of rural origin belonging to the middle class. It was, according to this scholar, not a

Politicians

The clergy had its greatest level of representation in the Cortes de Cádiz, but as time progressed they lost almost all influence over the legislative body. The presence of the Church in the Cortes of 1812 is another one of the elements that gave that legislative term a certain uniqueness. Pilar Chávarri explains this presence as being a product of the extraordinary intervention of the clergy in the electoral process of 1810. The church often filled the vacuum left by the political powers that were involved in war. All of the elections were realized with the celebration of three masses in whose homilies the electors were exhorted to use "maturity and discernment."[55] From the beginning, as Callahan has shown, the Spanish Church was radically opposed to Napoleon, who they described as the "thief of Europe, the Attila of this century, enemy of God and of His holy Church," "the greatest heretic of all." For most of the regular and secular clergy the struggle against Napoleon was experienced as a sacred war, a "Holy Crusade" against an invader that had to be defeated by any means necessary.[56] When in 1809 elections were called, the Church saw the possibility of recovering from the *regalismo* and disentailment practices of Godoy. From this possibility stemmed the high hopes they held for the convening of the Cortes. Most of the deputies from the clergy came from the secondary levels of the ecclesiastical hierarchy, especially university professors and prebendary lecturers, a group well inclined toward political debate. The elected were not a monolithic group. Those committed to political and ecclesiastical reform were, to be sure, a minority among the clerics who were deputies. In the end those who proved to be most coherent as a group were the clerics who defended the traditional interests of the Church, since they were the nucleus of opposition to liberalism.[57] In the legislature of 1822 the Church's representation remained notable. It was higher than that of businessmen and professionals, with the exception of lawyers. The legislatures of 1834 and 1836 reflect the change in the tendencies of the relationship between the Church and the liberal system. This notwithstanding, the Church was

---

bourgeoisie in the traditional sense of the concept – it was not solely composed of an urban class linked to commercial and industrial activities, but included some noble elements as well. Herr (1989: 721–727) presents a social framework of purchasers similar to Rueda's analysis for the 1798 disentailment. However, Herr goes further in questioning the bourgeois nature of those purchasers, whether of rural or urban origin. In Herr's opinion, the landowners and most of the lawyers, clerics, and officeholders, etc. who constituted the nucleus of purchasers belonged to a group well-established in the old regime society, and therefore can not be considered a new emergent bourgeoisie.

[55] Chávarri (1988: 83).   [56] Callahan (1989: 92).
[57] Ibid. (1989: 95–95).

able to maintain a high level of representation in the political structure both in the *estamento de próceres* of 1834, as well as in the Senate.

More than one-third of the deputies throughout the period were employed by the state. Of these a little more than one-half were officeholders and the rest militarymen. The mean percentage of officeholders in the four legislatures covered here was of 18 percent, two points under those classified as *hacendados*. The Cortes of 1834 went eight points off of the mean, showing the lowest level of officeholders, while in the Cortes of 1822 this group held the majority of seats. The historical evidence of the era suggests that practically all of these were high officeholders. The most sizable number of them worked in the justice administration, followed by those in the Public Treasury, and, to a lesser degree, by other sectors of the administration.

Very little is known regarding the sociological characteristics of the men in the military in an era when they played such a decisive role. The mean percentage of members of this group in the four legislatures was of 15.6 percent, reaching its highest level of presence in 1834 and its lowest in 1822. Because of the scarcity of evidence, it is risky to generalize about the social composition or to propose a model of professional status for the Spanish army after 1834. Domínguez Ortiz has called attention to the changes that occurred within the Spanish army throughout the eighteenth century which brought about the rise of a renewed professionalism which was in part committed to the ideas of enlightened reformism.[58] Seco Serrano, however, prefers to speak of a "new army" born of "war and revolution" in the aftermath of 1808, in such a way that a dichotomy was created between the old officialdom of the old regime and the new order that had liberal leanings.[59] Until we have prosopographic studies that look at some of the sociocultural variables that characterized this group, however, it will be difficult to assess the possible ruptures or continuities of the group's social history. Only this type of analysis could clarify the real dimensions of the army's renovation as of 1808, as well as the social composition of its hierarchy and its relationship to liberalism.

I am convinced that the division posited by Busquets between an absolutist aristocratic army and a liberal bourgeois army completely lacks any historical base.[60] It is also very possible that the foundations of contempo-

---

[58] Domínguez Ortiz (1976: 400).   [59] Seco Serrano (1984: 17).
[60] Busquets (1982: 15).

Politicians

rary militarism can be found in the military culture forged between 1834 and 1867 which responded to the insufficiencies of civil Spanish society. The British ambassador in Madrid captured this reality perfectly when in 1839 he wrote in a report: "These men," referring to the influential group of generals that the Duke of Bailén led, "make up the modern nobility of Spain. Most of them trace their origins to the American conflicts and have been almost invariably the donors of patronage since the death of Ferdinand VII, and they are together the head of a party that, although it makes no noise, is capable of frustrating the projects of the businessmen called to counsel the queen, unless these belong to their own group."[61]

The last group with a significant representation was the professionals, among those ranks lawyers were most important. The categorization of lawyers is often erroneous. In its literal sense the category should include all those men with degrees who worked on their own, mediating between state justice and civil society. However, it is common to find cases of individuals who ended up fulfilling brilliant careers in the justice administration, in which case they should fall in the category of government officeholders.[62] Lawyers had always made up the bulk of the Spanish political class. Under absolutism political careers followed a well-defined path. It usually began with a law degree and a doctorate in laws, and tended to proceed to positions in courts, mayoralties, and *corregimientos* and culminate with a seat as councilor.[63] The electoral system and the competition between parties, as has been noted previously, made the mechanisms of access to the political class more flexible, shortening the duration of the rise of a political career. This notwithstanding, the social origins of lawyers did not undergo any significant transformations until the second half of the nineteenth century. The mechanisms of access to careers in law, as well as to all other careers requiring university degrees, remained closed to most of Spanish society.[64] Although some of the older institutions like the *colegios mayores* had begun to decline, there were still very few families that could cover the cost of a career or who could count on the social connections needed to be placed in an

---

[61] Janke (1974: 294).

[62] José María de Calatrava, for instance, participated as a lawyer in the Cortes de Cádiz. In 1820 he attained a position in the Spanish Supreme Court and later was nominated its president. After a long exile, in 1834 Calatrava was restored to the Supreme Court and granted a chair in the Council of State. He was minister several times and president of the cabinet.

[63] Gómez-Rivero (1988: 87–100) provides a series of professional biographies that support this assertion.

[64] Burdick (1983: 17–30), in her study of the Madrid writers, arrives at this same conclusion. Burdick combines occupational data with the variables of status and family backgrounds.

educational institution.[65] The legal field, and the professional world in general, continued to be accessible exclusively to those groups to which it had been accessible during the old regime.

The last group represented in the chart, the merchants and financiers, made up the most significant minority group in each of the four legislative terms. Those who, according to traditional notions derived from Marxist and liberal social categories, would have been the authentic bourgeoisie, only reached an average of 7 percent of the positions in the different legislatures. Almost all of those in this group were important businessmen, that is to say, they represented a commercial and financial elite of provincial origins but also had very strong ties to Madrid. The prominence that many of these men achieved as historical representatives of liberalism has kept their value as representatives of a sizable social group from being appreciated. Actually, the Mendizábal, Collado, and Salamanca families were fundamentally representative of a minority of powerful capitalists with strong ties to the state which was well established by the second half of the eighteenth century, as we have seen in previous chapters. They had only modest interest in commerce, and almost none in industry. It is true that their liberal political actions often favored the interest of commerce and industry in general, but we should not forget that these same actions were also in tune with the interests of elite landholders, among whom the nobility was prominent. While the old titled families of the nobility were always well represented in the Parliament, those members of the commercial world outside of Madrid's financial elite or those derived from in industrial sectors like that of Catalonia were perennially on the margin of political decision making. This marginalization would have important consequences in the middle and long term for the consolidation of a representative system in Spain.

The occupational structure of the groups that controlled executive power holds a certain relation, although with some variations, to that seen for the legislatures. For obvious reasons, the executive is always in need of people who are somewhat specialized in the field in which they are going to exercise their mandate. In the absolutist system this professional specialization was just as important as loyalty to the monarch and the clique that surrounded him. The representative systems introduced the value of political professionalism to the detriment of technical specialization. This notwithstand-

---

[65] Alcalá Galiano, in his memoirs (1955: 256), recognized that his family was not in its best moment when he was born, but he still found himself in an advantaged position which provided him with the necessary contacts and economic support to achieve a career.

Table 5.3. *Ministers, 1800-1853. Occupational structure*

Ocuupation		%
Officeholders	37	31.1
Military	26	21.8
Lawyers	30	25.2
Other professions	6	5.1
Diplomats	14	11.8
Finances/Commerce	5	4.2
Landowners	1	0.8
Total	119	

Source: Author's compilation from AHPM and AHN data; *Diccionario Enciclopédico Hispano-Americano de Literatura, Ciencia y Artes* (Barcelona: Montaner y Simón, 1887-1910); *Enciclopedia Universal Ilustrada Europeo-Americana* (Madrid: Espasa Calpe, 1930-1933).

ing, political careerism was subordinate to another kind of loyalty, which centered on ideological affinity. As a result, it is in the cabinet that we find the most distinguished members of the clientele or party of those in power at any given moment, hence providing fertile ground for the type of analysis I want to undertake. Even so, in the cabinet we can always see a higher level of professional skills and specialization than in the parliament.

Table 5.3 records the occupations of 119 ministers of the first half of the nineteenth century. It is more difficult to establish their political affiliation, since this is a formative period for the tendencies that would dominate the second half of the century. Of these, 45 (38%) have been identified as *moderadoes* and 32 (or 27% of the total) as *progresistas*. The remaining 42 (35%) either belonged to a period when liberalism was not yet divided, did not demonstrate a concrete political tendency, or had leanings that are not known to us. Looking at the data as a whole allows us to see the predominance of those occupations with ties to services to the state. A little less than two-thirds of the ministers were either government officials, diplomats, or members of the military. Among the officials those in the administration of justice far outnumbered those in other administrations, with a level of 68%. This is to say that they were mostly jurists who had risen in their careers through a system that, as had been pointed out previously, worked on a combination of patronage and personal promotion. After the administration of justice, the ministers served mostly as officials in the public treasury or as diplomats, although the latter was a group with some unique characteristics. While the jurists were present in all of the administrations, diplomats and those officials of the public treasury both generally served in those related to their specialization.

A significant portion of the ministers whose careers necessitated having strong ties to the state belonged to families with long traditions in this kind of occupation. In at least 47 of the 77 registered cases (61%), a minister was directly related to someone who had been employed in the bureaucracy. The father of Luis López de La Torre, for example, had been Councilor of the Public Treasury and General Director of Postal Services.[66] Canga Argüelles was the son of a former councilor from Castile and belonged to a family with a long tradition of service to the monarchy.[67] This tendency toward nepotism was especially prevalent among the families of diplomats. Manuel Bermúdez de Castro, for instance, was the son of a man who had been a diplomat under Charles IV, serving in London and other European cities. His brother Salvador, who was given the title of Duke of Ripalda, was also a distinguished diplomat.[68]

Besides those occupations related to service to the state, only professionals stand out as almost one-third of the occupational spectrum of the sample. As with the deputies, the predominance of lawyers was almost complete, and sometimes it is difficult to distinguish their occupational status from that of government officials. Among the latter, the level of occupational continuity in the family was not as pronounced as with the others. I have been able to detect ten cases (or 27.7%) in which there are direct family links in the profession, a number which might go up if more information was found. In any case, we must consider that a university degree offered a pretty secure route to social ascent.

Once again the sample shows only a very small presence of merchants and financiers in the cabinet, although the political relevance of its representatives was enormous. Among the five registered cases are Mendizábal, Istúriz, and Salamanca, persons whose historical importance will be apparent to the reader. All of them, as pointed out earlier, represented the large commercial financier capital with very strong ties to the state. This was a group that by their social and economic practices were closer to the old

---

[66] AHN, Estado, Carlos III, Exp. 1853.   [67] AHPM, P. 21000, p. 431.
[68] AHPM, P. 27142, p. 242.

Politicians

Table 5.4. *Ministers, 1800-1853. Political affiliation and occupation*

Occupation	Moderados	%	Progresistas	%
Officeholders	11	24.5	8	25.0
Military	6	13.3	10	31.2
Lawyers	15	33.3	9	28.2
Other professions	3	6.7	2	6.2
Diplomats	6	13.3	1	3.2
Finances/commerce	3	6.7	2	6.2
Hacendados	1	2.2	0	0.0
Total	45		32	

Source: Author's compilation from AHPM and AHN data; *Diccionario Enciclopédico Hispano-Americano de Literatura, Ciencia y Artes* (Barcelona: Montaner y Simón, 1887-1910); *Diccionario Enciclopédico Espasa Calpe* ; F. Caballero, *Fisonomía de los procuradores a Cortes de 1834-1836* (Madrid: 1836); J. Rico y Amat, *Historia política y parlamentaria de España* (Madrid: Escuelas Pías, 1860-61);

regime than to a system of free competition, but whose political practice was undoubtedly revolutionary.[69] The industrial bourgeoisie was not directly represented in the executive power of the first half of the nineteenth century.

As Isabel Burdiel has shown, a person's political leanings also seem to have had no direct relation to his occupational position, nor with the social implications that could be derived from this position. Some historians have exaggerated the commercial and professional bourgeoisie's identification with *progresismo*, while they have presented *moderantismo* as the option of landholders and of the part of the aristocracy that the liberal revolution assimilated.[70] Such a thesis ignores the fact that practically all of the Spanish politicians of the period had agrarian or rural backgrounds, regardless of their *progresista* or *moderado* affiliation. Table 5.4 shows the relation between political affiliation and occupation for seventy-seven ministers between 1800 and 1853. The only areas which show an important dichotomy are the military and the diplomatic professions, with men from the former group

---

[69] Mendizábal, for instance, made most of his fortune in the business of provisioning the army, first in his municipality, and then on a national scale when he became a partner with the Bertrán de Lis family, which was also well connected in the networks of the state client economy. See Janke (1974: 5-9).

[70] Burdiel (1987: 164); Marichal (1977: 97).

showing a greater tendency toward *progresismo*, and the latter leaning more heavily toward *moderantismo*. Little can be said about the social significance of the former's political tendencies before further research is undertaken. One possible explanation could be found in the fact that the greatest presence of militarymen among the ministers coincided with the regency of General Espartero, whose supporters may have been recruited among his military fellows. This is, however, a partial hypothesis about a group which requires greater attention from researchers. The case of diplomats can be related to the more endogamous character that this occupation seemed to have. We have to keep in mind that political affiliation did not correspond directly with class position but rather was founded on personal conviction, strongly mediated by a habitus based on loyalty. This loyalty best manifested itself through a variety of social practices among which the family played a crucial role. The experiences of the Cano Manuel and Pezuela families are a clear example of this tendency. Being both provincial families of landowners, bureaucrats, and professionals, belonging both to local elites, the Canos embraced *progresista* positions and the Pezuelas moderate ones during two generations of political activism.[71] Mariano Torres Solanot, a minister in the times of Espartero, passed the *mayorazgo* of an Aragonese noble family established in the province of Zaragoza. Tiburcio Torres Guillén, Mariano's paternal uncle, had been a knight of Santiago and the intendant of Zaragoza. His maternal grandfather had also been a knight of Santiago, as well as the intendant of Badajoz. Valentín Solanot, his maternal uncle, presided over the Junta de Aragón during the war of independence. He had also been appointed perpetual city councilman for Zaragoza in representation of the noble estate and attained a nomination of *caballero de Carlos III*.[72] Despite his family's *progresista* leanings, the clan was related to the Bardaji family, whose *moderado* affiliation was well known. The most extreme case of political polarization among groups of the same social standing is that of the Zumalacárregui family. Among the eleven children of D. Miguel de Zumalacárregui, a notary and wealthy proprietor, several followed ecclesiastical careers, two joined the military, and at least two others became lawyers. What is most interesting about the family, however, was that it also included among its ranks one liberal minister and one of the most doctrinaire absolutist political leaders of the period. The two coexisted

[71] On the Cano Manuel family see Suárez (1989: 39 and 82). On the Pezuela family see Gómez-Rivero (1988: 99); AHPM, P. 25459, p. 186.
[72] AHN, Estado, Carlos III, Exp. 1837.

Politicians

at the very time when the clash between the groups they represented was at its most violent.

Otazu has detected something similar in defining the political behavior of the business elite tied to the capital during 1833 and 1839. Some of these *hombres de negocios*, most of them involved in military provisioning, backed Mendizábal's *progresista* politics and made the implementation of his policies much easier (Manuel Cantero, Juan Muguiro, Manuel Gil de Santibáñez, Antonio Jordá, José Safont, Jaime Ceriola, Juan Guardamino, Juan Sevillano, Joaquín de Fagoaga, Francisco de las Rivas o Fernando Fernández Casariego, etc.). But there were others from this business elite who were *moderados* and who figured prominently in the following decade (1840–50). They were the Gaviria, Remisa, Finat, Salamanca, Pérez Seoane, Santamarca, Moreno, Nájera, and O'Shea. Otazu adds, however, that the dichotomy does not hold when one or the other businessman had the opportunity, as they often did, to embark upon profitable business ventures that challenged their political convictions. At that moment political convictions disappeared as if by magic.[73]

Geographical origins

Most historians agree that the balance of regional equilibrium on which absolutism was founded collapsed during the second half of the eighteenth century. this interpretation sees a process that began early in the seventeenth century, when the regions of the Spanish periphery developed faster than that interior. While Castile, Extremadura, and the interior of Andalusia remained agricultural, regions like Catalonia initiated a slow but continuous process of industrialization. Commercial activities intensified, especially in the coastal cities of the north as well as in the main ports of the Mediterranean. Such growth prompted social change and provoked social conflict. By the end of the century, according to Fernández de Pinedo, the process of surplus accumulation that characterized the whole period reached a saturation point. Groups that benefited from this process – landowners and merchant bourgeoisie – became the protagonists of an inevitable social breakup.[74] The problem, according to Roberto Fernández, was that economic growth required a more suitable environment. Technical or func-

---

[73] Otazu (1987: 307). [74] Fernández de Pinedo (1980: 161).

Table 5.5. *Geographic origins: Council of Castile, 1621-1788, and ministers, 1800-1853*
Regional distribution of the Spanish population, 1797-1860

	Councilors							Ministers	
Place of origin	1621-1700		1700-1746		1746-1834			1800-1853	
North	46	25.6%	12	11.6%	26	21.0%		23	19.3%
Northeast	14	7.5%	7	6.7%	13	10.5%		17	14.3%
North Plateau	44	23.6%	13	12.5%	14	11.3%		8	6.7%
South Plateau	7	3.7%	12	11.6%	11	8.8%		6	5.1%
Madrid	33	16.6%	14	13.5%	11	8.8%		5	4.2%
Extremadura	19	10.1%	2	1.9%	2	1.6%		8	6.7%
Andalusia	21	11.3%	19	18.3%	18	14.6%		28	23.5%
Levant	0	0.0%	22	21.1%	28	22.6%		16	13.4%
Colonies	3	1.6%	2	1.9%	0	0.0%		6	5.1%
Foreigners	0	0.0%	1	0.9%	1	0.8%		2	1.7%
Total	187		104		124			119	

Regional distribution of the Spanish population
(percentage of the total population)

	1797	1860
North	7.8	7.7
Northwest	14.4	14.9
North Plateau	14.9	12.8
South Plateau	11.2	9.6
Extremadura	4.1	4.6
Andalusia	19.8	20.4
Levant	27.8	30.0

Sources: A) "Consejeros" and ministers: (1621-1746) J. Fayard, *Los miembros del Consejo d Castilla (1621-1746)* (Madrid: Siglo XXI), 215; J. Fayard, "Los ministros del Consejo Real de Castilla (1746-1788)," *Cuadernos de Investigación Histórica*, Madrid, VI (1982), 116-117.
(1746-1834) Fayard's data plus author's compilation from AHPM data.
(1800-1853) Author's compilation from AHPM, AHN data.
B) Population: M. Artola, *La burguesía revolucionaria (1808-1869)* (Madrid: Alianza, 1989), 68-69.

tional reforms in the juridical framework of the absolutist monarchy were inadequate. In order to achieve political and economic stability, changes in the conception of class relations were necessary.[75]

An analysis of the regional origins of the 119 ministers of this sample reflects this geopolitical transformation, but with different dynamics than are customarily presented by historians. Some years ago David Ringrose pointed out some dissimilarities in the regional origins of the Madrid bourgeoisie. Most members of the council of ministers came from the mainly agrarian provinces of Andalusia. However, northerners were predominant among the merchant and banker community.[76] Thus, agrarian regions provided the political class of the Spanish "bourgeois revolution," not the areas with a commercial and industrial orientation. According to Ringrose this fact responded to a geopolitical trend begun at the end of the seventeenth century. My own data reinforce Ringrose's assertions, adding evidence to the argument of the nonexistence of a new political class in liberal Spain.

Table 5.5 compares the regional origins of the nineteenth-century ministers with the members of the old Council of Castile studied by Janine Fayard. The cabinet (*consejo de ministros*) absorbed executive functions that were performed by the Council of Castile before the liberal revolution. Both institutions made up the executive power before and after the crisis of the old regime. Analyzing the regional origins of the members of the institutions from a historical perspective, one may notice long-term tendencies. The main change in the regional composition of the political elite took place during the seventeenth century rather than in the first half of the nineteenth. The interior of Spain (two Plateaus plus Madrid) provided 44% of the *consejeros* in the times of the last Austria rulers, while the same regions only provided 29% of the liberal ministers. By contrast, the number of politicians from the peninsular periphery increased since 1665. Only the Northwest shows an ascending tendency in this same period – from 7.5% to 14.3%. Most of those politicians were from Asturias. The Levant region offers the most radical change, moving from having no members during the seventeenth century to 22.6% at the end of the eighteenth. However, this region, which includes Catalonia, declined in its number of representatives during the liberal period. Furthermore, there is only one minister from Barcelona – the only Catalan – among the 119 that make up this sample.

---

[75] Fernández (1985: 52).   [76] Ringrose (1986: 316).

Politicians from Andalusia, however, increased to the point of becoming a majority within the liberal cabinets.

Comparing these percentages to the regional distribution of the Spanish population we may detect three tendencies. First, only in the northern regions was representation in power institutions disproportionately superior to their demography. Second, the drop in Castilian politicians corresponded to its demographic decline. Finally, the demographic vitality of Spanish eastern regions at the end of the eighteenth century, especially Catalonia, did not correspond to their representation in the national government. The presence of northerners (Basques, Montañeses, Riojanos, etc.) both in the government administration and the business community deserves more detailed research. Catalonia developed a model of regional integration which presented early social and economic particularisms compared to other Spanish regions.

Another element that defined the sociology of the Spanish political class was its predominantly migratory character. Most ministers in this sample were born far from Madrid. Almost two-thirds of them – 61% – came from the rural countryside; the rest belonged to families established in provincial capitals or local urban towns. Thus, most politicians experienced the style of life in the Spanish *pueblos* before they were sent to the capital to complete a professional or political career. I think this detail is essential for understanding their social origins and, in particular, some basic features of their social culture. Almost half of the ministers – 45% – who came from urban areas were Andalusians. Madrid provided 15% of the urbanites. Colonial cities such as Mexico, Lima, or Buenos Aires provided 16%. The remaining 24% came from several provincial capitals which could be considered urban only by their administrative functions, not by their style of life. Only one minister in the whole sample was from Barcelona.

Family backgrounds

The provincial and rural origins of the ministers in this sample must be considered in relation to the status of their families to complete this sociological analysis. Looking for the heros of the bourgeois revolution, historians have emphasized political ideologies rather than evaluating social origins and behaviors of the politicians. Even when the approach has been more sociological, historians have focused on those specific cases that allow them to demonstrate the ascent of a new class. The use of Mendizábal's life

Politicians

story exemplifies this type of interpretive model. Coming from a family from the middle ranks of the Cádiz merchant community, Mendizábal climbed up to the highest spheres of political and economic influence. Could one find a better example of bourgeois ascent?

However, Mendizábal represented a minority in a realm dominated by individuals whose social origins and political careers were not the result of a process of social ascent. To the contrary, most ministers in this period belonged to well-established families, in most cases with *ilustre* backgrounds. In the social vocabulary of the period, belonging to a *familia ilustre* meant to have noble ascendancy. Behind this label lurked a habitus characterized by the inertia of certain traditional practices of their social stratum. Of course, by 1840 having noble lineage did not have the same legal implications that it had during the absolute monarchy. However, belonging to a *familia ilustre* was in itself promise of social success since it assured, or at least facilitated, certain mechanisms of solidarity that almost always had nothing to do with political networks.[77] Leaving the project of offering a more detailed analysis of this habitus of exclusivity for the next chapters, here I only intend to discuss evidence replete with historical implications: the majority presence of the political class of liberalism in the lineages of the *familias ilustres* with origins in the provinces. From this perspective the liberal revolution once again seems to be the product not of an ascendant bourgeoisie, but rather the result of a combination of forces from different social strata often tied by familial bonds and personal loyalties that stemmed mostly from the middle and low ranks of the nobility of the old regime.

Combining primary sources from notarial and *Ordenes Militares* archives, with information from biographical and genealogical literature, I have traced the familial records of the 119 ministers in the sample. Table 5.6 shows a breakdown of the group according to evidence (or lack thereof) of an *ilustre* familial past. This data must be accepted with some reservations although it nonetheless does demonstrate a pattern. It is true that noble pedigrees were at times dispensed without a clear, actual noble past. One generation's social ascent was enough for the following to dare to try to rewrite their family history so as to stake a claim to noble status. But we should not minimize the importance of these documents, especially if they

---

[77] Antonio Alcalá Galiano used the influence of his uncle Villavicencio to attain his first job in the Council of State. Don Antonio recognized the enormous distance between his own political ideas and those of his uncle; however, familial solidarity exceeded political differences. Alcalá Galiano (1955: 399 vol. I).

Careers, business, and fortunes

Table 5.6. *Ministers, 1800-1853. Familial status*

Hidalguía (Gentleman)	66	55.4%
Old aristocracy	12	10.1%
Title from the eighteenth century	5	4.2%
New title	13	11.0%
None of above	23	19.3%
Total	119	

Status	Moderados		Progresistas		Unknown	
Hidalguía (Gentleman)	21	46.7%	23	71.9%	22	52.4%
Old aristocracy	7	15.5%	0	0%	5	12.0%
Title from the eighteenth century	2	4.5%	1	3.1%	2	4.7%
New title	7	15.5%	4	12.5%	2	4.7%
None of above	8	17.8%	4	12.5%	11	26.2%
Total	45		32		42	

Source: Author's compilation from: A. García Carraffa, *Enciclopedia heráldica y genealógica hispanoamericana*. (Madrid: A. Marzo, 1952-1964), 82 vols.; *Diccionario Enciclopédico Hispano-Americano de Literatura, Ciencia y Artes* (Barcelona: Montaner y Simón, 1887-1910); AHPM and AHN data.

were from far back, as most of them were. Although there have been no systematic studies done, it is known that on occasion a family's noble aspirations were rejected because of lack of evidence. The way these credentials were eventually put to use points to a culture impregnated with the values of the old regime. The fact that the Mendizábal family and the Esparteros never flaunted their family pasts in the same way that the Cano Manuels and the Alcalá Galianos did, although all four were political friends, is symptomatic of this culture. Almost two-thirds of the 119 ministers had ancestors of clear noble lineage originating in the old regime, although, of course, at different levels of importance in the social hierarchy. Those at the highest levels were a small but extremely significant 14.3% of ministers who belonged to the old aristocracy or from families with titles granted throughout the eighteenth century. It is significant that they outnumber ministers with family origins in commerce, finances, or industry.[78] The greatest number of ministers, as would be expected, came from families whose surname's im-

[78] They were people like Toreno, Miraflores, Rivas, Ofaliá, Nibbiano, Amarillas, et al.

Politicians

portance was merely symbolic. That is to say, the family name reflected more a social status, in the Weberian sense, than a position of wealth or power. This was the case of Agustín Argüelles, *el divino* Argüelles, as his followers called him. The second son of a family of medium nobility which had a significant patrimony. He had to rely on a kind of political charity to be included in the list of parliament members in 1834. This notwithstanding, Don Agustín did not let his prestige and family connections go to waste when seeking employment in the Court. The patronage of his *paisano* and friend Jovellanos started him on an expansive political career that lasted until his death in 1844.[79]

Very few of the ministers in the sample belonged to families that had only recently risen in the social scale. I have already mentioned the notable example of the Mendizábal, Espartero, and Salamanca families. This was also the case with some families of medium-sized agrarian property owners in regions with active rural economies.

A larger number of ministers were from families who belonged to what the end of the nineteenth century would know as local *caciquismo* or political bossism, and what in the period with which we are concerned can be called local notability. The Díaz-Caneja family, for example, were from a small locality in the province of León and counted among its ranks one minister of Gracia y Justicia, one bishop of Oviedo, and several lawyers. The wealth of Díaz-Canejas came originally from their agrarian properties. They proved their noble heritage at Valladolid in 1774 and members of the family had used noble titles since the seventeenth century.[80]

The most numerous and therefore more representative social group, however, was of ministers who originated from families of the middle nobility. This was a group that because of its intermediate status was able to have representatives in both the high and low levels of the social hierarchy. Those who immediately stand out are the ministers who belonged to bureaucratic dynasties, as did José Canga Argüelles. His family was of the lesser nobility and distinguished itself in its members' service to the state. His paternal grandfather held several positions in provincial administration. His maternal grandmother lived off the rents received from the lands of his *mayorazgo* in the region of San Justo, next to Gijón. As I have noted earlier, his father served on the Council of Castile and José himself married the daughter of a high official of the Public Treasury. The different branches of

[79] Alcalá Galiano (1955: 353, vol. II); Burdiel (1987: 294).
[80] AHN, Estado, Carlos III, Exp. 1819.

the family had proven their nobility at the Chancery of Valladolid on several occasions, beginning in 1535. José himself entered the order of Charles III and in 1851 was selected for the more prestigious Order of Santiago. His sons kept the family tradition going, serving at the highest levels of the administration of the state and obtaining the titles of counts of Canga Argüelles.[81]

The Bardaji family's *mayorazgo* and residence were in Graus, the town from which the clan originated. They were an *ilustre* Aragonese family, some of whose members held high posts in the government administration and in service to the monarch. José Bardaji, the father of the government minister, besides being in the military was lord of Villanova y Albenozas. He had seven children with his wife Maria de Azara. The eldest, Vicente, arranged his life around the *mayorazgo* that he inherited. The family's high social standing can be inferred from the excellent social positions that the rest of the male children reached. Eusebio achieved highest honors in public life, Dionisio held the highest cardinalship that an ecclesiastic of his time could aspire to, and last, Anselmo reached the highest rank in his chosen military career.[82]

A significant 41 percent of these families from the middle nobility originated from the provincial urban nuclei. These were mostly families that combined activity in local political life with service to the state. Their wealth generally came from their agrarian landholdings, although they were also sometimes active in commercial and financial ventures. Francisco Martínez de la Rosa, for example, belonged to a Granada family that follows this model perfectly.[83] His uncle and godfather, Manuel Martínez Verdejo, was *caballero venticuatro* in the municipal government and attained a nomination of *caballero de Carlos III*. He had made his fortune in trade with the New World colonies exporting agrarian products from Granada. Francisco's father, Francisco Martínez, had been Honorary Treasurer of the Armada and worked with his brother on army provisioning contracts. The family of his wife, Luisa de la Rosa, was also well-established in the government bureaucracy of the city government. Francisco Martínez Verdejo inherited the fortunes of both his brother and his wife, who at her untimely death left him with two young sons. After his wife's passing Francisco kept a maid, a cook, a footman, and a doorman as household employees. He owned the luxurious

---

[81] AHN, Estado, Carlos III, Exp. 1806; AHN, Ordenes Militares, Santiago, exp. 208 (mod.).
[82] AHN, Estado, Carlos III, Exp. 1256.
[83] His ancestors obtained noble credentials in 1573, 1734, 1735, and 1777. AHN, Estado, Carlos III, Exp. 2362.

mansion he lived in on his property, as well as properties such as the Carmen de las Torres and a farm called Las Elviras, which had a profit margin of 24,000 reales a year. He was also the owner of various lands in the area of Maracena.[84] His brother left him the Mita Galán, a farm valued at 400,000 reales, as well as a house in Granada and a fairly large amount of gold and silver which he had saved. With this information the reader should be able to assess the Martínez de la Rosa's social position and place them right under Granada's grand aristocracy. This aristocracy, however, was not an idle nobility and were, of course, fairly enlightened. Francisco's father had founded an academy which the most notable personalities of Granada's Enlightenment attended. His father's notoriety among advanced social circles and the salons where intellectuals met no doubt favored the early intellectual development of Francisco Martínez de la Rosa.

Antonio Alcaláa Galiano tended to say that his was not a family name that was well known in the annals of his country's history, but he was not exactly an adventurer who rose in social rank as a result of the revolution, either.[85] On his father's side his lineage stemmed from the sixteenth-century fusion of two *ilustre* families who founded their *mayorazgo* in the area of Doña Mencia in Cordoba, where the family home was located. The maternal branch of his family included the Duke of San Lorenzo and the Marques of Mesa. The two branches of the family, as was often the case, were already related through marriage, and so Antonio's parents had to request a double dispensation from the church in order to marry. His paternal grandfather, who reached the rank of field marshal in the military, inherited the family *mayorazgo* and wore the habit of the order of Alcántara. The careers of this grandfather's sons – Antonio's uncles – all led into service to the state, as was so often the case with the men of the provincial nobility. Three of the four sons served in the military while one became a lawyer. The two youngest left their native province to install themselves in Madrid, where they came to occupy important positions in the administration of the treasury. One of the daughters of the family spent her life in a convent, while the other married a military officer who had the title of the Marquis of Medina. Antonio's two uncles from his mother's side of the family had also been sailors and knights of the order of Alcántara, while the married women of the family took the unmarried women into their care, as was customary. When Antonio Alcalá Galiano came into the world his family enjoyed an

[84] Sarrailh (1930: 9). [85] Alcalá Galiano (1955: 255, vol. I).

advanced social status, well off financially although not extremely wealthy, and with good prospects for future expansion of the family fortune. During his early childhood his parents' home was shared by his maternal grandmother and one of his paternal uncles. As Alcalá Galiano himself recognized, his extended family served as the means through which he would achieve financial success.[86]

Like most of the men of the political elite of his time, Alcalá Galiano used his family's social status to begin the process of becoming financially independent. Because he was from an *ilustre* family he was able to wear the uniform of the Spanish Royal Guard at the tender age of seven. But it was in 1807, just after turning eighteen years old, that his relatives invited him to move to the capital to begin to forge his career. His grandfather, a very distant and morally rigid man who survived several of his descendants, was very well connected in Madrid. Antonio's more important connections, however, came through his uncles Vicente and Antonio, both members of the Council of the Treasury. The former took the young Antonio into his home in the city. The war of 1808 temporarily delayed Antonio's administrative career, but it provided him with the opportunity to begin a very active political career.

The Peña Aguayo family, originally from Córdoba, was related to other families of Andalusia's urban middle nobility, like the Rosa and Heredia families. José de la Peña Aguayo was minister of the treasury in 1843. His father began his professional career in the army, although he soon left the service with the rank of second lieutenant of the cavalry. The family lived off the rent of his mother's *mayorazgo* in the village of Cabra.[87] His membership in the Heredia clan facilitated his entry into politics under the sponsorship of the Count of Contradi.

Alvaro Florez Estrada belonged to an old, well-established family of Pola de Somiedo, in Asturias.[88] His father was well known among *ilustrado* circles of their province. Alvaro was the eldest of eleven children, which meant he would inherit the family *mayorazgo*. His provincial *mayorazgo* did not, however, dictate his destiny, as he opted to follow a career in the state bureaucracy. His father's liberal ideas seem to have influenced him in this career choice. As a child Alvaro proved to be bright and seemed to have a good disposition for public life, and so his father decided to send him to Madrid under the sponsorship of his *paisanos* Campomanes and Jovellanos.

[86] Ibid., (1955: 259–260, vol. I). [87] AHN, Estado, Carlos III, Exp. 2342.
[88] Martínez Cachero (1961: 17).

Politicians

His first marriage to the sister of the count of Toreno ended when she died prematurely. He was later remarried to Maria Amalia Cornejo, the daughter of a member of the Consejo de Castilla. This marriage afforded him the opportunity to penetrate even more the elite world of the court and therefore to better his position in the government administration.

The last examples of this genealogical analysis will be of the families of some *hombres de negocios* who had noble lineages dating back to the old regime. This was the case of Joaquín Maria Ferrer y Cafranga, minister of state in 1840 and a *progresista* sympathizer. The Ferrer family seems to have originated in Mallorca and established itself in Guipuzcoa toward the end of the sixteenth century. The family had for a very long time enjoyed the privileges, prerogatives, and exemptions of the nobility, and as such had held honorary government posts.[89] They had always been involved in trade and finances. Melchor Ferrer, Joaquín Maria's grandfather, owned a commercial house in London, where he died. Vicente Ferrer Echeverría, Joaquín Maria's father, combined his military career with a business in government provisioning for the Spanish navy, providing the *armada* with products from England. He was appointed as royal accountant, which undoubtedly put him in a favorable position to be awarded government contracts. Joaquín Maria reached the rank of captain in the army, but he soon thereafter retired to pursue a career in business. He kept the family tradition of military provisioning and succeeded in the business, judging by how much he added to the family patrimony. The Ferrers enjoyed the *mayorazgo* of Echeverri, which was divided among the heirs when the property was disentailed. Among the papers Joaquín Maria left behind after his death was a document certifying the family's nobility, obtained by his grandfather in 1762. A family coat of arms decorated the palace Joaquín Maria had built in Pasajes. The interior of the palace, decorated in English style, is filled with portraits of his ancestors, genealogical diagrams, and the coats of arms of the various last names found among his lineage. The Ferrers' business proclivities and liberal *progresismo* were not in any way incompatible with the persistence of a certain mentality of their social class. After all, the Ferrer lineage had a history of over two hundred years.[90] Their example

---

[89] García de Carraffa (1952–1963: 34 vol. 166).

[90] Joaquín María Ferrer y Cafranga did not have sons to continue the family name. Nevertheless his daughters married members of *ilustre* families of the nineteenth-century elite. Flora, the eldest, married José Lemery, a military man who attained the highest rank of captain general. Aurora's husband, Juan Antonio de Seoane, came from a well-known family of Madrid bankers. He studied law and attained a position in the Spanish supreme court. Isabel, the youngest daughter, married a

makes two very important points: that one could participate in *progresista* cultural politics while at the same time take in and enjoy the benefits of an aristocratic social culture. Second, they are exemplary of a significant portion of the business bourgeoisie that in the nineteenth century repeated the same cycles of social ascent and reproduction that their ancestors had in the old regime.[91]

Conclusion: A new political class?

Judging by their social extraction, the men who led the liberal revolution in Spain did not constitute a new elite. The evidence given in this chapter shows that the politicians of this period came from a social spectrum that was already well established at the time of the revolution. They mostly came from a small number of families of the provincial nobility whose descendants either became professionals or were placed in the government bureaucracy or the church. This medium and lower nobility of the provinces was also joined by some members of the old aristocracy and by the financial and commercial elite, but these groups were always in the minority. As a unit the group's social classification was defined by their status as rentier proprietors. The studies available to us about the political sociology of the seventeenth and eighteenth centuries show a certain continuity with what I have found for the nineteenth century. The members of the Council of Castile studied by Fayard were systematically recruited from the medium and lower strata of the various nobilities. The same occurred with other sectors of the administration, whether it was national or local. If one could speak of the appearance of a new political class in Spain, it would be more appropriate to locate the period of change at the end of the seventeenth century rather than the beginning of the nineteenth.[92] In this Spain's example is not isolated or peculiar, as the country followed a pattern of development similar to other continental European countries.

Does this mean that society at the beginning of the nineteenth century was static, at least in terms of the development of its political elite? Does this mean that there was no mobility in this social space? Absolutely not. As I pointed out at the beginning of this chapter, what most surprised contem-

member of the Caballero family, whose main source of income these years came from the revenues produced by leasing its rural and urban properties. AHPM, P. 28758, p. 1016; AHN, Estado, Carlos III, Exp. 1795.
[91] AHN, Ordenes Militares, Alcántara, Exp. 163 (mod.).
[92] Contrary to the thesis of Morales Moya (1983: 1222) and Hernández Franco (1987: 131).

Politicians

poraries was the speed at which one could fulfill a political career, something which could seldom be done so rapidly before 1812. Without a doubt, the liberal revolution introduced a social dynamism to which the subjects of the absolute monarchy were unaccustomed. Historians have traditionally characterized this new dynamic as the result of a sudden social change that was the product of bourgeois ascent. The evidence presented in this chapter shows this is a misconception. Spanish society after 1812 offered more opportunities for social ascent, but the beneficiaries of this opening of channels were essentially the same social groups that were well established in power circles in the eighteenth century. Social mobility was then the result of horizontal pressures and not of the rise of a new social class. The political elite of liberalism was created in a process of reproduction and co-optation of elements whose social cohesion is noteworthy. Both social reproduction and co-optation were moved by kinship and friendship networks, as well as solidarity among *paisanos*. These networks, as the impetus for social mobility, were much more important than class conflict. These were mechanisms that guaranteed the dominance of an old elite through traditional social practices, while at the same time offering a sufficiently strong margin of social flexibility so as to not endanger the bases on which social order rested. These practices were already well in place during the old regime. The recent studies of Mauro Hernández and Christian Windler show that the elites of the old stratified society reproduced and at the same time renewed themselves through practices that were both from the estate and the liberal societies.[93] It was, without a doubt, a defense mechanism that assured continuity without creating obstruction. Under these presuppositions Morales Moya's thesis is valid. He states that the crisis of the old regime was the result of conflict between old elites rather than of opposing social groups. In the following chapter we will see the historical implications of understanding the political process that Spain underwent between 1750 and 1850 when viewed in this manner.

[93] Hernández Benítez (1991: chap. 9); Windler (1991: 1).

Part II

The museum of families

6

Habitus, solidarity, and authority

For many years historians have assumed that the revolutions between 1789 and 1848 brought about the end of Western European corporate societies.[1] The liberal state, according to this conception, developed a new social organization based on the principles of natural law and freedom of choice, rather than on inherited privilege. The old regime society in which social groups were defined by function, quality, power, and wealth was substituted by a new social order based on class.[2] The proponents of this point of view contend that in the new society, there was only one law for all citizens, and (at least nominally) everyone was equal before the law. The hierarchy of privilege and preferred treatment, sanctioned by law and tradition in the old order, no longer prevailed. The personal relationships, the bonds of loyalty and fealty, and the servile dependence of the traditional society were replaced by impersonal relationships imposed by the rule of law and by the power of money.[3]

These general assumptions resulted from an understanding of history – influenced by positivism and Marxism – according to which political, economic, and social change responded to an evolutionist logic of progression. "One of the corollaries of this evolutionist view," writes C. C. Harris,

> is the association of particular institutions with evolutionary stages or historical periods and the supposition that we are situated in the midst of a historical process which eliminates some social features and replaces them by others. According to this approach, universal aspects of social life – such as property or social position – have to have their specific institutional referents in the historical process. Substitution of feudal institutions by capitalist ones

[1] Blum (1978: 418); Palmer (1959: 5); Morris (1979).
[2] I. A. A. Thompson (1991: 53).   [3] Blum (1978: 440).

reflects, in Marxist historiography, basic changes in the evolutionary stage of the means of production. Social formations – traditionally known as modes of production – follow one another according to a logic in which material life (infrastructure) generally determines institutional changes (superstructure). Simple/primitive or pre-industrial societies – in the view of some defenders of the modernization paradigm – seen to be founded in collective systems of privilege (estates) and loyalty (kinship), while complex industrial/capitalist societies are based on individual economic relations (classes).[4]

This has been the logic followed by those aforementioned scholars who linked legal changes with the extinction of the estate societies in Europe between 1789 and 1848.

Developments in social and cultural history in the last two decades have challenged this evolutionist logic of historical understanding. Inspired by cultural anthropology and poststructuralist sociology, the history of family, gender, and everyday life emphasize the autonomy of sociocultural structures in relation to the economic and political ones.[5] Economic and social relations are not prior to or determined by cultural ones; they are themselves fields of cultural practice and cultural production which cannot be explained deductively by reference to an extracultural dimension of experience.[6] Transformations in the legal system or economic structure, therefore, do not necessarily imply cultural changes, or vice versa. Transformations of political culture and ideology normally occur faster than legal reforms and not always in response to alterations in the economy. Furthermore, the reception of new ideas by a select social group is extremely fast in comparison to how habits, costumes, and traditions change in any given society.

Most countries have at some point in their history experienced conflict between legal and economic change and sociocultural inertia. New ideological, legal, or economic developments may constitute a challenge to the habitus of already established social groups. These groups' response is a quiet resistance to changing their cultural habits. This habitus of cultural

---

[4] C. C. Harris (1990: 1–2); see also O'Connell (1976: 20).
[5] E. P. Thompson objected to the traditional reductionist Marxist interpretation of the dependence between base and superstructure. He emphasized class consciousness as "the way in which experiences (of productive relations) are handled in cultural terms: embodied in traditions, value systems, ideas, and institutional forms." Quoted in Trimberger (1984: 219). However, according to Thompson "class experience is largely determined by the productive relations into which men are born – or enter involuntarily." Thompson (1966: 10). As Lynn Hunt has pointed out, in Marxist models the social experience is, by definition, always primary Hunt (1989: 5). Roger Chartier (1982: 30) has questioned the classic Annales paradigm which characterized *mentalités* as being part of the so-called third level of historical experience.
[6] Hunt (1989: 7).

resistance is even stronger in those societies in which legal changes resulted from the will of an enlightened minority, instead of as response to the existence of new economic and social developments. That was the case of most continental European countries during the nineteenth century and is the case of many Third World countries today. The dual dynamics between politicoideological changes and habitus among the Spanish dominant groups is the subject of the second part of this book.

In this chapter and the next I am going to question the traditional assumption that changes in the Spanish legal system between 1812 and 1843 brought about the end of the old corporate society, at least in terms of dominant social practices. This assumption has been traditionally maintained by scholars who share the aforementioned evolutionist conception of history, whether they identified themselves as Marxist or non-Marxist historians.[7] Early politicized versions of the bourgeois revolution paradigm in Spain claimed a more deterministic linkage between class struggle and historical change.[8] However, in the last decade a more pragmatic approach has been developed to adjust the paradigm to the outcomes of new historical evidence. According to the proponents of this revised version, the bourgeois revolution was essentially a "juridical" revolution that radically modified the legal foundations of the estate society.[9] This process did not necessarily imply the substitution of one dominant social group by another but rather the imposition of a new liberal civil law and a new public state law that abolished the feudal order. Thus, the bourgeois revolution was the establishment of a new juridical system that implemented the liberation of property, the privatization of family, and the concentration of political power in the state. Nevertheless, despite the inversion of the paradigm terms – changes in the superstructure provoked the transformation of the base – the nature of the revolution, according to these historians, was in the end social since it provided the cradle for a new social order.

In preceding chapters I have attempted to demonstrate that the "Spanish revolution" was not the result of the ascent of a new social class but rather the product of the acceptance of modernization on the part of an old elite that coopted some bourgeois elements. Now I shall argue that the imple-

---

[7] Palacio Atard (1978: 81).
[8] See Bruguera (1953). A recent approach of this kind can be found in Peset (1990: 173). For this author, liberal politics constituted the best evidence to demonstrate the existence of a revolutionary bourgeoisie in Spain toward 1834. Peset follows a traditional reductionist interpretation of Marxist thought, linking liberalism with bourgeoisie and absolutism with aristocracy.
[9] Petit (1990: 11); Clavero (1979: 42–43); Shubert (1990: 4–5).

The museum of families

mentation of a new juridical order did not necessarily imply a revolution in social practices; although the legal framework changed, hidden social and cultural relations such as kinship, friendship, and patronage prevailed as basic structures for the social reproduction of Spanish society. Like the "old English society," Spanish society of most of the nineteenth century was based on property and patronage instead of class relations. It was a society dominated by an elite that held the political, economic, and social power of the community. In this hierarchically organized "old society," social agents were acutely aware of their exact relation to those immediately above and below them. Except for those at the very top, however, they were only vaguely conscious of their connections with those at their own level. Basic social relations depended on bonds of loyalty and personal dependency. The basis for social differentiation was determined by an equal combination of status and wealth.[10]

The persistence of the "old society" was not peculiar to Spanish history. In most continental European countries, up until 1914, the ruling classes maintained corporate practices of social reproduction, although the practice was not limited to this elite alone. As Arnold Mayer pointed out some years ago, "by virtue of historical practice and presumption the nobilities of land and office kept reproducing a governing class that not only staffed the state bureaucracy but also kept replenishing the higher echelons of political leadership. This unbrokenness in political personnel and direction, which had profound societal moorings, accounts for the feudal element surviving as more than a mere integument of the State."[11]

However, the persistence of the old society can only be deduced from an analysis of the basic practices of social reproduction. As cultural anthropologists and sociologists have pointed out, these relations belonged to the private sphere of social life. Historians who have claimed the end of the old society in the first half of the nineteenth century, nevertheless have focused almost exclusively on changes that took place in the public sphere: the codification of new juridical norms and the creation of new institutions. The persistence of the old social practices, however, has to be found in the concealed social and cultural practices that took place in the daily flow of the private life. This is a field scantily studied by historians, whether Marxist or liberal, who have tended to focus on the world of the state and production. The next pages will provide an analysis of private social and cultural prac-

[10] Perkin (1969: chap. II). [11] Mayer (1981: 135).

tices of the Spanish middle and upper classes. My intention is to reveal the existence of a long-standing contradiction between private and public discourses among the elements that constituted these social groups. While public discourse encouraged social practices based on merit, freedom of choice, and intellectual commitment – all values traditionally associated with a class society – their private discourse was determined by a habitus based on the practice of personal loyalty and collective solidarity – typical values of the old corporate society. To explain this contradiction we will need to understand the meaning and dynamics of both the public and private spheres.[12]

The public sphere can be defined as the arena for objective developments and communal projects. It refers to the collective discourse of social groups as they carry out control of politics and market developments. Commitment to modernization characterized the public discourse of the Spanish elite. Between 1750 and 1850 this discourse can be traced from the reformist positions of *ilustrados* to the radical policies of liberal *progresistas*.[13] The goal of both groups was to put the Spanish economy, political institutions, and culture at the same level with those already present in some European countries of the period.[14] The bulk of the Spanish middle and upper classes' public discourse consisted of policies of enlightened reformism, as well as liberal revolution. Debates in cafés or at the parliament, collective reading of political books, pamphlets, and press at the *gabinetes de lectura* (reading clubs), political discussions in the nightly *salones* and *tertulias* (social gathering), were some of the places and ways in which the public sphere was shaped.

However, the setting for the private sphere may be located in the hidden sociocultural practices of reproduction. It essentially concerns daily life decisions and strategies for the continuation of the family. "Most people,"

---

[12] On the concept of public/private see Senntet (1978: 16–17); Habermas (1989: chap. V); Davidoff and Hall (1987: 29f. and 454).

[13] In Spain, the generic term for the supporters of the Enlightenment was *Ilustrados*. Carr (1966: 175–176).

[14] As early as 1722 Melchor de Macanáz advised the future inheritor of the Spanish crown "to send every year two or three confidential advisers throughout Europe to get information on new scientific, political, and state affair developments." See M. Macanáz. 1722. "Auxilios para bien gobernar una monarquía católica." Quoted by Moreno Alonso (1989: 32). Alberto Lista, in his *Elogio de Floridablanca*, written in 1808, lamented the corruption of the Spanish administration which "contributed toward diminishing our political consideration in Europe," as well as the scientific and cultural backwardness of the Iberian peninsula when "arts and sciences had already reached a high level of perfection in the cultured nations of Europe." See A. Lista. 1809. Elogio histórico del Serenísimo Sr. D. José moñino, conde de Floridablanca . . . Quoted by Moreno Alonso (1989: 174).

as Gerald Sider has pointed out, "think about the future. They think about growing up, or old; about their children, present, past, and to come; about their parents; about personal and public events, occasions, festivals, and holidays, coming and past; about issues that we abstractly call "economic trends" and "political processes"; about the condition of their material possessions in conjunction with their needs and wants; about their relations to and with other people, and what is happening in these relations. And they watch and listen to their kith, kin, and others grapple with the same topics."[15] Thus, private discourse can be defined as the multiplicity of solutions implemented by individuals and groups, linked by affinity ties, to the challenges of everyday life. What make these answers different from the public discourse is the existence of affective conditions for their determination. In the case of the middle and upper classes, affective conditions are mainly determined by a will to preserve social domination.[16]

Private and public discourses can intersect, but both also have independent dynamics. Because private discourse concerns family reproduction and social domination, it is made up not only by objective categories such as wealth or legal status but also by more subjective ones like personal beliefs and fears, habits and customs, norms, and values: all those structures contained in what Bourdieu called the area of cultural and symbolic capital. While the dynamics of public discourse do not affect individuals or groups in the short term, private dynamics may have immediate consequences for the continuation of families in immediate generations. As a result, groups and individuals may adopt radical positions in the public sphere while at the same time remaining reluctant to advance changes that might alter their personal lives and the lives of their offspring. In societies with a good deal of social polarization – as was the case of Spain in the first half of the nineteenth century – the gap between public and private discourses becomes even greater. Because of the fast transformations of political culture in Spain after 1750, the distance between public and private discourses of the society was even more obvious. As a contemporary of the Spanish enlightened reformers pointed out, "ideas have changed, it is true, but only among the writers . . . . the people's ideas remain always immutable."[17]

In Spain, as in most of continental Europe between 1789 and 1848, the language of estates was substituted by the language of class in public

---

[15] Sider (1986: 3).
[16] On the concept of domination, see Bourdieu (1988b: 251); Kontos (1975: 116–132); Gould (1983).
[17] Palacio Atard (1964: 69). Quoted by I. A. A. Thompson (1991: 77).

Habitus, solidarity, and authority

discourse.[18] Certainly the word "class" had been frequently used by writers and politicians before that period, but in a way that suggested the combination of status and wealth. The use of class as a legal category associated with natural law and political economy emerged only at the beginning of the nineteenth century.[19] Merit and freedom of choice were central themes of public discussion in the 1810–12 parliamentary debate that enacted the first Spanish liberal constitution.[20] The goal of most radical deputies was to implement a meritocratic society that avoided the negative experience of egalitarian Jacobinism. The constitution of 1812 introduced Spain for the first time to the principle of individual freedom by the legal abolition of old estate privileges. Therefore the return to estate society occurred only temporarily between 1814 and 1820, and so the language of class imposed its hegemony over political culture and legislative practices.

Despite the introduction of the principles of personal freedom and merit in the legal system, however, basic social relations in Spain during the first half of the nineteenth century were dependent upon privilege and a complex system of personal dependence. Privilege was no longer a legal category anymore, as under the old regime, but it remained a cultural value especially crucial to dominant economic and political groups. Social mobility usually was the product of familial and personal loyalties instead of equal opportunity. Because historical analysis has focused almost exclusively on objective categories such as class, estate, and institutional change, cultural relations have remained ignored. As C. C. Harris has put it, "because a type of institutionalized group or practice disappears or is absent of a society, it does not follow that *that aspect* of social relations is absent, nor does it excuse us from investigating its significance in the life of that society at either the theoretical or cultural level. If it were true (which it is not) that history

---

[18] In England, John Millar was the first to establish a link between wealth and social position in defining social categories. His division of English people into three main groups ("landlords, capitalists, and laborers") according to the distribution of national wealth anticipated Marxist conceptions of class. David Ricardo and his "Socialist" school (William Thompson, Thomas Hodgskin, and others) were the first to elaborate an economic theory of class divisions. After the Ricardians, the analytical concept became an instrument for social and ideological conflict. See Perkin (1969: 27).

[19] The concept of "class" (vs. estates) became a loaded term in European political culture and legal practice due to the connotations it derived from the experiences of the French Revolution. The French revolutionaries developed a new political rhetoric, inspired by the enlightened philosophes who turned to the principles of reason and nature as their ideological foundations. As Lynn Hunt has pointed out, this new political culture provided the bases for "a new social and political order in which careers ought to be based on talent, rather than birth; that there should be no special privileges for castes, corporations or particular places; and that participation through elections and officeholding should be open to a broadly based citizenry" Hunt (1984: 213–14).

[20] Moreno Alonso (1989: 180); Pérez Ledesma (1991: 189).

records the replacement of feuding descent groups by antagonistic classes, it would not follow that the social relations in class societies are not structured by kinship categories and obligations, nor that relations in descent group societies were not hierarchically organized in terms of property. The societies concerned are differentiated, not in terms of the presence or absence of structural elements, but in the manner of their articulations."[21]

In this chapter and the next I will provide some examples which support these assertions as applied to Spanish society between 1750 and 1850. These examples refer to some Spanish families among the middle and upper classes, some of them well known for their involvement in liberal politics. Analyzing personal behaviors and public positions of their most prominent members, I will illustrate the contradictions between public and private discourses. Using these examples I attempt to demonstrate how social relations among the groups that made possible the Spanish revolution were not determined by conflict among antagonistic classes. To the contrary, social practices resulted from the will of already established dominant networks of families and friends. Although Spain toward 1850 possessed a new legal framework for the definition of social functions, basic old regime sociocultural practices of domination remained virtually unaltered.

A culture of domination

As I pointed out in the introduction to this book, I consider social relations always to be relations of domination, whether among individuals or among groups. The history of the Cabarrús family, my first example, illustrates how social groups who implemented political and social reforms in Spain euphemized their domination by means of a traditional culture based on the practice of loyalty and mutual solidarity, despite their public defense of freedom of choice and equal opportunity. This euphemized culture of domination can mainly be traced in the study of the private sphere rather than in manifestations of public life. Because most historians have focused on the public role of Francisco de Cabarrús, his life has been portrayed as a paradigmatic example of the new Spanish bourgeoisie that was imposing a novel form of domination.[22] I intend to demonstrate the flaws of this interpretation. Cabarrús's embracing of enlightened liberal ideas was new,

---

[21] C. C. Harris (1990: 3). On the persistence of pre industrial corporate practices in the construction of nineteenth-century working-class consciousness, see Sewell (1980: 277f.).

[22] Examples of this approach to the Cabarrús's experiences are Maravall (1990: 13); Elorza (1970); Garcia Regueiro (1987: 45–48).

but his social performance was not. Cabarrús represents not the new bourgeoisie but rather the self-reproduced provincial elite that became aware of the socioeconomic backwardness of Spain and decided to work for the modernization of its life. Contradictions between political and social practices – that is to say, between public and private practices – which characterized the historical performance of this elite stemmed from the fact that they did not constitute an alternative social class. They instead had to fight for the maintenance of their social domination while at the same time implementing reforms. This would prove to be a very difficult task in the extremely polarized society of Spain between 1750 and 1850.

The ambivalent experiences of Francisco de Cabarrús

Francisco de Cabarrús, first Count of Cabarrús and founder of the Spanish branch of the family, was born in Bayone (French Basque country) in 1752. Around his sixteenth birthday he was sent to Valencia, in the Spanish Mediterranean coast, to complete his training as an international merchant. The Cabarrús family owned a commercial firm established in Bayone specializing in trade and exchange operations between France, Spain, and the Spanish colonies. The firm held business connections in Valencia, Cádiz, and several seaport towns in America. One of these connections was with the commercial house of Antonio de Galabert, a family originally from Montpelier and established in Valencia, where the young Cabarrús was sent. The years of Francisco's apprenticeship in Valencia remain obscure. Given what we know about the sagacity of our character and his special aptitude for business, one can imagine that he was able to rise easily in the Galabert business. All we know of those years is his romance with Antonia, one of his boss's daughters, and their secret marriage. The secrecy was motivated by the young age of the couple, not by the choice of partners. After all, the wedding of the most outstanding *mancebo* (apprentice) with some member of his master's family was a normal step in the business community. Despite this premature marriage, which caused temporary disappointment for the Galaberts, the future relations between father and son-in-law were always cordial and both families shared business throughout their lives.

With familial support both from the Cabarruses and the Galaberts, Francisco and Antonia moved to Madrid around 1772. Once in the capital Cabarrú managed some soap factories that belonged to his in-laws and was quickly accepted into the commercial networks that controlled the city provision trade. This rapid integration into the town business world was only possible thanks to his family connections and the help that he found among the small, but influential, community of French bankers that operated in Madrid.[23] In a few years Cabarrús had business going in the most profitable economic sectors available at the time in Spain: the state and city provisioning, the wool trade, and the operations of exchange with other European countries, especially France.[24] His intelligence and special ability as a businessman allowed him to make a fortune in a brief period of time.[25] In less than ten years Cabarrú owned a luxurious house on Fuencarral Street, complete with an orchard private garden in the back, a symbol of distinction reserved only for aristocratic mansions. He always shared his table with friends, kin, or subordinates at dinner or lunch time, and never missed guests for his nightly social gatherings or card play.

Unlike any other member of the French business community, Cabarrús was able to achieve an intense level of integration into Madrid social circles. Cabarrús did everything possible to be accepted into private *ilustrado* social gatherings. He probably used a letter of presentation – as was customary – written by one or another of his friends and kin in the business community. His admission in 1776 to the elective Economic Society of Madrid – the *Matritense*, as it was popularly known – exemplifies his ability to make the right contacts and his potential for public life. Two years later he met Jovellanos in the private social gathering that met almost every day at the house of Campomanes. The meeting marked the start of a long friendship between the two personalities and, to some extent, the confirmation of Cabarrús's public career.

In 1782, one year after Francisco de Cabarrús became a Spanish citizen, he was nominated to be the director of the Philippines Company and co-founder and director of the first Spanish National Bank. These nominations were obviously not coincidental occurrences but rather the result of a long lobbying process that began in 1778, when he submitted to the king a first *memorial* (project) to improve national finances. In 1784 he was nominated an *ad honorem* member of the National Treasury Council. Five years later the King honored him with the title of "Count of Cabarrús" in recognition of his services to the Crown. By 1790 Don Francisco was a very influential person inside the administration. His innovative ideas helped in the short

---

[23] About this community see Zylberberg (1983: 275–281).
[24] Tedde (1988: 36).   [25] AHN, Diversos, Serie General, leg. 7.

term to improve the finances of the state and created new facilities for public and private credit. At the same time, because innovators always eventually come up against opposition by traditional cliques, he quickly became a target for political attacks.[26]

The troubles began in 1790 and came from different fronts. First, the Inquisition initiated an inquiry against him after he presented his *Elogio de Carlos III* in the *Matritense*.[27] The document contained a fervent defense of enlightened ideas. Unfortunately, it came out at a critical moment, a few months after the beginning of the revolution in France. The case was dismissed thanks to the moderation of the General Inquisitor and the favorable attitude of one of the three prosecutors. Despite Cabarrús's initial good luck with the Inquisition his enemies soon counterattacked. This time the accusation was made by groups who were working with him in the service of the National Treasury. Although his attackers were ostensibly accusing him of mismanagement of the National Bank of San Carlos because of some terrible mistakes he made, behind these accusations there were obscure political and personal interests. Actually, Cabarrús was no more than a scapegoat in a political confrontation between the supporters and the opponents of the *ilustrado* policies of the first minister, the Count of Floridablanca.[28]

The Count of Lerena, Secretary of the Spanish Treasury, was the head of the group that opposed Cabarrús.[29] The Count of Floridablanca was the political patron of both Lerena and Cabarrús, in their public careers. However, with the passage of time, Lerena became distant from the Floridablanca clique. Most contemporary testimonies, whether or not they came from supporters of enlightened policies, presented the Count of Lerena as a disastrous administrator, a conservative politician, and a greedy person. He was not only unlearned, wrote Jovellanos, in most skills related to his administrative duties he was also rather vindictive with his benefactors.[30] Less impartial was the opinion of Queen Maria Luisa, who directly called him ruthless and compared Lerena's personality to an uncut diamond.

---

[26] The Count of Floridablanca, who in fact shared with Cabarrús many opinions related to economic reform, wrote in 1789 that "the audacity of his [Cabarrús's] discourse and his ardent imagination, reflected in his written works as well as in his acts, disappointed many people and caused the number of his opponents to increase." Quoted by Tedde (1988: 37).
[27] García Regueiro (1987). [28] Alcazar (1953: 95–99).
[29] AHN, Diversos, Serie General, leg. 14-A. The September 26, 1855, edition of the newspaper *Eco del Comercio* printed a brief biography of Francisco de Cabarrús.
[30] Quoted by Sarrailh (1957: 86).

The museum of families

The confrontation between Lerena and Cabarrús came as a result of the way in which Cabarrús managed the bank of San Carlos and the relationship between this institution and the public Treasury.[31] In 1784 the bank reached an agreement with the Treasury to guarantee the provisioning of the national army. The state traditionally had awarded contracts for the provisioning of the army to independent businessmen who were free to find their own suppliers. The intervention of the bank implied a sort of nationalization of this economic sector. Moreover, the royal administration, inspired by the *ilustrado* political philosophy, encouraged the bank to find suppliers inside of Spain as a way to strengthen the national economy. The logic was accepted by Cabarrús and by the directors of the bank, but its outcome was disastrous. In the short term Spanish manufactures turned out to be more expensive than the same products acquired in international markets. In addition, prices of cereal grew up from 20 to 60 reales/fanega between 1784 and 1789 because of a series of poor crops.[32] As a consequence, the bank and the Treasury started to lose money, and incurred delays in the arrival of the supplies. In order to avoid any of the blame for this affair, Lerena accused the bank of incompetent management and its director, the count of Cabarrús, of being corrupt.

It is true that the Cabarrús commercial firm, in partnership with Aguirre (another financier of French background), had business deals with the bank of San Carlos, most of them in relation to army provisioning. There is no doubt that Cabarrús was taking advantage of his public position to favor his own financial firm. His father-in-law was also a member of the board of directors of the bank, and both Galabert and Cabarrús made commercial arrangements with other kin, friends, and fellow countrymen, using the bank as a platform. But this was not an exceptional practice for the time and is, after all, what the client economy was all about. Cabarrús was hardly alone in using his position as director of the bank to protect his and his family's interests. Given that Cabarrús's practices were not atypical, it would seem that the attacks of the count of Lerena were motivated by political or personal reasons rather than moral convictions. The enemies of Floridablanca chose Cabarrús because he was an easy target due to the cumulation of mistakes from his public performance. The culminating error of Cabarrús was his advice to the bank that led to a large investment in French public debt months after the revolution. Cabarrús, misguided by his

---

[31] A detailed description of this confrontation can be found in Tedde (1986: chap. 7).
[32] Castro (1987: 308–317). One fanega equals 55.20 liters.

own political convictions, put too much confidence in a future of stability and prosperity for revolutionary France. Reality was very different. In a matter of months political turmoil caused a fast devaluation of public stocks. The Spanish National Bank suffered seriously from this devaluation and Cabarrús seemed to many to be personally responsible for the financial disaster.

The exact purpose of the trip to France that Cabarrús was preparing in the month of June of 1790 remains unclear. Whether he was planning a routine business trip, as he alleged in his passport application, or attempting to extract capital from Spain and to escape justice is not an important matter.[33] By that time Cabarrús had already lost his battle with the count of Lerena. On the morning of the 25 June an *Alcalde de Corte* – as the criminal judges were called in Madrid – arrested Cabarrús in his house on Fuencarral street. Although the accusations were very confused and full of inconsistencies, the count remained in jail for the next five years, until his case was completely dismissed in 1795, the accused being declared innocent.

After the prosecution the public and private life of the count of Cabarrús was full of ups and downs, but it never recovered the shape it had before. He was restored to his position on the National Treasury Council and received a compensation of 6 million reales which he never fully collected because of the persistent public deficit.[34] He also obtained substantial contracts from the Spanish crown for the supply of the army, as well as advantageous privileges in the officially controlled trade channels with the colonies.[35] In 1797 Cabarrús was nominated minister of the State Council – the institution responsible for the design of Spanish international policies – and plenipotentiary ambassador of Spain to the French Republic. After the French invasion in 1808 he joined the group of Spaniards who collaborated with the Napoleonic government. It was an obvious choice for a person who firmly believed in the politics of the Enlightenment, not to mention his French background. He died in 1810 as National Secretary of the Treasury. His descendants once again suffered accusations and persecution after 1814, when the Spanish monarchy was restored, but this is part of another story that I will detail further along in this chapter.

[33] AHN, Diversos, Serie General, leg. 7. The testimonies collected by Ortega Costa and García Osma lead one to believe that Cabarrús intended to leave Spain permanently or at least for a long period of time. Quoted by Tedde (1988: 197).
[34] AHN, Diversos, Serie General, leg. 14-A.
[35] Included in the privileges that Cabarrús obtained from the Spanish crown was a special permit to bring African slaves to the American colonies. AHN, Diversos, Serie General, leg. 16.

The museum of families

As a businessman Cabarrús represents a common pattern in the Spanish business community of his time. He also, however, showed throughout his career some signs of distinctiveness. His originality was, no doubt, due to his strong political convictions. In this the enemies of Cabarrús severely misinterpreted his intentions. His economic behavior was that of an ardent politician, not a cautious banker. In 1788, after the death of King Charles III, he declared a substantial personal fortune evaluated in 12 million reales. Most of this money was made in the traditional activities of the Madrid client economy: the city and state provisioning, the arrangement of interest loans to the government, and the international exchange operations.[36] Thus, the first steps of Cabarrús's economic career were taken in a very conventional manner: with the aid of his family, friends, and *paisanos*, who helped him integrate himself in the classic controlled markets of the city. Even the few testimonies available on how the count used his surplus money those years do not provide any deviation from what one could consider a normal economic behavior.[37] However, after 1790 he demonstrated an extraordinary energy and sense of innovation more evident in his economic activities than in his political achievements. It seems that the political failure of the 90s encouraged him to find the way to demonstrate in practice the merits of his politicoeconomic projects. After the political failure, his economic strategies lacked the rationality that characterized the banker and businessmen during the 80s, becoming the strategies of the politician he was until his death. As a consequence he never attained the level of personal fortune that he had during the good years.

Although Cabarrús never abandoned the patronage of the state during most of his business operations, after 1795 he used this patronage to develop innovative economic projects. A few months after his confinement the count returned to his traditional mercantile activities. As a gesture of compensation for the years that he spent in jail the king granted him and his son a

---

[36] For instance, between 1781 and 1782 the financial firm of Cabarrús-Aguirre lent the crown a total of 55 million reales with commissions between 1% and 6% plus 0.5 monthly interest until redemption. According to the contract, these loans were to be redeemed in Cuba with silver from the colonial mines, cash from the colonial trade taxes, and other colonial goods; or the money was to be returned in *vales reales* – a sort of public debt which was used at times for economic transactions. AHN, Diversos, Serie General, legs. 3 and 17.

[37] AHPM, P. 29733, p. 653. This document addresses the desire of Cabarrús to guarantee the future well-being of his family by the means of the entailment of his property. The property to be entailed was land and real estate acquired by purchases between 1772 and 1780 in the region of Valencia.

Habitus, solidarity, and authority

special permission to ship African slaves to the Spanish colonies.[38] The count also received 6 million reales from the Spanish national Treasury. Cabarrús used part of this compensation to finance one of his most ambitious projects: the development of irrigated farming. Inspired by French and English literature on innovative agronomy, the *ilustrados* developed several programs to improve the productivity of Spanish agriculture.[39] This had been the intention of the Count of Cabarrús when as early as 1788 he began purchasing land in the hinterlands of Caraquiz and Uceda, both villages located to the north of Madrid in an area crossed by the Jarama and Lozoya rivers.[40] Indeed, his agrarian projects were well under way before his prosecution. Nevertheless, he went back to them in 1796 looking, as he wrote later, for a more secure and useful investment. In February of the same year the count had submitted a long report (*memorial*) to the king that detailed the advantages of implementing a policy that funded the construction of irrigation canals to improve agricultural output. The report included some specific projects, among them one to begin the construction of a canal between the Lozoya and the Jarama rivers. His lobbying could not have been more successful; within a month of receiving the *memorial* the king created a special superintendency to study Cabarrús's projects. By July the National Treasury reached an agreement with a Dutch commercial firm to borrow 50 million reales to subsidize some of the projects. By December the Lemaur brothers – French engineers hired by Cabarrús – were already working on the construction of what would be known as the Uceda irrigation canal.[41] In between, Cabarrús purchased extensive lots of land located in the areas where he thought canals would be constructed.

It was obviously no coincidence that the state was subsidizing the construction of an irrigation canal on the recently acquired properties of the Count of Cabarrús. An 1804 document written by the count explained that the project responded to a long-term calculated strategy of investment. "Both enterprises, the purchase of land and the construction of the canal," wrote Cabarrús, "held great appeal for me. First, because they constituted a

---

[38] Cabarrús was one of the few Spanish merchants who participated in a trade controlled by the English. There is evidence that he obtained permission from the Spanish crown on several occasions to ship slaves from Africa to the American colonies and return colonial products to Spain. AHN, Diversos, Serie General, legs. 16 and 53.

[39] In 1781 Cabarrús sent several letters to the Count of Floridablanca in which he explained for the first time his agronomic projects. AHN, Diversos, Serie General, leg. 5. Regarding the content and inspiration of these projects see García Sanz (1974: 34–36).

[40] Zylberberg (1979: 418).   [41] AHN, Diversos, Serie General, leg. 5.

good example for the public utility, the persistent goal of my life. Second, because they favored a natural tendency of my personality: the constant search for retirement. Third, because they assured a consistent position in case of new possible political troubles. Finally, because they served to kill the vulgarity that many people attribute to those who, only by a chance of destiny, have been born out of these realms (country)."[42] In sum, the logic of Cabarrús's investment practices after 1796 responded to a calculated strategy determined by political beliefs as well as the desire to achieve social status.

As often occurs with ideological projects, there existed a high risk of failure when put into practice. This is exactly what happened with Cabarrús's project. A miscalculation of the amount of time it would take to finish the irrigation canal, poor planning on the part of the engineers, shortages of financial resources from the National Treasury due to bureaucracy and the public deficit, and difficulties in finding skilled manual labor, were, according to Cabarrús, the main reasons for the failure.[43] A more detailed inquiry into the characteristics and development of the project disclose some miscalculations that call into question its economic viability. Its failure can be attributed to structural reasons, not to poor planning and failures in its implementation. Productive outputs were very low due to the poor land quality, lack of adequate technology, and adverse ecology.

Cabarrús nonetheless tried his luck at new economic adventures under the patronage of the state until the end of his life. This time he shifted from agrarian capitalism to a sort of planned industrial capitalism. Because of health problems he had to move to a bathing resort in the Catalan Pyrenees. Once there he familiarized himself with the industrial economy of the region and decided to work for the development of this sector. He very quickly developed a project for the construction of a transportation canal along the Llobregat River. He intended to transport coal from the Pyrenees to Barcelona. In 1805 he formed a company made up of one architect, an engineer, a French banker, and himself to undertake with project. At the same time he sent *memoriales* to the monarch looking for financial support.[44] The project, however, was interrupted by the French invasion, which precipitated the count's renewed involvement in political affairs. Thus, the Catalan projects died with the count in 1810. There is evidence, however,

---

[42] AHN, Diversos, Serie General, leg. 7.   [43] AHN, Diversos, Serie General, legs. 4 and 7.
[44] AHN, Diversos, Serie General, legs. 5 and 12.

that he made some investments in the Catalan cotton and pottery industries which brought few returns.

A cursory look at the patrimony that he left upon his death indicates the true nature of his economic strategies. After 1795 the bulk of his investments were in land and real estate, most of it related to his agricultural projects. He owned an estimated capital of 15.5 million reales, but most of this money was held as in mortgages and credits owed by the state. Because of this the distribution of the fortune among his descendants took a long time and was not completed until 1879.[45]

Description of Cabarrús's public life and business strategies show once again the duality of his social biography. On the one hand he seems to be champion of enlightened ideas, a politician who was prosecuted because of the audacity of his economic reforms, and, on occasions, an unusual businessman who compromised his surplus in favor of achieving patriotic goals. From this perspective, he could be seen – and most historians have preferred this interpretation – as an avant-garde leader of the Spanish revolutionary bourgeoisie. On the other hand, he was not exactly a model of the self-made entrepreneur; to the contrary, he constantly used the influence of his family, friends, and fellow countrymen to attain economic power. He, like no one else, was able to control the mechanisms of Madrid's client economy in which favor was the main element, and, despite his radical defense of the laissez-faire policy, he constantly used the state as a protective umbrella to ensure business security and the protection of his kin and friends.

A similar duality can be found in comparing Cabarrús's public social thought to his private social behavior. In many ways his *Letters about the Obstacles which Nature, Opinion and Law Present to the Pursuit of Happiness*, written in 1795, represented a break with moderate *ilustrado* reformism and initiated a new revolutionary way of thought.[46] However, many of the postulates he developed in his writings were in direct contradiction with his private behavior. In a broad sense, what he exalted in his written work was a society and state based on respect for individual values as an alternative to the predominant autocratic, transpersonalist conception of power and social relations. This approach implied a criticism of the foundations of the society of estates and, especially, to the role of the aristocracy in that society. Let us focus on the fourth letter, where Cabarrús questions the usefulness of

---

[45] AHN, Diversos, Serie General, leg. 49.   [46] Maravall (1990: 7–8).

The museum of families

hereditary nobility and the institution of the *mayorazgo* as means of preserving the continuity of lineage to study the contradictions of his dual discourse.

"Is the inherited nobility useful or necessary to the constitution of the state? Are those institutions which preserve the social function of the nobility useful or necessary?" These were the basic questions around which Cabarrús developed his argument.[47] He wanted to find an answer for them in the terms of utility, reason, and nature. These three words constituted central concepts of *ilustrado* thought. By utility the *ilustrados* meant that which was in the public interest. What they considered useful were those thoughts and actions that aimed to provide service of the community. "Reason" lacked the metaphysical content attributed by philosophical systems of the seventeenth century, becoming something more trivial.[48] That which was rational, associated with a view in which experience, rather than emotions or magic, was the fundamental criterion for the solution of problems. Nature, of course, meant for the *ilustrados* the original quality of things, the basic egalitarian condition of the human being before social integration. In the name of reason, utility, and nature our author passionately refuted the idea that a person could inherit a sense of virtue, intelligence, and the capacity to serve the community, qualities traditionally associated with the social function of the nobility.[49] These were qualities that any individual could attain. Cabarrús argued that no political society should be allowed to prevent the natural development of primitive human means such as hope, nature, and fear. Political systems that controlled those natural social mechanisms were acting against public utility.

Cabarrús was not denying the social role of the nobility as an educated and virtuous elite. He was instead questioning the process of its selection. In an appeal to common sense, civic morality, and public utility, he proposed a nobility based on personal merit, intellectual commitment, and freedom of choice. That new nobility should be recruited according to individual backgrounds in public service, education, talent, and personal virtue. In the social language of Cabarrús the word "merit" played a central role. Merit meant liberation, utility, and progress, while privilege was associated with uselessness, social injustice, and tyranny. Merit was also opposed to favoritism, bias, partiality, and nepotism – all of the practices that prevented the

---

[47] Cabarrús (1990: 127). All quotations in reference to this letter come from the 1990 edition.
[48] Maravall (1990: 9). [49] Cabarrús (1990: 127).

achievement of public happiness. "Select the nobility according to the personal merit of the individuals," wrote Cabarrús, "instead of by the merit of their ancestors."[50] In the future all noble nominations should be considered as a service to the state and consequently limited to the life of the nominees. Any talented person may have the opportunity to reach a position in the army, the church, and the service of the monarch, independent of the social condition of his or her family.

Criticism of the role of nobility in general, and the performance of the Spanish nobility in particular, was commonplace in *ilustrado* thought. It was, indeed, common to all European Enlightenment thought. However, nobody in eighteenth-century Spain went as far as Cabarrús in his criticism. Not only did he suggest a new code of ethics for the selection of the nobility, but he also proposed radical changes in basic social institutions as the patriarchal family and marriage in order to accomplish his goals. Regarding the former, Cabarrús called for a new legislation on paternal emancipation. "Once the individual reaches emancipation by law," wrote the count, "he becomes the ruler of his own happiness and destiny, the only limitation to his freedom being is duty to public utility."[51] Nobody can oppose a marriage decision when it is based on the affinity of temperaments and dispositions. "Nature," he added, "proves to be in opposition to preestablished arrangements as well as basic principles of religion too. Political society points to the division of fortunes to avoid social unbalance. Custom claims for the sanctity of marriage, a free election of the partner based on love as its best guarantee."[52] Cabarrús's defense of affective individualism is in my opinion one of the most revolutionary issues addressed in his writings.[53]

One last legal proposition was essential to Cabarrús's crusade for the establishment of a meritocratic nobility: the abolition of the entailed *mayorazgo* as a legal form of property transmission. The *mayorazgo* was precisely the legal warranty for the continuation of noble lineages; its abolition then proved to be essential. Nevertheless, as we saw in Chapter 3 this was an institution that was already in decline by the time that Cabarrús was clamoring for its suppression. On this issue the count was simply echoing the complaints made by most of his fellow *ilustrados*.

---

[50] Ibid., p. 132. [51] Cabarrús (1990: 133).
[52] Ibid., p. 133.
[53] On the impact of affective individualism in social relations see Stone (1979).

Cabarrús never intended an immediate destruction of the established order but rather its progressive transformation. "Should we infer," he wrote, "from the uselessness and inconvenience of the inherited nobility that it is to be radically destroyed? Not at all. Such a scenario would provoke unnecessary social unrest. Let the old nobility be as it has been thus far, but let us at the same time create the conditions for its further transformation. Time and law will do the rest, for in the end no anachronistic institution can survive."[54] Thus, although the crux of Cabarrús's proposals was revolutionary, he intended a gradual implementation by means of legal reforms. Nevertheless, his public discourse clearly attacked the strongest pillar of Spanish social order: the self-reproduction of its nobility.

Most scholars have emphasized Cabarrús's critique of the established social order and his influence on nineteenth-century revolutionary liberalism. Indeed, his ideas on personal merit were at the heart of the political discussion that took place in the revolutionary Cortes (Spanish parliament) of 1812. No author, however, has pointed to the fact that in December of 1780 Francisco de Cabarrús established his own family entailed *mayorazgo* before a notary in Madrid. When Cabarrús made this decision he was thinking of the continuation of his family, the future of his children's status, and the prestige of his lineage. Obviously, in this private document there was no room for his defense of meritocracy and equal opportunity. His intention was very specific: "to firmly establish his children with the honor and permanence which corresponded to his family."[55] Here it seems that honor does not result from public recognition of personal value but was rather a privilege to be inherited by people whose only merit was to have held his family name. Indeed, the legal document imposed the obligation to use the last name Cabarrús to any future inheritor of the *mayorazgo*. The count wanted to ensure the continuation of his lineage by means of family inheritance. Ironically, the radical critic of traditional estate society was acting in defense of the most traditional mechanism of social reproduction: the privilege of belonging to a kinship system. Although the *mayorazgo* was never approved, his attempt makes evident the discrepancy between Francisco de Cabarrús's discourse and his actions.

There is no doubt that our man was answering to a natural impulse common to all human beings who have a family: to care about the future of

---

[54] Cabarrús, op. cit. p. 132.   [55] AHPM, P. 20733, p. 653.

Habitus, solidarity, and authority

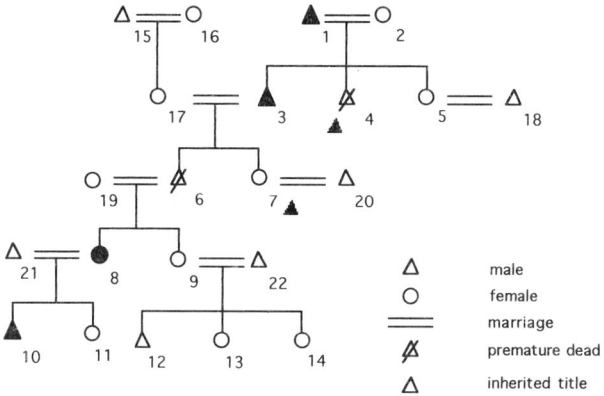

1. Francisco de Cabarrús, first Count of Cabarrús. 2. Antonia Galabert. 3. Domingo Cabarrús Galabert. 4. Francisco. 5. Teresa, princess of Caraman-Chimay, died in 1835. 6. Domingo Cabarrús Quilty, died 1834. 7. Paulina Cabarrús Quilty. 8. Paulina Cabarrús Kirkpatrick. 9. Enriqueta Cabarrús Kirkpatrick. 10. Cipriano Fernández Angulo, fourth Count of Cabarrús and Vizcount of Rambouillet. 11. Maria del Carmen Fernández Angulo Cabarrús. 12. Félix Vejarano Cabarrús. 13. María. 14. Antonia. 15. Tomás Quilty, Councilor of the General Treasure. 16. Francisca Cologán. 17. Rosa Quilty Cologán. 18. Prince Josef Rigout of Caraman. 19. Enriqueta Kirkpatrick. 20. Diego Martínez de la Rosa, lawyer. 21. Emiliano Fernández Angulo, landowner. 22. Félix Vejarano, lawyer and Count of Tajo.

Figure 6.1. Genealogy of the Cabarrús family, 1752–1900

his offspring. Nevertheless, he could have found other ways to accomplish this, at least ways that contradicted his moral principles less. His public proposals for the suppression of inherited nobility and the entailed *mayorazo* were, indeed, made in the name of a new morality, one which, according to him, should be based not on a tacit acceptance of a conventional code of ethics but instead on its sincere practice. In other words, this would be a moral practice opposed to the double standards that mostly characterized the social behavior of the Spanish elites. Double standards on morality, however, plagued Francisco de Cabarrús's life. We find two excellent examples of this in the way in which he acted at two decisive moments that would affect the future of his family: the election of a marriage partner for his son Domingo and the inheritance of his aristocratic title. Sometime in 1793, Domingo de Cabarrús Galabert – Don Francisco's eldest son (see Figure 6.1) – traveled to Andalusia to take care of some family business. On the journey he met Tomás Quilty, an older friend and political companion of his father.⁵⁶ Quilty invited Domingo to stay in his home, where he introduced him to his daughter Rosa, who would eventually become Domingo's wife. Tomás Quilty was a rich landowner, merchant, and entrepreneur of Irish origin established in Málaga.⁵⁷ His business was the export of agrarian products, especially sugar, grapes, lemons, and wine. Quilty was one of the most prosperous among the Málaga merchant community, made up mostly of foreign families.⁵⁸ The Cabarruses and the Quiltys had many ties in all spheres of life; both families had strong reasons for establishing close ties. In 1794 the Count of Cabarrús was attempting to alleviate the economic downfall provoked by his prosecution, and Quilty's money could have served as a warranty for his recovery. From the Quilty's vantage point, the fact that Cabarrús was regaining his position in the public sphere could serve the former's own political ambitions. Cabarrús's social status and public connections complemented Quilty's healthy financial status, circumstances which encouraged an engagement between the families. From February 1794 to March 1795 the Count of Cabarrús and Tomás Quilty exchanged correspondence to arrange the terms of the marriage between Domingo and Rosa. The arrangement is not exactly reminiscent of the passion of Romeo and Juliet. Domingo was eager to marry, but Rosa rejected the offer. It took several months of pressures and negotiations before Rosa accepted.

I have not found any evidence that points to the spontaneity, affectivity, and tenderness that the Count of Cabarrús was claiming should govern the free choice of marriage partners.⁵⁹ To the contrary, the abundant private correspondence among all subjects involved in the arrangement reeks of rigidity, coldness, calculation, and paternal control. There is no room for affectionate words, not a singe expression of individual tenderness. Indeed, the conjugal life of the couple was unaffectionate from the beginning. The first person to perceive this failure was Rosa's father, who reacted by accusing Domingo of being a capricious and irresponsible person.⁶⁰ It was obviously Rosa who suffered the worst consequences of this arranged marriage.

---

⁵⁶ Tomás Quilty, besides being a local notable – he held a position as *regidor perpetuo* (councilman for life) in Málaga – was minister in the National Council of the Public Treasury with Francisco de Cabarrús.
⁵⁷ AHN, Diversos, Serie General, leg. 46.
⁵⁸ See Villar (1982: 131).
⁵⁹ Notice that he was writing the letters at the same time he was negotiating his son's marriage of convenience.
⁶⁰ AHN, Diversos, Serie General, legs. 15, 42, 43, 47, and 49.

Habitus, solidarity, and authority

She led a lonely life in Málaga while her husband spent long seasons in Madrid. She died at the age of thirty-six while Domingo was in exile. The sad experience of Rosa Quilty best illustrates the nature of Francisco de Cabarrús's two-sided morality.

Double-standard morality can also be seen at another decisive moment in the life of Francisco de Cabarrús: the transmission of his aristocratic title to his son. I have no doubt that Cabarrús never felt uneasy about his title of count. It was a king's gift that recognized his services to the crown. He accepted it as acknowledgment of his talent and personal virtue and not the result of the reprobate privilege of inheritance. However, the same title has gone through an inheritance process almost a half dozen times from 1810 to today. It would be awkward, if not unfair, to blame Francisco de Cabarrús for the attitude of his successors regarding what he vehemently condemned: the right to inherit nobility. However, he never mentioned the merits of his son Domingo in reference to the inheritance of the title. Did he sincerely believe that Domingo fulfilled all requirements of talent, personal value, and public service that he demanded of one who was to hold an aristocratic title? Whether he believed it or not we have no evidence that he ever expressed it either publicly or privately. What we know indirectly through the opinions expressed by some of his contemporaries is that Domingo was not exactly an example of what his father would consider a talented man of merits. "He is an extravagant, whimsical, and arrogant person," wrote Tomás Quilty,

> who lives beyond his means using his wife's rents, that is to say, my money.... The entourage he took with him when he went to Cádiz some months ago was more appropriate for a duke; the entourage he brought with him on his way back was more appropriate for a prince.... One of his latest extravagances has been his decision to have a portrait of him and his wife painted, a caprice he cannot afford and which I have to pay for.... In the meantime, his father has not shown up with the money he had promised for the marriage.[61]

The animosity of Tomás Quilty toward his son-in-law was expressed throughout his daughter's marriage, until he died in 1804. Don Tomás could never stand the aristocratic costumes and tastes of Domingo. He was disappointed and felt cheated because, first of all, the son of the Count of Cabarrús showed no potential as a businessman or politician. He instead led

[61] AHN, Diversos, Serie General, leg. 47.

the life of a useless aristocrat. Second, he discovered that the capital promised by the Count of Cabarrús to the couple never arrived; thus, Domingo and Rosa were living entirely at the expense of the Quilty family. Things would change with the passage of time as Domingo took on more responsibilities in the Quilty business and in his own business. After all, he was only a twenty-year-old *señorito* (rich kid) when he married Rosa.

Despite his process of maturation, I do not think Domingo ever achieved the talent and the sense of service and discipline that characterized the life of his father. He served as Minister of the Public Treasury for a while under the Napoleonic government. As he explained in a document written in 1814, he reached this position thanks to the lobbying of his father.[62] After several years in exile and retirement to the properties inherited from his father and father-in-law, he returned to politics in 1834. This time he was nominated governor of the province of Palencia under the first liberal government of Francisco Martínez de la Rosa.[63] Once again, his return to politics was precipitated by familial connections rather than personal talent. His daughter Paulina had married Diego Martínez de la Rosa in 1818. When Francisco, Diego's brother, became prime minister both Diego and his father-in-law obtained political positions. Domingo de Cabarrús's term as governor was disastrous. In a matter of weeks his administrative style provoked strong opposition within the province. It is of course true that the politics of the time were extremely tense and polarized and that in such a mood it was almost impossible to implement any long-term program. Nevertheless, he was ejected from the provincial government in a matter of months, leaving behind a budget deficit and several gaps in its accounting. In the years that ensued he was accused of corruption and prosecuted, but thanks to the intervention of his kin and friends he was soon released.[64] Domingo de Cabarrús, already second Count of Cabarrús by right of inheritance, never returned to public life. Most of the fame that he attained during his life was due to his connections of family and friends, and he constantly used his surname as a magic tool to achieve social success and political power. He firmly believed in the inherent worth of his inherited aristocratic status as justification for respect and social domination. In 1816, for instance, our man complained because a public notary in Madrid was not using the title of count when addressing him in some private documents.

[62] AHN, Diversos, Serie General, leg. 9. [63] AHN, Diversos, Serie General, leg. 47.
[64] AHN, Diversos, Serie General, leg. 8.

His resentment was even stronger because this same notary was also improperly conceding a noble rank to Domingo's brother-in-law, his main enemy in those days.[65] In sum, Domingo was reproducing a culture that strongly contradicted his father's meritocratic philosophy. That was the culture transmitted by Francisco de Cabarrús to his son in the realm of their everyday private relations, a culture which obviously contradicted the ethics of his public discourse, but in the end the only practical behavioral code that the Cabarruses could use to maintain their social domination.

In fact, the principles expressed by Francisco de Cabarrús in his public discourse never took effect in the social practice of reproduction of his successors. Little by little, the family was becoming more aristocratic and less meritocratic. Domingo, the second Count of Cabarrús, had already followed the pattern of the traditional, dominant landed elite in the way that he conducted his social life and business strategies. Paulina Cabarrús Kirkpatrick, Domingo's daughter, was the third person to hold the aristocratic title. She married Emiliano Fernández Angulo, a land owner in the province of Cuenca and an obscure conservative politician.[66] Other branches of the family developed kinship ties within the old and new nineteenth-century aristocratic realm. At the beginning of the twentieth century the Cabarrús family was mainly one of lawyers and landowners, without any representation in the public sphere.

From the time of Francisco de Cabarrús the strategy of the family was oriented toward developing a combination of local power and a presence in Madrid. The Cabarrúses, like other ascendant Spanish families, turned their money and interests to the domain of agriculture.[67] They did so initially by attempting to create an entailed property, then later by starting a sort of agronomic experiment, and in the end, by becoming landowners through their linkage with other landed families. After all, land constituted the prevalent mean of production in Spanish economy. However, in turning their economic interests to agriculture, they also turned their vital experiences of social life. Although they practiced a fairly modern agrarian capitalism, they were forced to struggle for domination in traditional rural society. In the end they had no other choices but to accept the rules of tradition to ensure their continued authority. Something similar happened to their so-

---

[65] AHN, Diversos, Serie General, leg. 4.
[66] AHN, Diversos, Serie General, legs. 29 and 30.
[67] Héran (1990: 209f) provides an excellent case study of the development of family strategies of the landed elite in nineteenth-century Spain.

cial performance in the city. First they had to fight to find a place of strength in the Madrid client economy. Then, they had to struggle to maintain an equilibrium between urban influence and local dominations. Until Madrid changed its economic structure and the nature of its relation with its hinterland, the social composition of its elites would remain virtually unchanged. Consequently, cultural patterns of social behavior tended to favor traditional practices, despite the existence of new public discourses. Here, in part, lies the explanation to the ambivalent behavior of the Cabarrús family.

Local life and authority

Most of the people who controlled Madrid's political, social, and economic life were not born in the city. Some of them came from urban areas in the Spanish provinces, but the majority were born in rural towns far from the capital. Continuous demographic exchange between rural and urban worlds was one of the main characteristics of preindustrial societies.[68] It affected all social layers from the elites to the lower strata of society. Urban and rural populations actually became more stable once industrialization got under way, but in the meantime what prevailed was what David Reher has defined as a culture of mobility.[69] Table 6.1 shows how this traditional rural–urban interactive pattern characterized the composition of Madrid's politically and economically dominant groups. More than two-thirds of the individuals who make up the entire sample were born in rural areas. The other third came mainly from provincial capitals or large towns considered urban because of their functions as administrative and commercial regional centers, not because they were generating a style of life different from the one predominant in the countryside. Only a small portion of the elite was originally from any one of the three major Spanish urban centers of Madrid, Seville, and Barcelona.

Without a doubt, the reasons why these select groups decided to go to Madrid differed from the ones that motivated immigrants from the lower social ranks. Poor peasants from all around Spain were looking for a better life in the city. Their dream was to find a good master whom to serve or from whom to learn some kind of skill. However, bureaucrats, politicians, merchants, and financiers from the provinces were in most cases following a

[68] Poussou (1983: 27).
[69] Reher (1990: 299–304); Kertzer and Hogan (1985: chap. I).

Habitus, solidarity, and authority

Table 6.1. *Rural and urban origins of the Madrid middle and upper classes, 1750-1853* *

		%
1. Bureaucrats/Politicians		
Rural	165	58.10
Urban	90	31.69
Unknown	29	10.21
Total	284	
2. Merchants/Bankers		
Rural	174	76.00
Urban	30	13.10
Unknown	25	10.90
Total	229	
3. Professionals		
Rural	22	61.10
Urban	14	38.90
Unknown	0	
Total	36	
Total sample	549	

*Most individuals included under the category of "Politicians" were members of the Council of Ministers between 1800 and 1853. The category of professional includes lawyers, doctors, and pharmacists.
Source: Merchants.dat; Bankers.dat; Bureaucrats.dat; Professionals.dat; and Politicians.dat. See Appendix A.

tradition established by their families. As I have demonstrated in preceding chapters, most of them belonged to groups well settled in their places of origin or that, at least, held the necessary connections to fulfill an ascendant career. The origin of their wealth in most cases was the ownership of land. Their ultimate function, as Richard Herr has pointed out, was to link local dominant elites with central political power, a development that essentially explains the dynamics of Spanish history up to the 1930s.[70]

Understanding the interaction of rural and the urban realms is essential to making sense of the social and political experiences of dominant groups in nineteenth-century Spain. It explains some of the contradictory outcomes of modern Spanish history: the urge, on the one hand, to democra-

[70] Herr (1974: 57–59; 1978: 592 and 1989: 729).

tize political and social life by the groups who supported liberalism, and on the other hand the limits to this democratization process imposed by these same groups. This phenomenon also explains the sometimes ambivalent behavior of the political and economic elite regarding the modernization of social life – the experience of Francisco de Cabarrús provides a good example of this. At the base of these historical developments lies an economic explanation: the persistence of an agrarian economy and slow and incomplete industrialization. I would like to explore here some of its sociocultural implications.

I have intentionally used the word "interaction," rather than "dependency" or "subordination," to define rural–urban connections of the Spanish dominant groups. Provincial notables depended on the decisions made by the central government to retain control over local life, but at the same time central administrators were very concerned about the need to control local elites. Under absolutist rule the relation between these two sources of power was not always fully achieved. However, the liberal state reached an equilibrium that prevailed until the 1930s – what some historians have called the *Sistema Moderado* (Moderate System). The interest of the provincial elite in remaining connected to Madrid was not only a matter of personal status, familial prestige, or even a way of life. It was, above all, a matter of survival. Thus, the effects of this interactive system were not only reflected in the way in which political life was conducted. It could also be seen in the manner in which elites perceived and achieved social relations, more specifically, in the somewhat symbolic culture developed by the upper and middle classes to euphemize their domination.

To describe the elements that defined this culture, we should turn our attention once again to the domain of the private sphere. Publicly, first the *ilustrados* and later the *Liberales* praised the ideals of freedom, personal values, and egalitarianism. However, in their social practices most of them favored authority, familism patronage, and hierarchy.[71] In fact, what these dominant groups were doing was reproducing the prevalent culture of the Spanish rural community, a system of norms, meanings, values, and symbols aimed at the preservation of authority over inferiors and solidarity with their peers. The crux of this culture was not the relationship between classes but rather that between groups linked by ties of loyalty and deference. The instruments that determined social relations, as I already have pointed out,

---

[71] All of these being characteristic values of preindustrial societies. See Crone (1989: 99–117).

Habitus, solidarity, and authority

were family, friendship, neighborhood, and *paisanaje* (fellow countrymen's affinities) relationships. All these practices constituted habitus with a raison d'être of maintaining the traditional order of social domination.[72]

The problem is that the historian can barely find any open manifestations – in the form of declarations of principles or such – to define the nature of this habitus. Indeed, most public texts and political manifestations and actions during this period reflect just the opposite: public rejection of legal discrimination and authoritarianism. Scholars have linked this overt trend to the imposition of the bourgeois values as well as the urbanization of Spanish life.[73] However, manifestations of the underlying habitus remain hidden and only arise occasionally to the eyes of the historian. One of these few occasions occurred in the month of February 1816 and had as its protagonist once again Domingo de Cabarrús y Galabert, who had already become the second Count of Cabarrús.

Domingo de Cabarrús moved to Torrox with his family after the death of his father-in-law in 1804. Torrox is a small village in the southeast coast of Spain only a few miles from the city of Málaga.[74] In this western Mediterranean corner of the peninsula the Quiltys held large portions of land on which they cultivated a variety of products that were exported to Madrid and other European markets. A part of the land was vineyard that produced raisins and wine. Lemon and almond trees cultivated on the fertile hillsides provided another important portion of the products marketed by the Quiltys. The main feature of their agrarian enterprise, however, was the three sugar mills installed near the town, part of one of the few sugar production complexes in Europe at the time. The mills supplied themselves with sugar cane grown in the local fields. Some of the sugar was sold in the Madrid market, but portions were also sent to Marseille and Genoa. The contribution of the sugar produced in Málaga to the Spanish and European sugar market was always very small; actually, these Andalusian producers never could compete with their American counterparts, especially with these producers in Cuba. Nevertheless, they practiced an advanced form of

---

[72] Berdhal (1988: 44–76) provides a good example of habitus as a system of domination, using the case of the Prussian nobility between 1770 and 1848.

[73] In contrast, historians tend to understand the second half of the nineteenth century as a return to the domination of Spanish political life by the provincial agrarian oligarchies, establishing a sort of duality between both periods. To explain this paradox scholars recur to the use of the pact thesis. The new bourgeoisie established a tacit pact with the old landowning aristocracy to maintain law and order, thus eliminating the threat of a proletarian revolution.

[74] In the first half of the nineteenth century Torrox had about 4,100 inhabitants. See Madoz (1840: vol. XV, 112).

agrarian capitalism, and they provided an early but frustrated attempt at industrialization in southern Spain.[75]

The second count of Cabarrús spent his life between Torrox, Madrid, and Torrelaguna. In Torrox and Torrelaguna he had his estates, in Madrid his political interests. Torrelaguna is located only a few miles from Madrid, although the journey from the capital to Torróx took almost a week before the installation of the railroad at the end of the nineteenth century. The count lived most of the time in Madrid while his family stayed in Torrox. His son died there when he was only thirty-two; his daughter moved to Madrid after her marriage to Diego Martínez de la Rosa in 1818. The second and successive generations of Cabarrúses represent a clear example of the aforementioned landowning elite that had constant allegiance with both the capital and the village.

On February 12, 1816, the second Count of Cabarrús wrote a long personal letter to his son, also named Domingo (see Figure 6.1). Since the end of 1814 the only contact between father and son had been through private correspondence. The count, charged with collaborating with the Napoleonic regime, went into exile after the return of Ferdinand VII. The younger Diego was only fourteen years old when his father left Spain, a transcendental moment in the education of the person who would be the head of the Cabarrús family in the future. After a temporary stay in France and England, the Count of Cabarrús established his exile in Gibraltar, a place from where he could have better control of his family and businesses. Between January and March of 1816 he wrote daily letters – on some days he wrote two or three times – to his business agent, less frequently to his son, and almost never to his nineteen-year-old daughter.[76] This correspondence reflects the count's preoccupation with the perpetuation of his family and name. He was concerned, first of all, with his agent as the warrantor of this continuance in the short term, secondly with his son as the future head of the family, while the scarce communication with his daughter indicates the peripheral role played by women in the maintenance of the lineage.

These letters reveal how the count perceived the social role of his family while he was developing a strategy for controlling its future. Among them, the letter of February 12 deserves special attention because of its content and length. The content of the correspondence and, above all of this specific

[75] Unfortunately we know very little about this group; historians should pay more attention to them in future research.
[76] For further citations of these private letters, see: AHN, Diversos, Serie General, leg. 4.

letter, provide us with a fresh and direct picture of the culture of one representative family of Spanish liberalism. For this same reason it constitutes a perfect case study to analyze the habitus of the Spanish liberal dominant groups. In this private correspondence we find an unusual testimony in which a single agent defines, in simple, direct, and pragmatic terms, what ought to be the behavioral code of nineteenth-century elites that would allow the maintenance of their social domination.

In the advice given by Domingo de Cabarrús to his son there were two main scenarios in which aim the energies of social action: Torrox and Madrid. In the first, the emphasis was on the maintenance of authority, in the second the most important thing was the preservation of family influence. There was no separation between the two scenarios regarding the behavioral steps to follow, only a difference in the goals to pursue. In both scenarios, according to Don Domingo, any member of the family already held social recognition. That was the first series of values that the father was transferring to his son: "You arrived in the world under the auspices of a name, a family, and a fortune. You are the heir to the reputation, honor, uprightness, benevolence, private and public virtues of your ancestors." The message was very clear: because you are a Cabarrús, because you have been born inside of this family you already hold the necessary attributes to have a dominant position in society. The private advice of the second Count of Cabarrús radically contradicted the egalitarian principles of liberal ideology, a philosophy that he was publicly committed to defend just as his father before him had done. His private conception of the role of blood as an instrument to transmit social status was very traditional, if not reactionary.

With the acceptance of this principle of blood supremacy as a point of departure, the second Count of Cabarrús was also aware that its maintenance depended on the day-to-day behavior of each one of the family members, but especially on the social conduct of the head of the family. Conduct was a central word in the social discourse of our protagonist. Society already recognized the quality of the family. Most of the people of Torrox and Madrid, wrote Cabarrús, know "our goodwill disposition, our liberality, our talent, and our virtues," but to keep this cultural capital abreast, he told his son, you have to measure each one of your actions. This disposition may sometimes be contrary to "our convictions, habits, nature, and public interests. I know it is going to be difficult on occasions, but it is very important to be aware of the necessity to follow the rules imposed by religion, society, and business. In Spain people pay more attention to appearances than to the practice of virtue. This is the country of mimicry and hypocrisy." In this private social discourse Domingo de Cabarrús did not identify conduct with moral practice. He understood conduct as a symbolic instrument to keep and improve social prestige. H fatalistically recognized the prevalence of double standards in the moral practice of most Spanish people, but hypocritically advised his son to cultivate this culture of appearances. "It is not enough to be a good father, a good husband, a good son, or a good friend, what is most important is to convince the society that you really are like that, and that this is only possible with a scrupulous observation of social formality." Conduct in the private discourse of the second Count of Cabarrús had nothing to do with the values of modern individualism. It had more to do with a traditional conception of honor and *reputación* (reputation) which consisted most importantly with the acceptance of predefined models of symbolic behavior.[77]

In modern societies predefined models of behavior are considered intolerable restrictions on the expression of individuality. In the kind of society that the discourse of Cabarrús reveals, these predefined models were normal practice and necessary to maintain social equilibrium. That is why the language of social formality was so important. It was an instrument of the dominant groups to avoid social disruption and to preserve the established hierarchy. In the discourse of Don Domingo the language of social formality manifested itself in two basic practices, one symbolic and the other more empirical. The practice of symbolic actions was central in his advice: "I think," he wrote to his son, "that you did the right thing in adopting the local form of dress, but it has to be elegant. Make sure it is made with the best quality of material; although the form will be the same people must be able to recognize the refinement of your clothing. The workmanship is also very important: pick out the best tailor in the region, and I would suggest that you have your apparel made in Seville as I did, for it is very important that you not be censured for slovenliness. Also be very careful about the quality and external aspect of your harnesses and the trappings of your cart. Have them made in the city of Xeres, where you will find the most elegant and well-crafted work." Of symbolic value were also the count's complaints about the excessive weight of his son. To avoid obesity he advised an active life with no siestas, a restricted diet limited only to two meals a day, and, especially, the noble practices of hunting and horse riding. The overall

[77] On the meaning of honor and *reputación* in early modern Spain see Domínguez Ortiz (1979: 159); Maravall (1977: 17f.).

Habitus, solidarity, and authority

appearance of the household was of extreme importance. The count recommended maintaining three residences. The first was the one he already had in Torrox, located in the main square of the village because the owner has to live in the town. "It should always remain open, even when you are out of Torrox. This is the best way to communicate your continuous presence there, and the presence of your family." The second residence had to be located in Málaga; "You can use the house of your grandmother or just rent a decent but functional place." The last ought to be located in Madrid and "can be what was the main residence of your grandfather, Francisco de Cabarrús." Along with the household, the servants constituted an important symbol for prestige and family reputation. Because servants were part of the family "you should be very selective, always keeping a butler, a valet, and at least two maids, one of whom should be skilled at cooking. They must be honest, clean, and discreet. Avoid chatterboxes and gossipers. You should also hire a servant to keep in your confidence to protect you from dangerous situations. He has to be strong, preferably a young fellow who has served as a soldier or policeman. Be sure he is clean, good looking, courageous, and versed in fighting. Remember, the reputation of your servants, your reputation, and your house's reputation." The last recommendations of symbolic value were related to the practice of some forms of sociability. Visiting was extremely important: "Reserve Sundays for visits to the notable society of Málaga, as your maternal grandfather used to." Membership in formal religious and civil associations would guarantee control over public matters while at the same time being a sign of the Cabarrús's involvement in the life of the community.

The empirical aspect of Domingo de Cabarrús's language of social formality referred to the practice of patronage relationships. Friendship was the base of this kind of social practice. Even today, friendship remains a basic cultural form in Andalusian and Spanish social relations.[78] Friendship, normally an association between equals, transforms into patronage when a relationship becomes one of economic or power inequality.[79] At this point patronage is an institution for protection and corruption, a basic instrument to connect local authority with influence in provincial and central power institutions. Domingo Cabarrús identified patronage with *padrinazgo* (godfathership) and bribery. It was, according to the count, a necessary practice to succeed in the Spanish sociopolitical system: "a man

---

[78] Uhl (1987: 23f.).
[79] Pitt Rivers (195: 140); Campbell (1974: 224f.).

with only the protection of his personal assets is a lost man." In order to achieve protection our man advised the consolidation of a network of friends in a hierarchical scale, from the village to the capital. "I would like you," the letter to his son says, "to follow in your grandfather and my footsteps in this matter. Try to have correspondence with at least one of the most prominent persons in Madrid, another in Granada, and preserve friendship with the most possible number of local authorities in Málaga. Even more important is good relations with the people in their service, especially their personal secretaries and clerks. Do not forget every year at Christmas time to send sugar, raisins, rum, wine, and sweet potatoes to your protectors."

Cabarrús's understanding of social formality in both symbolic and empirical forms reveals his will to maintain the traditional social order of the old Spanish society. And this was a society based on the supremacy of status, hierarchy, subordination, protection, and corruption.[80] This is especially clear in his conception of the social relations inside of the local community and his role as the dominant agent. Authority and paternalism formed the key discursive values regarding the relations within the society of Torrox. Paternalism toward his subordinates, about three hundred families according to his own estimation, was of utmost importance. Authority over everyone in the community was central, especially over those who represented the middle strata of the society, because they could constitute a threat to his domination. When speaking about his relationship to his subordinates, his language becomes even more archaic. For instance, he never addressed the people who worked for him as his employees or his salaried workers but rather as his servants. There is no doubt that the nature of the labor agreements was purely capitalistic, that is to say, based in a contractual relation freely arranged according to the conditions of the market. However, labor relations were defined by the culture of hierarchy and service prevalent in Torrox society. In Cabarrús's discourse labor incentives played a role, but it was a secondary one. What prevailed was a paternalistic conception of labor relations: "be generous with your servants and with the poor people of the village in general. Help them with, surgical and medical expenses when you consider it necessary. You can do this by paying a yearly retainer to the doctors and surgeons in the village. Visit people when they are sick and help them on these occasions with food and solace. This is the appropriate

---

[80] On the role of corruption in the old society, see Rubinstein (1987: 265f.).

Habitus, solidarity, and authority

conduct for a gentleman and it agrees with the principles of religion while at the same time helping to create a favorable image among the common people in the village."

Maintenance of authority, however, was the main advice in the private discourse of Domingo de Cabarrús. In modern liberal societies authority ideally results from a compromise between the different powers that constitute the political and social body. In old regime society authority stemmed from the concentration of power in a leader or an elite who negotiated power through custom or religion, never in a political contract. Cabarrus's conception of authority coincides with the latter. "People in Torrox are wayward and false – they have to be controlled. If you make them prosperous their response will not be to please you but rather to take your position. As soon as a Torroxeño (someone from Torróx) makes a little money, all he wants is to lord over the rest of the people. There are only two options in Torrox: to command or to be commanded . . . By forgetting this you run the risk of being commanded by the most ignorant and greedy troublemakers and foolish people imaginable." In order to maintain authority he suggested establishing control over all levels of power: the city hall, the justice system, and the church. It was as simple as favoring in all these institutions people that belonged to the family's clientele, something very easily accomplished in a place where more than three hundred individuals were dependent on the will of the Cabarrúses.[81] In the correspondence, Don Domingo gave to his son all kinds of details about specific people whom he could (or could not) trust. The second Count of Cabarrús knew a great many details about the personalities, private life, attitudes, and dispositions of most people in Torrox – especially those he referred to as his servants. He advised his son on how to hold influence not only over their public lives but also over their private affairs. His understanding of authority was associated with the exercise of social control, a practice that absolutely excluded respect for the privacy and freedom of the individual.

Maintenance of authority also had its symbolic expressions. Manipulation of power structures was useless if not accompanied by the necessary preservation of public and private prestige. In the society of Torrox and Cabarrúses held the prestige ascribed to their noble condition, but to retain this cultural capital they had to also behave as superiors. This feeling of superiority was very important in the discourse of our protagonist. It had to

---

[81] About a quarter of the total population of Torróx.

be manifested in all relations with the entire population of the *pueblo*. Superiority over the most prosperous groups – the people immediately below the family – could be achieved through the maintenance of social distances. The second Count of Cabarrús recommended to his son not be intimate with anyone in the village, especially those in the middle and upper strata, because they always will be the competitors of the family. "If you have intimacy with one or several friends," wrote Don Domingo, "they will try to influence you. Remember that in Torrox friendship is always interested, especially with regard to those people like ourselves who have influential positions there, in the province and in Madrid. Nobody is going to look for a disinterested friendship. People will look for your intimacy only to manipulate you and to gain your favor and to have power over the community." To avoid these problems the count advised the practice of a splendid isolation. He recommended having friends outside of the village, better among kin or individuals in the same social sphere, but never inferiors within Torrox. Social isolation also would help to preserve the family's role as arbiter of the conflicts among the different groups within the *pueblo*. Maintaining a distance from communal petty business was basic to the preservation of superiority. The Cabarrúses have an obligation to be mediators in these conflicts, but never actors.

Finally, the symbolic language of superiority included very important rhetoric surrounding some forms of everyday community relations: "Do not visit anybody if they did not visit you beforehand. Avoid mixing with the people of the *pueblo* in collective celebrations. My feeling is that it is best to avoid all community celebrations if possible, but if it is not, to be sure that the place reserved for your person is appropriate to your status. Keep your seat in the Church separate, and be very scrupulous about the way in which you receive your visits at home. There, you have to always be prepared to receive people, with your clothes clean and appropriate and your home neat. Have a room ready exclusively for visits, try to make sure that it is always a servant who first greets the visitor, making sure he has to wait some minutes before you show up."

The discourse of the second Count of Cabarrús illustrates how Spanish landowning dominant groups perceived their social role as preserving domination. It reflects the ambivalent attitudes of most of these landowning elites regarding political organization on the one hand, and social practice on the other. In the end, Cabarrús's culture reflected the hierarchical and authoritarian nature of local life of nineteenth-century Spain. His experience was not an isolated one. It was the cultural experience of most landowning families who initially made up the bulk of the *ilustrado* minority and later of the *Liberal* political elite. This culture was in part the result of an unproductive agrarian economy that perpetuated economic and social polarization in most of the Spanish villages. The social habits of the politically and economically dominant groups resulted from their direct linkage to provincial and local life. It was the expression of a habitus based on the exercise of personal solidarity and local authority that survived the economic and, above all, political changes of the nineteenth century.

Conclusion

Using solely his ideological discourse as a tool of analysis, many scholars who have analyzed Francisco de Cabarrús have made him out to be an early champion of the Spanish revolutionary bourgeoisie. I do not mean to deny his role as a bourgeois and a revolutionary – only to take into account the contradictions between his public persona and his private behavior and the conservatism of his social actions. We have in Francisco de Cabarrús a person who thought boldly and acted cautiously. In his son Domingo we have a person who manifested sympathy toward innovative ideas and political practices, but whose social thought and action also proved to be very conservative, if not reactionary. The history of the family shows an experience of social ascent that culminated in aristocratization. In sum, we have in the Cabarrús family a good example of the complex dynamics that characterized the social history of the Spanish middle and upper strata between 1750 and 1850.

The experience of this family shows on the one hand many innovative elements; it also, however, makes clear numerous continuities with the past. Innovation appears in the political compromises and public performances of the family heads up to 1864, especially in the figure of Francisco de Cabarrús. Continuity, however, can be found in the social backgrounds of the family, the mechanisms used for social ascent, and the use and transmission of a very traditional culture to ensure social domination and the reproduction of the group. In sum, there was an atmosphere of innovation in the political activities of the family and one of continuity in that which concerns social performance. This is a small-scale example of what happened on the whole in Spanish society during the period selected for this study.

The museum of families

The Cabarruses, and the bulk of the political and economic elites who formed the core of *Ilustración* and liberalism, came from a similar social spectrum. They belonged primarily to the provincial middle and upper social ranks, most often families with noble backgrounds. As I have mentioned before, the pattern of social ascent that these groups represented was not new; rather it was as old as the establishment of Madrid as the capital of Spain in the sixteenth century. Although liberal politicians embraced the principles of individual merit and equal opportunity for social promotion, mechanisms for social ascent and reproduction among these groups remained virtually unchanged. Despite the new legal framework of the nineteenth century that recognized the equality of all citizens before the law, the means for social integration in the dominant political and economic groups continued to be based on the privilege of belonging to a family or to a network of mutual solidarity. Political and economic careers, such as the career of Francisco de Cabarrús, were based on the ability of the candidate to use familial connections and patronage, instead of on self-confidence in his personal merits. Only a relative minority – not precisely made up of newcomers – held the means and fulfilled the requirements to achieve integration in the dominant groups. The scarcity of individuals with social backgrounds in the world of industry and middle and low ranks of commerce among liberal politicians exemplifies the obstacles to the integration of new elements into these groups. At the same time, within the social framework of the provincial families of landowners, bureaucrats, professionals, high merchants, and financiers, the mechanisms of social promotion were anything but static. Within the boundaries marked by the networks of familial and patronage solidarities, this society was very dynamic and varied before and after the liberal changes occurred.

Continuity in the social composition of politically and economically dominant groups explains the contradictions between their promotion of political egalitarianism on the one hand, and the maintenance of a habitus of exclusivity on the other hand. In other words, the differences between their public and their private discourses. They embraced liberalism because that ideology was the agent of political stability and economic prosperity in northern Europe and America, because its economic principles were very much in line with their economic interests, and because they were attracted to its political message of freedom and progress against obscurantism and tradition. However, at the same time they had to maintain their domination in a society whose structure and organization was strongly opposed to the principles of the new ideology. Most of them, like Francisco and Domingo de Cabarrús, felt uneasy about carrying out this contradiction. They complained about the miseries of the Spanish sociopolitical system that encouraged corruption, they questioned the morality of Spaniards, especially of those who opposed their programs of political change. But in the end most of them adopted practical positions, rather than moral ones. At the same time that they endorsed liberalization of the political system they also maintained a culture based on the traditional principles of hierarchy, loyalty, and authority. Although some of them practiced a modern agrarian capitalism – again, Cabarrús fits the model – they behaved more like traditional landlords than modern entrepreneurs. That is why their political attitudes appeared to be patriotic, progressive, urban and bourgeois, while their social practices were indeed authoritarian, corrupt, and in opposition to the modernity of their political discourse.

7

Kinship, friendship, and patronage

Don Manuel Cantero and Don Manuel José del Pez both achieved brilliant careers in the administration of the Spanish Treasury, although no evidence suggests that they came into contact with each other in their administrative or their private lives. Cantero, who was much older than Pez, was already a well-established official when Pez entered the Treasury administration as an apprentice. They belonged to different generations in the administrative service of the Spanish monarchy. Nevertheless, one might imagine that the two had parallel experiences and more than one chance encounter in the offices and corridors of the ministry.

For several generations the Pez name was familiar among the highest ranks of the Spanish administration. Nobody knows exactly when this family began to occupy positions in the ministry of the Treasury, but around 1880 several dozen of its members were employed by this institution. By this time Don Manuel José del Pez was a very influential person with the ministry as well as the patriarch of his clan. The patronage of his kin and well-placed friends got him his first job in the ministry at the tender age of fifteen. Patronage was the only system of promotion he learned from his ancestors and it was the system he practiced his entire life. Don Manuel held a very cynical view of what the state administration was about. For him the administration was no more than a collection of conventional forms created to justify what it was in reality: a system of mutual favors run by the basic mechanisms of protection and bribery. That is why he carefully cultivated loyalty and friendship in his everyday professional relations. At the peak of his bureaucratic-political career Don Manuel was surrounded by a web of loyalists, most of them members of his large family. His son Adolfo became an *escribiente* (apprentice clerk) before he started his university studies. Federico and Antonio, also sons of Pez, held managerial positions in

Kinship, friendship, and patronage

the ministry before completing their law degrees. In almost all departments in the ministry one could find sons, nephews, sons-in-law, cousins, and other kin of Don Manuel, not to mention his protégés from outside the family. As one contemporary pointed out, wherever one looked in the ministry one could see plenty of *caras pisciformes* (fishlike faces).[1]

Don Manuel Cantero was born in 1797 in Aldeacueva, a small village of the Carranza Valley, in the mountains of the Spanish Basque country. He belonged to a propertied family of modest means. His father as well as his paternal and maternal uncles held positions as *regidores* (councilmen) in the Valley's city hall. Don Manuel was sent at a young age to his uncle's house in Madrid to begin a business apprenticeship. Once there, our protagonist joined the large circle of kin and *paisanos* from Carranza who were installed in Madrid's business and bureaucratic structures.[2] Canteroy used the patronage of influential people in this circle to attain a position in the administration of the Treasury. Business, politics, and bureaucracy constituted an interactive trilogy of activities in Cantero's life. Business helped politics, control over the mechanisms of the administration helped business, and politics helped both. In all three areas our man achieved brilliant results. As a politician he was an influential *progresista* in Mendizábal's circle. Beginning his political career in 1843, he served as mayor of Madrid and minister of the Treasury, and also headed other ministries. As a businessman he was an active participant in more than seven mercantile and financial companies established in the capital around 1850.[3] Despite his political and economic success Don Manuel Cantero never forgot his familial and geographic origins. He always thought of his kin and *paisanos* who remained in Carranza and helped those who migrated to Madrid. "He left the Valley to go to Madrid," wrote a member of the Carranza city hall in 1834, "invited by his kin and friends already established in the capital. Since then he has kept in contact with us and he corresponds consistently with his kin and *paisanos*."[4]

The biographies of Cantero and Pez show that the two probably followed

---

[1] *Pisciforme* in Spanish is applied to anything with the external aspect of a fish. Literally the surname "Pez" in Spanish means fish. The reader may catch the double meaning of the observation about the *caras pisciformes*.

[2] As a contemporary pointed out, people from Carranza had a tendency to emigrate to the Court and the Americas. Behind this emigration pattern was a system of property transmission that favored inheritance of the elder sons. Elders of propertied families provided their brothers with a kind of monetary compensation to help them start an administrative or business career. In time, these emigrants created networks of kin and regional solidarities to absorb new arrivals at the points of emigration. See *Diario de Madrid*, December 4 and 5, 1799, 1469–71, and 1473–75.

[3] Otazu (1987: 314). [4] AHN, Estado, Carlos III, Exp. 2222, p. 21.

similar career paths in the administration. Both were linked to solidarity networks that helped their career performances from beginning to end. Both maintained these ties of solidarity as basic mechanisms for selection and promotion within the administration and, most likely, in all spheres of social relations. Their personal experiences in decisive moments of their lives echoed one another. Despite their differences in age and political position, Cantero was a declared *progresista*, while Pez sympathized more with *moderado* conservatism. Both used the administration as an instrument for the reproduction of their affines, whether these were friends or family members. There was, however, a substantial difference between the two Manuels: while Cantero is the name of a real historical figure, Pez is only a fictional character in several of Benito Pérez Galdós's novels.[5]

I do not intend to confuse my readers by mixing reality and fiction – a blend that is not intended to be a treatise on the connections between literary and historical discourses. What I have attempted in emphasizing the similarities in these short biographies is to call attention to the persistence in Spain of a system of social relations built on bonds of loyalty and solidarity. Cantero's life provides us with historical evidence of this, while Galdós's character proves its existence as a cultural factor. My intention in this chapter is to study the persistence of this system of social relations and its historical consequences. I shall do it through an analysis of the nature of basic social relations among Madrid's dominant groups between 1750 and 1850.

Traditionally, historians have framed the discussion of these social relations in terms of class conflict. What characterized Spanish social history of this period, according to this conception, was the struggle between a new ascendant bourgeoisie and the old feudal dominant class to control power. I will argue that such conflict was not central to the evolution of Spanish dominant groups during those years. Although episodes of conflict between bourgeois and feudal elements did occur, they were secondary to a scenario dominated by group solidarity, rather than class conflict, and by social reproduction, instead of social substitution. I will argue again that relations based on family, friends, and patron–client ties are more important than class conflict to understand the social performance of Spanish dominant groups in our period. Of course, these were mechanisms for the mainte-

---

[5] Like many other Galdosian characters the Pez family has an independent life within the author's writings. The Pez family appears in various novels such as *La de Bringas*, *Fortunata y Jacinta*, *El amigo Manso*, *La desheredada*, *Torquemada en la cruz*, etc. See Pérez Gadós (1951: 1956–61, vol. VI).

nance of class domination. They were not, however, practiced by a new ascendant class but rather by the traditional bureaucratic, landowner, professional, and commercial groups. The use of family, friendship, and geographic affinities as basic mechanisms for social promotion was called the system of old corruption by Rubinstein. This term was applied to English society during its transition from an aristocratic rural-based society to a modern Victorian class-based society; it describes perfectly the conditions of Spanish society during the period of this analysis.[6] However, unlike England, practices of old corruption and features of the old society prevailed in Spain up to the first third of the twentieth century. Spain, as well as most of continental Europe up until 1914, was a model of social continuity in a very dynamic political context and an uneven yet active economic atmosphere. I will measure this social continuity through the enumeration and description of basic mechanisms used by the different social groups to perpetuate their dominance.

All groups in this study were holders of a significant amount of capital whether cultural – as defined by Bourdieu,[7] symbolic, or economic. These peoples used their capital to improve or maintain their social status. Economic capital was essential for almost everyone, but especially for ascendant groups. Despite the legal nature of social status before the changes introduced by liberalism, everyone knew that money was the best instrument of social ascent. Some groups, especially the bureaucrats, were particularly concerned with acquiring, improving, and preserving cultural and academic capital (educational background). Finally, those in the dominant groups depended upon the accumulation and preservation of symbolic capital. For already established groups – as we have seen in the case of the Cabarrús family – the maintenance of authority and social order was essential. For ascendant groups symbolic capital was necessary to attain social recognition. In sum, much of the social energy of Madrid's dominant groups was aimed at producing and reproducing the various forms of capital.

Strategies of reproduction are of central importance in understanding how people accumulate and reproduce the different forms of capital existent in a given society. Analysis of reproduction focuses on groups involved in the domination and control of power. Not all dominant groups follow the same patterns of reproduction. The variations are determined by the diversity of capital existent in society at a given historical moment.[8] Strategies

[6] Perkin (1969: 340–46) Rubinstein (1987: 265f).   [7] Bourdieu (1989: 13–14).
[8] Ibid. p. 386.

also do not always correspond with rational preestablished norms but rather consist of a number of very different practices that are objectively organized. These practices, which were not explicitly acknowledged or controlled, contributed to the reproduction of amassed capital.[9] Strategies are directly linked to the habitus of any social agent or group of agents. Bourdieu uses the example of handwriting to stress the connection between habitus and reproductive strategies. The same way that handwriting differs depending on whether one uses a pen, pencil, or chalk, and on the quality of paper or other material on which one is writing, reproductive strategies may be varied in form. At the same time, however, a reader will notice a characteristic style, regardless of the materials used. A certain consistency in the design of characters can be detected, an *air de famille* that will make the handwriting distinctive. In the same way, the behavior of one or several agents practicing under a similar habitus shares a certain style. Each action becomes a metaphor for the others, but in the end, these practices, whether played out in different scenarios, with different protagonists or under varied circumstances, are the result of the mise-en-scène of the structures of perception, thought, and action.[10]

Refusing the existence of rules but accepting the presence of tendencies, inclinations, and preferences, we may trace several kinds of reproductive strategies. First, the strategies of fertility, operating in the long term, are the basis of social reproduction since they ensure the continuity of the lineage. Second, we have strategies of succession, which control the transmission of familial patrimonies. These mechanisms were founded either in law, custom, tradition, or fraudulent practices. Third, the strategies of marriage, aimed at ensuring biological reproduction without challenging social status, were based on the promotion of equal alliances among individuals of similar social rank. Fourth, the strategies called "social investments" were those consciously or unconsciously aimed at the creation of social obligations. These obligations consist of assumptions of mutual reciprocity or recognition and may imply respect, exchange of favors, acknowledgement, fealty, or solidarity. Finally, the economic strategies – studied in detail in the first part of this book – concern the reproduction of wealth through the use of adequate investment and succession policies. In the next pages I would like to review the basic strategies of reproduction practiced by Madrid's dominant groups. Emphasis will be placed on methods of succession, marriage

---

[9] Ibid. (1989: 386–387; 1988: 122; 1972: 27). [10] Ibid. (1989: 387).

practices, and strategies for social investment, while strategies of fertility may appear somewhat marginal. This uneven treatment does not stem from the author's bias against the latter material but rather from the limitations of available sources.

Before beginning the analysis of specific reproductive strategies I will try to define the social origins of the different groups being studied. Knowing social origins will help us to characterize their social positions and to better understand mechanisms of social reproduction. This analysis is also essential to test whether or not there existed social interaction among the different groups, as well as provide insight into the nature of the social space in which they acted. Thus far, the portrait of society presented in this study may appear excessively static. Continuity, persistence, reproduction, co-optation, etc. are all terms that have often appeared in these pages. The reason for this repetition is directly related to the thesis that I am attempting to refute: that Spain experienced a social revolution between 1750 and 1850. The reader may ask if I intend to argue that nothing changed in Spanish society between 1750 and 1850.

The answer is no. A static society is impossible, just as there are no inactive organisms in nature. In fact, many of the families in this study were in the midst of social ascent themselves. Even the most stable groups experienced transformations throughout the period. Some were threatened by the natural processes of biological extinction, only a few experienced social decline, but none remained unaltered by the internal and external impacts of social activity. The social framework in which these dominant groups coexisted was a dynamic one. As some families succumbed to biological, economic, or social threats, new families rose to take their places. Dominant groups underwent a continuous process of reproduction but also of replacement.[11] Nevertheless, as I have mentioned before, this replacement also occurred in a social space marked by specific boundaries. Let me first fix these boundaries before I start with the analysis of strategies of reproduction.

Social origins and the social environment

The creation of categories for social classification is always a difficult task. If the people being classified lived two hundred years ago, the effort becomes

---

[11] This is to paraphrase Mauro Hernández's (1991: 178–186) assertion in reference to the social performance of the Madrid oligarchy of *regidores* (councilmen) between 1606 and 1808.

even more complicated. Either of the two most common categories used by today's sociology – based mostly on the level of income – are by no means sufficient because they do not take into account social status, which was still a very important factor for social distinction in the first half of the nineteenth century. Distinctions by status were made in state censuses, but they are particularly prominent in early-nineteenth-century biographies and memoirs.[12] Occupational categories may be more helpful for social classification for this period, but they can be problematic if we use them either generically or as an exclusive criterion. The use of detailed occupational categories, distinguishing subcategories within similar occupational levels, may seen more accurate for historical description but less useful for formulating analytical generalizations about the historical position of social groups. On the other hand, the use of occupation alone may also conceal social status. Most courtiers, for instance, belonged to old noble families while most lawyers did not. However, there were others of the king's servants whose nobility was either doubtful or nonexistent, while many lawyers, especially during the liberal era, held aristocratic positions inherited from their ancestors. Donoso Cortés, for example, obtained a law degree just like his father, who served on the Royal Council. The Cortéses were descendants of the famous *conquistador* of Mexico, and the family documented its nobility on several occasions throughout its history.[13]

Information available in the sources is always incomplete and sometimes may have been intentionally manipulated. Most notarial sources – wills, inventories, authorizations, etc. – during the second half of the eighteenth century provide occupational information for the proponents and their ancestors, but this custom became rare after 1814. Genealogical documents, because they were generally written up in order to obtain credentials of nobility, are also biased sources. They were normally a requisite for being granted a *hábito* in *Ordenes Militares* or to prove *hidalguía* (gentleman status) so as to become a member of an institution or to gain tax privileges. These documents generally provide accurate familial information, but their social value has to be carefully measured. In the case of the *Ordenes Militares*, if the aspirant belonged to a family with already established social status, there was no reason to misrepresent and the information is reliable, but if he was

---

[12] Most of the biographies compiled by Nicomedes Pastor Díaz and Francisco de Cárdenas in their *Galería de españoles célebres* began with a description of the noble condition (or its lack) of the subject studied.
[13] Burdick (1983: 24).

in the process of social ascent (the candidate was always male) then, falsehoods were more common. Another problem is the constant confusion between categories of status, occupation, and service in the social vocabulary of the period. Public and private documents mixed up these social definitions depending on the situation or on who was writing up the document. The minister Manuel Cortina, for instance, was labeled as a lawyer in one part of his will, while further up in the same document he is called an *hacendado* (landowner), a status that implied more social prestige and, undoubtedly, a better economic position.[14] The labels *hacendado* or *propietario* (owner) in the nineteenth century replaced what in the previous century were called *señores* (lords), or other similar estate titles. Finally, we should keep in mind that every social position has to be seen as a dynamic process subject to change through time.

Taking into account all of these insufficiencies it is impossible to avoid some inaccuracies, but using mainly occupational categories we can make some valid generalizations about the sociology of the dominant groups of Madrid between 1750 and 1850. To complement the sometimes deficient information inferred from occupational labels I will use data on property transmission. Transmission of property is an indicator of social mobility. A large amount of inherited property in a specific social group may be interpreted as a result of social reproduction, while the amassing of a fortune after beginning with none may indicate social ascent. I will also consider all information available on the noble status of the individuals and families being studied.

Some historians have minimized the value of *hidalguía* or aristocratic titles, if they were recently acquired, as a criterion for social classification. First, they claim that being an *hidalgo*, or using other symbols that might imply that condition – like the *Don* before a name – was less socially valuable in the period of this study. At the end of the eighteenth century the *Don* was commonly used by anyone who had attained a minimum level of social recognition but who did not necessarily come from noble ancestry.[15] Some-

---

[14] AHPM, P. 33573.
[15] Behind this debate lie two different historiographical positions. Those who emphasize the role of the bourgeoisie in the crisis of the Spanish old regime minimize the value of *hidalguía* or new aristocratic titles as a criterion for social classification. Many of these *hidalgos* and even some of the new marquises and dukes were, according to these scholars, merely aristocratized bourgeois. On the other hand, historians who claim the weakness of the Spanish bourgeoisie emphasize the social and symbolic value of *hidalguía* and aristocratization. On this debate see Tomás y Valiente (1986: 792); Morales (1988: 33); Herr (1989: 721); Hernández Benítez (1991: chaps. VI and XI).

thing similar happened, according to this point of view, with the condition of *hidalgo*. In some Spanish regions – the mountains of the north especially – the whole population held the right to be recognized as *hidalgo*, independent of their economic position. Besides, many Spanish *hidalgos* were as poor, or even poorer, than some of their plebeian counterparts. It seems that at times obtaining *hidalguía* was only a matter of having money and influence.[16] The candidate could bribe witnesses to help him prove to the judges that his family was of an ancient lineage and that he had *pureza de sangre* (pure blood). In the same way that some people could manipulate law and history to prove their *hidalguía*, many new aristocratic titles were the result of a rapid process of social ascent. Thus, behind some of the flamboyant titles of marquis or duke – argue the minimizers of early-nineteenth-century nobility – there were nothing but bourgeois ascendant families.

Although their evidence is essentially correct, I do not think it proves the devaluation of the importance of nobility and, consequently, its invalidation as a tool for sociological categorization. In all of Europe, part of the new titled aristocracy, as well as the low and middle ranks of nobility, consisted of ascendant bourgeois families, up until the twentieth century. Besides the lineages that in 1800 constituted the so-called old aristocracy could have also traced their family histories to the first recognition of nobility. Most of them were also people who originally emerged from the middle and lower ranks of the nobility; in some cases they were even bourgeois in origin.[17] It is true that the ranks of nobility became progressively more open to newcomers during the first half of the nineteenth century.[18] In Spain, for instance, the basis for awarding most new titles during this period, as well as *hábitos* of the *Ordenes Militares*, was a new meritocratic philosophy.[19] This

---

[16] Although there does not exist a systematic study on the number of *hidalguía* applications rejected by the institutions in charge of the inquiries, we know a few cases of families who attained the acknowledgement even though they did not possess the basic requirements to be *hidalgos*, e.g. not to have their blood mixed with non-Catholics. See Domínguez Ortiz (1983: 147–60).

[17] Some titles such as Marquis of Balbases and Estepa, Count of Pezuela de las Torres, Count of Villalvilla etc. were old in the period under study, but were originally created in the second third of the seventeenth century and conferred to banker families. Sanz Ayán (1989: 454). Hernández Benítez (1991: chap. 10) describes the case of the Negrete family, Counts of Campo Alange and Grandees of Spain in only two generations.

[18] After 1846 the purchase of a title was relatively easy in comparison with previous centuries, although they remained extremely expensive (between 16,000 and 80,000 reales plus taxes). Robledo (1987: 106).

[19] This spirit inspired the debates for the creation of the 1812 Constitution. See Varela Suances-Carpegna (1983). People like Floridablanca and Campomanes attained their aristocratic titles in return for their diplomatic and administrative services. Fayard (1982: 119).

Kinship, friendship, and patronage

meritocratic culture was founded on service to the state administration, not on the traditional medieval principles of military service, nor on the principles of bourgeois self-realization. So all indicators point to an opening up of the nobility to the ranks of the bourgeoisie, but this new accessibility somewhat invalidated the value of social distinction that noble lineage supposedly marked.[20] This helps to explain why most ascendant families pursued *hidalgo* credentials, encouraged the use of aristocratic symbols (coats of arms, surnames, genealogies, etc.), and endorsed nominations for aristocratic titles. Noble status in this period still signified a family's position as a holder of cultural capital. The suppression of legal privileges for the nobility by liberal politics changed the content of this capital. Nobility was no longer a legal status, but it continued to be a basic element for social distinction. In a world in which personal loyalties were still an essential part of social relations, belonging to a distinguished lineage or holding a prestigious surname tended to reinforce social success. Recent studies on the role of the aristocracy in nineteenth-century Europe are revising traditional assumptions. Despite the legal suppression of their traditional privileges, aristocrats continued to play a central role in European society, not only in terms of economic power but especially in areas of cultural dominance.[21] Nobility therefore cannot be used exclusively as a category for social analysis in our period, but it would be remiss to ignore its value as an instrument for social distinction and cultural domination.

Taking account of all the aforementioned informative limitations I have created Table 7.1. It includes the occupational breakdown for the fathers of the men in the four groups of my sample. I have decided not to establish a chronological division between the eighteenth and the nineteenth centuries – as I did when dealing with family fortunes – because it proved to be unnecessary. My initial attempt to do so showed no substantial differences in fathers' occupations between the two periods. Coincidences observed in the figures for bureaucrats and politicians, despite chronological differences, are a perfect example of what happened with the other groups. As occurred with occupational breakdowns in Chapter 4, the category of landowner/rentier is always the most confusing because it is not exactly an occupation. In the social vocabulary of nineteenth-century Spain the terms

---

[20] It is, however, unclear to what extent these new aristocratic families, at least in the upper levels, merged with the old titled nobility.
[21] Mayer (1981: chap. II); Bush (1984: 54); Cannadine (1982: 2); Bédarida (1979: 41); Price (1987: 358).

Table 7.1. *Social Origins: Occupational structure of parents of merchants, bankers, bureaucrats, politicians, and professionals*

Parents' Occupation	1750-1848 Businessmen		1766-1866 Bureaucrats		1800-1853 Politicians		1792-1858 Professionals	
Bureaucracy	10	8.8%	64	47.5%	24	32.4%	7	31.8%
Diplomacy	--		2	1.5%	12	16.2%	–	
Military	3	2.6%	13	9.6%	7	9.5%	1	4.5%
Court	7	6.3%	9	6.6%	2	2.7%	1	4.5%
Professions	2	1.7%	17	12.6%	10	13.5%	9	41.0%
Landowner/rentier	10	8.9%	26	19.3%	16	21.6%	3	13.7%
Commerce/finances	45	39.8%	4	2.9%	3	4.1%	1	4.5%
Farmer	30	26.5%	–		–		–	
Craftsman	–		–		–		–	
Other	6	5.4%	–		–		–	
Unknown	116		20		55		14	
Total sample	229		155		129		36	

Sources: Merchants.dat; Bankers.dat; Bureaucrats.dat; Politicians.dat; professionals.dat.

hacendado (landowner), *propietario* (owner), or rentier were all occupational labels that referred to similar social categories. They applied to individuals whose main source of income was rents from their properties, whether these were in the form of land, real estate, or public debt. However, most people in the other occupational categories also owned land, real estate, public debt, or stocks. They also obtained rents, in many cases very substantial amounts, from the tenants on these properties.

The higher amount of information on the fathers' occupation was found for bureaucrats (87% of cases), while for merchants I have been able to collect evidence only for less than a half of the known cases (49.3%). Around two-thirds of cases constitute the information available for the other groups – 61% for professionals and 57% for politicians. The parucity of details for merchants is not coincidental. Lack of occupational information in public and private documents has to be interpreted as a voluntary exercise of concealment. After all, the use of professional titles or categories of status in public or private documents was a recognition of social distinction.[22] If merchants scarcely used occupational labels it was simply because they did not have prestigious occupations. In fact, when they did use labels they often used the same ones of others in this sample. This sort of inferiority complex on the part of the commercial groups is a corollary of the value that positions of status still had in early-nineteenth-century Spanish society.

Looking at the percentages in Table 7.1, one can observe that the fathers' and son's occupational statuses coincide most closely in the case of politicians and bureaucrats. The structure for professionals shows some minor differences, while merchants appear as the most distinctive group. Thus, independent of the fact that in subsequent generations these merchants ended up establishing social connections through their families, we see here the diversity of their social backgrounds. About two-thirds of the bureaucrats and politicians – 65% and 68%, respectively – belonged to at least a second generation of public employees. The proportion among professionals is also high – 40% – while only 17.7% of the merchants' fathers held positions in the state administration. Similar disproportions can be found in the rest of the occupational categories. The highest proportion of professional backgrounds coincides with the professional group – 41% – while among merchants the figure is almost insignificant – 1.7%. Again, the percentages for this occupational category are very similar among politicians and bureaucrats – 12.6 and 13.5 respectively. The proportion of landowner/rentier backgrounds is substantial in the case of politicians – 23.8% – as it also is among bureaucrats and professionals – 19.3% and 13.7%. The percentage of merchants from landowner backgrounds is very low – 8.9%. Backgrounds in commercial and farming activities were, however, exclusive to the merchant/bankers group – 66.3% of cases – the proportion of this occupational category found among the remaining groups is insignificant.

These figures show us two main realities: first, that Madrid's dominant groups, with regard to their social origins, consisted not of a single class but rather of a coming together of people of different social origins. Second, despite this diversity of social backgrounds the levels of occupational continuity in second generations appears, especially among bureaucrats, politi-

---

[22] Remember the complaint of the second Count of Cabarrús when his notary did not address him properly.

cians, and professionals, as high as one might suspect. Regarding the first characteristic, the impression given is not one of a society undergoing a process of revolutionary transformation, nor is it one of a stagnant social space. Diversity in social backgrounds proves dynamic social activity. Variation in personal biographies is an unmistakable symptom of the existence of social dynamism. On the other hand, the high level of continuity in occupational structures alerts us to the societal limits placed on this pattern of dynamic activity. The impression given by this glimpse at the social origins of these groups is more of a society in transition than in revolution. This was a society with enough vitality to allow for the eventual renewal of its social components with new arrivals without altering the preestablished social order.

At the center of this society, controlling the positions of power, were the bureaucrats and politicians. Actually, distinctions between these two groups in our study may appear somewhat artificial. The distinctions are made for didactic purposes rather than as a reflection of reality; the different categories are due to the historical complexity of the time period of this study. It seemed inappropriate, when I created the different groups for the study, to include in the same category the members of the old *Consejos* with the ministers of the liberal cabinets. However, evidence in this and previous chapters demonstrates that, despite the differences in political frameworks before and after the liberal revolution, the social features of these two groups remained fairly constant. In other words, they belonged to the same social spectrum. At first they came from the traditional bureaucratic dynasties, a group recruited mostly from the middle and low ranks of the Spanish provincial nobility.

On a similar level with the bureaucratic dynasties we can locate those cases from landowning and professional backgrounds. In fact, social boundaries between high bureaucrats, landowners, and professionals are often difficult to establish. As I have mentioned before, most families in the high administration were also owners of land or real estate. On the other hand the world of professions was mainly reserved to those families who could afford the expenses of a career in the university. Paying for either secondary education or a university degree was certainly expensive during our period of study.[23] Education was normally paid by parents or other members of the

---

[23] Francisco Requena, former member of the Council of the Indies and General of the Royal Army, estimated the cost of the careers he provided to his six sons at a mean of 136,000 reales each. For the amount of money to cover one of those careers in 1817, the year the estimate was made, one could

Kinship, friendship, and patronage

family. Only a few people had fellowships, normally the result of church or aristocratic patronage. For some families university education was essential for the perpetuation of their social position, as was for the most part the case for bureaucratic dynasties. For others, it was a social and economic investment. The Dutari family, for instance, provided educations to all male members of its second generation. Thanks to this training, the Dutaris were able to place a family member on the governing board of the Bank of San Carlos. From this position José de Fagoaga Dutari was able to provide inestimable help to the weak finances of the family firm during the 1820s.[24] As in the case of the Dutaris, access to the university for business families occurred mostly in the second or third generations, when the family appeared to have enough capital and an interest in relocating their members in officeholding or public life. In general the university remained a domain of the Spanish upper classes: first, to those in control of land or real estate property, second, to those in the service of the state or the nobility with a regular source of income, and finally, to those in the world of business.

However, not all social biographies within these three groups (bureaucrats, politicians, and professionals) reflected a pattern of reproduction within the high ranks of the state service, the world of university professions, or in the transmission of land and real estate income. Nearly one-fourth of the cases of individuals in the high bureaucracy and politics had fathers who had been employees in the middle – or, less frequently, the low – levels of the state administration or in the provincial and local administrations. The proportion is higher among the cases that make up the professional sample – 37.3%.[25] The father of the influential Minister of State and prestigious bureaucrat Bernardo de Iriarte, for instance, was only a *capitan de milicias* (army captain).[26] José González Maldonado, member of the powerful Council of Castile, was the son of an *oficial* in the *Audiencia* of La Coruña. In its third generation the family had members in the high ranks of the army as well as the state administration. At least one of José's sons

---

buy a large house (even a building) in the center of Madrid. Only a tiny minority of Spanish society had the means to pay 136,000 reales on six different occasions. AHPM, P. 21777, p. 262.

[24] Juan Bautista and Domingo Dutari provided the money for the education of their nephews, José and Anacleto Fagoaga, at the University of Alcala. AHPM, P. 22207 and 22208, p. 52 and 208.

[25] Antonio de la Escalera, for example, a lawyer and for a while *corregidor* of the Andalusian town of Lucena, was the son of a provincial public notary. Asensio García Ordóñez, the pharmacist of the royal palace, was the son of an accountant in the provincial Treasury administration. See AHPM, P. 23109, p. 36; 23062, p. 183 and 789.

[26] See Mercader Riba (1983: 321 and 358); AHPM, P. 21693, p. 478.

became a landowning rentier.[27] These two cases exemplify the possibilities for social ascent within the service of the state. This pattern of mobility appeared to be stronger in some fields of the administration than in others. The army and the diplomatic field were very selective, while the Treasury administration, as we have seen in previous chapters, was more open and diverse in its sociological composition. However, if we take a collective view of particular forms of ascent we can find a significant pattern of repetition.

This pattern of social ascent in high administration, politics, and professions seems to be the dominant characteristic of the group of merchants and bankers of our sample. Unlike the other three groups, the social origin of more than two-thirds of merchants and bankers were in the world of business or in the low ranks of land ownership. Many came from the middle and lower levels of the central and provincial administrations, commercial and financial activities, and from various other professional activities. A few of them came from the commercial elite linked to the Cinco Gremios Mayores and the *cambista* financial elite, while the rest consisted of a middle group always in search of improving their social condition. Although the heart of Madrid's dominant group was made up of a number of well-established dynasties of officeholders, landowners, and professionals, it continually renovated itself, allowing the integration of new ascendant families. Commercial and financial activities, as one can infer from figures in Table 7.1, provided the easiest route to social ascent.

Does this dynamic social activity mean that Spanish society was experiencing a process of social revolution, at least in its middle and upper levels? Was this social mobility the effect of a process of substitution of one class for another, or the arrival of a new social class to the power structure? Absolutely not. The existence of social replacement does not mean that the traditional class structure was being replaced by a different one. Social mobility occurred, but on restricted scale, in a pattern in which limits were marked by the ability of new ascendant families to find patronage and status recognition. Continuity in occupational structure was stronger than renewal. With the exception of merchant and banker groups, repetition in occupational positions marked the general trend. This can be traced in the positions of the third generation of the people in the sample (Table 7.2). The immense majority of bureaucrats' sons attained occupations in the different levels of state service. At least one-fourth improved on their

---

[27] AHPM, P. 23077, p. 1334.

Table 7.2. *The positions of the sons at father's death: Bureaucrats and merchants*

Base: 200 cases Known: 168 cases (84%) Bureaucrats		%
Bureaucracy/similar	87	36.8
Bureaucracy/improved	63	26.7
Business	–	–
Army	67	28.4
Rentier	7	3.0
Church	11	4.6
Worse	1	0.5
Total number of sons	236	

Base: 229 cases. Known: 97 cases (42.3%) Merchants/bankers		%
Bureaucracy	40	32
Business/similar	49	39.2
Business/improve	16	12.8
Army	5	4.0
Rentier	1	0.8
Church	9	7.2
Worse	5	4.0
Total number of sons	125	

Source: Data base in Merchants.dat; Bureaucrats.dat.

fathers' positions with posts in high politics or within the administration. Careers in the army were also a favorite choice. Even in the normally ascendant business families more than half of third generation individuals repeated the occupation of their parents. Nevertheless, bureaucracy was for this group what the army was for the bureaucrats: the perfect occupation to achieve social recognition.

If we contemplate a new variable, the transmission of property, limitations in the composition of dominant groups appear even more evident. The information from family fortunes used in Chapter 1 through 5 show that most people in our sample inherited some kind of wealth. Inheritances usually came in the form of land or real estate property, but also often included cash, personal valuable, and stocks. Almost three-fourths of the patrimonies of merchants and bankers (72.6%) included some form of inherited wealth (Appendix B). On occasion, as was the case of the Iruegas and Carranza families, the level of inherited wealth is indicative of a previously acquired socioeconomic position.[28] The case of Juan Sixto García de la Prada, one of the richest merchants in Madrid toward 1800, was typical. He embarked upon a career in trade thanks to an inheritance of 300,000 reales from his uncle and benefactor.[29] That, of course, was a small sum when compared to the fortunes inherited by most noble families and many of the bureaucrat and politician families in the sample, but this modest amount proved to be very helpful to Juan Sixto's future social success. A family stipend, a small piece of land or, in the best of the cases, shares in an established commercial firm, were very common forms of property transmission among merchants and a helpful tool for starting a business career. Among bureaucrats and politicians the level of inherited property was even higher – 81% of patrimonies for the first, 86% for the latter. While many merchant families trasferred only modest sums of money for the installation of their successors in Madrid, most families in the bureaucracy, politics, and professions transferred substantial amounts of property. All groups had enough wealth for their members to be able to either help in the establishment of the family in Madrid or to ensure its continuity there. Even in those cases of indisputable social ascent, most of the members Madrid's dominant groups started out with a favorable social position.

Regardless of their level of wealth, persons from industrial or artisan backgrounds seem to have been barred from access to this dominant society. Some Madrid families accumulated industrial fortunes comparable to those of the traditional noble families or to the most successful merchants. That was the case of Gregorio Cruzada, owner of several chocolate mills and a soap factory, who held a fortune of more than 8 million reales when he died in 1848. Cruzada lived in a luxurious and comfortable house in the center of Madrid. Its interior was decorated according to the style and taste of the most distinguished society: damask in the curtains, over the thresholds and other gaps in the walls, in the chairs and couches; a main parlor with mirrors all around the walls, a large marble table in the center, and a Venetian crystal chandelier that lit the room during social gatherings; a main study with a mahogany wood desk, and so on. This exhibition of luxury suggests a

---

[28] AHPM, P. 23400, p. 902; 21409, p. 243; 20473, p. 534 and 21669, p. 642.
[29] The estimated value of Juan Sixto's fortune in 1804 was over 20 million reales. AHPM, P. 21039, p. 104; 21098, p. 204; 20043, p. 216 and 23028, p. 81.

bourgeois, if not an aristocratic, style of life for the Cruzada family.[30] However the Cruzadas, like other wealthy families of chocolate makers, carriage makers, jewelers, confectioners, etc., never attained public positions within the city government nor in national politics.[31] Nor did these families, despite their wealth, mix with other families of the economic and political dominant elite. As we shall see in the next section of this chapter, wealthy businessmen married noble landowning women to create webs of dominant families. None of these industrial families, however, became integrated into the dominant family networks.

Even among merchants and brokers, who provide the most examples of ascendant families in this sample, one can see the limits of complete integration. Most of the individuals who formed this group belonged to the same families, which in turn came from similar geographic areas. Toward 1800 belonging to an *hidalgo* family from the Valley of Carranza, even if this *hidalguía* was not associated with wealth, provided possibilities for success in Madrid's business world that could not be matched by persons from other Spanish regions belonging to non*hidalgo* families. By the middle of the century these northerners (Cameranos, Vascos and Montañeses) still accounted for the bulk of Madrid's business community.[32] This means that social ascent in Madrid society was not only a matter of personal value recognition or economic achievement; to be integrated into the dominant groups it was also necessary to fulfill some additional requirements. These were largely related to social status, but we should not conceive of status as a system of objective legal requisites. The requirements were instead the same during the old regime, and represented a collection of persistent cultural practices. These practices were mainly determined by the traditions, habits, customs, and perceptions of the social groups that formed the crux of these dominant groups in a long-term historical period. Social mobility within

---

[30] AHPM, P. 25697, p. 381.
[31] Isidro Tomé was a prosperous candlemaker who had two large shops on main streets of Madrid. In 1848 his fortune surpassed 4.1 million reales, very much above the mean fortune of high bureaucrats in our sample. Tomé owned houses in Madrid with a value estimated at 1.2 million reales. Part of his surplus was also invested in large tracts of land and several garden houses in the countryside. The carriage maker Fernando Rodriguez died with a fortune of 1.2 million reales. Similar sums were left by Gerónimo Daguerre, who owned several leather factories, and Juan Kastler, the German brewer installed in Madrid. Families of famous printers like the Ibarras held even greater patrimonies, not to mention some jewelers whose income levels according to the eighteenth-century *Catastro de Ensenada* were similar to high government employees. See AHPM, P. 25640, p. 496; P. 23084, p. 136; 23830, p. 13; 23090, p. 1646 and 21081, p. 543f. For information on the *Catastro*, see Ringrose (1985: 413f.).
[32] Otazu (1987: 299f.).

Madrid's middle and upper classes was affected by a kind of pruning effect related to one of the select groups that traditionally dominated the economic and political life of the capital.

How can we define the position of these selective groups within Spanish society? Did they form a new social class? All evidence points to the existence of a social collective consisting of a conglomerate of class and status positions in which it is possible to identify people from at least three different social layers. First, were those elements that belonged to the upper and middle levels of the Spanish nobility – from the old titled families to the middle ranks of the provincial *hidalguía*. They represent the most stable, continuous, and wealthy side of the collective. They were the people who controlled the best positions in the high administration, army, and politics and combined these occupations with the ownership of land and real estate property. In general they were old families, people of *rancio abolengo* (with evident noble backgrounds) but also included among their ranks ascendant families that prospered in the service of the crown. Most of them belonged to the provincial elites that connected the worlds of provincial life and central government power. Numerically they constituted an important piece of the social collective though not its majority. Nonetheless, they were its core in terms of moral authority and cultural hegemony.

The second layer was made up of the notables, a social term already used by contemporaries and fashionable in recent works of social history.[33] They were mainly provincial people and most of them belonged to families in the middle and lower ranks of the Spanish *hidalguía*. They formed a group distributed among the upper and middle societies in Spanish provincial cities, towns, and villages. They were the people who controlled municipal life and shared the exercise of local authority and social control with the old aristocracy and the church. These were families with very diverse occupational and income positions: from the well-established landowning groups to the poor *segundones*[34] of entailed *mayorazgos*, from university professionals to the less skilled employees in the service of a noble family or a local administration. They accounted for the bulk of Madrid's select society, and their social composition appears as a mixture of reproduction of old families and replacement of new ones.

Finally, a third layer formed by clearly ascendant elements, mostly from the lowest levels of the rural *hidalguía* (mainly from the north of Spain

[33] See Herr (1989: 723); Pilbeam (1990: 10–11); Price (1987: 97f.); Balmori (1984: 6); Burdiel (1987).
[34] In families with *mayorazgo* any son born after the elder one was called *segundón*.

where *hidalguía* was a universal condition) but also including persons with no noble status. Some of these ascendant elements may appear in the world of high bureaucracy and politics,[35] but the most common form of ascent occurred through their integration into the commercial and banking communities. They were a small part of the dominant groups, but they were also the most dynamic in terms of social replacement. Judging by their origins and social performance, they were the most clearly bourgeois elements in our sample. However, as I have mentioned before, their social performance depended exclusively on their ability to find protection from a member of an already established group. In the end, social mobility was in the hands of the dominant groups and used to guarantee the reproduction of the existent social order.

As I pointed out before, the occupational structure of fathers and sons in my study went relatively unaltered in the transition between the two centuries. Comparing our data with the figures offered by Janine Fayard and Mauro Hernández for the seventeenth and eighteenth centuries, and Ann Burdick's for the period 1833–43, one may reaffirm this continuity (Table 7.3). The fathers of men on the Council of Castile and *regidores*, a political elite and an urban oligarchy, show occupational structures similar to the bureaucrats and politicians of our sample. This may indicate that these four groups shared similar social origins despite their chronological distance. With some minor differences in professional origins, Burdick's writers belonged to a social spectrum between the middle and upper classes, very similar to the professionals in our sample. Thus, the crux of the Spanish dominant groups – that is to say, the Madrid dominant groups – was formed by elements that belonged to the same social spectrum in a long-term historical process. Unless we stretch the concept of the bourgeois so that it includes just about everyone, I hardly think they can be categorized as a new bourgeoisie. Nevertheless, they were responsible for the political, social, and economic transformations traditionally attributed to this social class. The impression regarding their social composition and social behavior is that of a collective formed by a conglomerate of class and status positions in which elements of the old regime were prevalent. They ensured their historical continuity by the practice of social co-optation, instead of class substitution.

---

[35] Andrés Simón Pontero, member of the Council of Castile under Charles III, belonged to a family of small farmers (*labradores honrados*) from the hamlet of Chillarón in the province of Cuenca. However, the Ponteros alleged to have pure blood, never tainted by Moorish or Jewish ancestry, and to have never engaged in manual labor.

Table 7.3. *Social origins, 17th-19th centuries: Occupational structure of parents of regidores of Madrid, councilors of Castile, and writers*

Parent's Occupation	1606-1808 Regidores		1621-1746 Council of Castile		1833-43 Writers	
Bureaucracy	121	45.2%	69	52.2%	6	11.7%
Military	21	7.8%	13	9.9%	4	7.8%
Court	23	8.5%	10	7.5%	2	3.9%
Professions	19	7.1%	–		15	29.5%
Landowner/rentier	47	17.6%	40	30.4%	12	23.6%
Commerce/finances	14	5.2%	--		3	5.8%
Farmer/craftsman	4	1.5%	--		5	9.8%
Shopkeeper	--		--		–	
Other	19	7.1%	--		4	7.8%
Unknown	209		116		69	
Total sample	477		248		120	

Sources: *Regidores:* Hernández Benítez (1995: appendix, XXV). Councilors of Castile: Fayard (1982: 226). Writers: Burdick (1983: 18-19). Rectifications have been made from the original figures to adapt the data to the categories in our table.

Established families demonstrated enough social flexibility to accept the incorporation of new ascendant families, but always within the limits of a pattern of "corrected mobility," that is to say, a mobility restricted only to those peoples who fulfilled the conditions imposed by a dominant social framework based on kinship and patron–client relations.

Family networks

Family was the basic instrument for the practice of social reproduction and corrected mobility that characterized Madrid dominant society. Despite the diversity in family unions that we will find within these dominant groups, two basic features prevail: a common cultural perception of the meaning of family as an essential instrument for maintaining dominance, and a common acceptance of solidarity as a central value for family relations. With regard to the first conception, the family becomes a transcendent entity to which the self is subordinated. The second conception consisted of an organizational

Kinship, friendship, and patronage

system based on kinship networks whose basic tool was the practice of familism.[36]

Sociologists, demographers, and social historians have traditionally emphasized the study of family structure to define social models. Early developments in sociology used as a starting point the assumption that human development in the last two centuries was related to a basic change in the structure of family. Extended family was the principal form of social organization in preindustrial societies, corresponding to a primitive division of labor, while the modern industrial world brought about a new family form based on the exclusive relationship between the couple and its offspring. In the realm of the extended family, social forms based on the practice of authority and subordination were prevalent, while the nuclear family was related to the practice of individual freedom. Following these corollaries, modernization theorists have tended to consider the nuclear family a sign of social and economic progress, while extended family is seen as a symptom of backwardness. On the other hand, those opposing modernization models have accused industrialization and its corresponding nuclear family form of destroying familial harmony and community life.[37]

These general assumptions have been systematically questioned by historical research in the last twenty years.[38] Taking the household as a basic unit of analysis, Peter Laslett and the so-called Cambridge school have challenged the belief that industrialization brought about a nuclear family form. In preindustrial Europe people practiced some form of family limitations as early as the seventeenth century. The age of marriage occurred later than theorists of traditional extended families suspected. Finally, using a careful method of family reconstruction,[39] these scholars arrived at the

---

[36] Familism is a practice which can be defined broadly as an overall orientation toward the family and the family members, and consists of dimensions such as loyalty to family members, subjugation of self to the family, obedience to familial demand, and economic support obligations, in conjunction with a host of other related kinship factors such as locality demands and obligations to extended family members. In many societies these interaction patterns are sufficiently routinized so that from generation to generation there is little change in the extent to which individuals are oriented to familial demands, needs, and obligations. See Aldrich, Goldman, and Lipman (1980: 184); Esposito (1989: 87–88).

[37] See Smelser (1959: 120); Winch (1977: 45f); Anderson (1979: 53f.); Wrigley (1972: 226–229 and 1977: 49–55).

[38] A review of the major developments in the history of family in the last twenty years can be found in Hareven (1990: 96); Stone (1980: 51–57); and Casey (1989).

[39] Mainly developed by the French historical demographers Louis Henry and Pierre Goubert. See Wheaton (1987: 287f.).

The museum of families

conclusion that the co-residential nuclear family constituted the basic form of household structure in most of Western Europe since the Middle Ages.[40]

Recent studies of Spain show similar conclusions regarding the predominance of the nuclear family.[41] However, these same scholars agree that the measure of household size – who lives with whom – is insufficient to define family relations. In his study of the world of nuclear co-residential families in early modern Cuenca, David Reher emphasizes the existence of a constant practice of familial interaction that extends beyond the frame of the simple household.[42] This interaction was mainly based on kinship ties, but also on relations of geographic and patron–client solidarity that in most occasions were inspired by the cultural practices of familial solidarity. Indeed, more recent developments in family history focus on the study of the family not only as a demographic structure but also as a cultural construction,[43] not as an aggregate of individuals living under the same ceiling but rather as a complex system of personal relations,[44] and finally not as a static unit in space and time but rather a dynamic element subject to alterations in a life cycle.[45]

If we apply a narrow demographic approach to define the household structure of Madrid's dominant families we will find that the nuclear family – the simple household – was predominant. From what we can infer from notarial wills, about two-thirds of bureaucrats', politicians', and professionals' households consisted of a couple and its offspring.[46] Merchant households presented a much more complex structure in which kin and apprentices appeared to be a part of the stem family, but nuclear families did constitute the bulk of this dominant society. Overall there are no signs of large groups of kin living in the same home. Since wills were normally written at the end of the family life cycle it is hard to know if these nuclear families were based on a three-generation pattern, but there are no signs of co-residence between the couple and married sons and daughters, at least not in a long-term family life cycle. Co-residence, when it existed, was only

---

[40] Laslett (1965, 1972); Wall (1983); Wrigley (1977: 71); Osmond (1981: 169–196); Hajnal (1983: 65f).
[41] Casey and Vincent (1987: 172); Chacón (1987: 154); Simón Tarrés (1987: 92).
[42] Reher (1990: 239).
[43] The cultural approach is as old as this field of study: Aries (1962); Demos (1970); Shorter (1976); Flandrin (1976); Stone (1977). Nevertheless, it is being revitalized in recent years: Burguière (1987); Seagalen (1980); Wheaton (1980: 3–26).
[44] Berkner (1975: 723f.); Medick (1976); Kertzer (1984: 202); Kertzer and Bettell (1987).
[45] Hareven (1977: 323).
[46] Wills are probably not the best source for this kind of demographic analysis, but the lack of censuses for the period studied makes them a valuable substitute.

temporary. The general tendency was for new couples to start their households apart from their base family. Finally, although these households registered the presence of servants more or less linked to family life, there is no indication that they should be considered as part of the family. Consequently, a household approach to the study of Madrid's dominant families gives us a model similar to the one invoked by Laslett and the Cambridge school as predominant in northern Europe in the same period. Furthermore, the Madrid model appears to be more advanced – relative to today's family models[47] – since the levels of co-residence were lower than in the nuclear households described by Laslett. Does this mean that a model based on independent nuclear families was predominant within Madrid's dominant society between 1750 and 1850? For the evidence we have seen so far attesting to the importance of fealty and solidarity as basic forms of social interaction, it would be difficult to argue the preponderance of any model based on the supremacy of individualized relations. Consequently, the use of household measures as a basic analytical category for the study of family history must be revised.

The problem is that household is not the same as family. The simple measure of household composition telss us of nuclear or extended family forms only in their external manifestations. It does not clarify the details of the internal dynamics of family life. Household statistics do not say very much about how individuals perceived family ties, about the symbolic value of family relations in other levels of social life, nor about internal conflicts in the acceptance or refusal of authority and subordination roles. What defines the nature of family forms is mainly the way in which family members interact with each other in time and space – mainly in a life-cycle. This is not to say that statistics cannot reflect social dynamics of family life, but in our case the simple logic of statistics proves to be insufficient. Let us see some examples.

I have already mentioned the Sáinz de Baranda family. Let me take you back to their home located in the Plaza de Santa Cruz, in the very heart of old Madrid. Toward 1790 the family was living in a comfortable apartment that occupied the second floor (*principal*) of a building of five levels. Close to their home was the commercial firm of Don Pedro Sáinz de Baranda y Gándara, where he ran his family's financial life. At this time his sons

---

[47] A decrease in the number of generations living together in the same household is one of the most characteristic features of the individualized family predominant in the twentieth century. See Modell (1989).

The museum of families

Vicente and Pedro were already learning the skills of commerce and finance, working long hours in the family business. Don Pedro's wife and a third son whose mental illness kept him from business and normal social life remained at home. Because Don Pedro emigrated to Madrid early in his life, he never provided shelter for his parents in his house in Madrid. There is no doubt that Pedro Sáinz de Baranda's household toward 1790 as well as the respective households of Vicente and Pedro later on fit Laslett's category of simple households, or what is generically called nuclear families. There are no signs of co-residence, only a family consisting of a couple and its three sons – one of them who would stay only until his eighteenth birthday. From this household structure one could deduce that the Sáinz de Baranda family was within the limits of the nuclear model. However, reality was far from this superficial appearance. Numbers tell us of a simple family structure, but a closer look at the everyday life of the Barandas shows us an intense family life that surpassed the limits of the household. Family ties were strong on both the matrilineal and the patrilineal sides. Ties can be deduced from family rituals, constant familial commitments for mutual help, and the practice of a carefully designed strategy for the continuation of the family. Weddings, baptisms, funerals, social visits, birthdays, etc., were some of the better known rituals that maintained a sense of family cohesion.

Despite the geographical dispersion of most of these families of immigrants, people often traveled to their home towns to be present on special family occasions. Don Pedro visited his home town several times in his life to see his parents, to be present at his brother's wedding, and to arrange patronage relationships with his nephews, nieces, and other kin.[48] The maintenance of ritualistic familial commitments was even stronger with his wife's family. Because the Azuelas and Gorritis were installed in Madrid as merchants and officeholders two generations before the Barandas, the number of kin in the capital was greater. Both of his wife's branches were better established in the structures of power of the city. For our protagonist, fulfilling family obligations with his in-laws was imperative to improving his social condition. A sign of his dedication toward this kind of family commitments can be seen in his involvement in the funerals of his in-laws. Following social norms, Don Pedro personally attended the funerals of his kin both near and far, friends, business colleagues, or neighbors as an act of symbolic passive Christian charity. In the case of his in-laws, however, the assistance

---

[48] The distance between Quintanahedo (Don Pedro's hometown) and Madrid required several days of travel through difficult mountainous roads. AHN, Diversos, Serie General, leg. 225.

he provided the family made his presence an act of active familial solidarity. Don Pedro was involved in funeral organization, acting as the executor of the will, the guardian of the children, or looking out for the widow and the family's interests.[49] Committing oneself to helping family was a constant practice among the successive generations of the Sáinz de Barandas. Don Pedro periodically sent money to his family in Quintanaedo and to his wife's family in Castrourdiales. Part of this money went toward the dowries for some of his female relatives, but it was also sometimes destined to finance the careers of nephews and cousins. According to the account of one of Don Pedro's sons, his father assisted more than eighteen kin by providing money for starting careers and dowries for marriages.[50] Finally, Don Pedro took special care to design a careful strategy for the continuation of his family. The main feature of this strategy was the arrangement of consanguineal marriages for his two sons Vicente and Pedro. Although first grade consanguineal marriage was strictly forbidden by Catholic law and custom, Don Pedro decided to marry his sons with Manuela and Josefa San Juan y Santa Cruz.[51] That was a sibling marriage between two brothers and two sisters, but they were also first cousins. What was the reasoning behind these marriages? The answer is the perpetuation of the family name and fortune. In sum, a good part of the Sáinz de Baranda family life existed outside of the boundaries marked by the nuclear family. Despite their immediate family structure, the way the Barandas perceived and acted in family life was not at all like what is now characteristic in contemporary nuclear families.

Households of bureaucrats, professionals, and property owners generally had simple structures. Nevertheless, what defined their family culture was also a firm commitment to the principles of loyalty, fealty, subordination, and mutual help in a common acceptance of the supremacy of familial relations in social life. We know, for instance, that most of the history of the Antonio Alcalá Galiano family took place in the frame of a simple household. Toward 1800 Don Antonio lived in Cádiz under the tutelage of his parents and in the company of his sister and several servants. Both his maternal and paternal grandparents lived in separate households. Two of his paternal uncles lived in Madrid, where they held positions in the Treasury council. His maternal uncles, as well as his father, served in the royal army and lived in the same town but in different dwellings. The only addition to

---

[49] AHN, Diversos, Serie General, leg. 217.   [50] AHN, Diversos, Serie General, leg. 226.
[51] Gacto (1987: 37–38).

The museum of families

the Galianos nuclear family was one of the mother's single sisters. *La tía*, as Don Antonio affectionately called her, played an important role in his life. She took care of him during his childhood, then accompanied him in his exile to England in 1823. *La tía* played the role of second mother and filled the emotional vacuum left by a father who spent most of his time far away from the family. Although the Galianos were a collective of nuclear families most of the time, they always preserved a strong sense of self-identification with their lineage and maintained a practice of mutual help within the familial group. When Don Antonio was born, his parents were caring for his paternal grandmother in their home, and continued to care for her until she died, and cared for one of his maternal uncles before he left for Madrid. In life-cycles that included two generations, the household changed its structure several times, although the nuclear form was prevalent. Nevertheless, both matrilineal and patrilineal sides lived close to each other in Cádiz. In his autobiography Don Antonio tells us about visiting his relatives in town and about his kinship ties to some of Cádiz's most powerful people. The influence of family connections in his political career was a constant. His first contacts with national politics came through the patronage of his paternal uncles, Vicente and Antonio. The first steps he took as an aspirant for a position within Spanish diplomacy were also taken due to the help of his uncles and other kin. Throughout his life he often sought the favor of one or another of his kin in order to achieve political goals. Mutual obligations, for instance, were used to promote the candidacy of his friend León y Pizarro during the French occupation. Along with his political ideas, the major sign of Don Antonio's self-identification was his family name, his feeling of belonging to a lineage. Family name in his culture was a credential of distinction and a key to social success. To be an Alcalá Galiano had implications that transcended the limits of the simple household and the obligations of the nuclear family. It implied a cultural perception of the family that emphasized its historical transcendence and its value as an instrument for social advance.[52]

In his autobiography José García de León y Pizarro reflected on this cultural perception. García León y Pizarro belonged to a family from Andalusia with a long tradition of service to the monarchy. His father was a lawyer who worked throughout his career with the Council of Indies. For a while the family lived in Quito, in the Spanish American colonies, where

---

[52] All the information on Antonio Alcalá Galiano has been collected in his memoirs. See Alcalá Galiano (1955: I–XI).

Kinship, friendship, and patronage

Pizarro's father occupied the position of governor. Other members of the family held different positions in the prestigious Council of State. Following family tradition, Don José achieved a brilliant diplomatic career, reaching a position on the Council of State. García León y Pizarro was one of those late-eighteenth-century *Ilustrados* who arrived in time to jump on the train of early Spanish liberalism. Despite their differences in age, Pizarro established a strong friendship with Antonio Alcalá Galiano and other young liberal figures during the French occupation. Pizarro later distanced himself from them because he could not digest their excessive romanticism. But I am not interested here in the political ideas of Francisco León y Pizarro but rather in his perception of the family. Pizarro, as most bureaucratic families in our study, belonged to a middle-high social layer of the provincial *hidalguía*. For him the family played a central role in the articulation of social life, which was reason enough for him to decide to record his memoirs. Unlike with other writers of his time whose autobiographies were intentionally written for the general public, Pizarro aimed his text at a more limited audience: his sons and relatives. By doing so, Pizarro was following a family tradition that his grandfather had begun and that his father followed. He admitted having preserved "the twelve volumes that his father wrote about his life." For him this manuscript was a sort of bible, a kind of spiritual and practical guide for action and behavior that he acknowledged having read several times during his life.[53] Like his father and grandfather, he wanted to introduce his sons and later descendants to the raw scenarios of real life by sharing his own personal and public experiences. In doing so Pizarro left us numerous details about historical facts and an especially vivid collection of anecdotes about personal life. Allow me to emphasize, among this collection of testimonies, his own conception of the social role of the family.

Family in the text of Pizarro is regarded as *un bien* that stems from human nature. Two kinds of goods harmonize human experience: the goods of fortune and those from providence. In the first category Pizarro includes what he considers mundane values: employment, wealth, and leisure. They are the result of personal effort, perseverance, luck, and commitment, but, like all human things, they are unstable, variable, and capricious. Destiny endows us with these goods and destiny takes them away. However, pro-

---

[53] José García de León y Pizarro was born in 1770 and died in 1835. See García de León y Pizarro (1953: 1–2).

vidential goods always remain and, according to our man, there is one that prevails over the rest. That one is the family.[54]

Family, fundamentally understood as the combination of name plus *reputación* (public esteem), is a transcendental entity in Pizarro's conception, an entity whose importance exists beyond the limits of the individual. He ordered his offspring to preserve the *reputación* that has been deposited directly by God in their name and family. This is why for Pizarro family has a kind of retrospective meaning: what one is depends on what one comes from. A person's fame is the result of the conduct and esteem stored up by ancestors and other family members; one's behavior is a contribution to the respectability of the group. In sum, what Pizarro was embracing is nothing other than the culture of the traditional family lineage.

Indeed, the prevalent model of family structure among Madrid's dominant groups was very much influenced by this traditional culture of family lineage. Fascination with ancestry was common to most European upper and middle-class families of the time. The linkage of lineage and *reputación*, however, may be more particular to Spain and other Mediterranean socieities.[55] This is not to say that our families were organized in the same manner as the clans of late medieval urban Italy, or like the aristocratic lineages of sixteenth-century Spanish towns.[56] There are no signs of hierarchical divisions between major or minor branches within our familial groups. Our families were less socially stable, more receptive to the incorporation of new ascendant elements, and lived in a more open social environment in which newcomers coexisted with old established groups. Unlike the traditional aristocratic lineages characteristic of the ordered and estate societies, Madrid family lineages in our period existed in what scholars have defined as the society of notables – that is to say, a society characterized by the survival of traditional social structures and habits of behavior that were slowly transformed mainly by economic change.[57] The notables' society was sustained during the nineteenth century by a political system based on a restricted electorate, which facilitated the maximum exercise of personal influence. However, unlike the modern class society, the social power of the notable was based upon status as well as wealth, and unlike the old ordered society, social ascent was more feasible. In many respects eighteenth-century Spanish society can be defined as a society of

---

[54] Pizarro (1953: 1).   [55] Pitt Rivers (1979); Peristiany (1976).
[56] Bennassar, B. (1983: 375); Amelang (1986: 205).   [57] Price (1987: 113).

notables, but the authentic era of Spanish notability started after 1812 and crystallized in the system of *Oligarquía y Caciquismo*. The persistence of status as a basic value for social relations in liberal Spain was particularly visible in the importance that Spaniards placed on the role of family lineage. Tenacious lineage fetishism, especially strong among middle and upper groups, brought about a family type with structure determined by the weight of kinship bonds. Thus, the prevalent family from among Madrid's dominant classes was one characterized by the existence of kinship networks.

In the past decade the field of family history has been paying more attention to the study of familial structures outside of the nuclear household. Kinship family networks appear as basic social structures in medieval and early modern European societies, both in rural and urban domains.[58] These structures based on the solidarity of kinship systems were not only typical among the middle and upper classes but also among the lower strata. They were not peculiar to rural and urban preindustrial societies but rather persisted throughout industrialization.[59] Among the lower classes they acted as instruments for social and economic mutual support. In the upper social groups these family networks were instruments for the preservation of social and economic domination. Some years ago Philip Greven demonstrated the effectiveness of kinship networks in the development of colonial American society. Linking household structure with patterns of landowning and inheritance, Greven discovered that family life in colonial Andover revolved around strong webs of kinship relations. Apparently, households consisted of nuclear families, but by studying their evolution through four generations, Greven arrived at the conclusion that the predominant family form was what he called the "modified extended" model.[60] To a certain extent, our Madrid families present a similar condition since most of them were immigrant groups that developed strong familial bonds in order to preserve their dominance. However, Greven's modified extended families had a much shorter life than our Madrid family networks. In Andover, networks weakened after the fourth generation and were almost entirely extinguished by the end of the nineteenth century. In Madrid, as well as in

---

[58] Smith (1979: 219f.); Plakans (1982a: 54); Segalen (1985); Wheaton (1987).
[59] Anderson (1979); Hareven (1990: 109).
[60] Greven (1970: chap. 8). He borrowed the concept of "modified extended family" from the sociologist Eugene Litwak (1960).

other Spanish regions, kinship networks were alive and used as forms of social domination until very recent times.

Madrid family networks functioned as associations of families related by economic and political interests, spatial proximity, sometimes by geographical origin, and on occasion by membership in religious and civil associations. Family networks were the instrument that provincial notable families most counted on to penetrate Madrid's dominant society and then maintain a continuous presence in it. Provincial *hidalgo* families, however, were diverse in their levels of wealth and social status, and so family networks were an instrument of continuity in the hands of the already established families, but they also provided the necessary means for the social ascent of regional groups.

A three-generation process constituted the basic demographic apparatus of our familial webs. After the third generation most families experienced signs of biological fatigue, but some family networks nonetheless survived for several centuries. Most of the networks that are object of this analysis originated in the second half of the eighteenth century, but they coexisted with other networks whose origins are found in the seventeenth century or even before. In fact, Madrid dominant society was a conglomerate of traditional well-established and ascendant immigrant families that for centuries used the same forms of social reproduction. Normally, Madrid family networks were the extension of others already existing in the provinces. If the original provincial family was wealthy and influential, the new immigrant's success was guaranteed from the start. In this case immigrants normally fell into already established networks. Something similar happened if the newcomer arrived in the capital under the protection of an already established family. However, on occasion newcomers from poor provincial families or from lateral branches of an established family were the ones who initiated new networks. In these new networks, the first generation was normally an example of social promotion. The second generation built the network and consolidated the group by developing coherent patterns of marital alliances and occupational endeavors. The third generation tended to expand the influence of the family to other social spaces. Successive generations then attempted to maintain the social rank attained by the family.[61]

Ascendant family networks were more frequent among merchants and bankers. The principal families of Madrid high commerce and finances were

---

[61] Balmori (1984: 2).

Kinship, friendship, and patronage

linked by kinship ties. They normally established those ties in the second and third generations, while successive generations tended to extend these alliances to other families of the high bureaucracy, politics, and aristocracy. The Iruegas family, for instance, connected with the Pérez family in its first generation (Figure 7.1). Both Iruegas and Pérez belonged to the guild of drapers, the strongest within the Cinco Gremios Mayores. Both placed members of the family in the highest rank of this powerful institution. In the third generation the Iruegas connected with the Sobrevilla, Bringas, Gonzalo del Río, and Aguirre families. Sobrevilla was a partner in the Iruegas firm and also held an important position within the Cinco Gremios Mayores. The Gonzalo del Ríos were one of the most important banking families established in Madrid at the beginning of the nineteenth century. In successive generations, the network formed by Iruegas-Pérez-Bringas ties connected with the Carranzas, another old banking family that received its noble title at the end of the eighteenth century, as well as with other notable families in Spanish politics, economy, and high society. The García de la Prada family provides a similar example. In the first generation they arranged a marriage with the Mazo family. The Mazos were from the same region as the Pradas and both families were already connected by kinship ties. The Mazos, however, were a family of bureaucrats and professionals of superior social status. In the second generation, the Pradas reinforced their ties with the Mazos through consanguineal marriages, while at the same time creating a marriage alliance with the Caballero family. The Caballeros were part of the Madrid business elite, but some members of the family were also bureaucrats and politicians. The Caballeros were linked to the Pérez family; thus, the Pradas were indirectly connected to other business elite families. In successive generations the Pradas reinforced their alliance with the Pérez family and other families within the business elite, but at the same time they diversified their familial strategy to join other influential groups in high politics, administration, and landowning. This strategy eventually connected them with the González Arnao, Muguiro, Collado, and Méndez-Vigo families, among others.

The Iruegas and the García de la Prada families are examples of ascendant business families. Their behavior applies to most merchants in this study, however. Many of the well-established aristocratic networks between 1750 and 1850 had ascendant origins in the preceding century. That was, for instance, the case of the Marquis of Miraflores's family. Miraflores, despite his commitment to *moderado* liberalism, was an aristocrat who held several

The museum of families

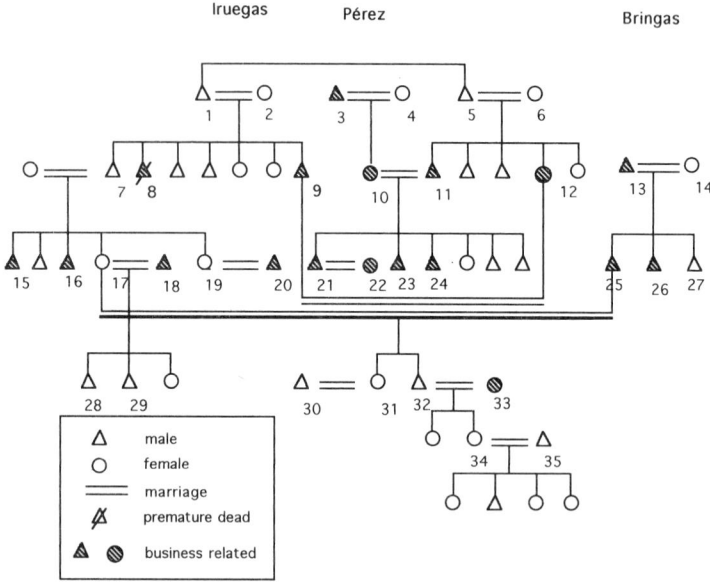

1. Marcos Iruegas Menoyo (Lorcio). 2. Rosalía Sotomayor (Lorcio). 3. Francisco Antonio Pérez (1720-1795, General Deputy of the CGM). 4. Ana Pérez (1724-1764). 5. Francisco Antonio Iruegas. 6. Antonia Aldana. 7. Bartolomé Iruegas Sotomayor (Inherited family entailed property in Lorcio). 8. Francisco Miguel (went to Madrid to work in the business of his uncle Lázaro about 1740). 9. Baltasar (1735-1813. General Deputy of the CGM). 10. Isabel Pérez. 11. Lorenzo Iruegas Aldana (1749-1795, General Deputy of the CGM and *Caballero of* Charles III). 12. Josefa. 13. Francisco Antonio Bringas López. 14. Antonia de la Presilla. 15. Gaspar Antonio Iruegas y Presilla. 16. Ramón Joaquín Iruegas y Presilla. 17. Angela Iruegas y Presilla. 18. Matias de Soldevilla (1741-1785). 19. Rosa Iruegas y Presilla. 20. Rafael Gonzalo del Río (1759-1919). 21. Lorenzo Iruegas Pérez (1748-1818). 22. Ana María de Aguirre. 23. Santiago Iruegas Pérez (businessman). 24. Lorenzo Iruegas Pérez (businessman). 25. Francisco Antonio Bringas Presilla (1756-1822). 26. Juan José (businessman). 27. Feliciano (lawyer). 28. Miguel Sobrevilla Iruegas (lawyer). 29. Gaspar (lawyer). 30. Antonio Barata (*militar*). 31. María Angela Iruegas Bringas. 32. Francisco Antonio Iruegas Bringas (businessman). 33. Polonia Carranza. 34. Maria Pilar Iruegas Carranza. 35. Manuel Cuevas y Chacon (*militar*, Count of Cuevas).

Figure 7.1. Family networks (Iruegas-Pérez-Bringas, 18th to 19th centuries)

titles and the status of *grande de España* (the highest rank within Spanish nobility). Toward 1850 his family constituted a network that included several well-known names of the Spanish new and old aristocracy.[62] The initiator of the network was a gentleman from the Carranza Valley who came to

---

[62] He married Vicenta Moñino Pontejos, who was the niece of the famous minister of Charles III and a descendant of the powerful Marquise of Casa Pontejos. AHPM, P. 21104, p. 389.

Kinship, friendship, and patronage

Madrid as a secretary of Philip V around 1740. This man, Antonio de Pando y Sabugal, belonged to one of these distinctive families of the Spanish provincial *hidalguía* that was well connected in Madrid. His family held a *mayorazgo* in his home town, but since he was not the eldest son, Don Antonio was forced to seek his fortune in Madrid. There he combined his administrative duties with business dealings – of course, mainly in the field of state provisioning. Don Antonio did very well, and when he died he left a fortune of more than 7 million reales that included several buildings in Madrid, land, company stocks, and livestock in the mountains. One of his brothers married the Countess of Villapaterna, and so the family attained an aristocratic title. In the second generation, the family improved its position by means of a carefully executed marriage strategy. One of his sons married his first cousin, Francisca de la Quintana y Pando. Francisca belonged to a family of powerful merchants from Bilbao who were also linked to several well-established bureaucratic families such as the Gardoquis. The other son inherited the title of Count of Villapaterna from his uncle, and married another titled aristocrat. Thus, in the second half of the eighteenth century, the Pandos had established a web that included people in the three basic influential scenarios of the time: the administration, the aristocracy, and the international commerce and finance.[63] In the third generation the Pandos continued the practice of wise marriage strategies, creating ties to other influential families. When the Marquis of Miraflores became a political celebrity he was considered a representative of the old aristocracy – he himself emphasized this in his written work. However, the Pando family in the nineteenth century was the result of a process of marital association between old aristocratic families and other ascendant families over no more than a century.

Marriage was a central piece in the consolidation of a family network. It was essential in order to protect the continuation of the family and in many occasions to improve its socioeconomic position. For these reasons people in our sample show a relatively high level of marriage unions (Table 7.4). Two-thirds of the bureaucrats and politicians were married, the proportion of married merchants and financiers was slightly smaller. The percentage of individuals who remained unmarried has a mean close to 13% for the entire sample. The proportion is a little below the 15% registered by Fayard

---

[63] AHPM, P. 17166 (complete); 20034, wp.; 20074, wp.; 20075, wp.; 20079, wp.; 20046, p. 493 and 20056, p. 315; 24673, p. 67.

Table 7.4. *Nuptiality among Madrid's dominant groups, 1750-1850*

		%
1. *Bureaucrats/politicians*		
Married	246	89.1
Single	30	10.9
Total known	276	
Unknown	8	
Total sample	284	
2. *Merchants/bankers*		
Married	172	85.5
Single	29	14.5
Total known	201	
Unknown	28	
Total sample	229	

Sources: Data from Merchants.dat; Bankers.dat; Func.dat; Polit.dat.

among the members of the council of Castile, and less impressive than the small 5% registered by Hernández among the Madrid urban oligarchs.[64] It is also close to Stone's figures for the landowning English aristocracy, which oscillated between 15% and 12% from 1650 to 1800. However, compared to other urban groups in early modern Europe the Madrid figure seems high.[65] In any case, Hernández's assertion that marriage was a social imperative for Madrid's urban oligarchs applies perfectly to our merchants, bureaucrats and politicians. In the case of ascendant families, prearranged marriages were still common. It would be naive, for instance, to think that a romantic ideal was behind the marriage of the Sáinz de Baranda brothers to their first cousins Manuela and Josefa San Juan y Santa Cruz.[66] The sisters San Juan y Santa Cruz were born in the valley of Arcentales, a hidden place in the north of Spain at several days traveling distance from the capital. One may suppose that their social life revolved entirely around the small village where they lived. On the other hand, the Sáinz de Baranda brothers socialized exclusively in Madrid, the place where they were born and raised. However, this difference in personal experience did not stand in the way of

[64] Fayard (1982: 288); Hernández Benítez (1991: 288).
[65] See Hernández Benítez (1991: 288). [66] AHPM, P. 19982, p. 473.

Kinship, friendship, and patronage

the doublt marriage. The brides were brought to the capital and, who knows how happily, they went through with the wedding. One thing is certain – the couples never split apart, although it is hard to imagine that they led a fulfilling conjugal life. Endogamic marriage was common among the merchant families. The Sáinz de Baranda brothers accepted their marriages as acts of obedience to the will of their family. The brothers, like most of their counterparts, probably did not see this demand as tyrannical or a violation of the personal will. To the contrary, this kind of marriage was part of their accepted culture.[67] Among ascendant and even established merchant families, marriages of convenience were an imperative to maintaining the stability of the business and the continuation of the family. Juan Francisco de Alday, the owner of a linen shop in the Plaza Mayor, described himself in his will as a single self-made man who worked hard to build a substantial fortune. He had employed in his commercial firm his two nephews, Ramón and Martín. In his will, Alday declared Ramón his sole heir, but on the condition that he not marry Manuela Martínez de Laguna, because she was not *de nuestra calidad* (of our same social stature). A few months after writing the will Alday arranged the wedding of his older nephew to Anacleta Mateo, the daughter of a well-established family of Riojano merchants. The arrangement document showed Alday's strong commitment to the continuation of his business firm and family name. The marriage was performed a few years later.[68]

Well-established families were less concerned with the choice of partner, so long as the person was of the same social rank. Antonio Alcalá Galiano, for instance, decided to marry his beloved fiancée despite his mother's opposition and the disapproval of his family. Alcalá Galiano's mother disapproved of the union not because she disliked the woman, but because the family of the bride was of inferior social status.[69] The couple went ahead with the wedding, but the marriage was a failure, in part because the relations between mother and daughter-in-law were never congenial. Pedro Girón, the marquis of Amarrillas, another moderate liberal, also went against his parents in his marriage choice. However, his rebellion did not cause the family significant turmoil, just a mild disappointment, since his partner's status was of the same aristocratic rank as the family.[70] These two examples illustrate that romantic love was an option amid Spanish dominant

---

[67] Seed (1987: 227f.). [68] AHPM, P. 21086, p. 820.
[69] Alcalá Galiano (1955). [70] Girón (1978: 130, vol. I).

The museum of families

Table 7.5. *Consanguineal marriage among Madrid dominant groups, 1750-1850: Wife's family connected at marriage*

1. *Bureaucrats/politicians*		
Family connection	72	29.3%
No evidence of connection	174	70.7%
Unknown	38	
Total sample	284	
2. *Merchants/bankers*		
Family connection	67	49.6%
No evidence of connection	102	60.4%
Unknown	60	
Total sample	229	

Source: Data from Merchants.dat; Bankers.dat; Func.dat; Polit.dat.

groups, but it was more frequent among established families, although statistics seem to indicate that it was not a widespread practice. Lawrence Stone's affective individualism did not pertain to Madrid's middle and upper groups.[71] Despite the prescriptions launched by some enlightened writers on the convenience of the free election of marriage, as well as the popularity of romantic literature, the levels of consanguineal and endogamic marriage remained very high. Affective individualism on the one hand and consanguinity and endogamy on the other are discordant tendencies in marriage practices. Noticeable levels of both consanguinity and endogamy are signs of biased unions, what common language calls marriage of convenience. Consanguineal marriages were significant among ascendant merchant families, but also frequent among landowner and bureaucrat families (Table 7.5).[72] Almost half of the merchants and bankers in our sample sought partners with their same blood or indirectly linked to their familial group. Bureaucrats and politicians did not follow such a drastic pattern, but consanguineal marriages were still common, judging by the 30 percent of cases in this sample. Among ascendant merchant families this kind of mar-

[71] Stone (1977).
[72] About a third of marriage and dowry contracts specify when a direct family connection existed. The rest of the cases have been deduced from genealogical reconstruction or by taking into account a combination of variables such as coincidence in surname, geographical origin, and social level.

riage choice was made to reinforce family economic positions. The predominant system of property transmission encouraged this kind of marriage. With the exception of families with *mayorazgos* what prevailed was the equal division of the patrimony among sons and daughters. The division of the inheritance could have devastating effects when the family owned a commercial firm. Marriage in the same family helped to avoid such inconveniences. Sometimes, however, families reached agreements that maintained the business part of the patrimonies intact. Consanguineal marriage in the second and third generations operated as a mechanism for the restoration of the old familial patrimony. This was a worthwhile practice not only among merchants but also among families whose wealth consisted mainly of property, as was the case for most bureaucratic dynasties and people in high politics. But, in particular, consanguineal marriage was especially a means to maintain the family's social rank and reinforce the strength of the lineage. It was a traditional practice that the high aristocracy used to ensure its continuity, but as we are seeing in these pages it was also a common instrument among middle and low noble families and other ascendant groups.

The Arizcun family provides an excellent sample of this tendency in the long term (Figure 7.2). The Arizcuns settled in Madrid at the beginning of the eighteenth century. They were part of the web of Navarrese business and officeholding families that controlled the political and economic life of the capital for some time. The pattern of installation and ascent of these groups is comparable to other cases that occurred during the days of the liberal revolution and later. The Arizcuns were a well-established family in their place of origin.[73] Successive generations of marriages among cousins helped to maintain the lineage's strength. This is why the Arizcuns did not encounter any difficulties in finding the necessary connections to improve their position in Madrid. Nicolás de Garro, Marquis of the Hormazas, who represented the pinnacle of familial achievement, held the surname Arizcun four times, inherited from two different branches of the family. The Arizcuns did not belong to the old aristocracy; they were a well-established family of the middle and low nobility that improved its social position. Most of their members were businessmen and administrative officials, not wealthy landowners. Nevertheless, they shared with the old aristocracy a culture of social reproduction that still was hegemonic in our period of study. Two

---

[73] Caro Baroja (1985: 286).

The museum of families

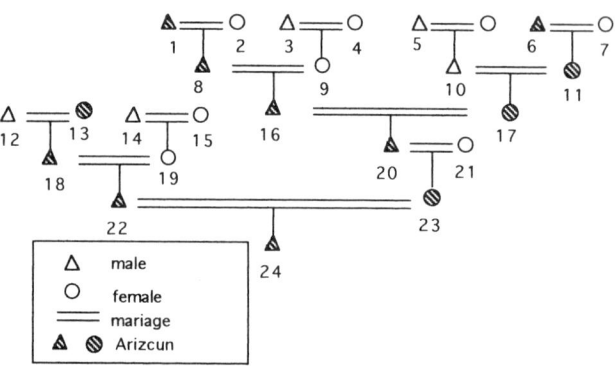

1. Martín de Arizcun. 2. María Jaimerena (married in 1623). 3. Juanes Beitorena. 4. Margarita de Echenique. 5. Pedro Mendinueta and María Peroscorena. 6. Juan de Arizcun. 7. María de Arráyoz. 8. Jerónimo de Arizcun (1627-1671). 9. Marigalant de Beitorena. 10. Miguel de Mendinueta (1618-?). 11 María de Arizcun. 12. Juan de Garro. 13. Graciana de Arizcun. 14 Juan de Micheltorena. 15 Catalina de Elizalde. 16. Miguel de Arizcun (1662-1720). 17 María Mendinueta Arizcun (1661-1628). 18. Juan de Garro Arizcun (1672-1741). 19 María Micheltorena. 20. Francisco de Arizcun (1685-?). 21. María Josefa Irigoyen. 22. Ambrosio de Garro (1703-?). 23. Josefa María de Arizcun (1724-?). 24. Nicolás Ambrosio (marqués of the Hormazas, 1746-1815).

Sources: Caro Baroja (1985: 265 and 281); AHPM, PP. 20067 and 20092 complete Protocolos).

Figure 7.2. Cosanguineal marriage in the Arizcun family, 16th–18th centuries

other practices defined restrictions on marriages: occupational and geographical endogamies. Occupational endogamy was traditionally very strong among Spanish dominant groups. It is a symptom of the importance of familial solidarity in social relations. To some extent it also indicates the relative closeness of dominant society. Occupational endogamy means economic endogamy, people choosing partners from their same socioeconomic level. But it also implies nepotism, one of the most blatant symbols of corruption in society of the time and a relatively normal practice. Janine Fayard called attention to the high proportions of members of the same family within the Council of Castile at different stages of its history. Fathers placed their sons within the council, uncles got positions for their nephews, as well as practicing favoritism at other kinship levels.[74] An average of 74 percent of the *regidores* in Madrid's City Hall were connected by family ties,

---

[74] Fayard (1982: 224f.); Hernández Benítez (1991: xxi, appendix).

Table 7.6. *Endogamic marriage among Madrid dominant groups, 1750-1850: Wife's fathers occupational position and geographic origin at marriage*

1. *Bureaucrats/politicians*					
Similar occupation	132	73.7%	Same geog. orig.	87	42.4%
Better position	46	25.7%	Different	118	57.6%
Worse position	1	0.6%			
Unknown	105		Unknown	79	
Total sample	284		Total sample	284	
2. *Merchants/bankers*					
Similar occupation	98	70.5%	Same geog. orig.	115	69.7%
Better position	37	26.6%	Different	50	30.3%
Worse position	4	2.9%			
Unknown	90		Unknown	64	
Total sample	229		Total sample	229	

Source: Data from Merchants.dat; Bankers.dat; Func.dat; Polit.dat.

according to the figures proportioned by Mauro Hernández's study. My own data also shows a high level of occupational endogamy (Table 7.6). Three-fourths of individuals within the three different groups tended to choose their partners from within the same occupational fields, which generally means they married at similar socioeconomic levels. Bureaucrats married the daughters of other bureaucrats. At the time of the marriage the union was usually uneven insofar as the bride's father generally held a higher position than the groom within the administration. In terms of social rank and economic condition, however, the unions were more equal. About one-fourth of the bureaucrats and politicians' marriages implied ascent for the husband's family. In these cases the groom normally belonged to the middle and low levels of the provincial *hidalguía*, while the bride was of a well-established family in Madrid – usually with an old aristocratic title. Ascendant marriages among merchants, however, usually meant integration into the high bureaucracy or politics. Men often married into families with recently acquired noble titles, but only rarely did they marry into the ranks of the old aristocracy. This means that intraoccupational marriage was more frequent among merchants, since this was the group with the largest number of ascendant elements in the sample. Geographic endogamy – marriage between people from the same region – was also a norm among the pre-

The museum of families

dominantly immigrant merchant community. It was the logical consequence of the high levels of consanguinity and occupational endogamies did not constrain interfamilial marriage. Families followed the lines of geographical solidarity and professional affinity to consummate marriage, but within these boundaries families connected with each other to favor the development of family networks. Endogamy and consanguinity were not impediments to demographic familial interaction but rather indicators of the strength of familism within the dominant groups. Marriage strategies that favored consanguinity and endogamy were aimed at maintaining a family- oriented social space.

The importance of these strategies marks a preference for prearranged marriages, or at least for marriages of convenience. They are indicators that subordination of individual affection to the will of the familial group was a prevalent practice in society. Their existence implies the maintenance of patriarchal authority within most of these familial groups. They framed the system of patronage that dominated relations to social promotion in Spain, since nepotism was its naturally accepted corollary. Finally, they constituted an irreplaceable instrument for the construction of family networks that determined social relations of Madrid dominant society.

The reproduction of the nuclear group was essential to the construction of the family network and the continuation of the lineage. Unfortunately, I do not have data on marriage age, which is indispensable to determining fertility trends. Because of its immigrant origin, Madrid's population tended to marry at later ages.[75] Late marriage was even more frequent among the middle and upper classes, since familial economies were more complex. Bureaucratic and commercial careers were very slow, aspirants had to wait many years before reaching a stable economic position. The councilors of Castile, for instance, married at a mean age of forty years, while the Madrid *regidores* married around the age of twenty-eight. Of course, women married at a much younger age, but still not early enough to take full advantage of their fertile years. Concern for ensuring descent was an important part of the demographic history of our families. I have compiled information on the number of children at the moment of writing the will for 110 cases of merchants and bankers and 226 cases of bureaucrats and politicians (Table 7.7). Children in my statistics means only descendants, not the

---

[75] Estimated age at marriage in Madrid between 1826 and 1837 was thirty for men and twenty-seven for women. See Carbajo (1987: 77).

Table 7.7. *Number of children in family at the moment of writing the will among Madrid dominant groups, 1750-1850 (Married cases only)*

1. *Bureaucrats/politicians*				
None	37	16.4%	Total children	572
1 - 2	73	32.3%	Mean	2.5
3 - 9	116	51.3%		
Total cases known	226			
Unknown	58			
Total married	246			
Total sample	284			
2. *Merchants/bankers*				
None	22	20%	Total children	201
1 - 2	66	60%	Mean	1.8
2 - 8	22	20%		
Total cases known	110			
Unknown	119			
Total married	172			
Total sample	229			

Source: Data from Merchants.dat; Bankers.dat; Func.dat; Polit.dat.

complete number of offspring by couple. According to these figures about 26% of bureaucrats and politicians – including bachelors – had neither sons nor daughters to whom they could transmit their patrimonies, the figures rises to 36% among commercial groups. These figures represent the difficulties of dominant groups to guarantee even the biological reproduction of their families. Nevertheless, if we compare our figures to others from earlier periods it is possible to detect a slight improvement. About 37% of Madrid *regidores*, according to Mauro Hernández's data, died without offspring to whom they could transmit their wealth and name. The proportion among the councilors of Castile in the study of Janine Fayard oscillates between 30% and 32%.[76] Merchants always had a difficult time producing descendants. Because many of them were involved in processes of ascent, they delayed marriage until they were financially secure. There were many more bachelors among the merchant group than among any other. Madrid

[76] Hernández Benítez (1001: 290); Fayard (1982: 288–89).

commercial firms were full of nephews, cousins, and *paisanos*. When there was no direct heir, fortunes were usually passed on to a patrilineal nephew. The proportion of families without heirs was also high among bureaucrats, landowners, and professionals, but their conditions were nonetheless better than they had been in the seventeenth and early eighteenth centuries.

There is no reason to conclude that a conscious strategy expalins this improvement because couples maintained a rather constant number of children through time. Bureaucrats and politicians tended to have larger families than merchants, and this trend did not change throughout the period studied. Between 1808 and 1814 many members of the Madrid elite were forced to abandon the city, but the negative demographic effects of war among these groups were mitigated by a rapid recovery after 1815. It is more likely that the relatively good outcomes in fertility were due to the general relief that mortality experienced in Spain during the second half of the eighteenth century.[77] Bachelorhood and the lack of heirs did not hurt the reproduction of our groups as dramatically as, for example, these factors affected the Egnlish elite studied by Lawrence Stone. Because of the predominant transmission system, having male descendants was imperative to the social reproduction of the English aristocracy up until recent times.[78] In Spain, however, the lack of male descendants only affected the continuation of the name once the *mayorazgo* disappeared as an economic and legal practice. In a transmission system characterized by the proportional distribution of wealth, the female element plays an equal role to the male element. Daughters were a positive resource to establish familial alliances and reinforce the economic strength of the group. In sum, our people found alternative ways to avoid the difficulties that persistent low fertility rates created for the continuation of family lineages. A calculated strategy of familial alliances and redistribution of wealth proved to be more effective than the unilineal transmission of the *mayorazgo*. This alternative implied a reinforcement of the use of family ties as an essential strategy of reproduction. Fertility practices of Madrid's dominant groups between 1750 and 1850 responded entirely to the needs of these family strategies that found their greatest expression in the widespread creation of family networks.

Madrid networks resemble the webs of familial solidarity and patronage that characterized elite social life in southern Europe and Latin America

---

[77] Carbajo (1987: 104f.). [78] Stone (1986: 48f.).

Kinship, friendship, and patronage

during the last two centuries. The use of family connections as a resource for the articulation of political and economic life was common to all European societies before industrialization and political modernization. What distinguishes Madrid from other cases in Northern Europe and North America[79] is its persistence through time, as well as its extreme importance until recent times. The use of family relations in politics and business is still a frequent practice in places like Spain, Italy, or Greece, not to mention Latin America. We are aware of this because of the ugly side of this practice: widespread corruption. Cases of economic and political corruption in Spanish politics, for instance, most often occur along lines of familial connections. However, episodes of political stability and economic growth have also happened in periods of strong familistic activity. The history of the interaction between family and politicoeconomic life is better known in Latin America than in Southern Europe, perhaps because of the influence of Anglophone scholarship.[80] Until we improve our knowledge in this field the use of Latin American models seems a suitable option.

Madrid's elite family type resembles the notable family networks analyzed by Balmori Voss and Wortman and, to some, extent, the Mexican elite grandfamilies studied by Lomnitz and Pérez-Lizaur.[81] Nevertheless, I find at least two differences between my case study and these Latin American models. Networks and grandfamilies in Latin America appear not to be as dependent upon the culture of family lineage as they were in Madrid. For this same reason I see more historical continuity in the families and forms of reproduction in Madrid than in Latin American cases. The oldest notable networks in the study of Balmori, Voss, and Wortman started in the eighteenth century. In Madrid new ascendant family networks shared the city's social space with others that had originated in previous centuries. New families connected to old families but always within a social realm limited to those who never depended on manual labor or were involved in industrial activities. With the exception of racial prejudice, Latin American kinship networks appeared to be more receptive to newcomers than the Spanish ones. Nevertheless, the similarities between Latin American and Spanish family models are greater than the differences. In both spaces family ties

---

[79] See Lamb Coser (1974); Stone (1975); Firth (1971).
[80] Cubitt (1982); Felstiner (1976); Ladd (1976); Barbier (1972); Kennedy (1973); Brading (1973); Burkholder (1978); Safford (1972); Kicza (1984); Lewin (1979); Tutino (1983).
[81] Lomnitz and Pérez Lizaur (1987).

constituted an essential instrument for the articulation of elite (and non-elite) social life until present times.[82] This social practice has produced similar results in the history of both social spaces since 1800. After all, connections between family life and public life – expressed in the practice of political and economic patronage – are still headline material for tabloids in both geographic areas.

Paisanos, friends, clients, and patrons

Richard Ford, in his *Gatherings from Spain* described nineteenth-century Madrid as the Spanish center of patronage and fashion. "From being the seat of the court and government," Ford said, "it attracts from all parts those who wish to make their fortune; yet the capital has a hold on the ambition rather on the affections of the nation at large. The inhabitants of the different provinces think, indeed, that Madrid is the greatest and richest court in the world (though its equivalent would be an English secondary city), but their hearts are in their native localities. *Mi paisano*, my fellow-countryman, or rather my fellowcountryman, my fellow parishioner, does not mean Spaniard but Andalusian, Catalonian, as the case may be."[83]

After the culture of familial solidarity, relations of mutual help between friends and *paisanos* complete the portrait of social practices within Madrid dominant groups. The boundary between friendship and *paisanaje* was not always tangible. Most of the time relations between *paisanos* involved ties of friendship, but on occasions *paisanaje* and friendship were not complementary. In those cases the relationship resulted either out of mutual convenience or from the obligations between a client and his patron. It is impossible to know the nature of the relationship in each specific circumstance, but one may infer that when it involved individuals from similar social positions the relationship kept its bargaining character, whereas when involving people from different social levels the relationship probably became one of influence and subordination.

It seems like patron–client relations were more prevalent than relationships "among equals" when someone helped another get installed in the

---

[82] Herán's study of the Andalusian Vázquez family offers an excellent sample case for Spain. The Vázquez, an *hidalgo* family that began its ascent at the end of the eighteenth century, carefully designed a familial strategy to create an influential network in southern Spain. Today, the Vázquezes form part of a constellation of a political and economic elite which controls the regional economy.

[83] Ford (1906: 11).

Kinship, friendship, and patronage

capital.[84] Newcomers always arrived with some kind of contact. It tended to be a letter of introduction or recommendation from some provincial notable that the person was to deliver to an influential person installed in the court. On many occasions these immigrants relied on the help of some member of their families, but even then the relation became one of dependence and subordination, that is, a patron–client relation.

I have already shown, through a number of personal histories, the details about the reception of beginners and the basic steps that they had to take in order to succeed in the city. We have seen some singular stories, a lot of unsubstantial occurrences, and a few failures. At this point, more than emphasizing the importance of patronage, I want to call attention to its survival as a hidden mechanism for social promotion within Spain's dominant groups up to recent times. This survival is especially notorious because it overcame the legal corrections introduced by liberal politicians in the first half of the nineteenth century. Still we need to study better this aspect of Spanish history: we get to know more details about the specific forms that patronage adopted in Spanish society in different historical moments. We need to scrutinize hidden processes, discover its protagonists, follow the threads to disclose the webs. It is a difficult process requiring patience and sometimes good luck in finding adequate sources of information, but it is not an impossible task. We have to go more frequently to notarial archives and especially to private archives, many of them still in the hands of the original families.

Patron–client relations among merchants and bankers usually followed the lines of familial solidarity and *paisanaje*. There is an astonishing coincidence in the regional composition of the merchant communities in places as distant as Madrid, Cádiz, Mexico City, and Buenos Aires in our period of study (Table 7.8). In all of these places, what we could call the Imperial Circuit, there was a preponderance of families from the mountain valleys of northern Spain. This immigration pattern responded to the way in which Spain articulated its economy after 1492 and especially once the court was installed in Madrid. Imperial policies introduced radical modifications in the organization of Spanish economic and social spaces. What we see after the sixteenth century is a disruption of late medieval Castilian urban net-

---

[84] Contemporaries labeled this relation with the name of *Compadrazgo*. See Pitt Rivers (1955: 137–141).

Table 7.8. *Geographic origins of merchants in Madrid, Cádiz and Buenos Aires, 1730-1830*

	Madrid (1750-1830)				Cádiz (1730-1823)	
Place of origin	(A)	%	(B)	%	(C)	%
North	146	79	298	34	1174	37.3
Northwest	7	3.7	84	9.6	204	6.5
Center	24	13	339	38.6*	133	4.2
South	1	0.5	15	1.7	1318	41.7*
Levante	3	1.6	83	9.4	189	5.9
Foreigners	4	2.2	59	6.7	139	4.4
Total	185		878		3157	

	Buenos Aires (1778-85)	
		%
From Spain		
Castile, Galicia, Santander	49	34.5
Andalucia	12	8.5
Catalonia	2	1.4
Basques	49	34.5
Other		
European (non Spanish)	9	6.3
Buenos Aires	18	12.7
Other American colonies	3	2.1
Total	142	

*Many of this merchants registered in the *matrícula* as Madrileneans or Andalusians were the second or third generations of immigrants from other Spanish regions, especially from the north.
Source: (A) 1750-1850. Author's compilation see chap. I, It refers mainly to merchants of the CGM. (B) 1830. Ringrose (1986: 306). (C) Ruiz Rivera (1988: 40, 51-57). Socolow (1978: 186)

works and the growth of key points in the imperial circuit.[85] In the context of these historical changes the losers appeared to be some Castilian production centers in favor of the commercial ports of the Cantabric rim and its hinterlands. Part of the social consequences of this historical interference

[85] Ringrose (1985).

Kinship, friendship, and patronage

can be seen in the development of these networks of solidarity and patronage controlled by a relatively homogeneous social group. The result of this homogeneity was the development of a culture of social relations common among all merchant communities of distant cities in the imperial circuit. Brading talks about the deep feeling of self-identification with their motherland among the members of Mexico's merchant community, minaly formed by Basques and Montañeses (from Santander). Compatriot relationships were an essential practice in the development and social action of this community. They represent a loyalty deeply rooted in a particularly communal orientation of religious practices and economic solidarity.[86] Both groups were famous for their noble pretensions and their passion for genealogy. Kicza describes elite reproduction of Mexico City as the result of the action of a network of client solidarity, in which individuals and groups identified primarily by their similar, though remote, geographic origins. Since 1742, the Mexican Consulate has been divided into two parties: the Basque and the Montañés.[87] Similar patterns of social activity have been described by Socolow for Buenos Aires and by myself for Madrid.[88]

Still, we know little about the nature of the society that they came from. Because they were from mountain communities dominated by an economy of small farmers, scholars have tended to emphasize their social egalitarianism and their relatively modest social origins. Their commitment to noble cultural values, these scholars stress, resulted from their origins in a society in which everybody had the right to consider himself a noble. *Hidalguía*, the basic condition of nobility in Spain, was a universal status among the inhabitants of these northern regions; consequently it cannot be considered as a symbol of social differentiation. These conceptions have been influenced by more general classic interpretive models of the characteristic mobility of mountain societies. One of the corollaries of these models is that in these agropastoral societies people are equals in poverty, they are usually described as communities of small landowners sharing mediocrity.[89] New approaches to the history of mountain communities are questioning this traditional view. By a minute examination of the social

---

[86] A product of it was the organization of some religious institutions such as the Cofradía de Nuestra Señora de Aránzazu and Cristo de Burgos, the hospital of *Vizcainas* etc.; also the nonreligious Sociedades de Amigos del País. Brading (1971: 107).
[87] Kicza (1983: 277f.).
[88] Socolow (1978).
[89] Poitrineau (1983: 6f.); Rosenberg (1988). In Spain this position appears particularly in the works of social anthropologists. Gilmore (1980: 4–8) offers a summary of the main works in the field.

structure of mountain communities and the forms of socioeconomic emigration these new approaches are bringing about the end of the egalitarian myth.[90] My own research points in this direction – as I have shown, not all of the people within the Madrid merchant community were the same. Some came from extremely humble social backgrounds, but most of them held enough resources to start their economic careers, a few of them even belonged to wealthy established families. My feeling is that, instead of being equals in the poverty of the mountain community, *montañés* migrants belonged to a middle-high spectrum within a society where clear social differences existed even though they were not as marked as in the communities of the plain. Thus, social self-esteem was not an artificial feeling among these immigrants, but rather responded to real differences in the status acquired in their places of origin. Familial solidarity, *paisanaje* bonds, mutual friendship, or all of these practices in the form of patron–client relations, were, finally, mechanisms for the maintenance of an already acquired social position.

Patronage was even more widespread among the rest of our dominant groups. Different authors, for instance, have referred to the cliques that controlled politics at different moments throughout the eighteenth century. Some of these groups were eventually known by a regional attachments of their components. Thus, writers have talked about the *círculo murciano*, referring to the acolytes that surrounded Floridablanca, or the *círculo Asturiano*, alluding to the people under Jovellano's patronage. For centuries the mechanisms of political promotion within the Spanish state were based on the relation between an aspirant (*pretendiente*) and his protector. They frequently involved kinship or *paisanaje* ties, but it was above all a patron–client relation. Once the aspirant arrived in Madrid he rushed to government offices, presenting his letter of recommendation, waiting in lines, and bribing government employees. This generalized social practice can be traced not only in the evidence of historical facts but also in the use of a specific social language that can be found in private and public texts. Later in the nineteenth century the practice of regional solidarity and patronage crystallized in *caciquismo*. During the years of the liberal revolution patronage shifted to the control of notables within the *moderado* and *progresista* parties. At this time, patronage was administered through the *Jefe Político* and the *Gobernador Provincial*, new institutions created for the maintenance

---

[90] See Fontaine (1990: 1433–50).

of political control. It was almost a mathematical formulation: whoever was in power and controlled the electoral system won the elections. Under these circumstances the use of the military was a resource in the hands of the opposition to neutralize the power of the patronage system.

Conclusion: A class society?

In this chapter I have argued that relations between kin, friends, and *paisanos* were more important than class conflict in the social articulation of Madrid's dominant groups. I have stated that these were relations of solidarity among affines, or of mutual bargaining among partners, and most frequently of subordination between clients and patrons. Does this mean that class relations did not exist in this society? Did interactions among kin, friends, and *paisanos* oppose class relations? Absolutely not. After all, not all people in Madrid's dominant society were of the same social level, and not all friends and *paisanos* held the same social position. Not all members within a family network had to have the same social standing, and patron–client relations involved, on many occasions, relations of class subordination. I do not intend to deny the existence of class relations and class conflict among Madrid dominant groups – what I suggest is that these kinds of social relations were not the only nor the most significant in explaining historical change in Spain between 1750 and 1850. The end of the old regime in Spain, as in the rest of Europe, was not the result of a confrontation between a decadent feudal class and a vigorous ascendant bourgeoisie. Social relations during those years cannot be described as a conflict between two antagonistic classes and the eventual triumph of one over the other. Nor can we say that there were a series of tacit agreements and a mutual give and take between two traditional enemies (the bourgeoisie and the aristocrats) who finally came to realize that the real threat stemmed from the revolutionary impulses of the popular classes. These pages have offered enough evidence to show that if such a conflict existed, it was not the moving historical force in our period.

Instead of the traditional picture of a stagnant society of estates and a liberated society of classes, I see the social dynamic within Spanish dominant groups with less liberal enthusiasm. I do not perceive that the practices that characterized social relations in the old regime dissipated with the liberal revolution. Most of them continued and some were even reinforced. I do note, on the other hand, that old regime society created mechanisms to guarantee the renewal of its managerial groups. As I have demonstrated, social mobility existed before and after Spain had a constitution and a civil code, but this mobility was corrected by the persistence of a traditional culture and a slow economy. Given this framework I do not see the emergence of a new class imposing a new culture of social relations. The societal process of time seems to be one of adaptation, replacement, and even renewal, through episodes of social ascent. In conclusion, I do not believe that liberalism's disruptive effects on politics had its parallel with regard to the social practices and social composition of dominant groups in Madrid.

8

Conclusion: Rethinking the Spanish revolution

More than sixty years have passed since Spanish politicians and intellectuals began to debate the bourgeois revolution and the existence of a bourgeoisie in the nineteenth century. As in most European countries, their preoccupation was at the center of heated political discussion.[1] At that time Europe was caught between the advance of Fascism and the impulses of the Bolshevik revolution, and many sought theories that could explain the current historical situation. One of those explanations revolved around the bourgeoisie and its central role in the development of capitalism. The democratic right – from conservatism to the most radical liberalism – tended to blame the rise of fascism and communism on the failures of the bourgeoisie in the nineteenth century. Interest in the role of the bourgeoisie among politicians and intellectuals also came from another front: those pursuing an effective strategy for the culmination of the proletarian revolution. The debate about the bourgeois revolution, then, involved many participants, though for different reasons.

In Spain the concepts of bourgeoisie and bourgeois revolution have played a central role since the 1920s in the debate over Spanish modernity.[2] This debate has unfortunately stayed true to its origins, remaining highly politicized. Obviously this polarization is due to the persistence of Francoism, which favored the prolongation of the discussions of the 1930s. Spain's political atmosphere is also the reason why, until recently, this intellectual debate was played out at a largely theoretical level, far from archival research.

In the following pages I will summarize the origins of the bourgeois

---

[1] This factor has been emphasized by Romanelli (1991: 32).
[2] The bourgeois revolution, a Spanish historian recently pointed out, constitutes in Spain an obligatory point of reference. See Petit (1990: 11).

revolution paradigm and look into the present state of the discussion. The Spanish model has developed in the context of larger European research and debate on the subject; thus I will try not to lose sight of the more general context. The ultimate objective is to contrast the results of my research with the present state of the discussion on the bourgeoisie and the bourgeois revolution in Spain.

The bourgeois revolution in Spanish historiography

The intellectual foundations of the debate are rooted in the nineteenth century, when the first explanations were formulated. On the one hand was the liberal tradition, which exalted all that was bourgeois as a sign of progress toward a freer world, while, on the other hand, the Marxist tradition demonized the bourgeois as a new agent of human exploitation. Both conceptions, as mentioned earlier in this study, stemmed from an evolutionist understanding of historical process, according to which all change corresponded to a logic of progression.[3]

In Spain the influence of the liberal tradition has been secondary, and Marxism has dominated discussion of the role of the bourgeoisie in the development of Spanish capitalism. The first steps in this debate were, in fact, taken in the 1920s and 30s by members of the leftist parties who characterized Spain as a bourgeois capitalist system in which a socialist revolution was necessary to improve living conditions.[4]

The failure of the Second Republic and the defeat of democracy in the civil war led to stronger pessimism regarding the strength of the Spanish bourgeoisie, and this was reflected in the first academic works on the subjects. For Ramos Oliveira, defeat in the civil war was due to the secular debility of the bourgeoisie.[5] Pierre Vilar emphasized the persistence of agrarian structures that "put material, juridical, and psychological obstacles in the way of capitalism."[6] The academic debate regarding the bourgeois revolution began in the wake of these two works, and it has continued to the present following two basic lines of interpretation.

---

[3] Skocpol (1979: 3–43); Tipps (1973: 199–210). On Marx and Engels's insights regarding the bourgeoisie and its revolutionary role in history, see Hamilton (1991: 4–9); Comninel (1987: 28–32).

[4] The main arguments of the debate on the Spanish bourgeois revolution were traced by Juan Sisinio Pérez Garzón in a rigorous article published in 1980. For the main part, I followed this author for my exposition of this issue up to the 1980s.

[5] Quoted by Alvarez Junco (1985: 144).

[6] Vilar (1947: 66–69).

Conclusion

I will call the first approach the "classic interpretation" because it follows the traditional model outlined by Marx and Engels in the *Communist Manifesto*. It adheres to the archetype of the French Revolution, and it continues in part the analyses begun in the 1930s. Those who follow this line of interpretation do not deny the existence of a revolutionary bourgeoisie in Spain in the nineteenth century, but they do question its ability to democratize the political structures of the country and to introduce a fully capitalist system. Gil Novales, following an interpretive line opened by Tuñón de Lara in the 1970s, argues that in order to bring a revolution to fruition a bourgeoisie needs to gather popular support, as occurred in France. For this to happen a country needs a strong and resolute bourgeoisie, capable of neutralizing popular rebellion and channeling the revolution toward its own interests. The weak Spanish bourgeoisie, however, were not capable of this. The revolutionary impulses they demonstrated in 1812 and especially in 1820 were tempered by the threat of popular rebellion in the 1830s. In the end the bourgeoisie "was to follow the path of collaboration with absolutist power" and with the landholding upper classes. This led to their aristocratization and in some cases to their refeudalization. The peculiar form that the Spanish bourgeois revolution took led Spain through the dictatorships of the nineteenth century, problems with the colonies, and the perpetual dissatisfaction of the people, straight to Francoism.[7]

None has dealt with the matter in greater detail than the members of what are now called the schools of Vicens Vives and Pierre Vilar. Pragmatic and innovative, both historians followed Marxist thinking influenced by Gramsci, Hobsbawm, and Thompson, introducing nuances to interpretations of how the bourgeois revolution developed in Spain. Influenced by Vicens Vives's thesis, according to which the only authentic Spanish bourgeoisie in the nineteenth century was the one found in Catalonia, Solé Tura also speaks of a failure of the revolution that would not be corrected until the second half of the twentieth century. According to this author, in fact, it was only in Francoism that the bourgeois revolution came full circle.[8] On the other hand, Fontana's work describes the Spanish revolution as following the "Prussian route to capitalism," rather than the change to democracy that characterized the French revolution. The revolution did occur, but it came from the top down, as opposed to what happened in France. Consequently, "the fall of the old regime in Spain took place under an alliance

[7] Tuñón (1977: 98); Shubert (1990: 14); Gil Novales (1985: 54–58).
[8] Solé-Tura (1970: 286).

between the liberal bourgeoisie and the *latifundista* (landowner) aristocracy. . . . This is why we can explain what is unexplainable in the French model: that the landed aristocracy sided with the revolution, as well as a vast portion of the peasantry."[9] These thoughts were presented in the midseventies and were elaborated upon in a subsequent work in which the author seems to question the social character of the Spanish revolution. "The French revolution was a social revolution," while in the Spanish case the deputies "had not wanted a social revolution and omitted any form of upheaval that would have introduced more profound reforms and moved the peasant masses to their side."[10] In this reasoning we see once again Gil Novales's thesis that the bourgeoisie feared popular revolution.

Since the beginning of the 1970s another line of interpretation has appeared inspired by the debate over the transition from feudalism to capitalism.[11] At issue is the mode of the transition from feudal to capitalist modes of production. This process places greater emphasis on the relations of production and less on political revolution. For this reason the framework of the analysis turned from the discussion of ideas and attitudes to economic relations and legal changes, from the realm of political and social history to the domain of economic and juridical history. In the framework of this debate the bourgeois revolution is the period of transition between the different modes of production, and so economic and legal aspects are stressed more than sociopolitical ones. Defining the role of the bourgeoisie becomes a secondary consideration, but the idea that the transition occurred under the guise of a social revolution is never abandoned.[12] The followers of the "transition line" of interpretation have logically centered their attention on the processes of disentailments and on the suppression of the seigniorial system.[13] Both events serve as models for the Spanish bourgeois revolution. For these historians there is no doubt that the revolution was completed since the determining factor is the existence of a framework of capitalist relations, and these were achieved during the nineteenth century.

---

[9] Fontana (1975: 162).
[10] Quoted by Pérez Garzón (1980: 123).
[11] For an update of the transition debate in the late 1980s, see Mooers (1991).
[12] Hilton (1984: 91); Pérez Garzón (1980: 123).
[13] Tomás y Valiente and Simón Segura were the first to consider disentailment as a key piece in the process of the Spanish bourgeois revolution. They based their argumentation on the fact that the bourgeois were the major purchasers of disentailed property. In the last two decades this thesis has been the object of debate in an extraordinary proliferation of disentailment studies. See Simón Segura (1973); Tomás y Valiente (1971 and 1986: 779–98); Rueda (1986); Herr (1989: chap. XX).

Conclusion

By reducing the concept of bourgeois revolution to a mere change in the relations of productions, this group of historians has even been able to fix concrete dates for its completion. Enric Sebastiá, one of the most prominent members of this school, places it between 1834 and 1843, when the feudal system was ended. What occurred between those dates "were the most profound changes seen in the last millennium. In a period of just years the seigniorial regime succumbed to the forces of revolution. A world of feudal privileges gave way to a society based on contractual relations."[14] The bourgeoisie, of course, provided the impetus for this process, although in Sebastiá's work this is taken as a given, and juridical changes take the center stage because they led to this framework of contractual relations.

Bartolomé Clavero follows a similar line of reasoning, claiming that the bourgeois revolution was, first and foremost, a juridical revolution. The dates of this revolution are fixed even more precisely, between 1835 and 1837. Although in Clavero's argument the process that led to the revolutionary rupture was instigated by the downfall of what he called the "feudal block," the revolution does not have to be considered a social rupture. Despite the antifeudal and bourgeois character of the revolution, it did not bring about a change in the composition of the dominant block. This was, above all, a political revolution that introduced a new juridical order, liberating property, privatizing the family, and centralizing the state, in order to consolidate a system of contractual relations.

The bourgeois revolution is a social revolution only to the degree to which in the middle term the juridical transformation provoked changes in class conditions, but it was not the result of a previous social alteration.[15] Clavero's thesis seems suggestive in its conclusion but contradictory in its exposition. He first speaks of a progressive tearing away of the bourgeoisie from the feudal block in order to explain the process that led to the juridical revolution. Later, however, he states that the revolution did not come as a result of an alteration of the social composition of the dominant block. What happened to this independent bourgeoisie? How and by whom was the anti feudal position articulated? Beyond this, why call a revolution "bourgeois" when it originated from a social block dominated by persons who were not bourgeois? It is little wonder that Fontana, from his less heterodox Marxist perspective, criticizes the "juridical illusion" which Clavero seems to accept when he considers that the imposition of liberal civil and public law as not

---

[14] Sebastià (1987: 13).
[15] Clavero (1979: 41–43). See also from the same author (1976: 35–54).

The museum of families

being a product of class struggle. Clavero is undoubtedly the victim of an unyielding adherence to Marxism.[16]

These same contradictions have been repeated by the diverse versions of the bourgeois revolution given by those following this line of interpretation. We have seen how Clavero proposes the existence of a political revolution which maintains the dominance of the same social block. Sebastiá, on the other hand, sees a social revolution in which the bourgeoisie and the peasantry stand up to feudalism. This bourgeoisie, however, did not seem to constitute a compact block, since after 1843 a part of it allied itself with the aristocracy while another part united with the middle sectors of society and the workers in order to fight the remnants of feudalism. For Alarcón Caracuel the bourgeois revolution represents the "the juridical and political consecration of the bourgeoisie as a dominant class." In his analysis this bourgeoisie, which has accumulated economic power, is solely responsible for the revolutionary process.[17] Pedro Torres, in the meantime, says in his study of the fall of the seigniorial regime in the south of Valencia that the revolution pitted "merchants and agrarian landowners against the aristocracy and feudal laws that obstructed the free development of commercial capitalism and the penetration of agriculture by capitalism." The revolution did not limit itself to simply changing the juridical superstructure but rather was accompanied by social struggle and class conflict.[18]

As we can see, within the Marxist tradition there exists a wide variety of positions and conjectures that range from those who see the bourgeoisie as weak and as having begun a revolution they did not finish, to those who see no gray areas – who say that, indeed, there was a bourgeoisie and that it had fulfilled its revolutionary missions. What is most surprising in the midst of all this confusion, however, is that all of these positions have been taken with little to no knowledge of the people and groups that supposedly made up this bourgeoisie. Everywhere there is mention of the bourgeoisie, but no one describes the group and nobody has studied it in a systematic manner.

Bourgeoisie and bourgeois revolution are terms that are widely used as basic points of reference in most work about the nineteenth century, but they are used as wild cards, to support explanations of very general processes. This is how Marxist historiography has used the terms, but it is also the case among those who belong to a liberal tradition, with the possible exception of some Catalonian historians. Miguel Artola, who sensibly pre-

[16] Fontana (1979: 25–32).   [17] Alarcón Caracuel (1975: 21–23).
[18] Torres (1981: 393–94).

Conclusion

fers to use the term "liberal revolution," nonetheless places an agrarian bourgeoisie at the center of his argument, without specifying who made up this group.[19] Marichal, whose position is somewhat tempered in the Spanish translation of his original English text, gives center stage to an urban bourgeoisie who he claims led the revolution between 1834 and 1844.[20] Similarly, Comellas and Palacio Atard also consider the bourgeoisie's role to have been central to the liberal revolution, but they, again, do so in an excessively broad and confusing manner.[21] Both Marxist and liberal historiographies are definitely in agreement when they speak of the existence of a new ascendant class that, either through alliances or on its own, was able to take control of the means of production and transform juridical structures so as to accommodate capitalism. Neither of these strains of thought, however, has detailed the characteristics of this class through a systematic study of it.

In recent years the picture has seemed less bleak. Spain has undergone many changes, as has Europe. Political debate is a lot less charged, allowing people to work less ideologically and more pragmatically. But this same process has also been occurring in other European countries, making what is happening in Spain seem a part of a more general tendency. It has been more than three decades since Cobban suggested that seeing the major conflict in eighteenth-century France as a clash between a feudal aristocracy and a capitalist bourgeoisie was an insufficient or, rather, an incorrect way of explaining the French revolution. Since that time dozens of studies have been published about the social classes that participated in the French revolution. The only conclusion that can be drawn from this abundance of information – Marxists and non-Marxists seem to agree on it – is that although there had been intense class conflict, the landholding elite of the old regime survived the revolution and was able to regenerate itself in the high society of the nineteenth century.[22] The debate is, nonetheless, ongoing.

The same is true for Germany, where historians have focused on the problem of defining the country's "particular" way of incorporating a capitalist system.[23] Here we also see debates about the weakness of the bourgeoisie and its ability to bring about an authentic bourgeois revolution. Also being questioned is the bourgeois-capitalist character of German so-

---

[19] Artola (1978: 93f.).   [20] Marichal (1977: 2–5 and Spanish edition 1980: 118f.).
[21] Comellas (1970); Palacio Atard (1978).   [22] Price (1987: 96); Hunt (1984: 213).
[23] See Reddy (1987: 14–23).

ciety in its transition from the nineteenth to the twentieth centuries. Researchers seem less preoccupied with bourgeois revolution, stressing instead either the "Prussian road" to capitalism or the "reformist road."[24] The debate has only begun to clear up in recent years, with empirical studies about the class system and the formation of the bourgeoisie. Blackbourn and Eley have shown that there was nothing excessively "peculiar" about the German route to capitalism relative to the rest of Europe. They simply warn against using closed models of interpretation, especially ones that establish a causal relation between social class and political positioning.[25]

This penchant for diversification also seems to be a tendency of late Anglo-Saxon Marxism, which tries to avoid the analytical schemes established by Perry Anderson. Work in the field is abundant, first with those influenced by Thompson and his conception of class relations that privileges the cultural, and second by the existence of a large number of empirical studies about the history of dominant groups. They have concluded that England's revolution was not essentially different from the rest of Europe's, that each country's revolution depended on imbalances and combinations in the nature of capitalist development.[26] Nevertheless, in England the debate over the bourgeois revolution is of secondary importance. Nobody questions the existence of a well-established middle class; what researchers pursue is an understanding of its role in the history of the last four centuries.

Given this general context for work on early modern and modern Europe, it should come as no surprise that in Spain the model of the bourgeois revolution should be questioned. What is interesting, though, is that challenges to the model have come not from persons identified with the liberal traditions but rather from many researchers with a Marxist background. Alvarez Junco, for example, has pointed to contradictions in the model when it is applied to concrete cases. It now seems more doubtful whether Marx and Engels's model, rooted in Hegelian dialectics, can be found in practice. If what we mean by bourgeois revolution is a violent change that

---

[24] Kossok (1983: 92f).
[25] Eley offers a definition of bourgeois revolution in which it is necessary to distinguish "between two levels of determination and significance – between the revolution as a specific crisis of the state, involving widespread popular mobilization and a reconstruction of political relationships, and on the other hand the deeper process of structural change, involving the increasing predominance of the capitalist mode of production, the potential obsolescence of many existing practices and institutions, and the uneven transformation of social relations." See Blackbourn and Eley (1984: 82–83). A similar analysis was applied to the Spanish case by Acosta Sánchez as early as 1975.
[26] Mooers (1991: 4 and 171).

Conclusion

causes political, social, and economic upheaval, then there were, indeed, very few bourgeois revolutions. In most countries capitalist transformation has occurred slowly and unevenly, the entire process sometimes lasting over a century. History has shown that evolutionary processes, and not revolutions, are what have moved capitalism, and so we always have to look out for the "peculiar" nature of each case.

In the case of Spain this process has lasted some one hundred sixty years. Applying the term "revolution" to the process is, then, simply making historical pieces fit into a puzzle that is in itself a poor tool for the study of history.[27] Alvarez Junco proposes abandoning a model that forces us to constantly move in the terrain of the exception to the rule. Rather than looking at subphases or intermediate situations, we should come up with new analytical schemes to look at the whole. We should distinguish, for example, the liberal oligarchic revolution of the early nineteenth century from the radical democratic ones of later years. "The most common form of transition from one political and social structure to another," concludes Alvarez Junco, "is evolution – revolution is exceptional and only affects certain spheres of social activity."[28] Along similar lines, Lufolfo Paramio has suggested that the distance between theory and practice in the paradigm of the bourgeois revolution should lead us not to change the terms of discussion but rather to change the paradigm.

However, research and not theoretical speculation should be responsible for inverting the terms or changing the paradigm. Fortunately, in this area the academic outlook seems to have improved. In recent years historians have been increasing our knowledge of the concrete processes and the persons who moved them, which is where research should have begun years ago. Results are still partial and uneven, but in some areas they are satisfactory. We have a much greater understanding of the business bourgeoisie and of some of the sectors of the powerful elite. Most of these works, however, use the old regime as a historical marker, or only begin their analysis for the period after 1834. With this information it is still difficult to reconstruct the characteristics of the dominant group at the time of the revolution. These studies also tend to be regional, and so a global perspective often escapes us. This notwithstanding, some conclusions can be drawn, especially for the second half of the eighteenth century.

Everything seems to indicate that there were many cities where important

---

[27] Alvarez Junco (1985: 145). [28] Ibid., 149.

nuclei of merchants settled, but there were only a few where they were truly influential. Their importance was felt in Cádiz, Málaga, Madrid, Bilabo, Barcelona, and probably in some other cities, but social prominence in all these places remained in the hands of the local nobilities.[29] In other areas like Santander or Valencia, the merchants were not even integrated into the local elite.[30] With the exception of Barcelona and some areas in the Basque country, the world of trade was apart from industrial investment and productive spheres. However, it was very common for members of these groups to invest in land and to be granted titles of nobility. While in Madrid, Cádiz, and Málaga the merchant bourgeoisie tended to consist of immigrants from very distant areas, the ports of the Mediterranean and the north both saw a greater integration of city and region, and so trade was more truly local. Barcelona was actually the only urban nucleus with an influential trade community that was originally from the region, but even there the nobility set social standards. We still know very little about the dominant groups of the local and provincial levels, but there does not seem to be anything to indicate that these groups saw a radical change in composition during the period. Recent work on disentailments, especially Herr's, has shown that local elites were strengthened but that their composition was left intact.[31] Among those who bought disentailed lands were merchants, professionals, and farmers, but by far the group that most benefited from disentailments was the old landowning elite, most of whom were from the nobility. We know a little more about Madrid's power elite,[32] but this knowledge lacks continuity. The period of transition from the old regime to liberal society is a vacuum yet to be filled. Our fragmentary knowledge of the period has made it difficult to judge whether there existed a bourgeoisie with the ability to lead a revolution. I have attempted, with this study, to fill this vacuum.

Bourgeoisie, gentlemen, notables? What kind of a revolution?

The concept of bourgeoisie is, of course, not easily defined, since its meaning has changed throughout history depending on where it is used. As

---

[29] Bahamonde Magro (1981 and 1986); Caro Baroja (1985); Cruz (1986 and 1990); Fernández (1982); García Baquero (1966); Otazu (1987); Ramos Santana (1987); Tedde (1983); Villar (1982); Zylberberg (1979 y 1983).
[30] Franch (1986); Maruri (1990); Eiras (1981). [31] Herr (1989: 747).
[32] Fayard (1982); Hernández Benítez (1991).

Conclusion

Romanelli has shown, the concept is not objective but relational, hence the historical variability of its definition.[33] Spanish historians' use of the term, however, stems from roughly two concrete points of reference: on the one hand is the Marxist tradition and on the other is the Sombartian. The models of both traditions were constructed with very different historical settings in mind. As mentioned earlier, the Marxist tradition has been dominant, but it was often the case that historians used a mix of both traditions, adding to the confusion. For this reason appraisals of the groups that made up this class have gravitated between being either excessively restrictive or exaggeratedly open. Vicens Vives, for example, wrote that between 1750 and 1833 the bourgeoisie consisted exclusively of "merchants without *almacén abierto* (open warehouse) and the manufacturers and industrialists in cotton and silk. In the true sense of the word, the only Spanish bourgeoisie can be only found among the merchants of Cádiz and the manufacturers and merchants of Catalonia."[34] Vicens obviously came up with this definition at a time when still very little was known about the importance of other merchant communities outside of Catalonia and Cádiz. Following a similar reasoning, Jover uses an occupational criterion to define the group. When he speaks of the bourgeoisie he means merchants, bankers, entrepreneurs, and some professional sectors.[35]

Marxist historiography has, however, expanded the social definition of the concept of bourgeoisie. First, it has stressed the importance of the agrarian element in the composition of the Spanish middle sectors. Historians like Fontana, Bernal, and Tomás y Valiente speak of an agrarian bourgeoisie that instigated the changes that occurred in Spain between 1808 and 1868. This being said, the composition of this landholding bourgeoisie is fairly confusing. According to these historians the primary way of determining if someone is a member of the bourgeoisie is to look at his relationship to the modes of production. Any landowner who exploited his properties in a framework of capitalist relations of production is considered bourgeois. It goes without saying that this definition expands the social limits of the bourgeoisie extraordinarily.[36] In a recent article Mariano Peset suggests that the Spanish bourgeoisie's most dynamic elements at the end of the old regime were merchants and manufacturers. He says, though, that this class also included

---

[33] Romanelli (1989: 70). [34] Quoted by Rueda (1986: 162).
[35] Ibid. (1986: 164).
[36] Tomás y Valiente (1978: 19); Fontana (1985: 238); Herr (1989: 729).

The museum of families

professionals, artisans, guild masters, and a significant part of the lesser nobility that openly identified with the principles of liberalism.[37] Marc Baldó Lacomba's classification is much more specific, considering the bourgeoisie a class in formation and, consequently, a group with little cohesiveness. Unlike Peset, in whose classification the urban element is primary, Baldó considers the importance of rural areas. He first includes in his group a small number of well-off peasants, tenants, and small landowners. Second, he includes a large group consisting of elements of the lesser and medium nobility (former *mayorazgos*, agrarian proprietors, professionals, government officials, etc.). A third group consists of those who took part in the putting out system, that is to say, those who worked between the worlds of rural production and the market. This was a significant group in Spain. The fourth group in Baldó's classification was an important urban sector of guild artisans. The final stratum of the classification consisted of merchants, bankers, and manufacturers, groups that, according to the author, provided the greatest challenge to absolutism. According to these historians then, the old nobleman who liberated his *mayorazgo*, the urban artisan using free contracting to run his shop, the Catalan industrialist, and the high government official of noble ancestry all belonged to the same socially ascendant group: the bourgeoisie.[38] It is my opinion that such an amalgam of social types is anything but a social class.

To consider as bourgeois anyone who exploited his land in a more or less capitalist fashion or those who sympathized with liberalism is an oversimplification that does not help us to understand history. The problem is that the point of departure for all of these classifications is a very reductionist conception of social classes. As I pointed out at the beginning of this work, a social class is not simply a collective of individuals with the same position with regard to the relations of production. Other variables have to be taken into account, such as their social origins, the nature and origin of their wealth, or how their position is determined by cultural practices based on tradition, systems of values, and ideas.

Throughout this work I have presented a series of biographies of persons who lived in the same era, many of whom shared ideas, collaborated in financial ventures, and who often shared similar political outlooks. With few exceptions I think all of them could be considered "bourgeois" in any of the

---

[37] Peset (1990: 172–74). [38] Baldó Lacomba (1988: 214–18).

Conclusion

classification systems detailed here. Despite all of these similarities, the diversity found in their social origins, the nature and origin of their wealth, and their social behavior, leads me to think that they did not constitute a new social class. They instead represent a conglomerate of classes that were characterized by their socially dominant position. This is why throughout my study I have preferred to speak of dominant groups or of middle and high classes, conscious of their social diversity but also aware of their societal dominance. Whether they were a bourgeoisie or not is irrelevant; in my opinion the debate over whether or not there was a bourgeoisie lacks relevance. What I do believe is that the concept of bourgeoisie – here again I refer to Romanelli's work – as it has been used in Europe to define the groups that dismantled the old regime, is in all respects insufficient.[39]

The central element of this group, and its largest contingent, consisted of a number of families whose status and wealth had not been recently acquired. This is the impression given, for example, by the analysis of families from the political and administrative elite during the transition from the eighteenth to the nineteenth centuries. There is no room really to speak of an ascendant class in formation. Even in sectors like commerce and finance, where social mobility was most evident, ascent was regulated by traditional mechanisms of solidarity and loyalty. By far most of the families in this powerful nucleus belonged to the middle and lower levels of the provincial nobility. There were a fair number of persons with recently acquired wealth, but there were also a good portion taken from the old aristocracy. Many of the families held *mayorazgos*, which means that their wealth proceeded on the one hand from agrarian rents, what historians have called feudal rents. On the other hand their wealth came from salaries, from what Herr called the redistributive economy of the old regime. They were, though, the instigators of laws that dismantled the legal apparatus of the old regime. Although they were not themselves capitalists, many of them followed those who were in changing laws that favored the development of capitalism. Some historians refer to this group as a "bourgeois nobility," because they adopted positions traditionally attributed to the bourgeoisie.[40] This argument is based on the belief of an inherent incompatibility between the bourgeois capitalist and the noble landholder. A number of works on European history have already shown the superficiality of this argument. This

[39] Romanelli (1989: 71–73). [40] Torres (1981: 343).

The museum of families

forces us to rethink the role of the nobility in the crisis of the old regime and to consider the possibility that, in effect, this crisis could be explained partly as being a conflict between elites.[41]

As in France, Germany, or Italy, in Spain liberalism had its adherents both among the bourgeoisie and the nobility. And so another of the traditional theses – that of a pact between the nobility and the bourgeoisie – is no longer valid. The evidence provided by my analysis shows that such a pact would not have made sense. In reality, before the big changes of the era both groups were already united by a community of interests that, if not social, were definitely political and economic. Several historians have already warned against the illusion of the predominance of feudal relations of production. The *mayorazgo* was in decline many years before its abolition because the aristocracy had a difficult time making their manors profitable, and the church was divided as to how it should administer its wealth. These groups found alternative ways of exploiting their wealth, many of which were plainly capitalist. Disentailments and the abolition of the *mayorazgos* and manors did not pit the bourgeoisie against the nobility. They undoubtedly caused some anxiety among the ranks of the nobility, but this was more the product of ideological differences than class conflict. What was resolved in the liberal era was the old conflict between local elites and central power. Through the electoral system local elites finally found an appropriate way of controlling central power and maintaining their socially dominant status. What emerges from this process was not a new bourgeois society but rather a society of notables, that is to say, a society characterized by the survival of traditional structures and habits that only economic change could transform. The foundations of this society were authority and patronage, structures that were perfectly adaptable to the restricted electoral system and to the predominant client economy. *Cacipquismo,* the concept used to define political bossism of the era of the Restoration, was actually nothing but an extension of notability, but this is a matter which should be studied in greater detail.

From the point of view of occupations, the dominant social group was made up of agrarian and urban property holders, followed by administrative officials, professionals, and businessmen. But the vast majority of the latter three groups were to some degree or another also property owners. At least in Madrid, where political decisions and large business contracts were un-

---

[41] As Antonio Morales Moya (1983: 1246) suggested several years ago.

Conclusion

dertaken, there were very few industrial entrepreneurs among the power elite prior to 1850. I have also, of course, not been able to find among the elite any merchants tied to the putting-out system of artisans. It is true that these groups defended liberalism, taking active part in the urban militias and participating in conspiracies. But there was also a large number of noblemen among the ranks of these militias. There is some indication that after 1845 some centers of local power changed in social composition, making room for ascendant groups. The same was not true of central power, whose social composition remained fairly continuous.

It is interesting to see how the social biographies of prominent members of Madrid's dominant group are repeated through time. The establishment of political and economic institutions is surprisingly similar to patterns going back to the seventeenth century. Administrative officials, politicians, and professionals, as well as businessmen, were all immigrants to the city. Beyond this, the pattern of migration seems to remain continuous right up until the last third of the nineteenth century. In this model there is a consistent presence of persons from the agrarian south and southeast in political institutions, while commerce and finance were dominated by families from the valleys of the northern peninsular mountains. Another important characteristic is that most of the immigrants were employed by the state. For politicians and bureaucrats it was a way of life and an instrument of control and domination. The lives of large merchant companies and financiers, however, also revolved around the state. This means that the kind of society generated by the capital resulted from the city's function as political and administrative center. As Ringrose has shown, the reason the city became the seat of the state was merely political. It stemmed from a decision in which strategic interests and dynastic convenience prevailed and not as a function of Madrid's position in Castile's urban network. The city's society reflected this reality in which the state was the principal generator of wealth, not agriculture, commerce, or industry.

Although as far as the dominant group is concerned society was neither closed nor static, it also cannot be considered to favor aggressive social mobility. As I have pointed out, although the nucleus consisted of the same social groups, the prominent individuals and families were not the same ones throughout the period. There were distinguished episodes of rapid social ascent. This ascent occurred, however, within the framework of social relations that favored reproduction over renewal and replacement over substitution. As in traditional societies, kinship, friendship, and patronage relations were the dominant forms of class relations. It is not that there existed no class relations, just that they were not worked out through conflict but rather through mutual agreement, solidarity, and loyalty. Class conflict was seen at the margins of the dominant group, but rarely in the center. Examples of ascent also had very fixed limits. Those who had no direct or indirect ties to local elites or to the commercial dynasties of the north and Cádiz had a very difficult time joining the dominant group. In order to rise socially one had to pass through the filters of patronage networks that controlled the social work of the capital. Mobility was then restricted by status so that, for example, wealthy artisan families could not become members of the powerful elite.

Networks of kinship, friendship, and patronage were basic social mechanisms of the old corruption. One of the objectives of the revolution was precisely to rid society of the abuses that this system encouraged, hence the reforms of liberal civil law and of state public law. But contrary to what Clavero states, these political reforms did not end the social practices of the old corruption in Spain or the rest of Europe, with the exception of England. As we saw for Madrid, families did not become more private than they had been, since marriages of convenience were still a common practice and the interests of the family came before those of the individual. Individuals also did not free themselves from the loyalties imposed by social promotion. Equality of opportunity was no more than a juridical formula that in practice was regulated by traditional mechanisms of social reproduction. Recent research seems to indicate that the old corruption began to disappear from European societies as a result of economic, rather than political, progress.[42] The prevalence in southern Europe of these practices in recent times seems to be a product of the area's slow economic development. I do not mean to minimize the influence of liberal political order over the introduction of new social and economic relations, but to infer from this that a social revolution occurred seems erroneous.

Social practice cannot be reduced to simply being a set of relations of production or laws. It must also take into account cultural relations, which many Spanish historians have failed to do. They have consequently found social revolution where there was only superficial change. Some years ago Tuñón de Lara pointed to the fact that nobody goes to bed an aristocrat and wakes up bourgeois simply because their legal status has changed.[43] This is

[42] Price (1987: 358); Blackbourn and Eley (1984: 151).
[43] Tuñón (1977: 98).

Conclusion

true of the individuals in the socially dominant groups of the Spanish capital. We have seen how they were mostly from families of local notability, generally of noble ancestry, whose wealth stemmed from a combination of rents and salaries. Although they managed their properties using capital methods, they do not seem to constitute a modern class of agrarian entrepreneurs. Most actually preferred to lease their properties and live far away from them. I do not think these circumstances should be overlooked as we evaluate the social behavior of this group. Because of their regional origins most had been raised in a culture that blended practices of social exclusivity and authority. These were fundamental mechanisms for the maintenance of domination in a highly polarized society. In their places of origin these families spoke a carefully symbolic language that helped them maintain their positions of power. This language consisted of coats of arms, illustrious family names, selective socialization, etc. This is what in local Spanish tradition is known as *señoritismo*, which is no more than an extension of old noble exclusivity. Authority was maintained through old and new institutions which the *señoritos* tended to control. I think that this culture was deeply rooted in the mental world of many of the men of the dominant group, to the point of constituting an habitus.

This habitus does not necessarily have to be in agreement with political practice, as some historians have suggested. In this study we have seen how an individual could be very liberal in his ideas and public activity, while remaining feudal in his social behavior. Alcalá Galiano described one of his uncles, a minister of the council of Hacienda, as a republican who nonetheless practices a Catholicism of the era of the counterreformation. The mayor of Sáinz de Baranda at one point complained about the way in which teaching positions in schools were being handed out. This same person, however, for years had an ongoing battle within his family because he wanted his son to inherit a chaplaincy that he claimed was his by right of birth.

The problem has been that most historians, when studying the social positions of liberals, have focused exclusively on their political practices, on their public discourse. What they have failed to take into account is that there also exists a private discourse that is just as important when it comes to defining the behavior of a social group. I have used the example of the Cabarrús family to show how the two discourses were often contradictory. While public discourse was fundamentally ideological, their private discourse was essentially social and therefore was concerned with daily life and maintaining social dominance. And so the Cabarrús family maintained a public position of commitment of liberty and equality, but when it came to keeping control of their properties and ensuring their continuity the family relied on authority, exclusivism, and the old corruption. They acted like this not because they were weak, perverse, or traitors, but rather because it was the only way they could survive as a dominant group in a highly polarized society. Francisco de Cabarrús admired the social and economic egalitarianism he saw developing in North America, and he wanted to move Spain in that direction. Although his political, social, and economic projects followed that path, he still had to maintain his position as an agrarian proprietor in a society that was poor and socially unjust. The result was a blend of ideas and practice that, of course, did not lead to his ideal of modernization.

Despite its contradictions, the conglomerate of social classes that dominated Madrid's power centers was able to bring about a political change of enormous historical transcendence. I do not think that their liberalism should be understood as inhabiting exclusively the realm of relations of production, what has traditionally been understood by class position. Many of them were simply attracted to the message of modernization and progress. Others wanted to follow the example of countries like England or North America, where the new system seemed to be producing positive results. Most embraced liberal ideas for both reasons, because they truly wanted to improve Spanish society and because it was economically and socially beneficial for them to do so. This change was not the product of the rise of a new social class, nor did it significantly alter the social mechanisms of domination of the traditional elites, but it did plant the seeds for a long process of transformations that would continue in Spain until the 1970s. I agree with those who say that to call this a "revolution" is to exaggerate, but it is also a mistake to consider that its nature was above all social and that it was the work of an ascendant bourgeoisie. The changes that Spain saw between 1808 and 1853 were essentially political in nature and, because of their intensity and the speed with which they took hold, could be considered revolutionary. Let us then speak of political revolution within the framework of social continuity and slow economic development. For the sake of better historical understanding, let us call this era Spain's liberal revolution.

Appendix A: The sample

This list includes 549 names of people who lived in Madrid between 1750 and 1850 who have been used in this study. The selection was made taking into account the occupation of each individual according to the information available in the archives. The sample is random in the sense that the cases have not been extracted from a population census or a statistically homogeneous group. Most of the information about the lives of our subjects comes from the Archivo Histórico de Protocolos de Madrid. Only a few of our cases have been documented in the Archivo Histórico Nacional and the Archivo Histórico del Banco de España, but the information found in these archives has been especially useful.

The testaments and inventories (*particiones de bienes*) were our main source of information, although we have also used other notarial documents related to property, the market, and marriage. The probate inventories undoubtedly have been the most complete source of detailed information about family economies and their transformation. Nevertheless the families did not always make an inventory of the deceased's possessions before they were distributed. This only occurred when there were more than two inheritors and, for whatever reasons, an agreement regarding the distribution of the inheritance was not reached. The wills and the inventories of capital, dowries, and prenuptial agreements supplement in part the scarcity of inventories. Additionally, these sources have supplied information about family structures and cultural aspects. The *escrituras de poder* offer indirect information about the markets; they are particularly important for the study of mercantile and financial communities. The sales and loan contracts have added considerable supplemental information to this study.

With the information compiled from these diverse sources I have created five data bases, each with seventy-eight variables: Merchants.dat,

Appendix A

Bankers.dat, Bureaucrats.dat, Professionals.dat, and Politicians.dat. The computer processes all this data using SPSSX.

Per.: Period.
    1 = 1750–1783
    2 = 1783–1816
    3 = 1816–1850

Occup.: Occupation.
    1 = Merchant (CGM or similar)
    2 = Bookseller
    3 = Merchant in Catalan commodities
    4 = *Ropería*
    5 = Retailers
    6 = Specialized commerce
    7 = Bankers
    8 = Bureaucrats
    9 = Proprietors
    10 = Lawyers
    11 = Physicians
    12 = Apothecaries
    13 = Other professions
    14 = Military

Merchants
(Merchants.dat)

Name			Per.	Occup.
Acha		Francisco	1	1
Alday	Angulo	Ramón	2	1
Alday	Zubiaga	Juan Francisco	1	1
Alonso		Domingo	2	2
Altable		Manuel	2	1
Angulo	Guardamino	Ramón	2	1
Antuñano	Basualdo	Francisco Nicolás	3	1
Araujo		Tomás (de)	1	2
Arco		Simón (del)	1	1
Azuela	Marroquin	José (de la)	1	1
Baile		Pedro	2	3
Balmaseda	Mateo	Juan Domingo	3	1
Baños		Juan Manuel	1	1
Bárcenas		Adriano (de las)	2	1
Bárcenas	Indo	Francisco (de las)	3	1
Barreras		Francisco	2	1
Basualdo		Antonio	1	1
Basualdo		Manuel	2	1
Baura		Gaspar	2	3

278

The sample

Name			Per.	Occup.
Berriozábal		Juan Ignacio	3	6
Bitón	Santibáñez	José	3	6
Blanco		Saturnino	3	4
Braceras	Campo	Agustin	2	1
Brihuega		Juan Antonio	2	4
Bringas	Iruegas	Francisco Antonio	3	1
Bringas	López	Francisco	2	1
Bringas	Presilla	Francisco Antonio	2	1
Caballero	Mazo	Andrés	3	1
Caballero	Moral	Andrés	3	1
Cabañas		Francisco	3	6
Calera	Llaguno	Manuel	1	1
Campo		Miguel	1	5
Castillo		José	2	1
Cerrajería		Francisco	2	1
Céspedes		Valentín	3	5
Chávarri	Laiseca	Mateo	2	1
Dehesa	Ortiz	Bartolomé	2	1
Díaz	Sánchez	Eugenio	3	4
Elejalde	Larrieta	Bartolomé	2	1
Elejalde	Sáez	Juan Antonio	1	1
Entrambasaguas		Manuel	2	1
Escudero		Juan Antonio	1	1
Faba		Roque	1	5
Fernández	Casariego	Fernando	3	1
Fernández	García	Pedro	2	1
Fernández	Maruri	José	2	1
Fernández		Simón	3	5
Fourdinier		Roberto	2	6
Fuentes		Juan Agustín	2	1
Galarza	Goicoechea	Cristóbal	1	6
Galarza	Goicoechea	Francisco	2	6
Gandara		Manuel Antonio	2	1
García	Aldeanueva	Manuel	2	1
García	Angulo	Francisco José	2	1
García		Casmiro	2	1
García		Francisco	2	5
García	Gastón	Bartolomé	2	1
García	Herrán	Manuel (de la)	2	5
García	Olaya	Miguel	2	1
García	Pinillos	Pedro	2	1
García	Prada	Juan Sixto	2	1
García	Prada	Manuel	2	1

Appendix A

Name			Per.	Occup.
García	Santiago	Manuel	2	1
Garrido	Castillo	José	2	1
Gil	Martínez	Manuel	1	1
Gil	Martínez-Solórzano	Manuel	2	1
Goicoechea	Galarza	Martín	2	6
González	Aguilar	Francisco	1	1
González	Cacho	Nicolás	2	1
González	Villa	Domingo	2	1
Gorbea		Juan Francisco	2	1
Gozani		Juan Francisco	1	1
Gregorio	Pinillos	Gabriel	2	1
Gregorio	Pinillos	Juan	2	1
Guardamino		Francisco	2	1
Guardamino		Manuel Antonio	1	1
Haedo	Pico	Francisco	1	1
Hermoso	Daza	Juan	3	1
Hermoso		Miguel	2	1
Hermoso	Sáenz de Tejada	Dámaso	2	1
Hernandez	Santa Cruz	Victoriano	2	1
Heros	Fernández-Sierra	Manuel	2	1
Heros	Fernández-Sierra	Juan Antonio	1	1
Heros	Herrán	Juan Francisco	2	1
Heros	Herrán	Nicolás	2	1
Heros	Manzanal	Bartolomé	1	1
Herrera	Riva	Felipe	1	1
Hoyos	Ruiz	Manuel	1	1
Ibarra		Hilarión Joaquín	2	2
Ibarra		Joaquín	1	2
Ibarrola		Domingo	2	1
Ibarrola	Torre	José Antonio	2	1
Iñigo	Vallejo	Bernardo	2	1
Iruegas	Aldana	Lorenzo	2	1
Iruegas	Pérez	Francisco	2	1
Iruegas	Sotomayor	Baltasar	2	1
Jaúregui	Lordia	Juan Tomás	1	1
Larramendi	Aguirre	Santiago	2	1
Larrinaga	Goiri	Francisco	2	1
Layseca	Zorrilla	Francisco Martín	2	1
Llaguno	Cueto	Juan	1	2
López de Sa		José	3	1
López	Martínez	Felipe	1	1
López	Rodrigo	Juan	2	1
López-Angulo	Ventadés	Francisco Antonio	2	1

The sample

Name			Per.	Occup.
Losada	Quiroga	Manuel	2	2
Machón	Bringas	Juan Agustín	1	1
Madrazo	Peña	Bartolomé	1	1
Martínez	Escudero	José	1	1
Martínez	Lerdo	Eugenio	2	6
Martínez	Robledo	Juan	1	1
Martínez	Santidrián	Fernando	1	1
Martínez	Torre	Francisco	2	6
Martínez	Ventadés	Santiago	2	6
Mas		Francisco Jaime	2	3
Mazo		Francisca (del)	3	1
Mazo	García-Prada	Bernardo	2	6
Mollinedo	Arco	Francisco Antonio	1	1
Monjas	Pinilla	Antonio	2	4
Murua		Juan	3	1
Nieto	Marqués	Andrés	2	1
Nieto	Marqués	Pedro	1	1
Novales	Iruegas	Francisco	1	1
Ojeda	Sáenz	Andrés	1	1
Ortiz	López-Villa	Juan Ventura	2	1
Ortiz	Peña	José	1	1
Ortiz	Rozas	Juan Manuel	3	1
Ortiz	Taranco	Francisco	1	1
Ortiz	Tejera	Juan Antonio	2	1
Ortiz	Urbina	José	2	1
Ortiz	Velasco	Manuel	1	1
Ortiz	Zárate	Juan Antonio	2	1
Pabón		Bartolomé	1	1
Palacio	Cerro	Diego	2	1
Palacio	Velarde	Francisco	2	1
Palacios	Saravia	Joaquín	1	1
Paliza		Antonio (de la)	1	1
Pando	Garma	Francisco Antonio	2	1
Pando	Pando	José Francisco	1	6
Pando	Sabugal	Antonio	1	6
Pedrorena	Esponda	Miguel	1	1
Peña	de la Peña	Manuel (de la)	1	1
Peña	Rodrigo	Manuel (de la)	2	1
Pérez	Fernández-Otero	Francisco Antonio	2	1
Pérez	Roldan	José	2	1
Pérez	Sánchez	Diego	2	1
Posadillo	Llaguno	Domingo	1	1
Posadillo	Llaguno	Francisco	1	1

Appendix A

Name			Per.	Occup.
Posadillo	Llaguno	Juan Santos	2	1
Posadillo	Medina	José	2	1
Quijada		Antonio	2	1
Quintana	Pando	Francisco Ambrosio	2	6
Retes	Bustamante	Francisco María	2	1
Retes	Martínez-Viergol	Francisco Antonio	2	1
Ribacoba	Gorbea	Francisco Antonio	3	1
Rubio	Lombardo	Pedro	3	1
Ruiz	Prada	Juan Bautista	1	1
Ruiz	Santayana	Santiago	2	1
Sacristana		Francisco	2	1
Sáenz	López	Joaquín	2	1
Sáenz	Prado	Ignacio	2	1
Sáenz-Tejada	Hermoso	Policarpo	2	1
Sáinz de Baranda	Gándara	Pedro	2	1
Sáinz de Baranda	Gorriti	Pedro	3	1
Sáinz de Baranda	Gorriti	Vicente	2	1
Sáinz de Baranda	Santa Maria	Manuel	2	1
Saánz		Francisco Antonio	3	1
Santa Ana	Plaza	Manuel	2	1
Santibañez	Ibarra	José	1	1
Saracha	Haedo	Manuel	2	1
Sedano		Pedro	2	1
Segura	Soto	José Antonio	1	1
Sierra	Balgañón	Fernando	2	1
Sobrevilla	Menoyo	Manuel	1	1
Sobrevilla	Menoyo	Pedro	1	1
Sojo	Vezara	Manuel	1	1
Soria	Zaldivar	Francisco	2	1
Sorzano	Soria	Juan Manuel	2	1
Sorzano	Soria	Paulino	2	1
Torre	Gómez	Manuel Lucas	2	1
Torre	Herrera	Juan Domingo	2	1
Torre	Rauri	Manuel	2	1
Trápaga		Felipe	1	1
Trápaga	Maza	Juan Antonio	2	1
Trasviña	Palacios	Manuel	3	1
Urquijo		José Alejandro	2	1
Urtiaga		Nicolás	3	1
Valle	Luengas	Francisco	2	1
Valle		Manuel (del)	1	1
Velasco	Chávarri	José	2	6
Velasco	Chávarri	Manuel	2	1

The sample

Name			Per.	Occup.
Vergara	Sáenz	Juan Manuel	2	1
Villa		Francisco	3	1
Villar	Toral	Pedro	3	6
Viña	Urruela	Manuel	2	1
Wercruyse		Pedro	2	6
Wercruyse	Shelly	Pedro	3	6
Zabala		Pedro	2	6
Zorrilla		Francisco	2	1
Zorrilla	San Martin	Manuel	2	1
Zubiaga	Osejuera	Pedro	2	1

Bankers
(Bankers.dat)

Name			Per.	Occup.
Abrisqueta		Andrés	2	7
Aguirre		Manuel Francisco	1	7
Alvaro	Benito	Frutos	2	7
Aragorri	Olavide	Simón	2	7
Arecha		Domingo Javier	2	7
Avancino		Antonio	2	7
Avancino		Felipe	2	7
Barthelemi		Juan José	2	7
Bouhebent		Jaime	2	7
Carranza	Gainza	Tomás	2	7
Chávarri		Francisco Antonio	3	7
Daudinot		Pedro María	2	7
Drouilhet		Juan	2	7
Dutari	Galainena	Domingo	2	7
Dutari	Zuelgaray	Juan Bautista	2	7
Fagoaga	Dutari	José	3	7
Fernández	Gonzalo del Río	Luis	2	7
González de Lovera		Manuel	3	7
Joyes		Gregorio	2	7
Joyes	Blake	Joaquin	2	7
Murga	Aguirre	José Manuel	2	7
Norzagaray		Mateo	3	7
Pedrueza	Helguera	José (de la)	2	7
Pérez	Seoane	Manuel	3	7
Queneau		Agustín	2	7
Ravara		Felipe	2	7
Rossi	Gosse	Juan Bautista	2	7

Appendix A

Bureaucrats
(Bureaucrats.dat)

Name			Per.	Occup.
Acedo	Torres	Francisco	2	8
Acha		Domingo	2	8
Aleson	Bueno	Juan Jose	3	8
Alvarez	Mendieta	Luis	2	8
Anduaga		José (de)	2	8
Arjona		José Manuel	3	8
Armesto	Antonio		2	8
Aróstegui	Manuel		2	8
Arozarena		José Gabriel	2	8
Ayestarán		Juan Ignacio (de)	2	8
Azofra	Delgado	Jose	2	8
Cabanilles	Jose		3	8
Cabarrús	Lalane	Francisco	2	8
Calvo	Rozas	Ramon	3	8
Campo	Haza	Francisco	2	8
Canga-Argüelles	Ventades	Joaquín	3	8
Carrancio		Manuel Angel	2	8
Carrión	Rivas	Francisco	1	8
Castro	Arias-Somoza	Ramon Antonio	2	8
Catalan		Dionisio	3	8
Cisneros	Cabreros	Antonio Maria	2	8
Colón	Larreategui	Mariano	2	8
Cornejo	Castaño	Antonio	2	8
Cortés		Andres	2	8
Crota		Juan Bautista	1	8
Cruz	Cano	Ramon de la	2	8
Dehesa	Fernández	Francisco	2	8
Domínguez	Llorente	Pedro	3	8
Doz	Funes	Manuel	2	8
Elorza	Aspiazu	Rafael	3	8
Enríquez		Pedro Alfonso	2	8
Escobedo	Alarcon	Jorge	2	8
Espinosa	Brun	Antonio	3	8
Fernández	Mendivil	Francisco	1	8
Fernández-Isla	Alvear	Juan	2	8
Fitta	Huel	Juan Antonio	2	8
Fuertes	Sanchez	Julian	2	8
Gacel	Combe	Luis	2	8
Galvez	Lopez-Sales	Antonio	2	8
Garcia	Pando-Echalburu	Francisco	2	8

The sample

Name			Per.	Occup.
Gargollo		Tomas	1	8
Garro	Micheltorena	Ambrosio Agustín	1	8
Gazel		Luis	3	8
Gómez	Ibarnavarro	Pedro	2	8
Gómez	Labrador	Pedro	3	8
González	Calderón	Pedro	2	8
González	González	Tiburcio	2	8
González	Maldonado	José	3	8
González	Peñafiel	Manuel Gaspar	3	8
González	Tejada	Zenón	2	8
González	Yebra	Antonio	2	8
Gorbea		Francisco	2	8
Güel		Juan Ignacio	2	8
Gutierrez		Matias	3	8
Gutierrez	Solana	Ignacio	3	8
Henríquez	Luna	Gonzalo	2	8
Herrán		Francisco Jerónimo	2	8
Ibarrola		Francisco Antonio	2	8
Ibarrola	Layseca	Fernando	2	8
Ibarrola	Llaguno	Antonio	2	8
Indart		Pedro	2	8
Iriarte	Oropesa	Bernardo	2	8
Irusta		José (de)	2	8
Iturbide		Joaquín	2	8
Jacot	Ortiz-Rojano	Melchor	2	8
Jaramillo	Contreras	Antonio	1	8
Jiménez	Guazo	Manuel	3	8
Jonsansoro	Serralta	Vicente	2	8
Jovellanos	Ramírez-Mira	Melchor Gaspar	2	8
Larramendi		Juan	3	8
Larrea		Miguel José	3	8
Larrea	Ribera	Manuel	1	8
Larrumbide		José Antonio	3	8
León	Roldan	Francisco	3	8
Llaguno	Amírola	Eugenio	2	8
López	Ballesteros	Luis	3	8
López	Juana	José	3	8
Lorieri		Pedro	2	8
Losada		Luis	2	8
Marcoleta	Labarrieta	Domingo	2	8
Marin	Vaguer	Francisco	3	8
Martínez	Calinsoga	Mariano	2	8
Martínez		Domingo	1	8

Appendix A

Name			Per.	Occup.
Martínez	Mata	Pedro	2	8
Martínez	Salcedo	Antonio	3	8
Martínez	Sobral	Francisco	2	8
Martínez	Villeda	Ignacio	3	8
Mata		Cristóbal	3	8
Maturana		Vicente Joaquín	2	8
Melendro	Aguión	Gabriel	2	8
Mendinueta	Múzquiz	Jerónimo	2	8
Moñino	Redondo	Francisco	2	8
Moñino	Redondo	José Antonio	2	8
Morales	Guzman-Tovar	Juan	2	8
Moreno	Martínez	Domingo	3	8
Moreno	Martínez	José	2	8
Múzquiz	Aldunate	Luis	2	8
Múzquiz	Goyeneche	Miguel	1	8
Nava	Noreña	Juan	2	8
Nestares	Grijalba	Fernando	2	8
Nieto		Juan	2	8
Ondarza		Pablo	2	8
Orbaneja	Ortega	Miguel	2	8
Orovio	Goicoechea	Juan Antonio	2	8
Ortiz	Guinea	Diego Joaquín	1	8
Otondo		Pedro	3	8
Oyarvide	Heredia	Juan Manuel	2	8
Pardo		Manuel	3	8
Pastor		Joaquín	2	8
Paz	Merino	Juan Antonio	2	8
Pedrueza	Carranza	Francisco	2	8
Peñaredonda	Pastor	Francisco (de)	3	8
Pérez	Caballero	Juan Pablo	3	8
Pérez	Hita	José Faustino	2	8
Pérez		Julian Aquilino	3	8
Pezuela	Sánchez	Joaquín	2	8
Piña	Ruiz	Juan	2	8
Rada	Aguirre	Ignacio	1	8
Requena	Herrera	Francisco	2	8
Rico	Villademoros	Domingo	2	8
Riega	Rico	Manuel	3	8
Rivas	Gallardo	Agustín	2	8
Robles	Vives	Antonio	2	8
Rodriguez	Castillo	Pascual	1	8
Rodriguez	Rivas	Vicente	2	8
Romero	Aleson	Manuel	1	8

The sample

Name			Per.	Occup.
Romero	Uruzcun	José	3	8
Sáinz	Alfaro	Antonio	1	8
Salazar	Agüero	Francisco	1	8
Sampelayo		Manuel	3	8
Santa	Maria	Juan Antonio	2	8
Santa-Clara	Villota	Ignacio	2	8
Santelices		Casimiro	2	8
Santelices		Manuel	2	8
Sanz	Rozas	Ignacio	2	8
Sanz	Velasco	Tomas	1	8
Segovia	Herrera	José Maria	3	8
Sendoquiz	Aldana	Mateo	2	8
Sierra	Rubio	Nicolás	2	8
Sisternes	Feliú	Manuel	2	8
Soria		José Antonio	2	8
Torre		Dámaso (de la)	2	8
Tudela		Joaquín	3	8
Ugalde	Fernández	Juan José	2	8
Urrutia	Llano	Andrés	3	8
Ussoz	Mozzi	José Agustín	3	8
Valiente	González-Bravo	José Pablo	2	8
Vallejo	Alcedo	Felipe	2	8
Vega		Francisco Javier	2	8
Velo	Arce	Manuel Antonio	1	8
Veyan	Monteagudo	Antonio	1	8
Vilches		Gonzalo José	3	8
Vilches		Pedro Fernando	1	8
Villanueva	Pacheco-Alvarado	Antonio	2	8
Virto	Escribano	Jacinto	2	8

Professionals
(Professionals.dat)

Name			Per.	Occup.
Aramayona		Juan (de)	2	13
Calderón		José	2	12
Escalera		Antonio (de la)	3	10
Franseri		Antonio	2	11
Gámez		Juan	2	11
García		Burunda	2	11
García	Ordoñez	Asensio	3	12
García	Sevillano	Juan José	2	11
Giraut		Antonio	2	12

Appendix A

Name			Per.	Occup.
González	Arnao	Vicente	3	10
González	Espinosa	Domingo	3	13
Guardiola	Aragón	José	2	11
Guardiola		Lorenzo	2	13
Herrezuelo		Juan	3	13
López		José Severo	2	11
Lorente		Iñigo Antonio	2	11
Maroto		Juan Pablo	3	11
Norzagaray		Mateo	2	10
Onofrio		Antonio	2	11
Parrondo		Pedro Antonio	2	12
Peña		Juan de Dios (de la)	3	10
Piñera	Siles	Bartolomé	3	11
Rajoo		Juan	2	11
Ribes		José	2	11
Rico	Villaseñor	Lucas	2	10
Rivillo		Miguel	2	11
Rueda		Pedro Manuel	3	13
Sáenz	Azofra	Santiago	2	13
San Vicente		Manuel Esteban (de)	2	13
Sanchez	Tola	Melchor	3	11
Soldevilla	Juan	Bautista	3	11
Spino		Rafael	2	13
Torre		Eugenio (de la)	2	10
Vallano	Pablos	Manuel	3	10
Villazán	Herrera	Eulogio	2	13
Villegas		Francisco	2	12

Politicians
(Politicians.dat)

Name			Per.	Occup.
Aguilar		Manuel María	3	8
Aguirre	Solarte	José Ventura	3	6
Alava		Manuel Ricardo	3	14
Alcalá	Galiano	Antonio	3	8
Alvarez	Guerra	Juan	3	8
Alvarez	Mendizábal	Juan	3	7
Argüelles		Agustín	3	8
Armendariz		Agustín	3	8
Arrazola		Lorenzo	3	10
Balboa		Trinidad	3	14
Barata		Antonio	3	8

The sample

Name			Per.	Occup.
Bardají	Azara	Eusebio	3	8
arrio	Ayuso	Manuel	3	10
Benavides	Navarrete	Antonio	3	10
Bermúdez	Castro	Manuel	3	13
Bordiú	Góngora	Cristóbal	3	13
Bravo	Murillo	Juan	3	8
Burgos		Francisco Javier	3	8
Caballero		Fermin	3	9
Caballero	Pozo	José Antonio	2	9
Cabarrús	Galabert	Domingo	3	8
Cabello		Francisco	3	10
Calatrava		José Maria	3	8
Calatrava		Ramón Maria	3	8
Calderón	Barca	Angel	3	8
Calderón	Barca	Miguel	3	9
Calderón	Collantes	Santurnino	3	8
Calderón	Molina	Carlos	3	9
Calvo	Asensio	Pedro	3	8
Canga	Argüelles	José	3	8
Cano-Manuel	Ramírez-Arellano	Antonio	3	8
Cano-Manuel	Ramírez-Arellano	Vicente	3	8
Cantero	San Vicente	Manuel	3	8
Carranza	Helguera	Lucas	2	8
Carramolino		Juan Martín	3	10
Castro	Orozco	Francisco	3	10
Castro	Orozco	José	3	8
Cevallos	Guerra	Pedro	2	8
Cienfuegos		José	3	14
ollado	Parada	José Manuel	3	6
Cortázar		Modesto	3	8
Cortina	Arenzana	Manuel	3	10
Cuetos		Olegario (de los)	3	14
Diaz	Caneja	Joaquín	3	10
Díez	Ribera	Ildefonso	3	14
Egaña		Pedro	3	8
Egea		Mariano	3	14
Erroy	Azpiroz	Juan Bautista (de)	3	8
Escosura	Morrough	Patricio (de la)	3	8
Escudero		Francisco	3	14
Espartero		Baldomero	3	14
Fernández	Gasco	Francisco	3	8
Fernández	Navarrete	Juan	3	8
Fernández	Velasco	Bernardino	3	8

Appendix A

Name			Per.	Occup.
Ferráz		Valentin	3	14
Ferrer	Cafranga	Joaquín Maria	3	1
Florez	Estrada	Alberto	3	8
Frías		Joaquín	3	14
Gallego	Valcarcel	Antonio	3	14
García	Goyena	Florentino	3	14
García	Torre	José	3	8
García León	Pizarro	José	3	8
Garelli		Nicolás Maria	3	8
Garro	Arízcum	Nicolás Ambroso	2	8
Gil	Cuadra	Ramón	3	13
Girón		Pedro Agustín	3	9
Gómez	Becerra	Alvaro	3	10
Gómez	Labrador	Pedro	3	8
Gómez	Serna	Pedro	3	8
González	Bravo	Luis	3	10
González	Carvajal	Tomás	3	8
González	Romero	Ventura	3	8
Goyeneche	Múzquiz	Ignacio	3	8
Heredia	Bejines	Narciso	3	8
Heros		Martín (de los)	3	8
Infante		Facundo	3	14
Istúriz		Francisco	3	1
Lersundi	Ormaechea	Francisco	3	14
Llorente	Lannas	Alejandro	3	10
López		Joaquín Maria	3	10
López	Torre-Aillón	Luis	3	8
Luyando		José (de)	3	14
Luzuriaga		Claudio Antón	3	8
Martínez	Irujo	Carlos	3	8
Martínez	Rosa	Francisco	3	8
Mayans	Enriquez	Luis	3	10
Mazo	Garcia-Prada	Francisco (del)	3	8
Méndez	Vigo	Santiago	3	14
Mon		Alejandro	3	10
Moscoso	Altamira	José Maria	3	14
Nárvaez		Ramón Maria	3	14
Olózaga	Almandoz	Salustiano	3	10
Ortiz	Taranco	Manuel	3	8
Ortiz	Zúñiga	Manuel	3	10
Pando	Fernández-Pinedo	Manuel	3	8
Pando		José Maria	3	8
Parga	Puga	Jacobo	3	8

The sample

Name			Per.	Occup.
Pastor		Luis Maria	3	13
Peña	Aguayo	José (de la)	3	10
Pérez	Castro	Evaristo	3	8
Pérez	Moltó	Ignacio	3	8
Pezuela	Cevallos	Juan	3	8
Pezuela	Cevallos	Manuel	3	8
Pidal		Pedro José	3	10
Piernas	Abades	Luis	3	8
Pita	Pizarro	Pío	3	8
Porlier	Sopranis	Antonio	3	8
Queipo	Llano	José María	3	9
Ranz	Romanillos	Antonio	3	8
Remón	Zarco Valle	Antonio	3	8
Riva	Herrera	Manuel	3	8
Roca de Togores	Carrasco	Mariano	3	8
Rodil	Galloso	José Ramón	3	14
Ruiz	Vega	Domingo	3	10
Saavedra	Ramírez Baquedano	Angel	3	9
Salamanca	Mayol	Jose	3	7
Salazar		Luis Maria	3	8
San Miguel	Valledor	Evaristo	3	14
Sancho		Vicente	3	13
Sartorius		Luis José	3	13
Seijas	Lozano	Manuel	3	10
Silvela		Francisco	3	8
Torres	Solanot	Mariano	3	8
Ulloa		Francisco Javier	3	8
Vadillo		José Manuel	3	8
Valdés		Gerónimo	3	14
Vargas	Laguna	Antonio	3	8
Vázquez	Figueroa	José	3	14
Zumalacárregui		Miguel Antonio	3	10

Appendix B: Analysis of assets

B.1. Merchants. Percentage distribution of gross assets
(reales de vellón)

1750-1815	Initial capital	Final capital	Personal estate			Real estate		Business			Investment		
			1	2	3	4	5	6	7	8	9	10
Alday Angulo, Ramón	768,874	1,011,280	1.96	9.32			24.00	15.88	35.82	13.02		
Alday Zubiaga, J. Fco	743,632	668,845	1.19	9.64			28.35	37.84	14.12	8.86		
Alonso, Domingo		1,313,740	3.97	5.80			72.78	17.45				
Araujo, Tomás (de)	144,920	1,309,367	1.42	12.63		15.27	21.64	23.38	25.66			
Basualdo, Manuel		1,573,212	0.95	0.08		28.85		56.91				13.21
Bringas, Fco Antonio		6,388,595	0.55	0.87	0.56	88.25		2.62	8.59	1.18		
Caballero Moral, Andrés	1,662,436	12,648,775	0.20	10.30	9.52	4.36	1.32	41.50	28.09	3.01		40.58
Campo, Miguel (del)	70,453	241,765	5.07	12.79	7.93	21.86		41.50		10.85		
Chavarri Laiseca, Mateo		5,992,298	8.60	10.00		21.53	22.31	20.40	15.47	1.69		
Elejalde Larrieta, Bmé.		1,149,683	1.82	3.49	6.22	5.65	14.50	26.78		41.54		
Entrambasaguas, Manuel	243,697	2,553,335	2.15	11.11	1.01		13.92	38.64	33.17			
Fernández García, Pedro		558,000					52.00	26.77		21.23		
Fourdinier, Roberto		2,232,994	0.85	0.41	0.18	62.97	14.81	11.72				9.06
Galarza Goicoechea, Crist.		2,692,609	1.21	4.28			57.48	36.16		0.87		
García Aldeanueva, Manuel		1,600,000	3.10	20.42	10.61		12.77	42.30	10.80			
García Gastón, Bartolomé		996,496	6.41	67.53	0.79			13.98	11.29			
García Olaya, Miguel		295,752	5.50	6.30	1.35	26.75	13.99	7.00		39.11		
García, Casimiro		1,731,438	3.32		0.62		24.74	71.32				
García, Francisco		316,792	5.89	39.09	33.58			11.63				
Gil Martínez-Solórzano, M.		820,134	6.93	3.67	0.60		31.18	43.30		14.32		9.81
Gonzalez de Villa, Domingo		120,500	5.64	9.11				20.65	6.51	58.09		
Gorbea, Juan Francisco		1,126,184	4.22	7.12	1.01		38.29	27.86	15.38	6.12		
Hermoso, Miguel		1,246,180	1.29	10.21	1.57	7.46	43.51	18.64	5.70	8.60		3.02
Heros, Manuel		485,294	4.33	18.05			39.47	27.32		10.83		

Nombre									
Ibarra, Joaquín		2,185,263	1.81	25.96			42.92	14.97		5.41
Ibarrola, Domingo		1,311,449	2.97	1.35		8.93	46.97	41.08		7.63
Iñigo Vallejo, Bernardo		1,191,168	1.38	5.25		28.91	26.12	16.10		22.24
Iruegas Sotomayor, B.		5,208,724	0.93	1.83		10.17	3.23	28.55	19.14	7.60
Jauregui, Mateo	90,000	1,065,098	1.56				11.58	26.77	9.55	50.54
Losada Quiroga, Manuel		763,631	2.37	0.68		23.58	69.78	2.22		1.37
López Rodrigo, Juan		1,165,776	4.20	12.32			31.30	22.62	17.22	12.34
Machón, Juan Agustín	1,567,700	4,610,030	0.75	7.85	2.02		49.96		7.77	12.09	4.28	15.28
Martínez de la Torre, Fco.		846,036	4.02	5.14		13.19	2.56	67.70	7.39	
Martínez de Robledo, Juan		2,035,337	0.14	1.12			55.89	42.85		
Martínez de Ventadés, S.		1,010,458	1.16		1.53	4.23	2.88	3.42	44.13	42.65
Martínez Escudero, José		765,475	7.48				8.85	69.86		13.81
Martínez Lerdo, Eugenio		997,206	2.92	21.48			22.75	27.51				25.34
Mas, Francisco Jaime		479,952	6.87	5.47		25.50	53.82	8.34		
Mazo, Bernardo (del)		10,262,245	0.91	11.39		1.46		66.79	19.45	
Nieto Marqués, Pedro		1,680,000	2.17	5.10			16.30	31.20		15.71
Pabón, Bartolomé		162,359	2.03	24.63	24.64		12.12			36.58
Palacio Cerro, Diego		1,280,702	3.68	13.66	7.82		27.25	27.50		20.09		29.52
Pando Sabugal, Antonio		7,134,985	1.04	15.57	14.86	29.54		10.22	8.45	2.30
Pando y Pando, José	3,567,492	4,637,694	3.66	0.58		32.24	11.03	17.61	2.18	2.54		18.02
Pérez Roldán, José		3,820,024	3.28	0.56		37.21		35.74	2.14	18.45		30.16
Pérez Sánchez, Diego		2,823,564	1.16	1.92	14.90	5.59	23.03	2.45	48.87	2.08		2.62
Posadillo Llaguno, Dom.	154,850	951,562	2.24	1.31	29.49	9.20	14.96	39.33		3.47
Posadillo Llaguno, Fco.	20,000	1,096,793	3.14	1.44			6.50		79.58	9.34
Quijada, Antonio		2,913,302	0.69		2.52	61.01	17.54	18.24		
Sacristana, Francisco		265,656	10.26				16.69	3.75	27.68	41.62
Santa Ana, Manuel		354,364	7.34		12.35	17.88	12.80	12.27	20.71	16.65
Sáinz de Baranda Gándara	45,000	581,508	5.88	3.98	1.71	7.74			39.87	42.53
Sáinz de Baranda Sta. Mª		337,006	7.21	3.01			29.36	58.71		
Sedano, Pedro		339,022	12.52		5.22		23.36	28.78	30.12	
Segura y Soto, José Ant.		272,327	7.17	2.87			36.41	14.28		39.27

B.1. (cont.)

1750-1815	Initial capital	Final capital	Personal estate		Real estate		Business			Investment		
			1	2	3	4	5	6	7	8	9	10
Soria Zaldívar, Francisco		4,976,258	1.27	31.36	0.10		30.77	36.50				
Trápaga, Felipe		489,394	2.78	2.10			12.51	55.91		26.70		
Valle Luengas, Francisco		1,499,382	2.88	1.53			16.05	15.91	17.61	23.34		
Valle, Manuel		384398	6.91	5.29		22.68	41.89	16.23	28.64			
Velasco Chavarri, Manuel		650,690	2.86	1.52		1.04	66.02	29.60				
Viña Urruela, Manuel		261,734	0.53	4.66				85.90	8.91			
Wercruyse, Pedro		2,418,916	6.69	3.46	0.78		34.59	55.26	19.72	7.56		15.48
Zubiaga, Pedro		521, 865	1.85	0.21			19.80	34.60				
Total			3.42	7.89	3.07	9.89	22.61	27.12	10.63	11.48	0.07	3.82

Key: 1. Domestic; 2. Silver/Cash; 3. Rural; 4. Urban; 5. Commodities; 6. Credit; 7. Public Debt; 8. Stocks; 9. Industry; 10. Loans

Sources: Alday Zubiaga, AHPM, P. 21086 (1792); Alday Angulo, AHPM, P. 21094 (1800); Alonso, AHPM, P. 19994 (1808); Araujo, AHPM, P. 18140 (1752); Arco, AHPM, P.19967 (1779); Basualdo, AHPM, P. 21613 (1804); Bringas, AHN, Títulos y familias, leg. 2225 (1810); Caballero, AHPM, P. 21782 (1812); Campo, AHPM, P. 17880 (1757); Entrambasaguas, AHPM, P. 21775 (1815); Fernández, AHPM, P. 21104 (1787); Fourdinier, AHPM, P. 21878 (1803); Galarza, AHPM, P. 20033 (1770); García, AHPM, P. 21754 (1802); García, Fco. AHPM, P. 21745 (1799); García Aledeanueva, AHPM, P. 21116 (1798); García Gastón, AHPM, P. 22863 (1805); García Olaya. AHPM, P. 21415 (1794); Martínez-Solórzano, AHPM, P. 21659 (1790); González de Villa, AHPM, P. 21690 (1808); Gorbea, AHPM, P. 22425 (1807); Hermoso, AHPM, P. 21077 (1785); Heros, AHPM, P. 18823 (1785); Ibarra, AHPM, P. 21084 (1787); Ibarrola, AHPM, P. 23396 (1813); Iñigo, AHPM, P. 21690 (1808); Iruegas, AHPM, P. 23400 (1815); Jaúregui, AHPM, P. 22848 (1802); López Angulo, AHPM, P. 21048 (1793); López Rodrigo, AHPM, P. 19990 (1804); Losada, AHPM, P. 21745 (1799); Machón, AHPM, P. 17638 y 21105 (1774 y 1788); Martínez Escudero, AHPM, P. 18817 (1780); Martínez Lerdo, AHPM, P. 23041 (1804); Martínez de Ventadés, AHPM, P. 21078 (1786); Mas, AHPM, P. Elejalde, AHPM, P. 19973 (1787); Martínez de la Torre, AHPM, P. 21109 (1791); Pabón, AHPM, P. 21796 (1788); Palacio, AHPM 21092, 21612 y 23025 19514 (1791); Mazo. AHPM, P. 23398 (1814); Nieto, AHPM, P. 17166 (1763); Pando Pando, AHPM, P. 20034 (1776); Pérez, AHPM, P. 23570 y 20069 (1791-1807); Posadillo (1789-1807); Pando Sabugal, AHPM, P. 21802 (1801); Pérez Roldán, AHN, Diversos, Títulos y Familias, leg. 2579 (1803); Posadillo, Fco., AHPM, P. 19983 (1797); Quijada, Laguno, AHPM, P. 21415 (1794); Sacristana, AHPM, P. 21096 (1802); Sáinz de Baranda, AHN, Diversos, General, Leg. 218 (1815); Sáinz de Baranda Santa AHPM, P. 21874 (1799); Santa Ana, AHPM, P. 22531 (1803); Sedano, Pedro, AHPM, P. 21096 (1802); Segura, AHPM, P. 20374 (1782); María, AHPM, P. 21921 (1783); Valle, AHPM, P. 19962 (1768); Valle Luengas, AHPM, P. 21885 (1812); Velasco, AHPM, P. 21.109 (1791); Viña, Trápaga, AHPM, P. 21408 (1814); Wercruyse, AHPM, P. 21754 (1802); Zubiaga, AHPM, P. 19973 (1787); Soria, AHPM, P. 21086 (1791).

B.2. Merchants. Percentage distribution of gross assets
(reales de vellón)

1816-1850	Initial capital	Final capital	Personal estate		Real estate		Business			Investment		
			1	2	3	4	5	6	7	8	9	10
Antuñano Basualdo, Fco		1,309,367	1.42	12.63		15.27	21.64	23.38	25.66			
Baura, Gaspar	31,553	1,329,990	1.02	0.73			35.52		60.31	2.42		
Berriozabal, Juan I.	1,884,547	7,555,262	0.75	4.34		2.92		40.68	50.58	0.71		
Bitón Santibáñez, José		621,190	0.39	4.17		28.85		26.42	40.17			
Blanco, Saturnino		386,203	8.52			50.67	40.81					
Brihuega, Antonio		651,371	2.68	8.45			44.15	9.89	34.83			
Cabañas, Francisco		1,437,604	1.72	7.11	2.66	57.61	23.49	7.41				
Díaz Sanchez, Eugenio		307,294	8.79	2.45		16.54	50.81	21.40				
Fernández Casariego, Fdo.		22,799,389	0.16	0.03	0.35	37.07	6.38	40.43		15.58		
García de la Herrán, Manuel		80,949	10.71				89.29					
Hermoso Daza, Juan		150,604	14.08	23.26			46.48	14.18	2.00			
Larramendi, Santiago		1,104,714	5.62	10.00		3.27	32.12	25.41	16.36			
López de Sa, Juan		265,816	6.75	19.87		39.63	25.14	8.61		7.22		
Mazo, Francisca		16,879,404	0.33	0.58	16.71	5.31	5.63	12.32	6.56	2.47	0.68	49.41
Murua, Juan		1,593,507	2.25	2.21	22.22	52.02	11.04	10.26				
Palacios, Joaquín		849,870	1.64	2.25			34.65	38.27		23.19		
Peña Rodrigo, Manuel		1,573,928	0.96				11.83	30.54	1.82	39.35		15.50
Ribacoba Gorbea, Fco. A.		1,675,149	0.98	4.98	5.47				88.57			
Rubio, Pedro		849,924	0.95	1.20	22.22	7.85	23.47	8.74	2.96	4.01		
Sáinz de Baranda Gorriti		1,536,680	6.32	2.92	38.77	24.08		27.91				28.60
Sáinz, Francisco A.		303,954	4.46		1.20	20.73	51.09	22.52				

B.2. (cont.)

1816-1850	Initial capital	Final capital	Personal estate		Real estate		Business		Investment			
			1	2	3	4	5	6	7	8	9	10
Trasviña Palacios, Manuel	102,000	8,501,488	0.37	17.28	0.37	7.49	5.02	25.46	27.09	0.42		16.50
Urtiaga, Nicolás		1,201,200	2.52	3.08		93.40	1.00					
Villa, Francisco		788,682				23.81	15.27		18.28	3.33		39.31
Villar Toral, Pedro		1,559,682	1.38	11.00	0.06	70.97	10.14	6.45				
Zabala, Pedro		1,586,910	0.90	3.72	28.22	4.79	10.47	51.90				
Total			3.30	5.47	5.32	21.63	22.90	17.39	14.43	3.80	0.02	5.74

Sources: Angulo, AHPM, P. 23027 (1816); Antuñano, AHPM, P. 23028 (1822); Baura, AHPM, P. 23000 (1816); Berriozabal, AHPM, P. 23063 (1828); Bitón, AHPM, P. 24589 (1838); Blanco, AHPM, P. 24585 (1833); Mazo, AHPM, P. 23081 (1835); Cabañas, AHPM, P. 25058; Fernández Casariego, AHPM, P. 25609 (1848); García de la H., AHPM, P. 22277 (1816); Hermoso, AHPM, P. 24299 (1837); Larramendi, AHPM, P. 21098; López de Sa, AHPM, P. 24743 (1838); Murua, AHPM, P. 24571 (1836); Peña, AHPM, P. 23401 (1816); Ribacoba, AHPM, P. 23060 (1824); Rubio, AHPM, P. 21783 (1821); Sainz, AHPM, P. 23400 (1816); Sáinz de Baranda Gorriti, AHN, Diversos, General, Leg. 218 (1845); Trasviña, AHPM, P. 25174 (1843); Urtiaga, AHPM, P. 24683 (1835); Villa, Francisco, AHPM, P. 23830 (1835); Villar Toral, AHPM, P. 29994 (1842); Zabala, AHPM, P. 23401 (1816).

B.3. *Merchants. Net assets* *
(*reales de vellón*)

1750-1815	Final capital
Angulo, Ramón	12,000,000
García Prada, Juan Sixto	22,000,000
Haedo Pico, Francisco	506,332
Olavarrieta, Juan A.	1,165,776
Pando Garma, Francisco, A.	695,345
Peña, Juan Manuel	581,868
Pérez Frenández-Otero F.	7,644,461
Ruiz Prada, Juan Bautista	769,543
Vergara Sáenz, Juan M.	668,476
Zorrilla, Fco	1,102,780

*This table includes a few cases in which we have found only information on net assets total amount. This information has been obtained not in probate inventories, rather in wills, personal letters or similar documents. Is why it is impossible to determine the composition of the family fortune.

Sources: García Prada, AHPM, P. ; Haedo, AHPM, P. 18822 (1784); Olavarrieta, AHPM, P. 19990 (1804); Pando, AHPM, P. 19991 (1805); Peña, AHPM, P. 18822 (1784); Pérez, AHPM, P. 21086 (1792); Ruiz Prada, AHPM, 18995 (1798); Vergara, AHPM, P. 21402 (1807); Zorrilla, AHPM, P. 18824 (1786).

B.4. *Bankers. Percentage distribution of gross assets*
(reales de vellón)

1750-1815	Initial capital	Final capital	Personal estate		Real estate		Business			Investment		
			1	2	3	4	5	6	7	8	9	10
Aguirre, Manuel Francisco	15,000	4,758,272	2.50	0.88	15.29	1.08		52.79		2.50	2.60	22.36
Aragorri Olavide, Simón	18,934,810	22,114,903	14.33	67.19	11.79					0.39		6.30
Avancino, Antonio		306,393	0.60	30.10	7.75	8.88		14.30	37.40	0.97		
Carranza y Gainza, Tomás		16,616,750	1.11	0.58	16.07	7.74	1.13	61.23	1.19	3.66	7.29	
Dutari, Juan Bautista		9,893,669	6.60	2.40	1.41	27.86		53.73		4.63	3.37	
Fdez. Gonzalo del Río, Luis		6,997,773	2.00		8.40	5.45		33.30	20.40	3.55		26.90
Pedrueza y Helguera, José		4,954,859	1.69		2.11			63.63				32.57
Queneau, Agustín	600,000	2,149,762	3.27	47.00	3.63	9.83	8.18	10.45	16.58	1.06		
Ravara, Felipe		2,423,705	4.01	18.52	8.31	7.60	1.16	36.18	9.45	2.09	1.66	11.02
Total												
(Only initial capital)												
Abrisqueta, Andrés	134,997		7.50				23.50	69.00				
Arecha, Domingo Javier	58,953		8.00	92.00								

1816-1867

Name											
Aguirre Solarte, José V.	3,942,000	7,217,721	1.01	4.50	2.31	15.00		1.35	75.83		
Caballero y Mazo, Andrés	3,710,000	17,426,041	0.71	9.46	11.82	23.46		34.31	20.24		
Collado Parada, José M.		69,441,431	0.19	12.00	31.23	10.83		16.61	15.00		14.14
Chavarri, Francisco Antonio	5,992,289	6,264,118	0.88	2.00		32.87		6.85	25.00		32.40
Chavarri, Basilio	2,837,947	9,267,306	2.40	1.88	8.91	24.58		61.16			1.07
Gil de Santivañez, Manuel		9,440,219	1.17	5.42	31.58	32.75		24.00	5.08		
Gonzalez de Lovera, Manuel		1,849,981	2.37	1.05	2.14			39.51	23.51	0.63	
Pérez Seoane, Manuel	440000	18,180,439	3.85	0.30		17.00	10.76	46.00	21.35	11.50	20.03
Maltrana Monasterio, Ant.		16,324,095	0.66		2.44	23.21			54.86		18.83
Norzagaray, Mateo	409,427	23,479,370	0.42	0.26	2.56	9.92		77.63	9.21		
Ruiz de la Prada, Manuel	10,922,172	15,955,607	1.20	0.86	17.07	3.96		3.48	49.31		24.12
Soriano Sanchez, Antonio		15,391,384	0.11	0.08	45.07	10.40		25.37	15.40	3.57	
Soriano Moreta, Ricardo		7,378,172	3.00	2.60	28.96	2.74		1.05	53.63	2.55	4.84
Total			1.38	3.11	14.16	15.90	0.83	25.95	28.34	0.47	7.79

Sources: Aguirre (1784) AHPM, P. 21102; Aragorri (1785-1806) AHPM, P. 21653 y 21764; Avancino (1810) AHPM, P.21883; Carranza (1794) AHPM, P. 21669; P. Dutari (1785) ABE, Secretaría, Libro 18648; Fernández Gonzalo del Río (1801) AHPM, P. 21095; Queneau (1794) ABE, Leg. 782; Rávara (1802) AHPM, P. 22848; Pedrueza (1793-1807) AHPM, P. 20473 y 22993. Abrisqueta (1788) AHMP, P. 19974; Arecha (1778) AHPM, P. 19114. Aguirre Solarte (1848) AHPM, P. 25609; Caballero (1862) AHPM, P. 27462; Collado (1865) AHPM, P. 27380; Chávarri (1842) AHPM, P. 24983; Gil de Santibañez (1862) AHPM, P. 27272; González de Lovera (1818) AHPM, 23405; Maltrana (1867) AHPM, P. 28275; Pérez Seoane (1831-1859) y Norzagaray (1814-1856) ver Cayuela Fernández, J. (1986, pp.478-489); Ruiz de la Prada (1851) AHPM, P. 25778; Soriano Sánchez (1845) AHPM, P. 25307; Soriano y Moreta (1856) AHPM, P. 26109.

B.5. Bureaucrats. Percentage distribution of gross assets
(reales de vellón)

1790-1860	Final capital	Personal estate		Real estate			Profession Business			Investments		
		1	2	3	4	5	6	7	8	9	10	11	12
Councilors of Castile													
1790-1809													
Pérez de Hita, José Francisco	621,508	10.86	7.94	25.29	55.91								
Santa Clara Villota, Ignacio	254,531	1.46	16.65			1.08				26.69	38.66		15.46
Salazar Agüero, Francisco	587,000	2.38	0.41		61.19			36.02					
Mata, Cristobal (de la)	359,554	11.82	80.95							7.23			
Herrán, Francisco	524,604	3.11	31.02							36.85	24.01		5.01
Fitta Huel, Juan Antonio	1,327,226	8.02	32.46		55.38	4.14							
Ondarza, Pablo	220,594	22.66	71.78	5.56									
Rico Villademoros, Domingo	222,998	7.55	6.06		9.76		20.75			39.50	16.38		
Total		8.48	3.86	15.13	8.30	2.59	4.50	0	13.79	9.88	0	2.56	
1839-1860													
Martín Vaguer, Francisco	1,600,910	1.52	12.84		80.09		1.32	1.51			2.72		
Cabanilles, José	1,475,436	0.74	47.53	1.18	39.41		9.32			1.82			
Vilches, Gonzalo José	557,363	6.04	4.99		38.54	43.06		7.37					
Arjona, José Manuel	75,428	28.30			70.37						1.33		
Total		9.15	16.34	0.29	57.10	10.77	2.66	2.22	0	0.46	1.01	0	0

Key: 1. Domestic; 2. Silver/Cash; 3. Agrarian Rents; 4. Rural; 5. Urban; 6. Salaries; 7. Credits; 8. Commodities; 9. Public debt; 10. Company stocks; 11. Industry; 12. Loans

Source: Pérez de Hita, AHPM, P. 18193; Santa Clara Villota, AHPM, P. 21659; Salazar Agüero, AHPM, P. 22520; Mata, AHPM, P. 22969; Herrán, AHPM, P. 23388; Fitta huel, AHPM, P. 21689; Ondarza, AHPM, P. 21690; Rico, AHPM, P. 21769, 21786; Martín Vaguer, AHPM, P. 23089; Cabanilles, AHPM, P. 25219; Vilches, AHPM, P. 25288; Arjona, AHPM, P. 27102.

B.6. *Bureaucrats. Percentage distribution of gross assets (reales de vellón)*

1779-1864	Final capital	Personal estate			Real estate		Profession Business			Investments			
		1	2	3	4	5	6	7	8	9	10	11	12
Councilors of the Public Treasury 1790-1816													
Múzquiz Goyeneche, Miguel	3,628,425	3.95	58.82		12.36	5.91					18.96		
Garro Micheltorena, Ambr.	14,490,966	4.97	10.71		34.50	22.08		5.01	4.07	8.54	5.89		4.23
Rodríguez Rivas, Vicente	887,393	23.62	56.74		1.29						18.35		
Orbaneja Ortega, Miguel	1,626,693	4.45	12.17			38.55		8.68		32.93	0.42		2.80
Iturbide, Joaquín	254,476	17.97	79.22		2.81								
Martínez Sobral, Francisco	337,446	3.16	62.14			4.10				15.11	15.49		
Vega, Francisco Javier (de la)	1,351,035	2.70	10.81				2.73	39.71		19.83	24.22		
Ibarrola, Francisco Antonio	876,457	2.41	8.20		35.46			5.38		27.50	10.00	11.05	
Martínez de la Mata, Pedro	4,765,537	1.04	1.63		20.54	15.41		23.84		19.12	8.89		
Nieto, Juan	1,520,084	5.17	5.19		19.95	1.39				68.30			9.53
Dehesa Fernández, Francisco	590,825	5.88	10.84		2.03			11.74		32,60	36.91		
Cabarrús Lalane, Francisco (de)	4,151,276	2.77	19.84		63.51					13.88			
Campo y Haza, Francisco	2,041,599	5.59	6.03		0.72	12.31		4.75		59.75	8.36		2.49
Total		6.44	26.33	0	14.86	7.67	0.21	7.62	0.31	22.89	11.35	0.85	1.47
1836-1864													
Pérez Caballero, Juan Pablo	3,604,819	4.01	8.71		62.40	2.50		11.78		10.60			
Espinosa Brun, Antonio	116,003	12.15	78.12					9.73					

305

B.6. (cont.)

1836-1864	Final capital	Personal estate		Real estate			Profession Business			Investments			
		1	2	3	4	5	6	7	8	9	10	11	12
Domínguez Llorente, Pedro	278,676	13.37	26.22			23.55	18.92			17.94			
Pardo, Manuel	-332,732	9.12	8.74				21.77				60.37		
Larramendi, Juan	329,843	12.90	87.10										
Pérez, Julián Aquilino	19,773,284	1.19	4.45		4.35	52.07		0.80	30.15		0.95	0.21	5.83
Canga Argüelles, Joaquín	1,697,626	5.11	9.12		71.90		7.33		6.54				
Total		8.27	31.78	0	9.54	21.43	5.81	4.23	4.31	5.01	8.76	0.03	0.83

Key: 1. Domestic; 2. Silver/Cash; 3. Agrarian Rents; 4. Rural; 5. Urban; 6. Salaries; 7. Credits; 8. Commodities; 9. Public debt; 10. Company stocks; 11. Industry; 12. Loans

Source: Múzquiz, AHPM, P. 18695; Garro Micheltorena, AHPM, P. 20067; Rodríguez Rivas, AHPM, P. 21855; Orbaneja Ortega, AHPM, P. 21741; Iturbide, AHPM, P. 21745; Martínez Sobral, AHPM, P. 21418; Vega, AHPM, P. 21697; Ibarrola, AHPM, P. 23093; Martínez de la Mata, AHPM, P.22993; Nieto, AHPM, P. 23036; Dehesa Fernández, AHPM, P. 22873; Cabarrús Lalane, AHN, Diversos, Serie General, legs. 7, 8,13, 35, 49, 54; Campo y Haza, AHPM, P. 21774, 21775; Pérez Caballero, AHPM, P. 23083; Espinosa Brun, AHPM, P. 24619; Domínguez Llorente, AHPM, P. 23090; Pardo, AHPM, P. 24744; Larramendi, AHPM, P. 25626; Pérez, AHPM, P. 25942; Canga Argüelles, AHPM, P. 27950.

B.7. Bureaucrats. Percentage distribution of gross assets
(reales de vellón)

1790-1837	Final capital	Personal estate		Real estate			Profession Business			Investments		
		1	2	3	4	5	6	7	8	9	10	11	12
Council of State													
García-Pando Echalburu, Fco.	258,116	40.22	50.48							9.30			
Paz y Merino, Juan Antonio	1,282,567	3.91	2.41		11.41						44.37		37.90
Enríquez, Pedro Alfonso	2,147,904	7.07			19.31	15.52		49.30		8.22	0.58		
Pedrueza Carranza, Francisco	1,625,453	2.50	8.41		33.02			9.56		46.15	0.36		
Irirarte Oropesa, Bernardo	493,312	48.96	49.83								1.21		
Anduaga, José	1,932,411	10.77	1.46			13.05				57.57	17.15		
Heredia Bejines, Narciso	3,744,973	4.26	2.71	2.63	48.83	31.05		2.59		1.60			6.33
Larrea, Miguel José	84,000	26.19	33.33							11.90	28.58		
Total		17.98	18.58	0.33	14.07	7.45	0	7.68	0	16.84	11.54	0	5.53

Key: 1. Domestic; 2. Silver/Cash; 3. Agrarian Rents; 4. Rural; 5. Urban; 6. Salaries; 7. Credits; 8. Commodities; 9. Public debt; 10. Company stocks; 11. Industry; 12. Loans

Source: García-Pando, AHPM, P. 21107; Paz y Merino, AHPM, P. 20087; Enríquez, AHPM, P. 22993; Pedrueza Carranza, AHPM, P. 20473, 22991, 21403; Iriarte Oropesa, AHPM, P. 21693; Anduaga, AHPM, P. 22277; Heredia Bejines, AHPM, P. 21775; Larrea, AHPM, P. 20200.

B.8. *Bureaucrats. Percentage distribution of gross assets*
(reales de vellón)

1788-1846	Final capital	Personal estate			Real estate			Profession Business		Investments			
		1	2	3	4	5	6	7	8	9	10	11	12
Other Councils													
Losada, Luis	263,967	8.65	13.08		20.73			4.19		17.58	35.77		
Fernández Isla Alvear, Juan	6,048,219	1.20	1.00		46.50	12.15		7.12		5.10		26.93	
Lorieri, Pedro	173,587	14.17	15.45		3.15	48.80				3.59	18.43		
Santa María, Juan Antonio	2,022,681	0.96	13.23		17.59	15.24				3.59	82.22		
Total		6.24	10.69	0	17.59	15.24	0	2.83	0	6.57	34.11	6.73	0
Alesón y Bueno, Juan José	142,677	59.59	37.92		30.76					17.96	9.38		9.65
Jacot Ortiz Rojano, Melchor	1,534,499	1.01	0.16			33.73				1.49	63.71		
López Juana, José	1,896,326	13.55			10.25	21.09							
Total		24.72	12.69	0	10.25	18.27	0	0	0	6.48	24.36	0	3.22

Key: 1. Domestic; 2. Silver/Cash; 3. Agrarian Rents; 4. Rural; 5. Urban; 6. Salaries; 7. Credits; 8. Commodities; 9. Public debt; 10. Company stocks; 11. Industry; 12. Loans
Source: Losada, AHPM, P. 21042; Fernández Isla, AHPM, P. 22424; Lorieri, AHPM, P. 22974; Santa María, AHPM, P. 21692; Alesón, AHPM, P. 22279; Jacot, AHPM, P. 21670; López juana, AHPM, P. 25371.

B.9. *High administration (other than ouncilors). Percentage distribution of gross assets (reales de vellón)*

1787-1835	Final capital	Personal estate			Real estate			Profession Business			Investments		
		1	2	3	4	5	6	7	8	9	10	11	12
Justice Administration													
Sisternes Feliu, Manuel	62,821	19.95	36.29		43.76								
Ugalde Fernández, Juan José	80,512	47.40	4968							2.92			
Carrancio, Manuel Angel	406,777	24.19	7.76		2.22		4.31			61.52			
Ussoz Mozzi, José Agustín	258,580	4.48	39.26		49.92					6.34			
Total		24.10	33.24	0	23.97	0	1.07	0	0	17.70	0	0	0
Public Treasury													
Gorbea, Francisco	953,166	8.67	41.90		10.72	13.89		5.04				19.78	
Azofra Delgado, José	1,823,250	0.27	4.16							46.59	95.57		
Marcoleta, Domingo	487,827	30.53	22.88										
Arozarena, José Gabriel	288,494	27.11	72.89										
Indart, Pedro Fermín	2,291,161	2.60	26.55		14.18	3.88		1.68		24.44	26.67		
Melendro Aguión, Gabriel	533,267	4.17	8.55		2.26	59.63		22.57					2.82
Güel, Juan Ignacio	3,533,456	4.23	11.50		4.43	29.43	1.78	4.17		17.60			26.86
Otondo, Pedro	632,197	3.55	2.85							29.62	63.98		
Cortés, Andrés	263,057	4.38	0.92			70.71				20.73			
Gazel Combe, Luis	848,847	6.05	46.71		3.26					8.76			38.48
Moreno Martínez, Domingo	777,602	2.39	7.15		11.18	6.34		6.23		58.99	7.72		
Total		8.54	22.36	0	4.18	16.71	0.16	3.60	0	18.79	17.63	1.79	6.19

Key: 1. Domestic; 2. Silver/Cash; 3. Agrarian Rents; 4. Rural; 5. Urban; 6. Salaries; 7. Credits; 8. Commodities; 9. Public debt; 10. Company stocks; 11. Industry; 12. Loans

Source: Sisternes, AHPM, P. 21745; Ugalde, AHPM, P. 22975; Carrancio, AHPM, P. 22869; Ussoz, AHPM, P. 23056; Gorbea, AHPM, P. 21656; Azofra, AHPM, P. 20927; Marcoleta, AHPM, P. 21658; Arozarena, AHPM, P. 23390; Indart, AHPM, P. 23391; Melendro, AHPM, P. 21693; Güel, AHPM, P. 23400; Otondo, AHPM, P. 22280; Cortés, AHPM, P. 22282; Gacel, AHPM, P. 20735; Moreno Martínez, AHPM, P. 24683.

B.10. *Bureaucrats. Middle ranks administration. Percentage distribution of gross assets*
(*reales de vellón*)

1780-1838	Final capital	Personal estate			Real estate		Profession Business			Investments		
		1	2	3	4	5	6	7	8	9	10
Martínez, Domingo	292,780	9.72	43.83	10.55			35.90					
Armesto, Antonio	-11,208	9.44	3.28		81.28		6.00					
Castro Arias Somoza, Ramón	72,094	62.74	8.21				15.00	14.05				
Santelices, Manuel	155,921	12.34	11.33	76.33								
Soria, José Antonio	244,410	23.58	17.12					18.55	40.50			
Jonsansoro Serralta, Vicente	423,256	15.80	13.09	23.62				25.99	21.50			
Gálvez López Salees, A.	214,152	19.43	13.26	11.02			27.43	9.85	3.51			
González de Tejada, Zenón	106,362	38.90	61.10									15.50
Rivas Gallardo, Agustín	159,793	3.07	15.67	17.49			17.17	46.60				
Pastor, Joaquín	259,977	10.10	55.72				6.87	27.31				
Santelices, Casimiro	536,064	1.12	3.12			2.42	2.44		90.90			
Gutierrez, Matías	289,371	1.76	37.87				1.38		0.69			
Tudela, Joaquín	243,360	7.27	3.95					88.78				
Gutierrez Solana, Ignacio	101,151	34.82	14.38				30.85	19.95				
Total		17.86	21.57	9.92	9.97	0.17	10.21	17.94	11.22	0	1.10

Key: 1. Domestic; 2. Silver/Cash; 3. Rural; 4. Urban; 5. Salaries; 6. Credits; 7. Public debt; 8. Company stocks; 9. Industry; 10. Loans

Source: Armesto, AHPM, P. 19519; Castro, AHPM, 20470; Galvez, AHPM, P. 21750; Gutierrez Solana, AHPM, P. 23081; Martínez, AHPM, P. 17644; Pastor, AHPM, P. 22863; Rivas, AHPM, P. 21686; Santelices, Manuel, AHPM, P. 22959; Soria, AHPM, P. 21677; Tudela, AHPM, P. 21788; Ugalde, AHPM, P. 22975.

B.11. *Professionals/Agentes/Procuradores. Percentage distribution of gross assets (reales de vellón)*

1789-1848	Final capital	Personal estate			Real estate			Profession Business			Investments		
		1	2	3	4	5	6	7	8	9	10	11	12
Procuradores													
Aramayona, Juan	117,229	24.30	4.33					26.89		8.73	44.48		
González Espinosa, Domingo	590,006	8.66	27.52					37.12		16.44	17.97		
San Vicente, Manuel Esteban	1,926,345	6.18	27.15		0.52	36.86		12.85		8.99			
Herrezuelo, Juan	399,085	3.52	18.28			66.61		2.60		20.39	2.95		
Rueda, Pedro Manuel (de)	135,716	3.83	0.67			22.10		50.06			13.09		
Total		9.30	15.59	0	0.10	25.11	0	25.90	0	10.91		0	0
Lawyers													
Guardiola, Lorenzo	808,498	3.78	7.97	5.74	75.77			6.74					
Torre, Eugenio (de la)	817,935	3.47	8.58		0.20	11.98		11.12		43.34	21.04		0.27
Norzagaray, Mateo	52,538	88.75	11.25										
Escalera, Antonio (de la)	558,898	3.00	18.64		60.28	12.68		5.40					
Ballano Pablos, Manuel	825,526	3.00	5.60		3.73	20.87		8.34		79.33	1.16		
Peña, Juan de Dios (de la)	682,430	12.65	7.56		39.13			18.63			3.70		
Total		19.11	9.94	0.96	29.85	7.59	0	8.37	0	20.44		0	0.04
Physicians													
Guardiola de Aragón, José	419,338	7.31			61.93	30.76							
Onofrio, Antonio	98,280	25.44	74.56										
Aramayona, Juan (de)	117,229	24.30	4.3							44.60			26.80
Rivillo, Miguel	92,228	5.71	84.75		3.53			3.49		2.52			
García de Burunda, Miguel	338,123	5.07	33.94					7.83		5.38	46.00		1.78
Rajoo, Juan	69,850	5.32	14.26		80.42								
Gámez, Juan	1,412,073	3.46	58.50				1.44			0.80	35.80		

B.11. (cont.)

1789-1848	Final capital	Personal estate			Real estate			Profession Business			Investments		
		1	2	3	4	5	6	7	8	9	10	11	12
López, José Severo	231,442	31.77	33.79				32.03			2.41			
Soldevilla, Juan Butista	320,058	14.48	55.69		3.74		6.29			9.01	10.79		
Maroto, Juan Pablo	2,017,595	0.71	1.79		26.50	71.00							
Total		12.36	36.16	0	17.61	10.18	3.98	1.13	0	6.47	9.26	0	2.85
Apothecaries													
Parrondo, Pedro Antonio	241,985	2.18	11.08		3.52			10.36	16.53	56.33			
Calderón, José	458,932	10.81	2.61	3.20		50.25		10.13	21.65		1.35		
Giraut, Antonio	291,835	6.31	3.02			19.36		17.95	15.83	23.68	13.85		
Villegas, Francisco	273,406	16.40						14.37	21.62	47.61			
García Ordoñez, Asensio	621,167	7.26	7.28			20.75		14.70	17.72	32.39			
Total		8.60	4.80	0.60	0.70	18.10	0	13.50	18.70	32.0	3.0	0	0
Agentes de negocios													
Sáenz de Azofra, Santiago	6,003,764	2.27	45.70		0.50	5.36		5.55		19.18	6.38		15.06
Spino, Rafael	205,675	16.83				55.23		27.94		45.12			
Villazán Herrera, Eulogio	209,580	13.96	16.02					24.90					
Total		11.10	20.60	0	0.10	20.20	0	19.50	0	21.4	2.1	0	5.0

Key: 1. Domestic; 2. Silver/Cash; 3. Agrarian Rents; 4. Rural; 5. Urban; 6. Salaries; 7. Credits; 8. Commodities; 9. Public debt; 10. Company stocks; 11. Industry; 12. Loans

Source: Aramayona, AHPM, P. 21704; González Espinosa, AHPM, P.22993; Herrezuelo, AHPM, P. 21782; Rueda, AHPM, P. 22288; an Vicente, AHPM, P. 23570; Guardiola23037; Torre, AHPM, P. 22995; Norzagaray, AHPM, P. 23104; Escalera, AHPM, P. 23109; Ballano, AHPM, P. 23069; Peña, AHPM, P. 23067; Guardiola de Aragón, AHPM, P. 22425; Onofrio, AHPM, P. 21052; Aramayona, AHPM, P. 21704; Rivillo, AHPM, P. 21874; García Burunda, AHPM, P. 21684; Rajoo, AHPM, P. 22989; Gámez, AHPM, P. 21763; López, AHPM, P. 21403; Soldevilla, AHPM, P. 21783; Maroto, AHPM, P. 25628; Parrondo, AHPM, P. 22213; Calderón, 21765; Giraut, AHPM, P. 22998; Villegas, AHPM, P. 21695; García Ordoñez, AHPM, P. 23062; Sáenz de Azofra, AHPM, P. 20927; Spino, AHPM, P. 21660; Villazán, AHPM, P. 22995.

B.12. *Politicians. Percentage distribution of gross assets*
(reales de vellón)

1805-1879	Final capital	Personal estate			Real estate			Profession Business			Investments		
		1	2	3	4	5	6	7	8	9	10	11	12
1805-1815													
Ministers													
Garro y Arízcun, Nicolás Ambr.	12,390,415	3.00	10.72		26.37	18.33		14.43		9.11	10.84		7.20
Caballero Pozo, José Antonio	6,500,000	6.46	2.77		69.23					21.54			
Porlier Sopranis, Antonio	1,340,191	3.96	18.71							59.01	18.32		
Total		4.47	10.73	0	31.87	6.11	0	4.81	0	29.89	9.72	0	2.4
1815-1879													
Cevallos Guerra, Pedro	7,472,403	1.05	0.16		30.92			0.40		67.47			
Pérez de Castro, Evaristo	1,662,333	15.69	4.95				16.37			62.99			
Canga Argüelles, José	2,199,733	2.85	5.21		20.84	37.14	3.97			27.87			2.12
Fernández Gasco, Francisco	448,153	16.21	8.54		72.57			2.68					
Riva Herrera, Manuel	41,379	8.12	46.83		34.85						10.20		
García de la Torre, José	541,869	16.79	5.96		33.18			3.36		34.07	6.64		
Aguirre Solarte, José V.	7,217,721	1.01	4.50		2.31	15.00		1.35		75.83			
Burgos, Javier (de)	2,918,813	3.74	6.89	5.68	29.33	7.02	0.55			0.19	28.78	17.82	
López, Joaquín María	1,070,159	3.00	7.72		78.82	4.61					5.85		
Silvela, Francisco	1,079,180	4.05	0.65		94.45			0.27		0.58			
Gallego Valcárcel, Antonio	840,470	4.64	3.97		69.24	12.98		1.64					7.53

B.12. (cont.)

1805-1879	Final capital	Personal estate			Real estate			Profession Business			Investments		
		1	2	3	4	5	6	7	8	9	10	11	12
Gil de la Cuadra, Ramón	1,125,959	83.12	2.66										14.22
Ferrer y Cafranga, Joaquin Mª	3,963,302	3.56	4.36		12.74	40.48				3.54	35.32		
Calderón de la Barca, Angel	1,848,138	0.42	30.46		1.78					21.13	46.21		
Cortázar, Modesto	491,443	47.11	18.90		2.60	31.39							
Collado Parada, José M.	69,441,413	0.19	12.00		31.23	10.83		16.61		15.00	14.14		
Remón Zarco del Valle, Antonio	1,366,274	3.62	2.59		2.78					42.73			48.28
Salamanca Mayol, José (de)	219,547,300	4.57	1.08		11.57	42.07		17.82		22.89			
Cortina Arenzana, Manuel	7,426,684	1.58	11.55			17.77				20.49			48.61
Total		11.65	9.42	0.3	27.85	11.54	1.1	2.32	0	20.78	7.74	0.94	6.36

Key: 1. Domestic; 2. Silver/Cash; 3. Agrarian Rents; 4. Rural; 5. Urban; 6. Salaries; 7. Credits; 8. Commodities; 9. Public debt; 10. Company stocks; 11. Industry; 12. Loans

Source: Garro Arízcun, AHPM, P. 2092; Caballero, AHN, Títulos y Familias, leg. 14, AHPM, P. 22980; Porlier, AHPM, P. 21410; Cevallos, AHPM, P. 25030; Pérez de Castro, AHPM, P. 25720; Canga Argüelles, AHPM, P. 21000, 24994, 25132; Ferneandez Gasco, AHPM, P. 25267; Riva Herrera, AHPM, P. 25219; Garcia de la Torre, AHPM, P. 25446; AHPM, P. Aguirre Solarte, AHPM, P. 25609; Burgos, AHPM, P. 26804; López, AHPM, P. 25764; Silvela, AHPM, P. 26376; Gallego, AHPM, P. 26813; Gil de la Cuadra, AHPM, P. 27101; Ferrer, AHPM, P. 28758; Calderón, AHPM, P. 25248; Cortázar, AHPM, P. 27986; Collado, AHPM, P. 27380; Remón, AHPM, P. 27671; Cortina, AHPM, P. 33573.

B.13. *Politicians. Percentage Distribution of Gross Assets*
(reales de vellón)

1805-1879	Final capital	Personal estate			Real estate			Profession Business		Investments			
		1	2	3	4	5	6	7	8	9	10	11	12
Other politicians													
Carranza Helguera, Lucas (de)	3,008,141	1.68	5.29		18.14	59.47				13.00	2.42		
Mazo García de la Prada, Fco.	1,844,051	2.86	6.80		2.17	19.93		46.55		21.69			
Cabarrús Galabert, Domingo	4,150,000		1.36		38.50	29.85		1.09				29.20	
Goyeneche Múzquiz, Ignacio	3,700,000	3.98			45.42	24.46							26.14
Calderón de la Barca, Miguel	692,629	6.06	6.90		28.38	49.24		9.42					
Ortiz de Taranco, Manuel	2,532,683	0.86	25.22		61.08	1.38				4.15			7.31
Pérez Moltó, Juan Ignacio	3,973,583	2.64	22.54		14.86			5.20		11.44	26.12	7.55	9.65
Piernas Abades, Luis	1,712,043	3.56	6.08		24.26	59.92		1.03			3.10	2.05	
Calvo Asensio, Pedro	875,313	3.50	23.90		9.76	48.45		14.34			17.55	4.60	
Calderón Molina, Carlos		0.86	2.00		31.29	22.72		20.98					
Total	43,473,755	2.60	10.00	0	27.39	31.54	0	9.87	0	5.03	4.92	4.34	4.31

Key: 1. Domestic; 2. Silver/Cash; 3. Agrarian Rents; 4. Rural; 5. Urban; 6. Salaries; 7. Credits; 8. Commodities; 9. Public debt; 10. Company stocks; 11. Industry; 12. Loans

Source: Carranza, AHPM, P. 22988; Mazo, AHPM, P. 23054; Cabarrús Galabert, AHN, Diversos, Serie General, legs. 7, 8,13, 35, 49, 54; Goyeneche, AHPM, P. 25424; Calderón de la Barca, AHPM, P. 25683; Ortiz de Taranco, AHPM, P. 26369; Pérez Moltó, AHPM, P. 26607; Piernas, AHPM, P. 28482; Calvo Asensio, AHPM, P. 27375; Calderón Molina, AHPM, P. 28431.

Appendix C: Archival sources

Archivo Histórico de Protocolos de Madrid

Notarios	Protocolos
Aguado, José Mateo	20447–20474 (1764–1803)
Badiola, Juan Antonio	19095–19117 (1753–1791)
Bande, Domingo	22570–27272 (1835–1862)
Barreda, Lorenzo	19531–19546 (1756–1782)
Caldeiro, Manuel	26804–27380 (1854–1865)
Canosa, José Antonio	21395–21441 (1792–1814)
Carranza, Ramón de	23024–23030 (1800–1826)
Castañeda, Vicente	26606–26609 (1852–1854)
Castillo, Eugenio	24742–24748 (1837–1841)
Cavia y Díez, Clemente de	21635–21638 (1794–1802)
Celis Ruiz, José	25959–25961 (1858–1860)
Costa, Vicente (de la)	21152–21154
Cuende, Pedro	20010 (1780)
Culebras Acero, Matias	18695
Delgado, Miguel	19959–19994 (1760–1808)
Díaz Noriega, Juan Antonio	23034–23038 (1792–1796)
Elipe, Ventura	18211 and 18212 (1793)
Escribano, Francisco	21412–21422 (1781–1804)
Estepar, Santiago	21655–21696 (1786–1818)
Febrero, José	19622 and 19623 (1757–1771)
Fernández Izquierdo, Gervasio	22497–22504 (1797–1810)
Gaona Loheches, Jacinto	25055–25059 (1839–1842)
García de la Madrid, Juan	25424–25428 (1846–1848)
García Jimenez, Ramón	22988–23007 (1791–1811)
García Sancha, Mariano	26109–28279 (1856–1868)
García Villamañan, Pedro	21264–21270 (1778–1785)
Garamendi, José Maria	25219–25946 (1844–1858)
Garrido, Juan	23567–28480 (1805–1832)

Appendix C

Notarios	Protocolos
Gómez, Casimiro Antonio	21721–21788 (1782–1832)
González, de San Martín, Tomás	17876–17884 (1743–1792)
González Sáez, Julian	22959–22985 (1785–1811)
González, Diego Benigno	21100–21127 (1778–1812)
Granja, Santiago (de la)	24619–24621 (1837–1839)
Joaquín Virto, Fermín	22478–22485 (1790–1800)
López de Salazar, Antonio	22840–22887 (1789–1820)
López, Felix	20826–20835 (1768–1785)
Magano, Alejandro	21032–21055 (1780–1800)
Manuel Manrique, Jacobo	21868–21888 (1796–1813)
Manuel Merinero, Nicanor	21913–21921 (1789–1804)
Milla, Francisco	20913–20928 (1770–1793)
Montoya, Francisco	23825–23829 (1814–1826)
Paris, Miguel Tomás	19475–19521 (1756–1790)
Peñuelas, Luis Pérez	22462–22468 (1791–1795)
Pérez Alonso, Cipriano	27984–27986 (1861–1862)
Pérez Piñuelas, Luis	22461–22466 (1790–1803)
Pérez, Dionisio	25129–25134 (1837–1844)
Raya, Juan de	23093–23154 (1800–1839)
Reyes, Domingo (de los)	25697–25699 (1848–1849)
Revilla, Jacinto	25028–25032 (1836–1839)
Rodríguez Moya, Carlos	25446–25450 (1847–1849)
Rodriguez, Félix	20200 (1780)
Ruiz, Simón	21424–21433 (1793–1818)
Salaya, Ignacio de	21000–21018 (1803–1812)
Salaya, Ildefonso	25620–25628 (1843–1849)
Sancha y Prado, Tomás	22210–22289 (1788–1822)
Santin, Martin	25771–25778 (1847–1851)
Sanz Barea, Antonio	24683–24695 (1835–1842)
Sanz Barea, Claudio	26369–27671 (1851–1866)
Sanz, Claudio	23387–23437 (1804–1837)
Sauquillo de Frias, Miguel	19440–19442
Sierra, Miguel María	24989–24995 (1838–1842)
Terreros, Lorenzo	18768–18824 (1751–1786)
Urraza, Juan Antonio	21700–21704 (1797–1799)
Urruchi, Angel de	22424–22428 (1792–1799)
Valladares, Pedro	21070–21099 (1779–1805)
Velasco, Santiago	28480–28487 (1861–1866)
Vicuña, Cristobal de	23039–25147 (1800–1843)
Villa y Olier, Juan	20031–20105 (1770–1812)

Archival sources

Archivo Histórico Nacional

Sección de Diversos, Serie General. Papeles of the Cabarrús family, legajos 1–54.
Sección de Diversos, Serie General. Papeles of the Sáinz de Baranda family, legajos: 217–221; 223–226.
Títulos y Familias, legajos: 14; 2246; 2225; 2227; 2228; 2579; 2609.
Sección de Estado, Caballeros de Carlos III, expedientes: 286; 767; 933; 975; 994; 1114; 1256; 1309; 1325; 1369; 1412; 1491; 1515; 1722; 1789; 1791; 1795; 1798; 1815; 1818; 1819; 1834; 1894; 1896; 1924; 1997; 2175; 2195; 2222; 2265; 2280; 2302; 2308; 2342; 2344; 2352; 2389; 2441; 2486; 2520.
Ordenes Militares, Santiago, legajos: 280 (moderno); 570 (mod.); 603 (mod.); 616 (mod.).
Ordenes Militares, Alcántara, 163 (moderno); 169 (mod.).

Archivo de la Villa Madrid

Secretaría, legajos: 2–291–1; 2–247–86; 2–249–13; 2–247–85; 2–247–89; 2–247–78; 2–247–79; 2–247–80; 2–247–97; 2–247–98; 2–247–100; 2–247–47; 2–247–48; 2–247–64; 2–248–2; 2–248–11; 2–290–25; 2–291–10; 2–291–32; 2–291–33; 2–291–36; 2–359–6; 2–367–4; 2–242–2; 2–249–9; 2–249–11; 2–402–4; 2–402–7; 2–249–79; 2–249–80; 2–249–15; 2–255–15; 2–249–90; 2–403–26; 2–294–40; 4–186–55; 2–248–30; 2–292–28; 4–172–15; 2–429–3; 2–176–21; 2–402–13; 2–402–13; 2–402–12; 2–229–20; 2–230–6; 4–172–14; 4–172–13; 2–230–38; 169; 224–29; 247; 249; 256; 303–4; 429.

Archivo Histórico del Banco de España

Secretaría, libros: 272–75; 322–23; 342–67; 18558; 18559; 18560; 18561; 18563; 18564; 18565; 18566; 18567; 18568; 18569; 18570; 18571; 18572; 18573; 18574; 18576; 18604; 18608; 18611; 18627; 18648.
Secretaría, legajos: 453; 455–57; 468; 469; 480; 481; 483–86; 553; 567; 571–73; 593; 655; 705; 706–10; 725; 782–84.

References

Acosta Sánchez, 1975. *El desarrollo capitalista y la democracia en España*. Aproximación metodológica. Barcelona, Dirosa.
Alarcón Caracuel, M. 1975. *El derecho de asociación obrera en España (1839–1900)*. Madrid, Revista de Trabajo.
Alcalá Galiano. 1955. *Obrasescogidas*. Madrid, Biblioteca de Autores Españoles. 2 vols.
Alcázar, c. 1953. "España en 1792. Floridablanca. Su derrumbamiento del gobierno y sus procesos de responsabilidad política." *Revista de Estudios Políticos*. 93–138.
Aldrich, B. W., F. P. Goldman, and A. Lipman. 1980. "Urbanization and Familism: An Examination of the Influence of Urban Residence upon Kinship Orientation in Two Culturally Related Developing Nations: Portugal and Brazil." In *The Family in Latin America*. New Delhi, Vikas Publishing House.
Allen, R. C. 1988. "The Price of Freehold Land and the Interest rate in the Seventeenth and Eighteenth Centuries." *Economic History Review*, 2nd ser., xvi.
Alvarez Junco, J. 1985. "Sobre el concepto de Revolución burguesa" In M. C. Iglesias (Ed.), *Homenaje a José Antonio Maravall*. Madrid, C.I.S., 135–149. 1986. "A vueltas con la revolución burguesa." *Zona Abierta*, 36–37.
Alvarez Junco, J. and S. Juliá. 1988. "Tendencias actuales y perspectivs de investigación en historia contemporánea." In J. Faci (Ed.), *Tendencias en Histoia*. Madrid, ANEP-CSIC, 53–63.
Alvarez Morales, A. 1982. *Historia de las instituciones españolas. Siglos XVIII–XIX*. Madrid, Editoriales de Derecho Reunidas.
Alvarez Santalo, C. and A. García Baquero. 1980. "Funcionalidad del capital andaluz en vísperas de la primera industrialización." *Estudios Regionales*, 5: 101–133.
Anderson B. L. 1970. "Money and the Structure of the Credit in the Eighteenth Century." *Business History* (July): 85–101.

References

Anderson, B. L., and P. P. Cotrell. 1974. *Money and Banking in England. The Development of the Banking System, 1694–1914.* Newton Abbot, David & Charles.
Anderson, M. 1971. *Family Structure in Nineteenth Century Lancashire.* Cambridge, Cambridge University Press.
  1979. "The Relevance of Family History." *Sociological Review Monograph*, 28: 49–73.
Arensberg, C. M. 1963. "The Old World Peoples: The Place of European Cultures in World Ethnography." *Anthropological Quarterly*, 36: 75–99.
Ariès, P. 1960. *L'Enfant et la vie familiale sous l'ancien régime.* Paris, Seuil.
Artola, M. 1974. *Partidos y programas políticos, 1808–1936.* Madrid, Aguilar, 2 vols.
  1976. *Los Afrancesados.* Madrid, Turner.
  1978. *Antiguo Régimen y revolución liberal.* Barcelona, Ariel.
  1982. *La Hacienda del Antiguo Régimen.* Madrid, Alianza.
  1989. *La burguesía revolucionaria (1808–1869).* Madrid, Alianza.
Artola, M. (Ed.). 1978. *El latifundio. Propiedad y explotación. Siglos XVIII–XX.* Madrid, Servicio de Publicaciones Agrarias.
Asselain, J. Ch. 1984. *Histoire économique de la France du XVIIIe siècle a nos jours.* Paris, PUF.
Aston, T. H., and C. H. E. Philpin. (Eds.) 1987. *The Brenner Debate. Agrarian Class Structure and Economic Development in Pre-Industrial Europe.* Cambridge, Cambridge University Press.
Atienza Fernández, I. 1987. *Aristocracia, poder y riqueza en la España moderna. La Casa de Osuna.* Madrid, Siglo XXI.
Bahamonde Magro, A. 1981. *El horizonte económico de la burguesía isabelina: Madrid 1856–1866.* Madrid, Universidad Complutense, Tesis Doctoral.
  1986. "Crisis de la nobleza de cuna y consolidación burguesa (1840–1880)." In *Madrid en la sociedad del siglo XIX.* Madrid, CIDUR. Vol. I, pp. 326–375.
Bahamonde Magro, A., and J. Toro Mérida. 1978. *Burguesía, especulación y cuestión social en el Madrid del siglo XIX.* Madrid, Siglo XXI.
Bahamonde Magro A., and L. E. Otero Carvajal. 1989. "La reproducción patrimonial de la élite burguesa madrileña en la Restauración. El caso de Francisco de las Rivas y Ubieta, marqués de Mudela. 1834–1882." In *La sociedad madrileña durante la Restauración, 1876–1931.* Madrid, CIDUR, 524–635.
Bahamonde Magro, A., and J. A. Martínez. 1994. *Historia de España siglo XIX.* Madrid, Cátedra.
Bairoch, P. 1989. "Urbanization and the Economy in Preindustrial Societies: The Finding of Two Decades of Research." *Journal of European Economic History*, 18: 239–290.
Baldó Lacomba, M. 1988. "Fernando VII." In A. Domínguez Ortiz (ed.), *Historiade España.* Barcelona, Planeta, 179–306.

References

Balmori, D., S. F. Voss, and M. Wortman. 1984. *Notable Family Networks in Latin America*. Chicago, University of Chicago Press.
Barbier, J. 1972. "Elites and Cadres in Bourbon Chile." *Hispanic American Historical Review*, 52: 416–435.
Barceló, M. et al. 1987. "La transició del feudalisme al capitalisme: noves reflexions per a un debat necessari." *Manuscrits. Revista d'Historia Moderna.* 4/5, Bellaterra.
Barciela, C. (Ed.). 1989. *Estadísticas históricas de España. Siglos XIX–XX*. Madrid, Fundación Banco Exterior.
Basurto, R. 1983. *Comercio y burguesía mercantil en Bilbao en la segunda mitad del siglo XVIII*. Bilbao, Universidad del Pais Vasco.
Bédarida, F. 1979. *A Social History of England, 1851–1975*. London, Methuen.
Bennassar, B. 1983. *Valladolid en el siglo de oro*. Valladolid, Fundación Municipal de Cultura.
——— 1984. "Los inventarios post-mortem y la historia de las mentalidades." In *Actas del II Coloqio de Metodología Histórica Aplicada. La documentación notarial en la historia*. Universidad de Santiago de Compostela.
Berdahl, R. M. 1989. *The Politics of the Prussian Nobility. The Development of a Conservative Ideology. 1770–1848*. Princeton, N.J., Princeton University Press.
Bergeron, L. 1978. *Banquiers, negociants et manufacturiers parisiens du Directoire a l'Empire*. Paris, Mouton.
Berkner, L. K. 1975. "The Use and Misuse of Census Data for the Historical Analysis of Family Structure." *Journal of Interdisciplinary History*, 5: 721–38.
Bermejo Cabrero, J. L. 1982. *Estudios sobre la Administración Central española*. Madrid, Centro de Estudios Constitucionales.
Bernard, G. 1976. *Le Secrétariat d'Etat et le Conseil espagnol des Indes, 1700–1808*. Geneve-Paris.
Blackbourne, D., and G. Eley. 1984. *The Peculiarities of German History*. Oxford, Oxford University Press.
Bleiber, H. 1977. *Bourgeoisie und bürguerliche Umwälzung in Deutschland, 1789–1871*. Berlin: Akademic-Verlag.
Blum, J. 1978. *The End of the Old Order in Rural Europe*. Princeton, N.J., Princeton University Press.
Booker, J. 1974. *Essex and the Industrial Revolution*. Chelmsford, Mass., Essex County Council.
Botrel, F., and J. Le Bouil. 1973. "Sur le concept de 'clase media' dans la pensée bourgeoise en Espagne au XIXe siècle." In *Colloque International de L'Université de Bordeaux. La question de la 'bourgeoisie' dans le monde hispanique au XIXe siècle*. Bordeaux, Biere, 137–160.

References

Bourdieu, P. 1972. "Les stratégies matrimoniales dans le système de reproduction," *Annales: Economies, Sociétés, Civilisations*, 27: 1105–27.
    1977. *Outline of a Theory of Practice*. Cambridge, Cambridge University Press.
    1988a. *Cosas dichas*. Madrid, Gedisa.
    1988b. *La distinción. Criterios y bases sociales del gusto*. Madrid, Taurus.
    1989. *La noblesse d'état. Grandes écoles et esprit de corps*. Paris, Les Editions de Minuit.
Brading, D. A. 1971. *Miners and Merchants in Bourbon Mexico, 1763–1810*. Cambridge, Cambridge University Press.
    1973. "Government and Elite in Late Colonial Mexico." *Hispanic American Historical Review*, 53: 390.
Bravo Lozano, J. 1986. "Don Francisco de Horcasitas. Las posibilidades de Madrid a fines del siglo XVII." *Estudios de Historia Social*, 497–521.
Brewer, J. 1982. "Commercialization and Politics." In N. McKendrick, J. Brewer, and J. H. Plumb (Eds.), *The Birth of a Consumer Society. The Commercialization of Eighteenth-Century England*. Bloomington, Indiana University Press, 197–262.
Bruguera, F. G. 1953. *Histoire Contemporaine d'Espagne, 1789–1950*. Paris, Ophrys.
Burdick, A. V. 1983. The Madrid Writer in Spanish Society: 1833–1843. Ph.D. dissertation, University of California, San Diego.
Burdiel, I. 1987. *La política de los notables. Moderados y avanzados durante el Régimendel Estatuto Real*. Valencia, Edicions Alfonso el Magnánim.
Burguière, A. 1987. "The Formation of the Couple." *Journal of Family History*, 12: 39–56.
Burke, P. 1974. *Venice and Amsterdam: A Study of Seventeenth Century Elites*. London.
Burkholder, M. A. 1978. "Titled Nobles, Elites, and Independence: Some Comments," *Latin American Research Review*, 13: 290–295.
Bush, M. L. 1984. *The English Aristocracy. A Comparative Synthesis*. Manchester, Manchester University Press.
Busquets, J. 1972. "Los militares en al sociedad decimonónica." In *Historia social de España. Siglo XIX*. Madrid, Guadiana, 207–228.
    1982. *Pronunciamientos y golpes de estado en España*. Barcelona: Planeta.
Cabarrús, Conde (de). 1990. *Cartas sobre los obstáculos que la naturaleza, la opinión y las leyes oponen a la felicidad pública*, Madrid, Fundación Banco Exterior.
Cabrera Bosch, M. I. 1982. "El poder legislativo en la España del siglo XVIII (1716–1808)." In Artola, M. (Ed.), *La economía española al final del Antiguo Régimen. IV Instituciones*. Madrid, Alianza, 187–268.
Callahan, W. J. 1989. *Iglesia, poder y sociedad en España, 1750–1874*. Madrid, Nerea.
Cameron, R. E. (Ed.). 1967. *Banking in the Early Stages of Industrialization. A Study in Comparative Economic History*. New York, Oxford University Press.

References

Campbell, J. K. 1974. *Honour, Family and Patronage. A Study of Institutions and Moral Values in a Greek Mountain Community.* Oxford, Oxford University Press.
Cannadine, D. (Ed.). 1982. *Patricians, Power and Politics in Nineteenth-Century Towns.* Leicester, Leicester University Press.
Capella Martinez, M., and A. Matilla Tascón. 1957. *Los Cinco Gremios Mayores de Madrid. Estudio crítico-histórico.* Madrid, Cámara Oficial de Comercio e Industria.
Carbajo Isla, M. 1987. *La población de Madrid desde finales del siglo XVI hasta mediados del siglo XIX.* Madrid, Siglo XXI.
Carmona Pidal, J. A. 1986. "Aproximación a un noble madrileño: El marqués de Alcañices." In A. Bahamonde and L. E. Otero. (Eds.), *Madrid en la sociedad del siglo XIX.* Madrid, CIDUR. Vol.I, pp. 505–514.
Caro Baroja, J. 1966. *Las brujas y su mundo.* Madrid, Alianza.
——— 1985. *La hora Navarra del siglo XVIII español. Personas, familias, negocios e ideas.* Pamplona, Diputación Foral de Navarra.
Carrasco Canals, C. 1975. *La burocracia en la España del XIX.* Madrid, Instituto de Estudios de la Administración Local.
Carriere, C. 1973. *Negociants Marseillais au XVIIIe. siècle.* Marseille, Institut Historique de Provence.
Casey, J. 1989. *The History of the Family.* Oxford, Basil Blackwell.
Casey, J., and B. Vincent. 1987. "Casa y familia en la Granada del Antiguo Régimen." In *La familia en la España Mediterránea.* Barcelona, Crítica.
Castañeda Peirón, L. 1984. "Ensayo metodológico sobre los inventarios postmortem en el análisis de los niveles de vida material: El ejemplo de Barcelona entre 1790–1794." In *Primer Congrés d'Historia Moderna de Catalunya.* Barcelona, Diputacio de Barcelona, 757–769.
Castro, C. (de). 1987. *El pan de Madrid: el abasto de las ciudades españolas del Antiguio Régimen.* Madrid, Alianza.
Cerutti, M. 1989. "Burgueses y burguesías productoras." In M. Cerutti and M. Vellinga (Eds.), *Burguesía en industria en América Latina y Europa meridional.* Madrid, Alianza, 11–21.
Chacón Jiménez, F. 1987. "Notas para el estudio de la familia en al región de Murcia durante el Antiguo Régimen." In *La familia en la España Mediterránea.* Barcelona, Crítica.
Chapman, S. D., and S. Chassagne. 1981. *European Textile Printers in the Eighteenth Century. A History of Peel and Overkampf.* London, Heinemann Educational.
Chartier, R. 1982. "Intellectual History or Sociocultural History?" In D. LaCapra and S. L. Kaplan (Eds.), *Modern European Intellectual History: Reappraisals and New Perspectives.* Ithaca, N. Y. Cornell University Press.
Chaussinand-Nogaret, G. 1970. *Les finances du Languedoc au XVIIIe siècle.* Paris.

References

1976. *La noblesse au XVIIIe siècle: de la féodalité aux Lumières*. Paris, Hachette.
Chávarri Sidera, P. 1988. *Las elecciones de diputados a las cortes generales y extraordinarias (1810–1813)*. Madrid, Centro de Estudios Constitucionales.
Christaller, W. 1966. *Central Places in Southern Germany.* Englewood Cliffs, N.J., Prentice-Hall.
Clavero, B. 1976. "Para un concepto de revolución burguesa," *Sistema. Revista de ciencias sociales,* 13, 35–54.
 1989. *Mayorazgo y propiedad feudal en Castilla (1369–1863)*. Madrid, Siglo XXI.
Clavero, B., and P. Ruiz Torres. 1979. *Estudios sobre la revolución burguesa en España.* Madrid, Siglo XXI.
Clay, C. 1974. "The Price of Freehold Land in the Later Seventeenth and Eighteenth Centuries." *Economic History Review,* xxvii.
Cobban, A. 1964. *The Social Interpretation of the French Revolution.* Cambridge, Cambridge University Press.
Comellas, J. L. 1962. "Las Cortes de Cádiz y la Constitución de 1812." *Revista de Estudios Políticos.* 126: 85–92.
 1970. *Los Moderados en el poder, 1844–1854.* Madrid, CSIC.
Comninel, G. C. 1987. *Rethinking the French Revolution. Marxism and the Revisionist Challenge.* London-New York, Verso.
Crone, P. 1989. *Pre-Industrial Societies.* Oxford, Blackwell.
Cruz, J. 1986. "Cambistas madrileños en la segunda mitad del siglo XVIII." In A. Bahamonde Magro and L. E. Otero Carvajal (Eds.), *Madrid en la sociedad del siglo XIX.* Madrid: CIDUR. Vol. I, pp. 454–474.
 1990a. "Propiedad urbana y sociedad en Madrid, 1749–1774." *Revista de Historia Económica,* 2: 239–69.
 1990b. "Revolucionarios con clase. Vida, cultura y fortuna de la familia Sáinz de Baranda, 1750–1850." *Espacio, Tiempo y Forma,* 25–50.
Cubitt, D. J. 1982. "La composición social de una élite hispanoamericana a la Independencia: Guayaquil en 1820." *Revista de Historia de América,* 94: 7–31.
Cuenca-Esteban, J. 1990. "The Markets of Latin American Exports, 1790–1820: A Comparative Analysis of International Prices." In L. L. Johnson and E. Tandeter (Eds.), *Essays on the Price History of Eighteenth Century Latin America* Albuquerque, University of New Mexico Press.
Curtin, P. D. 1984. *Cross-cultural Trade in World History.* Cambridge, Cambridge University Press.
Curzon, G. N. 1966. *Persia and the Persian Question.* New York, Barnes & Noble.
D'Aulnoy, Comtesse d'. 1874. *La cour et la ville de Madrid vers la fin du XVIIe siècle* . . . Paris, E. Plon.
Dahrendorf, R. 1959. *Class and Class Conflict in Industrial Society.* London, Routledge and Kegan.

References

Daumard, A. 1970. *Les bourgeois de Paris au XIXe siècle.* Paris, Flammarion.
Davidoff, L., and C. Hall. 1987. *Family Fortunes. Men and Women of the English Middle Class, 1780–1850.* Chicago, University of Chicago Press.
de Vries, J. 1976. *The Economy of Europe in an Age of Crisis, 1600–1750.* Cambridge, Cambridge University Press.
   1984. *The European Urbanization, 1500–1800.* London, Methuen.
Deane, P. 1986. *La primera Revolución Industrial.* Barcelona, Ariel.
Demos, J. 1970. *A Little Commonwealth: Family Life in Plymouth Colony.* New York, Oxford University Press.
Diefendorf, J. M. 1984. *Businessmen and Politics in the Rhineland, 1789–1934.* Princeton, N.J., Princeton University Press.
Domínguez Ortiz, A. 1976. *Sociedad y estado en el siglo XVIII español.* Barcelona, Ariel.
   1978. "Algunas notas sobre banqueros y asentistas de Carlos II." *Hacienda Pública Española*, 55: 167–76.
   1979. *Las clases privilegiadas en el Antiguo Régimen.* Madrid, Istmo.
   1983. *Sociedad y mentalidad en la Sevilla del Antiguo Régimen.* Seville, Servicio de Publicaciones del Ayuntamiento de Sevilla.
Doyle, W. 1980. *Origins of the French Revolution.* Oxford, Oxford University Press.
Earle, P. 1989. *The Making of the English Middle Class. Business, Society and Family Life in London, 1660–1730.* Berkeley, University of California Press.
Eiras Roel, A. 1981. "La burguesía mercantil compostelana a mediados del siglo XVIII: mentaliad tradicional e inmobilismo económico." In A. Eiras Roel (Ed.), *La historia social de Galicia en sus fuentes de protocolos.* Santiago de Compostela, 521–64.
Eisenstadt, S. N. 1984. *Patrons, Clients and Friends. Interpersonal Relations and the Structure of Trust in Society.* Cambridge, Cambridge University Press.
Elorza, A. 1970. *La ideología liberal en la Ilustración española.* Madrid, Tecnos.
Escudero, J. A. 1975. *Los orígenes del Consejo de Ministros,* Seville, Publicaciones de la Universidad.
Esposito, N. J. 1989. *Italian Family Structure.* New York, Peter Lang.
Fayard, J. 1982a. *Los miembros del Consejo d Castilla (1621–1746).* Madrid, Siglo XXI.
   1982b. "Los ministros del Consejo Real de Castilla (1746–1788)." *Cuadernos de Investigación Histórica*, 6: 109–136.
Felstiner, M. 1976. "Kinship Politics in the Chilean Independence Movement." *Hispanic American Historical Review*, 56: 58–80.
Fernández, R. 1982. "La burguesía barcelonesa en el siglo XVIII: la familia Gloria." In P. Tedde (Ed.), *La economía española al final del Antiguo Régimen.* Madrid, Alianza, 1–151.

References

Fernández, R. (Ed.). 1985. *España en el siglo XVIII. Homenaje a Pierre Vilar*. Barcelona, Crítica.

Fernández de Pinedo, E. 1980. "Coyuntura y política económicas." In Tuñón de lara (Ed.), *Historia de España VII. Centralismo, Ilustración y agonía del Antiguo Régimen*. Barcelona, Labor. 11–173.

Fernández García, A. 1971. *El abastecimiento de Madrid en el reinado de Isabel II*. Madrid: CSIC.

Firth, R. 1971. "The Nature of English Kinship." In *Readings in Kinship and Social Structure*. New York, N. Graburn, 385–389.

Flores, A. 1964. *La sociedad de 1850*. Madrid, Alianza.

Fontaine, L. 1990. "Solidarités familiales et logiques migratoires en Pays de montagne à l'époque moderne." *Annales ESC*, 6, 1433–1450.

Fontana, J. 1971. *La quiebra de la monarquía absoluta, 1814–1820*. Barcelona, Ariel.

1975. *Cambio económico y actitudes políticas en la España del siglo XIX*. Barcelona, Ariel.

1979. *La crisis del Antiguo Régimen, 1808–1833*. Barcelona, Crítica.

1979. "Sobre revoluciones burguesas y autos de fe." *Mientras Tanto*, 1: 25–32.

Ford, R. 1906. *Gatherings from Spain*. London, J. M. Dent and Co.

Franch, R. 1986. *Crecimiento comercial y enriquecimiento burgués en la Valencia del siglo XVIII*. Valencia, Institució Alfonso el Magnànim.

Freeman, S. T. 1970. *Neighbors: The Social Contract in a Castilian Hamlet*. Chicago. University of Chicago Press.

Furet, F. 1971. "Le catéchisme révolutionnaire." *Annales: Economies, sociétés, civilisations*, 26: 255–289.

Gacto, E. 1987. "El grupo familiar de la edad moderna en los territorios del mediterráneo hispánico: una visión jurídica." In *La familia en la España Mediterránea*. Barcelona, Crítca.

Gallard, D. M. 1797–1808. *Almanak Mercantil o Guía de Comerciantes*. Madrid, Imprenta de Ramón Ruiz.

Garcia Baquero, A. 1976. *Cádiz y el Atlántico*. Seville, CSIC, 2 vols.

Garcia Carraffa, A. 1952–1964. *Enciclopedia heráldica y genealógica hispanoamericana*. Madrid, A. Marzo.

García de León y Pizarro, J. 1953. *Memorias*. Madrid, Revista de Occidente.

García Regueiro, O. 1987. "Cabarrús y el 'Elogio de Carlos III': el encausamiento de un 'Ilustrado'." *Boletín de la Real Academia de la Historia*, 45–103.

García Sanz, A. 1974. "Agronomía y experiencias agronómicas en España durante la segunda mitad del siglo XVIII." *Moneda y Créito*.

1986a. "El interior peninsular en el siglo XVIII: un crecimiento moderado y tradicional." In R. Fernández (Ed.), *España el siglo XVIII. Homenaje a Pierre Vilar*, Barcelona, Crítica, 630–680.

References

1985b. "Auge y decadencia en los siglos XVI y XVII: economía y sociedad en Castilla." *Revista de Historica Económica*, III: 11–27.
García Sanz, A., and R. Garranbou (Eds.), 1985. *Historia agraria de la España Contemporánea*. Barcelona, Crítica, 2 vols.
García-Cuenca Ariati, T. 1982. "El Consejo de Hacienda (1746–1803)." In M. Artola (Ed.), *La economía española al final del Antiguo Régimen*. Madrid, Alianza, 405–502.
Gil Novales, A. (Ed.). 1980. *El Trienio liberal*. Madrid, Siglo XXI.
  1985. *La revolución burguesa en España. Actas del coloquio hispanoalemán celebrado en Leipzig los días 17 y 18 de 1983*. Madrid, Universidad Complutense.
Gille, B. 1963. *Documents sur l'etat de l'industrie et du commerce de Paris et du Département de la Seine*. Paris, Impr. Municipale.
Girón, P. A. Marqués de las Amarillas. 1979. *Recuerdos (1778–1837)*. Pamplona, EUNSA, 3 vols.
Gómez-Ferrer, G. 1986. "La clase dirigente madrileña en dos novelas de 1890." In A. Bahamonde Magro and L. E. Otero Carvajal (Eds.), *La sociedad madrileña durante la Restauración, 1876–1931*. Madrid, CIDUR, 534–556.
Gómez-Rivero, R. 1988. *Los orígenes del Ministerio de Justicia*. Madrid, Ministerio de Justicia.
Gramsci, A. 1971. *Selections from the Prison Notebooks*. New York, International Publishers.
  1979. *Scritti Politici*. Rome.
Greven, P. J., Jr. 1970. *Four Generations: Population Land and Family in Colonial Andover, Massachusetts*. Ithaca, N.Y., Cornell University Press.
Guimera, A. 1985. *Burguesía extranjera y comercio Atlántico. La empresa comercial irlandesa en Canarias, 1703–1771*. Santa Cruz de Tenerife, CSIC.
Habermas, J. 1989. *The Structural Transformation of the Public Sphere. An Inquiry into a Category of Bourgeois Society*. Cambridge, Mass., MIT Press.
Hajnal, J. 1983. "Two Kinds of Pre-Industrial Household Formation System." In R. Wall, J. Robin, and P. Laslett (Eds.), *Family Forms in Historic Europe*. Cambridge, Cambridge University Press, 65–104.
Hamilton, E. J. 1969. *War and Prices in Spain, 1651–1800*. New York, Russell and Russell.
Hamilton, R. H. 1991. *The Bourgeois Epoch. Marx and Engels on Britain, France, and Germany*. Chapel Hill, University of North Carolina Press.
Hareven, T. 1977. "The Family as Process: The Historical Study of the Family Cycle." *Journal of Social History*, 7:322–29.
  1991. "The History of the Family and the Complexity of Social Change." *American Historical Review*, 96–1: 95–124.
Harris, C. C. 1990. *Kinship*. Buckingham: Open University Press.

References

Harris, J., and P. Thane. 1984. "British and European Bankers, 1880–1914: An Aristocratic Bourgeoisie." In Pat Thane (Ed.), *The Power of the Past: Essays for Eric Hobsbawn*. Cambridge, Cambridge University Press.

Harrison, J. 1990. "The Economic History of Spain since 1800." *Economic History Review*, XLIII: 79–89.

Hatch, E. 1973. *Theories of Man and Culture*. New York, Columbia University Press.

Herán, F. 1990. *Le bourgeois de Séville. Terre et parenté en Andalousie*. Paris, PUF.

Hernández Benítez, M. 1995. El poder difuso. Estudio de una oligarquía urbana (Madrid, 1606–1808). Madrid, Siglo XXI.

    1986. "Reproducción y renovación de una oligarquía urbana: los regidores de Madrid en el siglo XVIII." *Anuario de Historia del Derecho Español*, 637–681.

Hernández Franco, J. 1984. *La gestión política y el pensamiento reformista del Conde de Floridablanca*. Murcia, Universidad de Murcia.

    1987. "Una familia de la 'nueva clase' política del siglo XVIII: los Robles Vives," *Cuadernos de Investigación Histórica*, 131–152.

Herr, R. 1974. "El significado de la desamortización en España." *Moneda y Crédito*, 131:55–94.

    1975. *España y la revolución del siglo XVIII*. Madrid, Aguilar.

    1977. "Spain." In David Spring, (Ed.), *European Landed Elites in the Nineteenth Century*. Baltimore, Johns Hopkins University Press.

    1978. "La élite terrateniente española en el siglo XIX." *Cuadernos de Investigación Histórica*, 2: 591–615.

    1986. "Hidalguía y desamortización bajo Carlos IV." In *Desamortización y Hacienda Pública*. Madrid, Ministerio de Hacienda. Vol. 2, pp. 463–478.

    1989 *Rural Change and Royal Finances in Spain at the End of the Old Regime*. Berkeley, University of California Press.

Hilton, R. 1984. "Feudalism in Europe: Problems for Historical Materialists." *New Left Review* (Sept.-Oct.).

Hughes, H. S. 1977. *Consciousness and Society. The Reorientation of European Social Thought, 1890–1930*. New York, Vintage Books.

Huizinga, J. H. 1968. *Dutch Civilisation in the Seventeenth Century*. London, Collins.

Hunt, L. (Ed.) 1984. *Politics, Culture, and Class in the French Revolution*. Berkeley, University of California Press.

    1989. *The New Cultural History*. Berkeley, University of California Press.

Janke, Peter. 1974. *Mendizábal y la instauración de la monarquía constitucional en España (1790–1853)*. Madrid, Siglo XXI.

Jiménez Blanco, J. 1972. "Estructura social e ideologias." In *Historia social de España, Siglo XIX*. Madrid, Guadiana.

References

Jovellanos, G. M. 1956. *Obras publicadas e inéditas de Don Gaspar Melchor de Jovellanos.* Madrid, B.A.E.
Jover Zamora, J. M. 1992. *La civilización española a mediados del siglo XIX.* Madrid, Espasa Calpe.
Juliá, S. 1989. "De poblachón mal construido a esbozo de gran capital: Madrid en el umbral de los años treinta." In A. Bahamonde and L. E. Otero Carvajal (Eds.), *La sociedad madrileña durante la Restauración, 1876–1931.* Madrid, CIDUR, 138–149.
—— 1994. In David Ringrose and Cristina Segura (Eds.), *Madrid. Historia de una capital,* Madrid, Alianza Editorial.
Kamen, H. 1981. *La Esopaña de Carlos II.* Barcelona, Crítica.
Kany, C. 1970. *Life and Manners in Madrid: 1750–1800.* New York, AMS Press.
Kennedy, J. "Bahian Elites, 1750–1822." In *Hispanic American Historical Review,* 53: 415–39.
Kenny, M. 1960. "Patterns of Patronage in Spain." *Anthropological Quarterly,* 33.
—— 1968. "Parallel Power Structures in Castile: The Patron-Client Balance." In J. G. Peristiany (Ed.), *Contributions to Mediterranean Sociology. Mediterranean Rural Communities and Social Change.* Paris, Mouton, 155–162.
Kertzer, D. I. 1984. "Anthropology and Family History." *Journal of Family History,* 9: 201–6.
Kertzer, D. I., and C. Bettell. 1987. "Advances in Italian and Iberian Family History." *Journal of Family History,* 12: 87–120.
Kertzer, D. I., and D. P. Hogan. 1985. "On the Move: Migration in an Italian Community, 1865–1921." *Social Science History,* 9: 1–24.
Kicza, J. E. 1983. *Colonial Entrepreneurs: Families and Business in Bourbon Mexico City.* Albuquerque, University of New Mexico Press.
Kontos, A. (Ed.). 1975. *Domination.* Toronto, University of Toronto Press.
Kossok, M. 1983. "Historia comparativa de las revoluciones de la época moderna. Problemas metodológicos y empíricos de la investigación." In G. Brendler (ed.), *Las revoluciones burguesas. Problemas teóricos.* Barcelona, Crítica.
Krieger, L. 1957. *The German Idea of Freedom: History of a Political Tradition.* Chicago, University of Chicago Press.
Kroeber, A. L., and C. Kluckhohn. 1963. *Culture: A Critical Review of Concepts and Definitions.* New York, Random House.
Ladd, D. M. 1976. *The Mexican Nobility at Independence, 1780–1826.* Austin, University of Texas Press.
Lafuente, M. 1951. "Madrid en 1850, o aventuras de Don Lucio Lanzas." In E. Correa Calderón (Ed.), *Costumbristas españoles.* Madrid, Aguilar, 29–57.
Lamb Coser, R. (Ed.). 1974. *The Family: Its Structure and Functions.* New York, St. Martin's Press.

References

Landé, C. H. 1977. "The Dyadic Basis of Clientelism." In S. Schmitt (Ed.), *Friends, Followers and Factions*. Berkeley, University of California Press.

Lane, F. 1973. *Venice, a Maritime Republic*. Baltimore, Johns Hopkins University Press.

Laslett, P. 1965. *The World We Have Lost – Further Explored*. London, Methuen.

(Ed.). 1972. *Household and Family in Past Time*. Cambridge, Cambridge University Press.

Lasso de la Vega, M. Marqués del Saltillo. 1951–53. *Historia nobiliaria española*. Madrid, Maestre, 2 vols.

Lefebvre, G. 1963. *Etudes sur la Revolution française*. Paris, PUF.

LeRoy Ladurie, E. 1978. *Montaillou: The Promised Land of Error*. New York, G. Braziller.

Lewin, L. 1979. "Some Historical Implications of Kinship Organization for Family-Based Politics in the Brazilian Northeast." *Comparative Studies in Society and History*, 21: 262–292.

Lisle-Williams, M. 1984. "Merchant Banking Dynasties in the English Class Structure: Ownership, Solidarity and Kinship in the City of London, 1850–1960." *British Journal of Sociology*, 34: 333–362.

Litwack, E. 1960. "Geographical Mobility and Extended Family Cohesion," *American Sociological Review*, 25: 385–394.

Llorens, V. 1968. *Liberales y románticos. Una emigración española en Inglaterra (1823–1834)*. Madrid, Castalia.

Lomnitz, L., and M. Pérez-Lizaur. 1987. *A Mexican Elite Family, 1820–1890: Kinship, Class, and Culture*. Princeton, N.J.: Princeton University Press.

Lynch, J. 1989. *El siglo XVIII. Historia de España*, Barcelona, Crítica.

Madóz, P. 1840. *Diccionario geográfico-estadístico-histórico de España y sus posesiones de ultramar*. Madrid.

Madrazo Madrazo, S. 1984. *El sistema de transportes en España, 1750–1850*. Madrid, 2 vols.

1986. "La lógica 'Smitheana' en la historia económica y social de Madrid. A propósito de una traducción reciente." *Revista de Historia Económica*, IV: 609–617.

Maluquer de Motes, J. 1989. "El ascenso de la burguesía industrial: el caso catalán." In M. Cerutti and M. Vellinga (Eds.), *Burguesía en industria en América Latina y Europa meridional*. Madrid: Alianza, 181–201.

Maravall, J. A. 1990. "Cabarrús y las ideas de reforma política y social en el siglo XVIII." In Count of Cabarrús, *Cartas sobre los obstáculos que la naturaleza, la opinión y las leyes oponen a la felicidad pública*. Madrid, Fundación Banco Exterior, 7–34

Marichal, C. 1977. *Spain (1834–1844). A New Society*. London, Tamesis Book.

References

1980. *La revolución Liberal y los primeros partidos políticos en España: 1834–1844.* Madrid, Cátedra.
Marín Perellón F., (Ed.). 1988. *Plannimetria general de Madrid.* Madrid, Tabaprés.
Martí, C. 1981. "Afianzamiento y despliegue del sistema liberal." In Tuñón de Lara (Ed.), *Historia de España, VIII. Revolución burguesa, oligarquía y constitucionalismo (1834–1923).* Barcelona, Labor.
Martín Aceña, P., and L. Prados de la Escosura. 1985. *La nueva Historia Económica en España.* Madrid, Tecnos.
Martínez Andaluz, A. 1986. "Préstamo privado y elites en el Madrid Isabelino (1856–1868)." In A. Bahamonde Magro and L.E. Otero Carvajal (Eds.), *Madrid en la sociedad del siglo XIX.* Madrid: CIDUR. Vol. I, pp. 492–504.
Martínez Cachero, L. 1961. *Alvaro Florez de Estrada. Su vida, su obra política y sus ideas económicas.* Oviedo.
Martínez Martín. J. 1986. Lecturas y lectores en la España Isabelina (1833–1868). Madrid, Universidad Complutense, Tesis Doctoral.
Maruri Villanueva, R. 1990. *La burguesía mercantil santanderina, 1700–1850. Cambio social y mentalidad.* Santander, Universidad de Cantabria.
Marx, K. 1920. "Die moralisierende Kritik und die kritische Moral." In F. Mohring (Ed.), *Aus dem literarischem Nachlass von K. Marx und F. Engels.* Stuttgart.
Marx, K., and F. Engels. 1934. *Manifesto of the Communist Party.* London, Martin Lawrence.
Mas Hernández, R. 1978. "La actividad inmobiliaria del marqués de Salamanca en Madrid (1862–1875)." *Ciudad y Territorio*, 3: 47–70.
—— 1986. "La propiedad urbana en Madrid en la primera mitad del siglo XIX." In Angel Bahamonde and Luis E. Otero (Eds.), *Madrid en la sociedad del siglo XIX.* Madrid, CIDUR. Vol. I, pp. 24–87.
Matilla Quizá, M. J. 1982. "Las compañías privilegiadas en la España del Antiguo Régimen." In M. Artola (Ed.), *La economía española al final del Antiguo Régimen.* Madrid, Alianza, 271–401.
Mayer, A. J. 1981. *The Persistence of the Old Regime. Europe to the Great War.* New York, Pantheon Books.
Maza Solano, A. 1953–57. *Nobleza, hidalguía, profesiones y oficios en la montaña, según los padrones del Catastro del Marqués de la Ensenada.* Santander, Centro de Estudios Montañeses.
McDonogh, G. 1986. *Good Families of Barcelona.* Princeton, N.J., Princeton University Press.
Medick, H. 1976. "The Proto-Industrial Family Economy: The Structural Function of Household and Family during the Transition from Peasant Society to Industrial Capitalism." *Social History*, 1–2: 291–315.

References

Mercader Riba, J. 1983. *José Bonaparte rey de España (1808–1813). Estructura del Estado español bonapartista.* Madrid, CSIC.

Mesonero Romanos, R. de. 1851. *Escenas Matritenses.* Madrid, Librería de Gaspar y Roig.

1964. "El curioso parlante: Contrastes." In E. Correa Calderón (ed.) *Costumbristas españoles.* Madrid, Aguilar.

1975. *Memorias de un setentón.* Madrid, Tebas.

Millerson, G. 1964. *The Qualifying Associations: A Study in Professionalisation.* London, Routledge & Paul.

Miraflores, Marqués de. 1834. *Apuntes histórico-críticos para escribir la historia de la revolución en España, desde el año 1820 hasta el año 1823.* London.

Modell, J. 1989. *Into One's Own: From Youth to Adulthood in the United States, 1920–1975.* Berkeley, University of California Press.

Molas, P. 1977. *Comerçi estructura social a Catalunyai València als segles XVII i XVIII.* Barcelona, Curial.

1985. *La burguesía mercantil en la España del Antiguo Régimen.* Madrid, Cátedra.

Moliner Prada, A. 1988. *Joaquín María López y el partido progresista. 1834–1843.* Alicante, Diputación Provincial.

Mooers, C. 1991. *The Making of Bourgeois Europe. Absolutism, Revolution and the Rise of Capitalism in England, France and Germany.* London, Verso.

Moore, A. 1984. "Peoples of the Old World Revisited: The Cultures and Communities of Spain." In *Cultures and Community in Europe. Essays in Honor of Conrad M. Arenberg.* Delhi, Industan Publishing Corporation, 36–58.

Morales Moya, A. 1983. Poder político economía e ideologia en el siglo XVIII español: la posición de la nobleza. Madrid, Universidad Complutense, Tesis doctoral.

1987. "Actividades económicas y honor estamental en el siglo XVIII." *Hispania*, 167: 959–76.

1987. *Reflexiones sobre el estado español del siglo XVIII.* Madrid, Instituto Nacional de la Administración pública.

Moreno Alonso, M. 1989. *La generación española de 1808.* Madrid, Alianza.

Morodo, S., and E. Díaz. 1966. "Tendencias y grupos políticos en las Cortes de Cádiz y en las de 1820." *Cuadernos Hispanoamericanos*, 201–27.

Morris, R. J. 1979. *Class and Class Consciousness in the Industrial Revolution, 1780–1850.* London, Macmillan.

Mouffe, C. (ed.) 1979. "Hegemony and Ideology in Gramsci." In *Gramsci and Marxist Thought.* London, Routledge & Kegan, 168–204.

Nadal, J. 1981. "Industrialización y desindustrialización del sudeste español, 1820–1890" in *La industrialización europea. Estadios y tipos.* Barcelona, Crítica.

References

1985. "Bonaplata, pretexto y símbolo." In J. Nadal and J. Maluquer de Motes (Eds.), *Catalunya, la fàbrica d'Espańa. Un siglo de industrialización catalana, 1833–1936.* Barcelona.

1987. *El fracaso de la revolución industrial en España, 1814–1913.* Barcelona, Ariel.

O'Connell, J. 1976. "The Concept of Modernization." In C. E. Black (Ed.), *Comparative Modernization. A Reader.* London Free Press, 13–24.

Osmond, M. 1981. "Comparative Marriage and the Family." *Journal of Comparative Sociology,* 22: 169–96.

Ossowski, S. 1956. "La visión dichotomique de la stratification sociale." *Cahiers Internationaux de Sociologie,* XX.

Otazu, A. de 1987. *Los Rothschild y sus socios en España, 1820–1850.* Madrid, O. Hs. Ediciones.

Palacio Atard, V. 1964. *Los españoles de la Ilustración.* Madrid, Guadarrama.

1978. *La españa del siglo XIX, 1808–1898.* Madrid, Espasa.

Palmer, R. R. 1959. *The Age of the Democratic Revolutions: A Political History of Europe and America, 1760–1800.* Princeton, N.J., Princeton University Press.

Paredes, J. 1991. *La organización de la justicia en la España liberal. Los orígenes de la carrera judicial: 1834–1870.* Madrid, Civitas.

Pérez Díaz, V. 1987. *El retorno de la sociedad civil. Respuestas sociales a la transición política, la crisis económica y los cambios culturales de España, 1975–1985.* Madrid. Instituto de Estudios Económicos.

Pastor Díaz, N., and F. Cárdenas. (eds.) 1842–46. *Galería de españoles célebres contemporáneos.* Madrid, Boix, 9 vols.

Pérez Galdós, B. 1951. *Obras completas.* Ed. by F. Sainz de Robles. Madrid, Aguilar, 6 vols.

Pérez Garzón, J. S. 1978. *Milicia nacional y revolución burguesa. El prototipo madrileño, 1808–1874.* Madrid, CSIC.

1980. "La revolución burguesa en España: los inicios de un debate científico, 1966–1979." In Tuñón de Lara (Ed.), *Historiografía española contemporánea.* Madrid, Siglo XXI, 91–138.

1988. "Isabel II." In A. Domínguez Ortiz (Ed.), *Historia e España.* Barcelona: Planeta, 307–432.

Pérez Herrero, P. 1988. *Plata y libranzas. La articulación comercial del México Borbónico.* Mexico, D. F., El Colegio de México.

Pérez Ledesma, M. 1991. "Las Cortes de Cádiz y la sociedad española." *Ayer,* 1: 167–206.

Pérez Moreda, V. 1983. "En defensa del censo de Godoy: observaciones previas al estudio de la población activa española de finales del siglo XVIII." In G. Anes, L. A. Rojo, and P. Tedde (Eds.), *Historia económica y pensamiento social.* Madrid, Alianza, 283–300.

References

Peristiany, J. G. 1976. *Mediterranean Family Structures.* Cambridge, Cambridge University Press.
Perkin, H. 1969. *Origins of Modern English Society.* London, Ark Paperbacks.
Peset, M. 1990. "Propiedad y crédito agrario." In Carlos Petit (Ed.), *Derecho privado y revolución burguesa.* Madrid, Marcial Pons, 157–185.
Petit, C. 1979. *La compañía mercantil bajo el régimen de las Ordenanzas del Consulado de Bilbao, 1737–1829,* Seville.
  (Ed.) 1990. *Derecho privado y revolución burguesa.* Madrid, Marcial Pons.
Pinkney, D. 1950. "Paris capitale du coton sous le Premier Empire." *Annales: Économies, Sociétés, Civilisations,* 55–60.
Pitt-Rivers, J. A. 1955. *The People of the Sierra.* London, Weidenfeld and Nicolson.
  1968. "Honor y categoría social." In J. G. Peristiany (Ed.), *El concepto del honor en la sociedad mediterránea.* Barcelona, Labor.
Plakans, A. 1982. "Ties of Kinship and Kinship Roles in an Historical Eastern European Peasant Community: A Synchronic Analysis." *Journal of Family History,* 7, Spring: 52–75.
  1984. *Kinship in the Past: An Anthropology of European Family Life, 1500–1900.* New York, B. Blackwell.
Poitrineau, A. 1983. *Remues d'hommes. Les migrations montagnardes en France 17e–18e siècles.* Paris, Aubier Montaigne.
Pollard, S. 1965. *The Genesis of Modern Management. A Study of the Industrial Revolution in Great Britain.* Cambridge, Mass., Harvard University Press.
Poussou, J. P. 1983. *Bordeaux et le sud-ouest au XVIIIe siecle; croisance économique et atraction urbaine.* Paris: Editions de l'Ecole d'Hautes Etudes en Sciences Sociales.
Prados de la Escosura, L. 1988. *De imperio a nación: crecimiento y atraso económico en España, 1780–1913.* Madrid, Alianza.
Price, R. 1987. *A Social History of Nineteenth-Century France.* London, Hutchinson.
Ramos Santana, A. 1987. *La Burguesía Gaditana en la época Isabelina.* Cádiz, Cátedra Adolfo de Castro. Fundación Municipal de Cultura.
Reddy, W. 1987. *Money and Liberty in Europe. A Critique of Historical Understanding.* Cambridge, Cambridge University Press.
Reher, D. 1990. *Town and Country in Pre-industrial Spain. Cuenca, 1550–1870.* Cambridge, Cambridge University Press.
Ringrose, D. 1970. *Transportation and Economic Stagnation in Spain, 1750–1850.* Durham, N.C., Duke University Press.
  1985. *Madrid y la economía española, 1560–1850. Ciudad, Corte y País en el Antiguo Régimen.* Madrid, Alianza.

References

1986. "Ciudad, pais y revolución burguesa: Madrid, del siglo XVIII al XIX." In A. Bahamonde and Otero Carvajal, L. E. (Eds.), *Madrid en la sociedad del siglo XIX*. Madrid, CIDUR. Vol. I, pp. 302–23.

1987. *Imperio y península. Ensayos sobre historia económica de España (Siglos XVI–XIX)*. Madrid, Siglo XXI.

1988. "Poder y beneficio. Urbanización y cambio en la historia." *Revista de Historia Económica*, VI: 375–395.

Robertson, I. 1988. *Los curiosos impertinentes. Viajeros ingleses por España desde la accesión de Carlos III hasta 1855*. Madrid, Serbal/CSIC.

Robledo Hernández, R. 1984. *La renta de la tierra en Castilla la Vieja y León (1836–1913)*. Madrid: Servicio de Estudios del Banco de España.

Rodríguez Casado, V. 1953. "La revolución burguesa del XVIII español." *Historia de España. Estudios publicados en la revista Arbor*. Madrid.

Romanelli, R. 1989. "Borghesia, Büegertum, bourgeoisie. Itinarari europei di un consetto." In J. Kocka, (Ed.), *Borghesie europee dell'Ottocento*. Venice, 69–94.

1991. "A propósito de la burguesía. El problema de la élite terrateniente en la Italia del Ochocientos." *Ayer*, 2: 29–48.

Roover, R. 1957. *L'evolution de la lettre de change, XIVe–XVIIIe siècles*. Paris, Armand Colin.

1963. *The Rise and Decline of the Medicis Bank*. Cambridge, Mass., Harvard University Press.

1974. *Business, Banking and Economic Thought in Late Medieval and Early Modern Europe*. Chicago, Chicago University Press.

Rosemberg, H. 1966. *Bureaucracy, Aristocracy and Autocracy. The Prussian Experience, 1660–1813*. Boston, Beacon Press.

Rosemberg, H. G. 1988. *A Negociated World, Three Centuries of Change in a French Alpine Community*. Toronto, University of Toronto Press.

Rozman, G. 1973. *Urban Networks in Ch'ing China and Tokugawa Japan*. Princeton, N.J.: Princeton University Press.

Rubinstein, W. D., 1987. *Elites and the Wealthy in Modern British History. Essays in Social and Economic History*. New York: St. Martin's Press.

Rueda, G. 1986. *La desamortización de Mendizabal y Espartero en España*. Madrid, Cátedra.

Ruiz Martín, F. 1970. "La banca española hasta 1782." In *El Banco de España. Una Historia Económica*. Madrid, Banco de España.

Ruiz Rivera, J. B. 1988. *El Consulado de Cádiz. Matrícula de comerciantes, 1730–1823*. Cádiz, Diputación Provincial.

Ruiz Torres, P. 1981. *Señores y propietarios. Cambio social en el sur del Pais Valenciano, 1650–1850*. Valencia, Institución Alfonso el Magnánimo.

Russel, C. 1979. *Parliament and English Politics*. Oxford, Oxford University Press.

References

Safford, F. 1972. "Social Aspects of Politics in Nineteenth Century Spanish America: New Granada, 1825–1850." *Journal of Social History*, 5: 344–370.

Sánchez Albornoz, N. (Ed.). 1985. *La modernización económica de España*. Madrid, Alianza.

Sánchez Bella, I. 1974. "La reforma de la administración central en 1834." In *III Symposium de Historia de la Administración*. Madrid, Instituto de Estudios de la Administración, 655–688.

Sanz Ayán, C. 1988. *Los banqueros de Carlos II*. Valladolid, Universidad de Valladolid.

Sarrailh, J. 1930. *Un homme d'Etat Espagnol: Martínez de la Rosa, 1787–1862*. Bourdeaux, Feret et Fils.

——— 1957. *La España ilustrada de la segunda mitad del XVIII*. Madrid, Fondo de Cultura Económica.

Saville, J. 1969. "Primitive Accumulation and Early Industrialization in Britain." *Socialist Register*, vi.

Schama, S. 1988. *The Embarrassment of Riches. An Interpretation of Dutch Culture in the Golden Age*. Berkeley, University of California Press.

Schumpeter, J. A. 1962. *Capitalism, Socialism and Democracy*. New York, Harper Torchbooks.

Sebastiá, E., and J. A. Piqueras. 1987. *Pervivencias feudales y revolución democrática*. Valencia. Edicions Alfons el Magnanim.

Seco Serrano, C. 1984. *Militarismo y civilismo en la España contemporánea*. Madrid, Instituto de Estudios Económicos.

Seed, P. 1987. *To Love, Honor and Obey in Colonial Mexico. Conflicts in Marriage Choice, 1574–1821*. Stanford, Calif., Stanford University Press.

Segalen, M. 1980. *Mari et femme dans la société paysane*. Paris, Flammarion.

——— 1985. *Quinze generations de Bas-Bretons: Parenté et societé dans le Pays Bigouden Sud, 1720–1980*. Paris

Sennet, R. 1978. *The Fall of Public Man: On the Social Psychology of Capitalism*. New York, Vintage Books.

Sewell, W. H., Jr. 1980. *Work and Revolution in France. The Language of Labor from the Old Regime to 1848*. Cambridge: Cambridge University Press.

Shorter, E. *The Making of the Modern Family*. New York, Basic Books.

Shubert, A. 1990. *A Social History of Modern Spain*. London, Unwin Hyman.

Sider, G. M. 1986. *Culture and Class in Anthropology and History. A Newfoundland Illustration*. Cambridge, Cambridge University Press.

Simón Palmer, M. C. 1969. "El colegio de San Mateo." *Anales del Instituto de Estudios Madrileños*, IV, 326–328.

Simón Segura, F. 1973. *La desamortización española del siglo XIX*. Madrid, Instituto de Estudios Fiscales.

References

Simón Tarrés, A. 1987. "La familia catalana en el Antiguo Régimen." In *La familia en la España Mediterránea*. Barcelona, Crítica.

Skinner, W. 1977a. "Regional Systems in Late Imperial China." In *Second Annual Meeting of the Social Science History Association*. Ann Arbor, Mich.

——— 1977b. "Cities and the Hierarchy of Local Systems." In *The City in Late Imperial China*. Stanford, Calif., Stanford University Press.

Skocpol, T. 1979. *States and Social Revolutions: A Comparative Analysis of France, Russia, and China*. Cambridge, Cambridge University Press.

Smelser, N. 1959. *Social Change and the Industrial Revolution: An Application of Theory to the British Cotton Industry*. Chicago, University of Chicago Press.

Smith, A. 1937. *An Inquiry into the Nature and Course of the Wealth of Nations*. New York, Random House.

Smith, C. A. 1976. *Regional Analysis*. New York: Academic Press, 2 vols.

Smith, R. (Ed.). 1979. *Land, Kinship and Life-Cycle*. Cambridge, University Press.

——— 1979. "Some Issues Concerning Family and Their Property in Rural England Household." In R. Smith (Ed.), *Land, Kinship and the Life-Cycle*. Cambridge, Cambridge University Press.

Soboul, A. 1981. *Comprendre la Revolution: problemes politiques de la Revolution française (1789–1797)*. Paris, Maspero.

Socolow, S. M. 1978. *The Merchants of Buenos Aires. Family and Commerce*. Cambridge, Cambridge University Press.

Solá, A. 1986. "Mentalitat i negocis de l'élite económica barcelonina de mitjan segle XIX." In *Orígens del món catalá contemporani*. Barcelona, Fundació Caixa de Pensions, 149–181.

Solé-Tura, J. 1970. *Catalanismo y revolución burguesa*. Madrid, Edicusa.

Solís, R. 1987. *El Cádiz de las Cortes. La vide en la ciudad en los años de 1810 a 1813*. Cádiz, Silex.

Stone, L. 1965. *The Crisis of the English Aristocracy*. Oxford, Oxford University Press.

——— 1972. *The Causes of the English Revolution, 1529–1642*. New York, Harper & Row.

——— 1979. *The Family, Sex and Marriage in England, 1500–1800*. New York, Harper & Row.

——— 1981. "Family History in the 1980's." *Journal of Interdisciplinary History*, 12: 51–57.

Stone, L., and J. C. Fawtier Stone. 1986. *An Open Elite? England 1540–1880*. Oxford, Oxford University Press.

Suárez, F. 1982. *Las Cortes de Cádiz*. Madrid, Rialp.

Taylor, A. J. (Ed.). 1975. *The Standard of Living in Britain in the Industrial Revolution*. London, Methuen.

References

Tedde Lorca, P. 1983. "Comerciantes y banqueros madrileños al final del Antiguo Régimen." In G. Anes, L. A. Rojo, and P. Tedde (Eds.), *Historia económica y pensamiento social*. Madrid, Alianza, 301–331.

    1988. *El Banco de San Carlos (1782–1829)*. Madrid, Alianza.

Thomas, D. 1983. *The Royal Company of Printers and Booksellers of Spain, 1763–1764*. New York, Troy.

Thompson, E. P. 1966. *The Making of the English Working Class*. New York, Vintage.

    1971. "The Moral Economy of the English Crowd in the Eighteenth Century." *Past and Present*, 50: 76–136.

Thompson, I. A. A. 1991. "*Hidalgo* and *pechero:* the language of 'estates' in early-modern Castile." In P. J. Corfield (Ed.), *Language, History and Class*, Cambridge: Basil Blackwell.

Thompson, K. (Ed.). 1985. *Readings from Emile Durkheim*. New York,

Tipps, D. C. 1973. "Modernization Theory and the Comparative Study of Societies: A Critical Perspective." *Comparative Studies in Society and History*, 15: 199–226.

Tomás y Valiente, F. 1971. *El marco político de la desamortización en España*. Barcelona, Ariel.

    (Ed.). 1986. *Desamortización y hacienda pública*. Madrid, Ministerio de Agricultura, 2 vols.

Tone, J. 1990. "The Moral Economy in Navare." Paper presented to the 21st Annual Meeting of the Society for Spanish and Portuguese Historical Studies.

Toro Mérida, J. 1986. "El registro de sociedades mercantiles (1885–1900)." In Angel Bahamonde and Luis E. Otero (Eds.), *Madrid en la sociedad del siglo XIX*. Madrid, CIDUR. Vol. I, pp. 528–532.

Torras Elías, J. 1989. "Mercados españoles y auge textil en Cataluña en el siglo XVIII. Un ejemplo." In *Haciendo Historia: Homenaje al profesor Carlos Seco*. Madrid, Universidad Complutense, 213–18.

Torrente Fortuño, J. A. 1969. *Salamanca bolsista romántico*. Madrid: Taurus, 3 vols.

Tortella Casares, Teresa. 1986. *Indice de los primitivos accionistas del Banco Nacional de San Carlos*. Madrid, Archivo Histórico del Banco de España.

Tortella, G. 1973. *Los orígenes del capitalismo en España*. Madrid, Tecnos.

    1989. "Madrid, capital del capital durante la Restauración." In A. Bahamonde and L. E. Otero Carvaja (Eds.), *La sociedad madrileña durante la Restauración, 1876–1931*. Madrid, CIDUR, 338–349.

Trimberger, E. K. 1984. "E. P. Thompson: Understanding the Process of History." In T. Skocpol (Ed.), *Vision and Method in Historical Sociology*. Cambridge, Cambridge University Press.

Tuñón de Lara, M. 1977. *Estudios de historia contemporánea*. Barcelona, Laia.

References

(Ed.). 1983. *Revolución burguesa, oligarquía y constitucionalismo (1834–1923)*. Barcelona, Labor.
Tutino, J. M. 1983. "Power, Class, and Family: Men and Women in the Mexican Elite, 1750–1810." *The Americas*, 39: 359–381.
Uhl, S. C. 1987. Friendship and Fealty in Southern Spain. State University of New York at Stony Brook, Ph.D. dissertation.
Varela Ortega, J. 1983. *Los amigos políticos*. Madrid, Alianza.
Varela Suances-Carpegna, J. 1983. *La teoría del Estado en los orígenes del constitucionalismo hispánico (Las Cortes de Cádiz)*. Madrid, Centro de Estudios Constitucionales.
Vicens Vives J. 1968. *Coyuntura económica y reformismo burgués y otros estudios de historia de España*. Barcelona, Vicens Vives.
(Ed.). 1971. "Los siglos XIX y XX. América independiente." Vol. 5. de la *Historia de España y América. Social y económica*. Barcelona, Vicens Vives.
Vicens Vives J., and J. Nadal Oller. 1985. *Manual de historia económica de España*. Barcelona, Vicens Vives.
Vilar, P. 1947. *Histoire de l'Espagne*, Paris, PUF.
1987. *Cataluña en la España Moderna*. Barcelona, Crítica, 3 vols.
Villacorta Baños, F. 1989. *Profesionales y burócratas. Estado y poder corporativo en la España del siglo XX, 1890–1923*. Madrid, Siglo XXI.
Villar García, M. B. 1982. *Los extranjeros en Málaga en el siglo XVIII*. Córdoba, Caja de Ahorros.
Wall, J. R. (et al.) 1983. *Family Forms in Historic Europe*. Cambridge, Cambridge University Press.
Wallerstein, I. 1980. *The Modern World System. Mercantilism and the Consolidation of the European World Economy, 1600–1750*. Vol. 2, New York, Academic Press.
Wareign, J. 1980. "Changes in the Geographical Distribution of the Recruitment of Apprentices to the London Companies, 1486–1750," *Journal of Historical Geography*.
Weber, M. 1978. *Economy and Society. An Outline of Interpretive Sociology*. Edited by G. Roth and C. Wittch. Berkeley, University of California Press.
Wheaton, R. 1980. "Introduction: Recent Trends in the Historical Study of the French Family." In R. Wheaton and T. Haveren (Eds.), *Family and Sexuality in French History*. Philadelphia, University of Pennsylvania Press.
1987. "Observations in the Development of Kinship History, 1942–1985," *Journal of Family History*, 12, 285–302.
Williams, R. 1981. *Culture*. London, Fontana.
Wilson, D. 1988. *Rothchild. A Story of Wealth and Power*. London, Andre Deutsch.
Winch, R. 1977. *Familial Organization: A Quest for Determinants*. New York, Free Press.

References

Windler, Ch. 1991. "Reformismo borbónico y formas de comunicación de las élites locales. Reflexiones metodológicas y resultados de un proyecto de investigación sobre la Baja Andalucia." In *La Burguesía en al España Moderna*, Madrid (forthcoming).

Wrigley, E. A. 1972. "The Process of Modernization and the Industrial Revolution in England." *Journal of Interdisciplinary History*, 3: 225–229.

— 1975. "A Simple Model of London's Importance in Changing English Society and Economy, 1650–1750." In D. Burgh (Ed.), *Aristocratic Government and Society in 18th Century England*. New York,

— 1977. "Reflections on the History of Family." *Daedalus*, 106: 71–85.

— 1987. *People, Cities and Wealth: The Transformation of Traditional Society*. Oxford, Blackwell.

Yun Casalilla, B. 1987. *Sobre la transición al capitalismo en Castilla. Economía y sociedad en Tierra de Campos (1500–1830)*. Salamanca, Junta de Castilla y León.

Zylberberg, M. 1979. "François Cabarrus, agriculteur eclaire, ou un banquier aux champs. Un exemple d'Agriculture nouvelle en Nouvelle-Castille à la fin du XVIIIe," *Melanges de la Casa de Velázquez*, XV: 415–450.

— 1983. "Un centre financier 'périphérique': Madrid dans la seconde moitié du XVIII siècle," *Revue Historique*, 546: 265–309.

Index

Abad de Aparicio, firm, 64
Abrisqueta, family, 72
agrarian capitalism, 140, 184, 193, 198, 207
Aguirre, family, 70, 72, 74, 76, 77, 82, 84, 239
Aguirre e Hijos, firm, 64, 82
Aguirre, Manuel Francisco de, 66
Aguirre Solarte, José Ventura, 64, 131, 132, 134
Alarcón Caracuel, M., 264
Alcalá Galiano, Antonio, 94, 142, 161, 162, 233, 235, 243, 275
  family, 158, 234
Alcaldes de Casa y Corte, 92, 118
Aldana, Antonia, 240
Alday, Juan Francisco de, 243
Alesón y Bueno, Juan de, 112
Almanak Mercantil, 63
Alvarez Junco, José, 266, 267
Alvarez Santalo, Carlos, 45
Alvaro Benito, Frutos, 64, 71, 76, 84
Amandi, firm, 64
Anderson, Perry, 266
Anduaga Mejia, Manuel, 64
Angulo, Ramón de, 19, 33
Aragorri, Nicolás de, Marquis of Iranda, 64, 72, 74, 84
Aranjuez, 36
Arcentales, valley of, 56
Argüelles, Agustín, 94, 159
Arizcun, family, 245

Artola, Miguel, 100, 143, 264
Avancino, firm, 64, 73
Ayala, valley of, 72
Azara, María de, 160
Azofra Delgado, José de, 119

Bahamonde, Angel, 63, 80
Bailén, Duke of, 147
Baldó Lacomba, Marc, 270
Balmaseda, Juan Domingo de, 64
Bank of San Carlos, 39, 60, 68, 81, 114, 115, 116, 179, 180, 221
Bank of San Fernando, 41
Barata, Antonio, 240
Barbería, Pedro, 64
Barcelona, 9, 16, 18, 21, 28, 55, 59, 83, 118, 156, 184, 194, 268
Barcenas, Francisco de las, 64
Bardají Azara, Dionisio 160
Bardají Azara, Eusebio 160
  family, 94, 152, 160
Barrueta, firm, 64
Bartelemi Hermanos, firm, 64
Basque Country, 4, 25, 33, 56, 72, 121, 177, 209, 268
Basurto, Ramón, 46
Baztán, valley of, 72, 135
Bermúdez de Castro, Manuel, 150
Beronda y de Espina, Juan, 64
Bilbao, 17, 22, 46, 62, 241, 268
Blackbourn, David, 266
Bonaparte, Joseph, 103, 126

343

Index

Bourdieu, Pierre, 12, 13, 174, 211, 212
bourgeois
  culture, 10
  revolution, Spain, 4, 5, 6, 10, 17, 23, 55, 56, 90, 129, 140, 155, 156, 171, 259, 260, 261, 262, 263, 264, 266, 267
  revolution, England, 12, 266
  revolution, Europe, 10, 11, 262, 267
  revolution, France, 12
  revolution, Germany, 12, 265, 266
bourgeoisie
  Catalan, 84, 261
  Castilian, 84
  Spanish, 3, 7, 176, 260, 261, 269
Brading, David, 255
Braudel, Fernand, 50
Bravo Lozano, Jesús, 56
Bringas López, Francisco, 39
Bringas
  family, 39, 239
  firm, 40, 126
Bringas, Francisco Antonio, 19, 39, 40, 126, 240
Bringas, María Pilar, 40
Buenos Aires, 156, 253, 255
Burdick, Ann, 227
Burdiel, Isabel, 151
Burgos, Javier de, 136, 137, 138
Busquets, Julio, 146

Caballero del Moral, Andrés, 41
Caballero y Mazo, Andrés, 41, 64
  family, 33, 41, 74, 239
  firm 19
Caballero, José, 41
Caballero, José Antonio, 134
Caballero, Manuel, 29
Caballero, Marquis of, 103
Cabanilles, José, 111, 112
Cabarrús Kirkpatrick, Paulina, 189, 193
Cabarrús Kirkpatrick, Enriqueta, 189,
Cabarrús Quilty, Domingo, 189, 198
Cabarrús Quilty, Paulina, 189, 192
Cabarrús, Domingo, 138, 189, 190, 191, 192, 193, 197, 199, 200, 201, 202, 203, 204, 207
Cabarrús, family, 176, 177, 189, 194, 198, 205, 206, 275, 276
Cabarrús, Francisco, Count of Cabarrús, 58, 68, 86, 97, 100, 111, 114, 139, 176, 177, 178, 179, 180, 181, 182, 183, 184, 185, 186, 187, 188, 189, 190, 191, 192, 193, 196, 201, 205, 207, 276
Cabarrús, Teresa, Princess of Caraman-Chimay, 189
caciquismo, 159, 237, 256, 272
Cádiz, 17, 18, 22, 36, 45, 51, 52, 62, 80, 115, 141, 142, 143, 145, 157, 177, 191, 233, 2Index34, 253, 268, 269, 274
Calderón de la Barca, Angel, 137
Calderón Molina, Carlos, 139
Calderón, Carlos, 139
Calderón, Manuel, 139
Callahan, William, 145
cambista, 63, 64, 65, 66, 73, 77, 83, 222
Campo y Haza, Francisco de, 115
Campomanes, 162, 178
Canga Argüelles, José, 93, 132, 136, 150, 159, 160
  family, 113
Cano Manuel, family, 152, 158
Cantabrian, region, 25, 28, 34
Cantero, Manuel, 153, 208, 209
Capella, Miguel, 18
Carbajo Isla, María, 93
Carrancio, Manuel, 119
Carranza, family, 72, 73, 77, 224, 239
  firm, 73
Carranza, Domingo, 73
Carranza, Polonia, 240
Carranza, valley of, 33, 126, 209, 225, 240
Casa Gaviria, Marquis of, 64
Castile, 82, 94, 134, 138, 153, 273
Castro y Orozco, Francisco de, 128
Castrourdiales, 35, 72, 73, 233
Catalonia, 4, 8, 9, 44, 83, 138, 148, 153, 155, 156, 269

344

Index

Ceriola Flaquer, José de, 64
Ceriola, Jaime de, 64,153
Cevallos, Pedro, 135
Charles II, 59, 85, 97
Charles III, 73, 90, 128, 160, 179, 182
Charles IV, 134, 136, 150
Chávarri, Francisco Antonio, 64
Chávarri, family, 72
Chávarri Sidera, Pilar, 145
Chávarri, Basilio, 64
Cinco Gremios, 18, 19, 20, 21, 22, 27, 28, 29, 34, 36, 37, 40, 41, 44, 45, 66, 74, 80, 81, 111, 114, 115, 222, 239
Clavero, Bartolomé, 100, 263, 264, 274
client
   economy, 85, 121, 180, 182, 185, 194, 272
   solidarity, 255
   system, 55, 95, 125
   networks 122
Cobban, Alfred, 265
Cogolludo, Marquis of, 38
Cohen, Abner, 12
Collado, José, Marquis of Laguna, 41, 64, 132
   family, 131, 148, 239
Cologán, Francisca, 189
Colonilla, Marquis of, 64, 72,76
Comellas, José Luis, 265
consanguineal marriage, 233, 244, 245
Contradi, Count of, 162
Cornejo, Maria Amalia, 163
Cortázar, Modesto, 131, 132, 135
Cortés, Donoso, 214
Cortina, Manuel, 215
Council
   Castile, 91, 94, 96, 97, 101, 102, 103, 110, 112, 115, 154, 155, 159, 164, 221, 227, 242, 246
   Hacienda, 91, 94, 97, 275
   Indies, 110, 234
   State, 94, 97
Cruzada, Gregorio, 224
Cuevas y Chacón, Manuel, Count of Cuevas, 240

cultural
   capital, 9, 13, 199, 203, 217
   hegemony, 7, 9, 10, 226

Daudinot Bouhebent, firm, 64
Díaz-Caneja, family, 159
Diego, Antonio de, 136
disentailment, 4, 5, 46, 80, 101, 121, 135, 140, 144, 145, 262, 268, 272
domination, 10, 12, 100, 110, 174, 176, 177, 192, 193, 194, 196, 197, 199, 202, 204, 205, 206, 211
Domínguez Ortiz, Antonio, 100, 146
Drouillet, firm, 64, 72
Durkheim, 10, 11
Dutari
   family, 68, 72, 74, 76, 84, 86, 221
   firm, 64, 66, 70, 74, 75, 76
Dutari, Juan Bautista, 66

Eley, Geoff, 266
endogamy, 244, 246, 247,
   occupational, 248
   professional, 126
Engels, 261, 266
England, 60, 93, 163, 198, 234, 250, 276
   banking 62, 63, 71, 72,73
   revolution 266
   social conditions 74, 211, 274
Enlightenment, 161, 181, 187
Ensenada, Catastro de, 20, 93
Ensenada, Marquis of, 36
equal opportunity, 176, 188, 206
Espartero, Antonio de, 152, 159
Espinosa Brun, Antonio, 95, 111
Extremadura, 112, 153

Fagoaga Dutari, José de, 74, 221
Fagoaga Dutari, Joaquín de, 153
familial solidarity, 24, 246, 250, 252, 253, 256
familism, 196, 229, 248
family
   extended, 29, 162, 229, 231
   lineage, 236, 237, 250, 251

Index

family (*cont.*)
  networks, 144, 225, 228, 238, 248, 250, 251
  nuclear, 229, 230, 233, 234
  strategies, 250
Fayard, Janine, 97, 98, 116, 130, 164, 227, 228, 241, 246, 249
Ferdinand VII, 147, 198
Fernández Angulo, Cipriano, 189
Fernández Angulo, Emiliano, 189, 193
Fernández Angulo, María del Carmen, 189
Fernández Casariego, Fernando, 153
Fernández de Pinedo, Emiliano, 153
Fernández, Roberto, 83, 153
Ferrer Echeverría, Vicente, 163
Ferrer y Cafranga, Joaquín María, 132, 134, 135, 163
Finat, Andrés, 64
Florez Estrada, Alvaro, 162
Fontana, Josep, 261, 263, 269
Ford, Richard, 252
France, 63, 68, 93, 136, 141, 177, 198
  class conflict, 265
  commerce with, 178
  liberalism, 272
  revolution, 12, 179, 181, 261, 262, 265
Franch, Ricardo, 45
freedom of choice, 169, 173, 175, 176, 186
friendship, 25, 172, 178, 197, 201, 202, 204, 208, 211, 235, 252, 273
  networks, 165
  ties 27, 57

Galabert, Antonia de, 177, 189
Galabert, Antonio de, 177, 180
Gámez, Juan, 126
García Baquero, Antonio, 45
García de la Prada
  family, 37, 42, 239
  firm, 19, 38
García de la Prada, Fernando, 37
García de la Prada, Juan Sixto, 30, 37, 41, 224
García de la Prada, Manuel, 38, 126
García de la Torre, José, 131, 135

García de León y Pizarro, José, 234, 235, 236
García Sanz, Angel, 50, 51
García Sevillano, Juan José, 126
Gardoqui, family, 22, 241
Garelli, Nicolás, 94
Garro Micheloterena, Ambrosio, 95
Garro y Arizcun, Nicolás Ambrosio, Marquis of the Hormazas, 135, 245, 246
Gaviria, Antonio de, 64, 73, 139, 153
Germany
  liberalism, 272
  route to capitalism, 266
Gil de la Cuadra, Ramón, 132
Gil de Santibáñez, Manuel, 64, 153
Gil Novales, Alberto, 141, 261, 262
Girón, Pedro, Marquis of Amarrillas, 243
González Arnao, Vicente, 126
González de Lobera, firm, 64
González Maldonado, José, 221
González Yebra, Antonio, 103
Gonzalo del Río, firm, 64
Gonzalo del Río, Rafael, 239, 240
Gorbea, firm, 64
Gorbea, Francisco de, 121
Gordejuela, valley of, 121, 57
Goyeneche, Ignacio de, Count of Saceda, 86, 138
Gramsci, Antonio, 10, 11, 261
Greven, Philip, 237
Guardamino, Juan, 153
Güell, Juan Ignacio, 118
Guriezo, valley of, 41

habitus, 13, 152, 157, 169, 170, 171, 173, 197, 199, 205, 206, 212, 275
hacendado, 142, 143, 146, 215, 218
Hacienda, Ministry of, 92, 97, 101, 103
Harris, C.C., 169, 175
Heran, François, 144
Hernández, Mauro, 101, 165, 227, 228, 242, 247, 249
Heros, Bartolomé de los, 31
Heros, Juan Antonio de los, 31
Heros, Manuel de los, 33

Index

Herr, Richard, 101, 144, 195, 268, 271
Herrezuela, Juan de la, 126
hidalguía, 50, 73, 214, 215, 216, 225, 227, 235, 241
Horcasitas, Francisco de, 56, 57
Hunt, Lynn, 141

Ibarrola Layseca, Fernando de, 119
Ibarrola Llaguno, Antonio de, 115
ilustrado, 162, 173, 178, 179, 180, 183, 185, 186, 187, 196, 205, 235
industrial
  bourgeoisie, 87, 138, 139, 151, 225
  fortunes, 224
  investment, 50, 51, 81, 82, 83, 115, 130, 137, 139, 268
industrialization
  Andalucía, 137, 198
  Catalonia, 4, 83, 148, 153
  England, 62
  Europe, 251, 229
  Madrid, 63
  Spain, 4, 5, 21, 196
Iriarte, Bernardo de 104, 105, 221
Iruegas, family, 33, 39, 224, 239, 240
Iruegas, Baltasar de, 39, 240
Iruegas-Sobrevilla, firm, 19
Isla Fernández, family, 115
Istúriz, Francisco de, 150
Italy, 16, 236, 251
  liberalism, 272
Iturbide, Joaquín de, 95

Jordá, Antonio, 153
Jovellanos, Melchor Gaspar de, 159, 162, 178, 179
Jover, José María, 269
Joyes, Patricio, 64, 73
Junta de Comercio, 67, 116

Kicza, John, 255
kinship, 68, 165, 170, 172, 176, 228, 237, 246, 256, 273
  bonds, 237
  networks, 68, 144, 229, 237, 238, 251
  relations, 237
  system, 188
  ties, 193, 230, 234, 239
Kirkpatrick, Enriqueta, 189

Laslett, Peter, 229, 231, 232
Lerena, Count of 179, 180, 181
liberal revolution, 20, 105, 123, 125, 129, 151, 155, 157, 164, 165, 173, 220, 245, 256, 257, 265, 276
Lima, 156
Llaguno, Gregorio, 35
London, 16, 18, 55, 62, 63, 71, 93, 150, 163
López Ballesteros, Luis, 94, 103
López de La Torre, Luis, 150
loyalty, 26, 141, 149, 152, 169, 170, 172, 173, 176, 196, 207, 208, 210, 233, 255, 271, 274

Madóz, Pascual, 97
Málaga, 45, 51, 52, 139, 190, 191, 197, 201, 202, 268
Maltrana Monasterio, Antonio, 64
Marcoleta, Domingo de, 120
Martínez de la Mata, Pedro, 112
Martínez de la Rosa, Diego, 189, 198, 192
Martínez de la Rosa, Francisco, 160, 161, 192
Martínez de Laguna, Manuela, 243
Martínez Verdejo, Francisco, 160
Martínez, Jesús, 63
Marx, Karl, 11, 261, 266
Marxism, 169, 260, 264, 266
Marxist, 4, 11, 12, 15, 88, 148, 170, 171, 172, 260, 263, 264, 265, 266, 269
Matilla Tascón, Antonio, 18
Mayer, Arnold, 172
mayorazgo, 97, 98, 100, 101, 102, 103, 104, 112, 113, 118, 119, 135, 152, 159, 160, 161, 162, 163, 186, 187, 188, 189, 226, 241, 245, 250, 270, 271, 272
Mazo, family 239
Mazo, Francisca del, 41

Index

Mazo, Francisco del, 139
Medina, Marquis of, 161
Medinaceli, Duke of, 38
Mena, valley of, 40
Mendizábal, 97, 148, 150, 153, 156, 157, 158, 159, 209
merit 26, 74, 141, 142, 173, 175, 186, 187, 188, 191, 206, 217
meritocratic, 175, 193, 216
   nobility, 187
Mesa, Marquess of, 161
Mesonero Romanos, 74, 128, 129
Mesta, 66, 74
Mexico, 156
Mexico City, 17, 51, 253, 255
Miguelturra, 36
Miraflores, Marquis of, 14, 15, 239, 241
moderado
   affiliation, 136, 149, 151, 210, 239, 256
   system, 196
Molas, Pere, 18, 20
Moñino, José, Count of Floridablanca 102, 110, 179, 180, 256
Morales Moya, Antonio, 165
Muguiro, family, 74, 239
Muguiro Iriarte, Rafael, 64
Muguiro, Juan, 153
Muñoz Sánchez, José, Marquis of Remisa, 64
Murga, José Manuel, 72, 74
Murga Michelena, Bartolomé, 64
Múzqiz, Miguel de, 102

Nadal, firm, 64
Nafarrondo, firm, 64
Nestarés, Fernando de, 103
Norzagaray, Mateo de, 64

Oakes, James, 63
old regime, 3, 15, 18, 23, 61, 65, 71, 73, 87, 88, 89, 94, 98, 127, 128, 129, 130, 144, 146, 148, 155, 157, 158, 163, 164, 165, 169, 175, 176, 203, 225, 257, 261, 267, 268, 269, 271, 272

Ortiz de Taranco, Manuel, 139
Otazu, Alfonso de, 153

paisanaje, 197, 252, 253, 256
paisano, 61, 74, 86, 111, 119, 159, 162, 165, 182, 209, 250, 252, 257
Palacio Atard, Vicente, 265
Pando y Sabugal, Antonio, 241
Pando, family, 22, 241
Paramio, Ludolfo, 267
Paris, 16, 21, 50, 52, 55, 62, 68, 93
patron–client
   solidarity, 230
   relations, 228, 252, 253, 256, 257
   system, 59
   ties, 210
patronage, 26, 42, 115, 141, 147, 149, 159, 172, 182, 184, 196, 201, 206, 208, 209, 221, 232, 234, 248, 250, 252, 253, 255, 256, 272, 273, 274
Paz y Merino, Juan Antonio, 110
Peña Aguayo, José de la, 162
Pérez de Castro, Evaristo, 94
Pérez de Hita, José, 112
Pérez Donis, Diego, 41
Pérez Galdós, Benito, 134, 210
Pérez Ledesma, Manuel, 142
Pérez Moltó, Ignacio, 139
Pérez Roldán, firm, 19
Pérez Seoane, Manuel, 64, 153
Pérez, Francisco Antonio, 240
Pérez, Julián Aquilino, 95, 113
Pérez-Lizaur, Marisol, 251
Peset, Mariano, 269, 270
Pez, Manuel José del, 208
Philip IV, 73, 97
Philip V, 97, 241
Piñeira, Bartolomé, 127
Porlier Sopranis, Antonio, 136
Posadillo, Domingo de, 35, 36
Posadillo, family, 33, 35
Presilla, Antonia de la, 240
private discourse, 173, 174, 176, 200, 203, 206, 275
private sphere, 172, 173, 176, 196

Index

progresista, affiliation, 149, 151, 152, 153, 163, 164, 173, 209, 210, 256
public discourse, 173, 174, 188, 193, 194, 275
public sphere, 173, 174, 190, 193

Queneau, Agustin de, 68
Quilty, family, 190, 192, 197
Quilty, Rosa, 139, 189, 191
Quilty, Tomás, 189, 190, 191
Quintana y Pando, Francisca de la, 241

Rávara and Son, firm, 64
Reher, David, 194, 230
reputation, 69, 199, 200, 201
Riansares, Duke of, 64
Rico Villademoros, Domingo, 126
Rigal, firm, 64
Rigout of Caraman, Josef, Prince, 189
Ringrose, David, 8, 9, 93, 155, 273
Ripalda, Duke of, 150
Riva Herrera, Manuel de la 94, 131, 135
Rivas y Ubieta, Francisco de las, Marquis of Mudela 56, 57, 64, 153
Romanelli, Raffaele, 269, 271
Romero, firm, 64
Rosa, Luisa de la, 160
Rossi, Juan Bautista, 74
Rubinstein, William D., 74, 211
Rueda, Pedro Manuel, 124
Ruiz de la Prada, Juan Bautista, 37
Ruiz de la Prada, Manuel, 64
Ruiz de la Prada, Rosa, 126
Ruiz Garcia de la Prada, Manuel, 64

Sáenz de Azofra, Santiago, 124, 126
Sáenz de Prado, Ignacio, 33
Sáenz de Tejada, family, 33
Sáenz de Tejada, Antonia 104
Safont, José, 153
Sáinz de Baranda, family, 33, 231, 232, 233, 242, 243
Sáinz de Baranda y Gándara, Pedro, 231, 232, 275

Salamanca, José de, Marquis of Salamanca, 86, 97, 131, 132, 134, 136, 148, 150, 153, 159
Salazar Rogibal, Francisco de, 112
Salazar y Agüero, Francisco, de, 112
San Juan y Santa Cruz, Josefa, 233, 242
San Juan y Santa Cruz, Manuela, 233, 242
San Lorenzo, Duke of, 161
San Vicente, Manuel Esteban de, 124, 126
Sancho, Santiago, 33
Santander, 37, 41, 73, 135, 255, 268
Sebastá, Enric, 263, 264
Seco Serrano, Carlos, 146
Sevillano, Duke of, 64
Sevillano, Juan, 153
Seville, 45, 59, 194, 200
Sider, Gerald, 174
Silvela, Francisco Agustín, 134
Skinner, Williams, 7, 8
Smiles, Samuel, 86
Sobrado, Joaquina de, 35
Sobrevilla Iruegas, Miguel, 239, 240
social
  ascent, 119, 121, 122, 123, 125, 127, 150, 157, 164, 165, 205, 206, 211, 213, 215, 216, 222, 224, 225, 236, 238, 258, 273
  mobility, 140, 165, 175, 215, 222, 225, 258, 271, 273
Solanot, Valentín, 152
Soldevilla, Matias de, 240
Solé Tura, Jordi, 261
solidarity, 24, 122, 157, 169, 173, 176, 196, 205, 206, 210, 212, 228, 231, 233, 237, 255, 257, 271
  geographical, 248
  networks, 210
  regional, 30, 68, 256
Soriano, family, 64
Sotomayor, Rosalía, 240
Stone, Lawrence, 244, 250

Tedde, Pedro, 60
Thompson, Edward P., 11, 261, 266

349

Index

Tomás y Valiente, Francisco, 269
Toreno, Count of, 163
Torrecilla de Cameros, 33
Torres Solanot, Mariano, 152
Torres, Pedro, 264
Torrox, 197, 198, 199, 201, 202, 203, 204
Tuñón de Lara, Manuel, 261, 274

Ugalde, Juan Ignacio de, 122
Urquijo, firm, 64
Ussoz y Mozi, José Agustín, 119

Valencia, 18, 19, 45, 111, 126, 177, 264, 268
Vega, Francisco de la, 111
Vegamar, Count of, 64

Vejarano, Félix , Count of Tajo, 189
Velle, Count of, 64
Vicens Vives, Jaime, 261, 269
Vicente, Juan José de, 64
Vienna 17, 62
Vilar, Pierre, 9, 8, 83, 260, 261
Villar, Begoña, 45
Vizcaya, 31, 72, 84, 119, 135

Windler, Christian, 165
wool trade, 66, 73, 84, 178

Yun Casalilla, Bartolomé, 101

Zapater, firm, 64
Zumalacárregui, Miguel de 152